INTRODUCTION

Peace. What wouldn't we give to have a little more of it? Peace in our relationships.
Peace at home and at work. Peace despite painful memories. Peace in the midst of the
pressures and demands that threaten to crush us. Is there a way to find peace in all
these areas of our lives? What if we could build a moment of peace into every single
day of the year, intentionally opening our hearts to the peace God has promised? What
would it be like to live with less fear and anxiety and with more confidence and joy?

The mission of *The One Year Devotions for Women: Becoming a Woman at Peace*
is to help you take hold of the peace God is offering. This peace is far richer
and more satisfying than anything you or I can imagine.

When the Bible speaks of peace, it often uses the Hebrew word *shalom*.
Like many Hebrew words, this one contains depths of meaning that the
English word *peace* cannot fully convey. In addition to the idea of serenity,
tranquility, and the absence of conflict, shalom also means wholeness, heal-
ing, success, completeness, soundness, perfection, and good relationships.
Shalom sums up all the blessings God can give to those he loves.

I hope that as you join me this year, you will become a woman who is
capable of enjoying more of the peace God has for you. As his Spirit works in
your heart, I pray that God will show you how to spread his peace to others
so that they, too, might come to know that no matter what has happened in
the past or what might happen in the future, they are safe in God's keeping.

As you begin this year, remember the ancient prayer God instructed
Moses to pray over his people. Although first prayed thousands of years ago
in the midst of a Middle Eastern desert, the words emanate from the mind
of our eternal God, expressing his heart toward us today.

May the LORD bless you
    and protect you.
May the LORD smile on you
    and be gracious to you.
May the LORD show you his favor
    and give you his peace.

NUMBERS 6:24-26

—Ann Spangler

BEGIN WITH THE END

I am leaving you with a gift—peace of mind and heart.
JOHN 14:27

You have probably heard of Stephen R. Covey's book *The 7 Habits of Highly Effective People*. Covey's second habit for living effectively is to begin with the end in mind. What does he mean by that? Simply that there are two steps to creating anything. The first step involves envisioning exactly what it is you want to create, and the second involves making sure that your life is aligned with that vision so that every day you can do something toward achieving your goal.

To put flesh on the bones of this concept, Covey explains that before you build a house, you've got to know exactly what kind of home you want. Once you know that, you can have a blueprint drawn up and can develop construction plans. Before digging the first shovelful of dirt or hammering the first nail into place, you have to have a plan. After that, he says, "you put it into bricks and mortar. Each day you go to the construction shed and pull out the blueprint to get marching orders for the day. You begin with the end in mind."[1]

Similarly, if you want to live a life of greater peace, you need to begin by envisioning what that life will look like. Fortunately, you needn't develop this vision on your own because God has already provided it. He has also graciously offered a blueprint that, when followed, will lead to a life characterized by deeper levels of his peace.

Why not respond to his offer today by asking him to help you envision the rich and enduring peace he wants to give? Then use the devotions that follow as your "construction shed," a place where you can pore over God's blueprint and receive your marching orders for the day. As you go through the year, who knows what wonderful things may happen as you earnestly seek God's peace?

Consider taking a few moments now to commit the months ahead to the Lord. As the months unfold, I pray you will experience him drawing near, showing you how to put the bricks and mortar of a more peaceful life into place.

Father, I want to experience your peace in deeper ways. Please open my soul to your grace, so I will miss nothing of what you want to give me.

GOD UNDERSTANDS

The LORD is like a father to his children, tender and compassionate to those who fear him. For he knows how weak we are; he remembers we are only dust.

PSALM 103:13-14

I had a meeting recently with two people who were helping me get up to speed on social media. Both have extensive experience working with nontechies like me. During the course of our time together, they happened to mention a couple of phrases that caught my attention. For instance, when speaking with colleagues about a computer problem, they sometimes say, "There seems to be a problem between the keyboard and the chair." Translation: nothing's wrong with the computer; it's the person operating the computer who's causing all the difficulty. Or they'll talk about a "defective end user." Same translation.

As someone who's not a quick study when it comes to computers and technology, I've always appreciated how patient and nonjudgmental computer techs can be when it comes to dealing with people like me. Though "defective end user" doesn't exactly roll off the tongue, it does inject a note of humor and objectivity into their quest to help the less technologically gifted.

I like to think that God deals with us in a similar way. Seeing our struggles to live for him, he realizes that we are all "defective end users," and he does not judge us harshly. He knows how difficult it can be for us to get it, to respond to his leading or to do his will perfectly. He understands that, at times, our ignorance can create unintended havoc.

In the midst of your struggles, give yourself a break. Remember that you belong to a "tender and compassionate" God who wants to help you. Instead of imagining that he's disappointed in you or judging you, try to imagine him patiently extending his grace to help resolve whatever problem still exists "between the keyboard and the chair."

Father, you know I want to live for you. Yet sometimes I fail. When that happens, help me to get up and keep going, confident that you are there to help.

WHO'S WATCHING OVER YOU?

The LORD keeps watch over you as you come and go, both now and forever.

PSALM 121:8

I sometimes wonder if I'm spiritually hearing impaired. I wonder if God has to shout to get my attention or repeat things more times than he should have to so that I will finally get the message.

I remember hobbling into Dr. Shirley Kleiman's office one day, nearly bent over with pain from a back that had been twisted out of shape by an ill-considered roller-coaster ride. Dr. Kleiman is one of the best physical therapists my back has ever encountered, and it's tough to get an appointment with her. But I had prayed, and friends had prayed because I was heading out of town the next day on a business trip and didn't think I could endure the plane ride without some help. "Somebody must be watching over you," Dr. Kleiman commented as she walked into the room, acknowledging how hard it was to get a last-minute appointment.

The following week I made some repairs to the roof of my home. I'd postponed them as long as I dared, praying to make it through the winter without problems. That spring, one of the roofers who bid on the job had confirmed what I already knew. Portions of the roof were in a pretty sorry state. He couldn't believe we had made it through the winter without a leak. "Somebody must be watching over you," he said. Then a month later, after he and his men had completed the repairs and I was settling the bill, there it was again: "I can't believe that roof didn't give you trouble over the winter. Somebody must be looking out for you." This time the words sank in. I had prayed, and God had helped. He was looking out for me and my family. He knew exactly what we needed, and he had provided.

I wonder how much more peaceful our lives would be if we could finally settle the question of God's faithfulness. No matter what happens, whether life is hard or easy, each of us will enjoy more peace if we can learn to lean into the relationship we have with God our Father. He will watch over us, just as Psalm 121:8 promises. Today let us pray for the grace to trust in his watchful, loving care.

Father, thank you for watching over me, for hearing my prayers, and for preserving my life.

January 4
PAPER LOSSES

Let me reveal to you a wonderful secret. We will not all die, but we will all be transformed!

1 CORINTHIANS 15:51

A few weeks ago I was on the phone with my financial adviser. "Mark, I have to thank you," I said. "If it hadn't been for you, I would have sold everything at the absolute bottom of the market." It felt good to thank him now that my portfolio no longer looked so anemic. If Mark hadn't been there to temper my fear, I'm sure I would have gotten rid of everything, locking in my losses when the market was down by more than 50 percent. Fear can have such devastating effects.

That's true in our spiritual lives as well. God has promised us many things. He tells us that he is good, he is our loving Father, he will never fail us or forsake us. Such assurances may not be hard to believe when life is on an upswing. But what about those times when our lives resemble a bear market? How do we think about God when we've lost our livelihood, suffered an accident, fallen ill, been betrayed by someone we love? What then? Do we shake a fist? Do we tell ourselves that God doesn't care? Do we let doubt corrode our faith? At such times it can be tempting to throw up our hands, to say we've had enough of this God and his fantastic promises. But to do so would be turning our backs on everything we know to be true. It would be giving up our hope. It would be selling out and locking in our losses.

Fortunately God has promised to make everything right—if not now, then surely in the end. The last will be first. The hungry will be satisfied. Those who weep will laugh. As today's verse says, we will all be transformed. Because we are God's beloved children, we will live and not die. We will also, I believe, be given the grace to look back on earthly sorrows and recognize them for what they are: "paper losses." At times these losses are painful, frightening, and grievous—but they will one day be redeemed. Today, ask for the grace to keep believing. Refuse to lock in your losses, and instead choose to keep trusting in Christ.

Lord, today I choose to believe. Help me by your grace to
keep believing, no matter what happens.

I can never escape from your Spirit! I can never get away from your presence!

PSALM 139:7

One of my readers wrote to me recently in order to share an experience she had while singing a song about God's names. "There is a point in the song," she explained, "when all the music stops and the choir whispers every name of God that comes to mind. It was so powerful. It moved us all to tears. I felt like I needed to take off my shoes because I was standing on holy ground."

Her words reminded me of times in my own life when I have experienced the Lord in a particularly strong way. One of the most vivid was in Jerusalem. During the hottest part of a sweltering midsummer day, I decided to walk over to the Western Wall. Called the "Wailing Wall," it is part of the ancient retaining wall of the Temple Mount and Judaism's most sacred site. Although the heat was excruciating, that afternoon ended up being the highlight of my time in Israel. It's hard to describe the awe I felt, not because of the ancient stones, but because of a sense that I was in the presence of the Father.

I had been to the Western Wall on a previous trip and felt nothing out of the ordinary. But in that moment, in that place, all the devotion and reverence I had witnessed since I traveled to this ancient land seemed to coalesce. Sensing the greatness of God as never before, I was aware that I was standing in the presence of the one the Bible calls *Yahweh Shalom*, a name that means "the Lord is peace." I wish I could tell you that I commonly experience God in this way. I don't. But I will not forget the peace I experienced in that moment.

Fortunately, you needn't travel around the world to experience more of God. He is near right now, regardless of whether you are aware of his presence. As the year begins, join me in praying for the grace to become mindful of his presence and open to the peace he wants to give.

Father, bring me into your presence today. Help me this
year to experience you as Yahweh Shalom.

TRY HARDER?

*"Peace be with you," [Jesus] said. . . . They were filled with joy when they saw
the Lord! Again he said, "Peace be with you. As the Father has sent me, so I am
sending you." Then he breathed on them and said, "Receive the Holy Spirit."*

JOHN 20:19-22

Imagine that you are at the starting line of a race. You have been training for months. You've competed on this track before, but today you are
determined to win. As soon as the starting gun goes off, you break out in a
burst of speed. Amazingly, you keep it up, rounding the track twice and then
heading across the finish line. But guess what? Despite your heroic efforts,
and the fact that this was your best time yet, you lose again. It isn't for lack
of trying. Your problem is that you aren't properly equipped to win a race
against a Porsche!

That's only a rough analogy to highlight the fact that merely trying
hard won't win the race when it comes to living our lives as Christians. Even
though many of us are working very hard at it, we rarely, if ever, experience
the joy and peace that are promised in the Bible. So what's the problem?

Perhaps we are still holding the reins of our lives too tightly, afraid to
surrender ourselves to God's Spirit. Pastor Jim Cymbala points out that "the
irony of Spirit-filled living is that we have to give up power in order to gain
a greater power. How many times in your Christian walk," he asks, "have
you come to a place where you struggled to do something, so you just tried
harder? . . . How did that work out for you? Trying harder has never gone
well for me.

"Christianity is not a self-effort religion but rather one of power—the
ability and might of the Spirit. . . . The Spirit is the only one who can produce
self-discipline, love, and boldness. But to do so, he has to control us daily."[2]

Join me today in forsaking the temptation to retain control of your life.
Together, let us ask for the grace to surrender more fully to the Holy Spirit,
allowing God to guide and energize our lives with the power that comes
from him.

*Father, you know how afraid I am of letting go, even into your good
hands. Please help me to surrender myself to you daily, confident that your
Spirit, who lives in me, is more than able to do the things I can't.*

THE PEACE GOD PROMISES

*The LORD bless you and keep you; the LORD make His face shine upon you, and be
gracious to you; the LORD lift up His countenance upon you, and give you peace.*

NUMBERS 6:24-26, NKJV

More than thirty years ago, at a site just south of Jerusalem, archaeologists unearthed two rolled-up pieces of pliable silver, about the size of a credit card. Delicately etched on each plaque were words drawn from the priestly blessing enshrined in Numbers 6:

The LORD bless and keep you; the LORD make his face shine upon you
and give you peace.

Dating to the late seventh century BC, these small silver plaques contain the earliest written citations of Scripture ever found. Perhaps they also bear witness to what must surely have been a primordial longing of our species—the desire for peace.

But what exactly is peace? When most of us think of peace, we think of an absence of conflict or the sense of tranquility we sometimes feel after a walk in the park or a day at the beach. But the Hebrew word *shalom* is far brawnier than the English word *peace*, encompassing these ideas and more. Shalom contains the idea of completeness. It is the sum of all the blessings God can bestow—healing, prosperity, soundness, well-being, good relationships, perfection. It is what happens when God shines his face on you, when he turns toward you in all his greatness and brings you good.

After the daily sacrifice, the Israelite priests would extend their hands to pray this blessing over the people. As the priests prayed, it became customary for them to leave an opening in their fingers and for the people to cover their heads with their prayer shawls. They did this to express their reverence, believing the *shekinah* (the cloud of God's presence) was hovering over their heads and its light was streaming through the open fingers of the priests.

What a beautiful image of the kind of peace God has promised to those who love him. As you seek God for a greater measure of peace this year, ask him for his shalom. Today as you pray, bow down before the Lord in reverence, asking him to shine his face upon you and give you peace.

*Father, I want the shalom you promise. Please bless me and protect me,
smile on me, and be gracious to me. Show me your favor, Lord.*

January 8

BE GRATEFUL

Always be joyful. Never stop praying. Be thankful in all circumstances,
for this is God's will for you who belong to Christ Jesus.

1 THESSALONIANS 5:16-18

What does gratitude have to do with experiencing a life of greater peace? Gratitude is like a compass that can help us get our bearings. Imagine wandering in a great wilderness with no obvious way out. You've lost the trail completely. Alone and anxious, you wonder how on earth you will ever find your way home. It's a frightening and disheartening experience. But then you remember. Digging deep into your backpack, you find the compass. With it, you know you can make your way to safety.

Like the compass, gratitude helps us find our bearings. It points us in the right direction—toward God, who is the source of all our blessings. I try to remind my children of the importance of giving thanks. When they can't find anything to be thankful about, I start reminding them: a house to live in, a family who loves them, friends, sunshine, food, fun, freedom, health, and on and on and on. Living with gratitude is like living with your face to the sun. It orients you to goodness rather than complaint.

I wish I could tell you that my face is always oriented toward the sun, that I am always as grateful as I should be. I'm not. But when I need to dig myself out of a hole, I find that gratitude makes an excellent shovel.

Join me today in turning your back on all that is wrong in your life, on every complaint and shadow that haunts you. And turn your face toward God. Give him thanks and praise, remembering all the good he's ever done for you.

Lord, thank you for revealing yourself to me, for daily blessings, for rescue
and grace and mercy and goodness. Thank you for a future that is full of hope.
Give me a grateful heart, and keep my face always turned toward you.

January 9
SHALOM

The peace I give is a gift the world cannot give.
JOHN 14:27

I love the word *peace*. It captures the way I feel standing on the shores of Lake Michigan or the relief that comes from a great massage or the comfort I feel knowing my children are safe. Even so, the word itself begins to look rather plain, more like one of Cinderella's stepsisters than Cinderella herself, when you start comparing it to the Hebrew word *shalom*. Why? Because shalom far outshines it, containing, as it does, ideas of calm, completion, harmony, wholeness, healing, wellness, perfection, safety, soundness, success, prosperity. When there is shalom, life is as it should be. We are as we should be. Nothing is off kilter. To taste shalom is to taste paradise. It is to touch the life God intended us to have.

We know, of course, that this original shalom has been shattered by sin. Instead of shalom, myriad evils have entered our world. Fortunately, God has no intention of giving up on his original idea of creating a world full of peace. Instead, he sent his Son to make a costly sacrifice in order to restore the peace, which is why Paul spoke to the Romans, saying, "'How beautiful are the feet of those who preach the gospel of peace" (Romans 10:15, NKJV).

This year as you focus on becoming a woman at peace, don't settle for less than God intends to give you. Ask him to show you the things that make for true shalom. The peace you long for, the peace God promises, will only be fully established when Jesus comes again. But even now, those of us who belong to him can grow in our experience of his promised peace. To quote Etty Hillesum, a woman who perished in a Nazi death camp during World War II, "Ultimately, we have just one moral duty: to reclaim large areas of peace in ourselves, more and more peace, and to reflect it toward others. And the more peace there is in us, the more peace there will also be in our troubled world."[3]

Father, I pray that you will show me the way to peace. Help me grow in shalom as I seek to follow you. And as I do, help me spread your peace to others.

*Jesus replied, "The most important commandment is this: 'Listen,
O Israel! The LORD our God is the one and only LORD.'"*

MARK 12:29

Unlike our unruly tongues, our ears rarely get us into trouble, unless, of course, they stop functioning, as in the case of a man who doesn't hear the whistle of an oncoming train or a child who fails to register cries of warning as she edges too close to a cliff.

Although the Hebrew word *shema* (pronounced "shmah") is translated as "hear" or "listen," it means more than what we normally think of as hearing, which is a rather passive activity. Shema implies *acting* on what has been heard. That's why our English Bibles frequently translate the word shema as "obey."[4]

Many of the Old Testament prophets preceded their announcements with the phrase "Hear the word of the Lord." In other words, listen to what God is saying, and then do what he tells you to do. Though the New Testament was written in Greek, Jesus would have been familiar with this understanding, which is why he said, "Anyone with ears to hear should listen and understand" (Mark 4:9). Hearing God means not only listening to what he says but doing what he asks.

Fortunately this active way of "hearing" is a two-way street. We can be confident that when God *hears* our prayers, the implication is that he will *act* in accordance with our best interests. Listen to the words of the psalmist:

> I cried out to him with my mouth; his praise was on my tongue. If I had cherished sin in my heart, the Lord would not have listened; but God has surely listened and has heard my prayer. Praise be to God, who has not rejected my prayer or withheld his love from me!
> PSALM 66:17-20, NIV

If you want God to hear your prayers, make sure you are doing your best to hear his voice.

Father, when your Spirit descended on Jesus in the Jordan River, you said: "This is my dearly loved Son. Listen to him" (Mark 9:7). Help me to listen.

WICKED WAYS

Search me, O God, and know my heart; test me and know my anxious thoughts. Point out anything in me that offends you, and lead me along the path of everlasting life.

PSALM 139:23-24

In Psalm 139, David bravely invites God to search his heart, asking him to point out anything offensive. The King James Version says it more forcefully: "Search me, O God, and know my heart: try me, and know my thoughts: And see if there be any wicked way in me, and lead me in the way everlasting." The phrase "wicked way" vividly describes what is off kilter in a person's life. It can literally be translated as the "way of pain."[5]

Certainly the "way of pain" can be seen in personal experience. Sin deforms and destroys, spreading pain to whomever it touches. That is why God hates it.

Though we share God's hatred for sins like murder, rape, and theft, many of us find other sins more tolerable. What is so bad about a little bit of gossip, a touch of greed, an isolated flirtation with lust? These seem more like ways of pleasure than pain. And so we indulge them, refusing to consider where they will eventually lead us.

The way to the good life, to life everlasting, is to find peace with God by embracing what he thinks is good, whether or not it appears good to us. Remember the words of the proverb: "There is a path before each person that seems right, but it ends in death" (Proverbs 14:12). Join me today in asking God to uncover any way of pain that has burrowed its way into your heart, whether from your sins or the sins of others. May the Lord be gracious to you, healing, forgiving, and restoring. And may he lead you in the way everlasting.

Father, put a spotlight on my heart and show me what is there. Help me to repent of whatever displeases you, trusting that your grace is sufficient to deal with the things in my life that need to change.

PASSIONATE FAITH

May the God of peace make you holy in every way, and may your whole spirit and soul and body be kept blameless until our Lord Jesus Christ comes again.

1 THESSALONIANS 5:23

When I was growing up, it wasn't unusual for me to reach into our family's cookie jar and find the world's favorite cookies inside. You know the ones I'm talking about—those round black cookies with the delectable white frosting in between. Neither was it unusual to bite into one of those Oreos and find myself chewing on quite another treat than the one I thought I had just popped into my mouth. Instead of a sweet, luscious mouthful, I found myself chewing on dry crumbs. Someone had sneaked them out of the jar, eaten the creamy inside, and then put the two round cookies together again, hoping no one would notice. Of course, the culprits were my two younger brothers.

I tell the story, not merely to expose their crime, but to make the point that faith can be like those Oreo cookies. Think about it. The cream inside is what really makes those cookies work. Nobody would buy them without it. Likewise, the passion we have for Christ is what makes our faith work. Without that passion, that love relationship, everything else becomes tasteless and dry.

Many people who identify themselves as Christians just go through the motions, attending church and paying lip service to their faith while their hearts are far from God. Perhaps they never had a personal encounter with Christ, or perhaps they drifted away from their first love. This can happen slowly, under the radar. The passion we have for Christ begins to dissipate and then degrade. Finally it simply slips away, making the faith we profess dry and tasteless. Instead of having a vibrant faith, we become merely religious. When that happens, we desperately need the Holy Spirit to restore and renew us.

Pursuing peace apart from Christ will, in the end, prove to be the most fruitless of journeys. Only the peace he offers has the power to transform our lives and take us where we want to go.

Father, you know the state of my heart. Please show me what is there and give me more grace, more faith, and more passion to live for you.

LESSONS IN THE DARK

He uncovers mysteries hidden in darkness; he brings light to the deepest gloom.

JOB 12:22

I wish I were a quick study, not when it comes to learning subjects like math or physics, but in becoming more Christlike. But spiritual growth is difficult, and it's often counterintuitive. Jesus tells me to stop worrying, yet my sleepless nights persist. He tells me to turn the other cheek when my instinct is to raise the other fist. He talks of dying and carrying a cross when all I want to do is enjoy every minute of the life I have. Maybe I suffer from a mental block when it comes to spiritual things. I can't get it through my head that there's no such thing as an easy path for becoming the person Christ calls me to be.

Carol Kuykendall knows what it's like to follow a path she never would have chosen. Her husband, Lynn, had nearly been pronounced cured when the results of a recent MRI showed that his brain tumor was back. This time, Carol says, their fears are bigger because the cancer now has more devastating effects and the statistics for surviving it are worse. "Yet," she says, "as I look back at our earlier journey down this same unpredictable path, I remember how we discovered surprising doses of God's hope all along the way.

"There's a saying that you should 'remember in the dark what you learned in the light.' But as we begin this journey again, I'm remembering in the dark what I learned in the dark: that God gives us enough light to direct our paths, one step at a time, and what we need when we need it most."[6] Carol is able to share these hope-filled words, even though she and her husband are facing a difficult journey.

Perhaps you know someone who is suffering in ways you can hardly imagine. Take a moment to pray for that person now and determine to keep him or her in your prayers. As you do, ask God for the faith to realize that, no matter how unpredictable or difficult your own path may sometimes feel, he is using the darkness to teach you how to become more like the Christ you love.

Father, my default setting is toward ease and pleasure. Help me not to fall apart when life gets difficult, but to grow in faith and courage, trusting that you will bring light out of even the darkest times.

WHOLENESS

He made peace with everything in heaven and on earth by means of Christ's blood on the cross. This includes you who were once far away from God. You were his enemies, separated from him by your evil thoughts and actions. Yet now he has reconciled you to himself through the death of Christ in his physical body. As a result, he has brought you into his own presence, and you are holy and blameless as you stand before him without a single fault.

COLOSSIANS 1:20-22

As I write this, the media has been chasing a story about a prominent politician who fathered a child with a woman who had worked for his family for twenty years. The man's inability to control his desires damaged not only his wife, who is divorcing him, but his children, the maid with whom he had the affair, and the son she bore. For thirteen years this politician kept the secret until the media exposed it. He's one more example of a person who, despite his power, couldn't control himself.

This story is a microcosm of the human predicament. Fashioned for relationship with God, we are meant to be people of integrity, the same on the inside as we are on the outside. But sin has driven a wedge into our lives, creating an internal rift that alienates us from ourselves, from others, and from God. It's what makes us want to hide, to wear masks that make us look better and less broken than we are. The wholeness and integrity that God has for us, on the other hand, eliminates the need for deceit because we have nothing to hide. This is the internal peace, the *shalom* that Christ brings us as we continue to yield our lives to him, healing the divisions within us so that we can have peace with God, with others, and with ourselves.

As you pray for God's peace today, ask for the grace to admit your brokenness. Ask, too, for the faith to believe that God will heal you and make you whole.

Lord, you breathed life into the first man and the first woman. They were your perfect creations. In the midst of my brokenness, breathe your life. Heal me and make me whole, I pray.

January 15
THE WEAKNESS OF VIOLENCE

"Put away your sword," Jesus told him. "Those who use the sword will die by the sword."
MATTHEW 26:52

London Is Burning." That was one of the headlines during the violent August 2011 protests in England's capital city. The uproar began when police shot and killed a twenty-six-year-old man. In response, rioters created mayhem across London and other British cities, killing at least five people and injuring others. Whether the violence was a result of simple thuggery or social inequalities is a matter of debate. But what most people would not debate is that violence is no way to solve the problem.

Martin Luther King Jr. once elegantly explained why, pointing out that "the ultimate weakness of violence is that it is a descending spiral, begetting the very thing it seeks to destroy . . . adding deeper darkness to a night already devoid of stars. Darkness cannot drive out darkness; only light can do that. Hate cannot drive out hate: only love can do that."[7]

When I was a teenager, I was so frustrated by a family member's drinking problem that I was tempted to make a public spectacle of my anger, taking every last bottle of alcohol in the house and dumping the whole mess into the street. Maybe a heap of broken glass would finally make the point. Years later, after I had moved away from home and given my life to Christ, I realized that all my critical, argumentative comments had only added more darkness to the situation. So I resolved, instead, to do my best to love the person, pray faithfully, and speak the truth, but only when absolutely necessary. A few years passed and then, through an act of tremendous grace, the person I loved stopped drinking. That was more than twenty years ago.

Most of us aren't guilty of taking our anger to the streets. But what happens in our homes when ugly arguments and critical attitudes do violence to the spirit? Let's remember that hate is nothing but a ninety-pound weakling, too weak to win a fight with itself. Just as light is the only thing that can drive out darkness, the only thing strong enough to drive out hatred is God's love.

Lord, you know how easy it is to get hooked into negative attitudes and arguments at home. Please help my family and me to find better ways of dealing with our difficulties.

HIDDEN PAIN

Dear friends, never take revenge. Leave that to the righteous anger of God.

ROMANS 12:19

There are a thousand reasons why the peace we desire eludes us. I stumbled across one of them the other day when one of my daughter's friends confided in me. A solid athlete, Kaitlin was shocked and disappointed when she didn't make her high school track team. I had been praying for her to make the team because I thought her involvement in sports would be good for her. But I also knew that the competition would be fierce, especially for a girl who hadn't been training recently.

The day after Kaitlin got the bad news, she told me that none of the girls from her former middle school had made the team. She wondered if the coach had been biased against them. Stung by his perceived rejection, Kaitlin said she hoped the team would lose every meet, because maybe then the coach would know he needed her.

It hasn't worked out that way, and Kaitlin is still fuming. She can't seem to take responsibility for her own lack of discipline. Nor can she take hope from the positive feedback the coach gave her after the tryouts and his encouragement to try again next year.

My young friend needs the grace to experience her disappointment and then let it go. Why is that so hard? Because, I am guessing, her sense of righteous indignation is a shield against her pain. But this kind of shield actually keeps the pain alive because pain is the only thing fueling her desire for revenge.

What hurt or disappointment are you holding on to? Is it fueling attitudes that are stealing your peace? Ask God to show you exactly what's in your heart. And then ask him for the grace to let it go, replacing your hurt with his peace.

Show me, Lord, what is in my heart. Uncover the pain and the hurt. Let me look at it in the safety of your presence. And then give me the grace to let it go.

GETTING THE FACTS STRAIGHT

*Have you never heard? Have you never understood? The LORD is the everlasting God,
the Creator of all the earth. He never grows weak or weary. No one can measure the
depths of his understanding. He gives power to the weak and strength to the powerless.*

ISAIAH 40:28-29

Have you ever heard of "brain school"? It's an educational program,
also known as Arrowsmith, developed more than thirty years ago in
Toronto. Based on brain plasticity, the capacity of the brain to change and
heal itself if given the right kind of stimulation, the program has enabled
many children with learning disabilities to grasp what they're taught.

Many of these children have trouble with what educators call "working
memory." For instance, they will learn their math facts and then forget them.
Then they will learn them again and forget them again. No matter how hard
they try, they can't seem to hold on to the facts they've learned. Fortunately,
such children no longer need to be locked in this vicious cycle. By targeting
certain areas of the brain with exercises designed to improve specific brain
functions, the Arrowsmith Program enables children to increase their working memory so that they can retain the information they learn.

When it comes to retaining theological truth—truth about God—some
of us have our own problems with working memory. At times we seem to
have a solid grasp on God's goodness and love. Our faith sustains us through
many difficulties. But there are other times when we seem to lose the memory of who God is and what he has done for us. He seems distant. We feel
tired out by life's endless challenges. Fortunately, our spirits are as plastic as
our brains. Because of God's grace, it is possible not only to learn the truth,
but to remember it when life gets difficult. Today let us ask God to increase
our spiritual memory, so that with John Newton, the author of "Amazing
Grace," we, too, can say:

*Through many dangers, toils and snares
I have already come;
'Tis Grace that brought me safe thus far
and Grace will lead me home.*

RUNNING AWAY

I can never escape from your Spirit! I can never get away from your presence!
PSALM 139:7

My sister and I made a pact. We would run away from home together. Our parents weren't that bad, we agreed, but we'd both had enough of our older brother. It was time to go. Here's what we agreed on. The first one to wake in the middle of the night promised to wake the other. Together we would steal out of the house and make our way to a nearby park where we would live. The only hard part would be deciding which picnic table to camp under.

Ever felt like running away—even as an adult? I have. Maybe that's why I love Margaret Wise Brown's classic children's story, *The Runaway Bunny*. Perhaps you remember it. The book is about a mother rabbit and a baby bunny who has determined to run away from home. The bunny tells his mother that if she runs after him, he will become a fish and swim away from her. But his mother assures him that she will become a fisherman who will fish for him. Delightful images parade across the pages as the bunny thinks of ingenious means of escape while the mother even more ingeniously assures him of her love and determination not to let him go. In the end, the bunny gives up, deciding to stay home and be his mother's baby bunny.

A friend of mine suggested that Psalm 139 reminds her of *The Runaway Bunny*. As soon as she said this, I understood why it had always been one of my favorite psalms. Listen to how the psalmist describes his experience of God:

> I can never escape from your Spirit! I can never get away from your presence! If I go up to heaven, you are there; if I go down to the grave, you are there. If I ride the wings of the morning, if I dwell by the farthest oceans, even there your hand will guide me, and your strength will support me. (7-10)

Truly God is our great pursuer and protector. If you are tempted to run away from circumstances that are troubling you, read Psalm 139. Talk to God about everything that's difficult in your life, asking him to reveal his persistent, fatherly love.

Lord, "You saw me before I was born. Every day of my life was recorded in your book"
(Psalm 139:16). Help me on this day to experience your love and protection.

THE POWER OF A SINGLE PRAYER

*Pray in the Spirit at all times and on every occasion. Stay alert and
be persistent in your prayers for all believers everywhere.*

EPHESIANS 6:18

M ost middle-school children aren't crazy about praying out loud. Take
my youngest. At the end of each day, we pray together briefly, offering thanks and petitions and then usually closing with the Lord's Prayer. At
times, Luci will ask me to do the praying for her. But I remind her that God
hears from me all the time. "He wants to hear your voice too," I say. I wonder
if my daughter's reticence stems from the fact that she underestimates her
influence with God.

Perhaps that's true for most of us. We don't realize what a difference
one prayer can make. Author Fern Nichols tells of a time in her own life
when she felt prompted to pray for her husband, Rle, and her ten-year-old
son, Troy, while they were on a canoeing trip with friends in Canada. Sitting
down at the kitchen table, she prayed through passages from her Bible:
"Protect them from the evil one" (John 17:15, NIV); "'Because he loves me,'
says the LORD, 'I will rescue him; I will protect him, for he acknowledges my
name'" (Psalm 91:14, NIV). Because the urge to intercede was so strong, she
prayed for about an hour.

That night Fern received a call from her husband telling her that during the afternoon, he and Troy had been struggling for their lives in the icy
waters of the Fraser River. Their canoe had capsized, and they had spent
nearly an hour in the freezing, raging water until they and their friends were
finally rescued by helicopter. The paramedics told Rle that Troy would have
died from hypothermia had he been in the water for just ten more minutes.
Fern was startled to learn that they had been struggling at the same time she
had been praying.[8]

If you ask whether her prayer made a difference, Fern won't hesitate to
say so. Her story reminds us of how God can work powerfully through one
woman who prays. Because Fern paid attention to God's Spirit, he used her
prayers to keep four people safe. Now that's what I call influence!

*Lord, I remember that shalom also means "safety." Thank you for the way you
have kept me safe. Please use my prayers to bring shalom to others.*

January 20
SLOWLY, SLOWLY

*It is useless for you to work so hard from early morning until late at night,
anxiously working for food to eat; for God gives rest to his loved ones.*

PSALM 127:2

Hurry never brings out the best in me. Heaven help anyone who gets
between me and the goal I'm focused on achieving. Trying to squeeze
in a trip to the store before picking my daughter up at school, I am tempted
to speed. Waiting in line at the polls when I need to be home cooking dinner,
I start complaining. Worried that my daughter will miss the school bus, I nag
her—hurry, hurry, hurry!

John Ortberg once asked Dallas Willard for advice on how to grow
spiritually. The advice Willard gave surprised him, because instead of laying
out a complex set of instructions for what John should do, he simply said this:
Eliminate all hurry from your life.

Several years ago I traveled to Greece. It was a fascinating trip, despite
several mishaps. One woman in our group lost her passport on the concourse
in Detroit. Without it, she had to fly right back to Detroit from our stop in
Munich, missing the entire trip, a thirtieth anniversary celebration for her
and her husband. Another woman broke her ankle on a slippery side street
in Athens. And a third person hit his head and shattered his glasses when
he stumbled while sightseeing in Rhodes. After the trip, I kept hearing our
tour guide's voice in my mind. One of her favorite sayings continued to roll
across my brain. "Slowly, slowly," she would say as she took us to one ancient
site after another, attempting to explain the pace of historical change in that
land. It occurred to me that "slowly, slowly" would have been a good mantra
for the group to have adopted, perhaps helping us avoid at least some of the
mishaps suffered along the way.

What's your day like today? Filled with meetings? Scheduled to the
max? Spinning out of control? Whatever your day, week, month, year, or life
looks like right now, take a moment to think about how much more peace
you would enjoy if you could find a way to make "slowly, slowly" your own
personal mantra.

*Lord, I'm not in control of every aspect of my day, but I am in control of some. Show me
places in my life where I can slow down. Teach me to eliminate all hurry from my life.*

A TOOL THAT WORKS

The Lord answered, "If you had faith even as small as a mustard seed, you could say to this mulberry tree, 'May you be uprooted and thrown into the sea,' and it would obey you!"

LUKE 17:6

I love smartphones and the apps that come with them. Want the news? Just click on an app and you will soon know what is going on in Aruba or Afghanistan. Looking for the best price? Simply scan the bar code. I can't wait until someone develops an app that will cook dinner or clean the bathroom. But the app I really want, the one I would pay good money for, would be what I call the peace app. Feeling stressed? Just download it and you will feel as though you're living at a spa. Having a hard time in a relationship? This app will smooth things out. You've got the peace app!

Okay, enough of the ridiculous. When it comes to having peace, the only practical application I know of is faith. Faith enables us to stand up when we feel like lying down, to move forward when we want to run away. It's what enables us to please God, because without faith we can't begin to live the way he wants us to. The book of Hebrews tells us that faith "is the confidence that what we hope for will actually happen" (11:1). Scripture goes on to say that by faith, people have overthrown kingdoms, ruled with justice, received what God promised, quenched flames of fire, escaped death. It was by faith that their weakness was turned to strength (see Hebrews 11:33-34). If we want to have peace, then we have to have faith.

But faith isn't a matter of "trying harder." It is something supernatural, a gift from God to enable you to do what you cannot do on your own. It's also a gift that has to be used. If you fail to exercise it, living by your own wits, you will find that faith becomes a shriveled, feeble thing, unable to support you when you need it.

Ask God today to fill you with real faith, not in yourself, but in him. Remember what Jesus said: even faith the size of a mustard seed—and that's tiny—can do great things.

Lord, thank you for the gift of faith. Help me to use it so I can obey your commandments and hold fast to your promises. I want to take the risks that you ask. And as I do, increase my faith.

KEEP YOUR HEART PURE

Purify me from my sins, and I will be clean; wash me,
and I will be whiter than snow.

PSALM 51:7

Firearm experts point out that if a gun is never cleaned, it will eventually become a safety hazard. That's because every time you fire a gun, residue is left behind. This grime will eventually clog up the works, rendering the firearm unsafe to use. The same is true with our tongues. Every time we lash out in anger, every time we accuse, berate, gossip, criticize, or betray a confidence, a residue is left in our hearts that will make our tongues more harmful to ourselves and others.

Cleaning a handgun is fairly straightforward. After safely disassembling it, you wipe it with a cloth rag, removing as much of the caked-on carbon as possible. Then you apply a solvent and scrub the gun with a brush. After more wiping and scrubbing and brushing, you oil the components that need to be lubricated. Then you reassemble it and, presto chango, you have a gun that is much safer to use.

Cloth rags, solvents, and oil won't quite do it for our tongues, of course. But there is something we can do to make them less hazardous in the future. We can begin by recognizing negative patterns of speech, asking God to search our hearts and to show us where we have sinned. Then we can ask him for forgiveness. A clean heart will enable our tongues to function the way God intends, building others up rather than tearing them down.

"Have mercy on me, O God, because of your unfailing love. Because of your great compassion, blot out the stain of my sins. Wash me clean from my guilt. Purify me from my sin. For I recognize my rebellion; it haunts me day and night. Against you, and you alone, have I sinned; I have done what is evil in your sight. . . . Purify me from my sins, and I will be clean; wash me, and I will be whiter than snow. . . . Unseal my lips, O Lord, that my mouth may praise you" (Psalm 51:1-4, 7, 15).

LISTENING

*Understand this, my dear brothers and sisters: You must all be
quick to listen, slow to speak, and slow to get angry.*

JAMES 1:19

Because both of my daughters were born in China, I tell them they are my favorite Chinese characters. You probably know that the written form of Chinese contains thousands of characters, some of which require dozens of brush strokes to create. What's more, some of these characters are pictographs—pictorial representations of physical objects. The character for *sage*, for instance, is of particular interest. Consisting of a large ear and a small mouth, it implies that a wise person is someone who listens well and speaks little. When it comes to our search for peace, we should ask ourselves what life would be like if we developed larger ears and smaller mouths.

Why is it sometimes so difficult to listen? Perhaps because we think we know more than we do. A child complains about her homework for the hundredth time and we tell her to get to work and stop being lazy. But what if her complaints are a symptom of a learning disability and not laziness? Have we really listened, allowing ourselves to consider that more might be going on than "meets the ear"?

Some of us have difficulty listening because we have an urge to fix things. A wife tells her husband she feels down and he tells her she's got to start exercising more regularly. A friend worries about her son's inability to keep a job, and we tell her to stop worrying. She can't do anything about it anyway. Often our advice goes nowhere. That's because we're either telling people what they already know or offering advice they aren't ready to hear. In such instances, we often withhold the thing they need the most—a listening ear.

To fine-tune your listening skills, consider spending the next couple of days straining to hear what others are trying to say. Put down the phone, take a break from your computer, turn off those video games, and really listen to the people around you. Help them to experience more of God's peace by giving them your full attention.

*Father, give me the grace to hear what others are saying. Teach me wisdom
as I listen, both for words that are spoken and for those that are not.*

A MATTER OF INTERPRETATION

The eternal God is your refuge, and his everlasting arms are under you.

DEUTERONOMY 33:27

Pastor and author Charles Stanley tells about camping in the Canadian Rockies one night. During the night he awoke to find himself pinned down by a heavy weight. *A bear,* he thought, *lying on top of me!* Terrified, he lay perfectly still. After a while, hearing nothing and feeling only the heavy, immovable weight pressing down on him, he struggled out from under it.

Standing outside his tent, he realized that there had been no ravenous bear, only six inches of wet snow that had fallen during the night, causing the tent to collapse. Then he remembered—the previous day he had asked God for snow. An avid photographer, he knew that snow would provide a striking contrast to the rugged terrain of mountains and trees, especially if the view could be captured on black-and-white film.[9] Ironically, it was the answer to his prayer that had terrified him.

Stanley uses this experience to point out that the way we view life determines our response to it. Fear will color our response to everything. If, for instance, we think we are going to fail in a particular job, we probably will. Or if we think people won't like us, we will behave in ways that discourage positive relationships. Furthermore, if we think God doesn't care about us or doesn't want to help us, it will be very difficult to receive his help because we will be too busy focusing on our own challenges and difficulties.

The way to peace involves rejecting fear in favor of embracing the story God has already told us—that he is a good and loving Father who will provide for his children. And that underneath us, in every situation, are his everlasting arms.

Lord, sometimes I am afraid of my own shadow. Help me to overcome fear, not by trying to convince myself that the world is without danger, but by trusting that I am never without your help.

SIDE EFFECTS

Now you are free from the power of sin and have become slaves of God. Now you do those things that lead to holiness and result in eternal life. For the wages of sin is death, but the free gift of God is eternal life through Christ Jesus our Lord.

ROMANS 6:22-23

I get a chuckle from all those slick television commercials advertising expensive new medicines. Why? Because, by law, even the most sophisticated ad has to disclose the potential side effects of the medicine it is advertising. You've probably heard one that pushes a medicine that will rid you of arthritis pain. But then, in a reassuring tone, the voice goes on to say that in addition to all its wonderful benefits, this medicine might cause indigestion, diarrhea, and abdominal pain. Oh, and by the way, it might also cause a heart attack or stroke, which might lead to your death. Perhaps that reassuring voice is meant to signal that even if the worst should happen, at least you won't be in pain anymore.

Or what about this pitch for a drug to cure restless leg syndrome: "Tell your doctor . . . if you experience increased gambling, sexual, or other urges." Thanks, but I'd rather my legs get twitchy than take a medicine that makes me want to run off to Vegas with my life savings.

The Bible has its own share of prescriptions, for which the side effects are duly noted. Swallow the sin pill, for instance, and it will eventually lead to disaster, calamity, conflict, alienation, bitterness, ruin, and death. But the side effects that come from entrusting your life to God and to his Son Jesus Christ are love, joy, peace, patience, kindness, goodness, faithfulness, gentleness, self-control (see Galatians 5:22-23), and life everlasting (see John 3:16). No slick ads, just the truth that will set you free.

Lord, thank you for not hiding the consequences of living in a particular way. Help me not to seek an easy life but to seek a good life, blessed by your presence and held safely in your hands.

STAND UP STRAIGHT!

*Look at the lilies and how they grow. They don't work or make their clothing, yet
Solomon in all his glory was not dressed as beautifully as they are. And if God cares
so wonderfully for flowers that are here today and thrown into the fire tomorrow,
he will certainly care for you. Why do you have so little faith? . . . So don't be afraid,
little flock. For it gives your Father great happiness to give you the Kingdom.*

LUKE 12:27-28, 32

Take a moment to imagine that you are living in a two-hundred-square-foot house with four-foot-high ceilings. You have to shoehorn yourself into your bedroom every night because the room is so tiny. Your kitchen consists of a hot plate, a small sink, and a tiny fridge. Because the ceilings are so low, you have to stoop whenever you walk around. Stuck in a too-small house, you feel frustrated, cramped, and depressed, wishing you had a better place to live.

That's a picture of what life can be like when we fail to grasp who we are in Christ. Without believing we are daughters of the King, we struggle to feel good about ourselves, attempting to find our identity elsewhere. But no matter how successful or how beautiful we may be, no matter what relationships we pursue, we are never quite at peace. Always looking for something or someone to tell us who we are and to make us feel secure, we miss out on the joy and confidence that comes from resting in the Father's provision and following Christ wherever he leads.

If you are living in a too-small spiritual house, ask Jesus for the faith to step out of it so you can stand up straight and be the woman God is calling you to be. If you make the Kingdom of God your primary concern, Jesus assures you the Father will provide for your needs.

*Father, help me to grasp what it means to be your daughter. Give me the confidence to
follow your Son wherever he leads, knowing that ultimately, he will lead me home.*

January 27

PASS IT ON—OR NOT!

Don't point your finger at someone else and try to pass the blame!

HOSEA 4:4

I cut my teeth playing the popular board game Monopoly. I loved all the fake cash that enabled me to amass property, build hotels, and then charge outrageous rent to players unlucky enough to land on them. I was so intent on winning that I prayed God would give me an edge, then cried when I discovered he wasn't interested in doing so. Of course, I was only eight years old at the time. I've since learned that my fascination with the game is shared by people everywhere; more than one billion people have played it. Despite that, there is another game that's far more popular, one that most people on earth have played—not just once, but many times.

This game first took place in the Garden of Eden, and Adam and Eve were the first to play it. No, it wasn't croquet. It was the blame game. Remember what Adam said when God asked him about that bite-size chunk he'd taken out of the forbidden fruit? Quick as lightning, the first man pointed his finger at the first woman and said, "She made me do it!" Then Eve joined in the game, saying, "The serpent tricked me. That's why I ate it."

In our house, the blame game might go something like this. I blame Katie. Katie turns around and blames Luci. Luci turns around and blames the dog. And the dog turns around and bites the cat. Okay, we don't always play it in exactly that sequence with such disastrous results for the cat, but I assure you we play it. Your family probably does too. But what's the point? Does blaming others really make us feel better? And can any of us ever win such a game?

The truth is that playing the blame game on a regular basis is a terrific way to destroy the peace at home, at work, and at church. So remember: when you're dealing with blame, it's always a good idea to pass it on—not!

Father, please put a check in my spirit whenever I start to play the blame game. Help me to step back and think honestly about the things that are bothering me, taking responsibility as needed rather than passing my frustration on.

WHO ARE YOU TALKING TO?

*If you make the LORD your refuge, if you make the Most
High your shelter, no evil will conquer you.*

PSALM 91:9-10

Jim Cymbala says that "unbelief talks to itself instead of talking to God."[10] How's that for cutting straight to the problem of our lack of peace? I don't know about you, but my unbelief has talked to itself all night long at times, keeping me wide awake when everyone else was fast asleep. But what does that kind of conversation sound like?

For some it might sound like this: *I've got to figure out a way to make more money or we're going under. No way can we make it on my salary. But this economy is rotten. What am I going to do? I won't be able to pay the mortgage. The kids won't be able to go to the doctor. If we lose our house, we'll have to move and they'll have to change schools. The stress is going to tear my marriage apart. There's no way I can ever retire. I've got to figure out a way to make more money or we're going under.*

Notice how circular the talk is, just worry feeding on worry and ending up pretty much in the same place it began. Now, I'm not trying to downplay concerns that are serious and difficult. I'm just saying that we won't be able to resolve them by feeding on our unbelief, rather than confiding in God and feeding on the faith he gives.

What if the conversation went more like this: *Lord, I'm worried and afraid. Yet I know you're faithful and that you have promised to provide. Thank you for helping me pay the bills last month. I still don't know what to do, but you do. Instead of being afraid, I want to stay close to you, to put you first, to serve you and obey you and to trust that as I do you will be with me and my family. Lead me step by step. Help me to glorify you no matter what happens. I trust you, Lord.*

Soaking in God's Word, letting it shape the conversation we are having with ourselves and God, can help us stop conversing with unbelief. Remember, if you want to find peace, you've got to be careful who you talk to.

*Father, I want to be in communion with you and not with unbelief. Turn my
mind, my heart, and my prayers to you, the only one who gives real peace.*

BE CAREFUL WHAT YOU LISTEN TO

Avoid all perverse talk; stay away from corrupt speech.

PROVERBS 4:24

My youngest child, Luci, is a girl who always wants to be "in the know," and it's amazing what she can hear from a football field away. So I was surprised when during a conversation regarding who in our extended family does what, she seemed shocked when I told her my brother Mark manages a laboratory. Screwing up her face in a look that combined complete disgust with total shock, she exclaimed, "What? Uncle Mark manages a lavatory?"

Most of us have played the childhood game of Telephone, in which one person whispers a short sentence to the next person, and that person whispers it to the next person, and so on. Finally, the last person to hear the whispered message repeats what he's heard, often to gales of laughter because the original message has become so garbled. A couple of years ago, someone organized 1,330 children to play the game. The original sentence was "Together we can make a world of difference." After more than two hours and 1,330 repetitions, the sentence had morphed into "We're going to break a world record. Haaaa!"[11]

Considering how easy it is to misunderstand what others are saying, it's amazing how much credibility we give to our ears. Even when there is no maliciousness involved, it's easy for truth to morph into falsehood. Now mix a little negative energy into the picture, as when people pass on the latest bit of gossip or speak ill of others, and the potential for mischief grows exponentially.

If we want to become people who experience God's peace, we need to be careful not only to control our tongues, but to control our ears, limiting the kinds of things we allow ourselves to hear. The next time you get together with friends or watch television or sit around in the lunchroom chatting, be careful what you listen to. If someone starts gossiping, see if you can find a graceful way to change the subject or make an exit. Do whatever you need to in order to guard your ears, because doing so will also guard your heart, keeping it from passing judgment on others.

Father, help me to resist the temptation of listening to gossip. Make me aware of how fallible my ears are, so that I might use them to increase peace and not destroy it.

GOD DOESN'T WASTE ANYTHING

*"I know the plans I have for you," says the LORD. "They are plans for
good and not for disaster, to give you a future and a hope."*

JEREMIAH 29:11

Sometimes it's the little things that make your day. Last summer, the city started dropping off blue and gold recycling carts in my neighborhood. I was delighted to have a shiny new cart of my own with wheels and enough space to handle all the recyclables that wouldn't fit into the old bins. No more lugging dirty bins to the street, hoping nothing would spill out along the way. With the advent of my new cart, I became downright passionate about stuffing every bit of unwanted paper, metal, and glass into the cart. I wanted nothing to go to waste.

My approach to recycling reminds me of habits I have formed as a writer. I have found that inspiration comes in many guises—some painful, some beautiful, some surprising. I try to remember things that strike me, that make me smile or weep or wonder. Even the most mundane experience can be grist for my writer's mill, so I do my best to pay attention and take note of every possibility.

I think God shares this passion for not wasting anything. He knows that even the most painful, bewildering circumstances can produce a life of beauty and grace if we allow them to be molded by his creative hands. Like the writer, what matters to him is not so much the circumstance itself but what he intends to do with it.

What kind of life are you living right now? Are you married or single? Are you old or young? Are you living in a big house or one that's cramped and small? Perhaps you've reached rock bottom. You may be sitting in prison or struggling with a serious illness. Wherever you are, whatever your circumstances, remember that you belong to a God who lets nothing go to waste. Trust him to make something beautiful of your life, no matter how painful and confusing your circumstances may be.

Father, help me to realize that you are writing a good story for my life. When I am afraid or discouraged, remind me of your steadfast love and your creative power.

CHARACTER COSTS

*[Jesus] said to her, "Daughter, your faith has made you
well. Go in peace. Your suffering is over."*

MARK 5:34

I live in an older home, built in 1925. Though many people have commented on how much character the house has, I have come to realize that
character comes at a price. People love the wood floors, crown molding, and
gabled roof. But they don't realize that in the ten years we've lived in this
house, I have had to put in new windows, remodel the basement, rebuild the
screened-in porch, replace the boiler, repaint the interior and exterior, fix
the fence, replace some of the gutters, and do a host of smaller repairs. In the
process, I've gotten to know various plumbers, electricians, plasterers, paint-
ers, carpenters, and woodworkers.

Depending on the work that needs to be done, some of these craftsmen
begin by messing things up even more. Like the guy who does the plaster
work. I cringe whenever I see him twisting and turning a screwdriver into
a wall or ceiling in order to probe the extent of the damage that needs to be
repaired, even though I know that he has to do this before he can estimate
the cost of fixing it.

Sometimes God works in our lives in a similar way, bringing a problem
to light and then probing it painfully to show us the extent of the damage
he is determined to repair. Maybe it's a relationship issue. Take the case of a
woman whose marriage is collapsing. Finally, she and her husband seek counseling in order to heal the marriage. As they work through issues together, it
becomes clear that many of their marital difficulties are a carryover of problems she had with her father when she was a child. Though this discovery
may open the door to future healing, it also opens the door to deeper pain as
she looks back on a difficult childhood.

Like the craftsman who won't simply slap a patch of plaster on a deteri-
orating wall, God is not interested in quick fixes that do not solve our deeper
problems. When it comes to taking on the character of Christ, the process
can at times be costly. But his aim is to bring a deeper healing, true *shalom*.
And that should be our aim too.

*Father, thank you for showing me places in my heart that need more of your healing grace.
Help me to face whatever I need to in order to become the woman you want me to be.*

AH, THE PEACE

The temptations in your life are no different from what others experience. And God is faithful. He will not allow the temptation to be more than you can stand. When you are tempted, he will show you a way out so that you can endure.

1 CORINTHIANS 10:13

Here's a question. What's a five-letter word for peace that starts with the letter *b*? Stumped? Let me offer some clues. It's a place where treasures can be had for free. Both children and adults love to go there (dogs do too). And now for the clincher—it's a word that rhymes with *peach*. By now you know I'm thinking of the word *beach*. Some of the most peaceful moments of my life have been spent walking along a beach, feasting my eyes on sparkling blue water dancing in the sunlight. Ah, now that is my idea of peace.

To be sure, it's a fleeting sort of peace, an interlude between times that are more hectic, tense, or difficult. But even with these, there is a kind of peace that can endure. The only catch regarding this brand of peace is that it doesn't come easily. In fact, it is often the fruit of struggle.

Martin Luther once made a rather surprising statement: "My temptations," he said, "have been my masters in divinity." Rick Warren supports this idea, pointing out that temptation isn't necessarily a bad thing. Why? Because it can become a stepping stone to spiritual maturity, presenting not just an opportunity to do wrong but an opportunity to do right. Every time you choose to do the right thing, you become more like Christ.

"Character development always involves a choice," Warren says. "And temptation provides that opportunity." He goes on to say that "God develops real *peace* within us, not by making things go the way we planned, but by allowing times of chaos and confusion. Anyone can be peaceful watching a beautiful sunset or relaxing on vacation. We learn real peace by choosing to trust God in circumstances in which we are tempted to worry or be afraid."[1]

In light of these truths, it looks like I may need to revise my theory that peace = beach. Or maybe it does, as long as when we're enjoying the beauty of creation, we take the opportunity to resist temptation, becoming more like the Lord we love.

Lord, help me to recognize temptation when it comes, realizing that you are giving me an opportunity to grow. Strengthen me in your peace, I pray.

February 2
A TERRIBLE, HORRIBLE, NO GOOD, VERY BAD DAY

*Don't worry about tomorrow, for tomorrow will bring its own
worries. Today's trouble is enough for today.*

MATTHEW 6:34

This morning as I backed the car out of our narrow driveway, trying to navigate between piles of snow on either side, a chunk of the driver's side mirror tore off as it scraped too close to the fence. Moaning about my mistake, I dropped my daughter off at school. Moments later I heard a loud scraping noise as I exited the parking lot. (By now my moans had given way to heartfelt exclamations that I should not repeat here!) My car had clipped the edge of a small snowbank, scraping the bottom of the front passenger door. But how much damage, I reasoned, could a snowbank do? Several hundred dollars' worth, I discovered when I stopped to inspect the door.

By now I was beginning to feel that I had embarked on what Judith Viorst calls a "terrible, horrible, no good, very bad day."[2] Attempting to lift my spirits, I reminded myself that everyone makes mistakes. Then I tried countering my bad mood by counting my blessings, thanking God for sunshine, children, and snowflakes. Wait a minute, wasn't it snowflakes that had started all the trouble?

My dark mood hovered like an unbudgeable cloud. Then I thought of some wise advice offered by an elderly friend. Mary told me that whenever something bothered her, she asked herself whether the problem would matter fifty years from now. If the answer was yes, she gave herself permission to be upset. But a response of no helped restore her perspective. Since I couldn't convince myself that a damaged car would matter much in fifty years, I decided to stop wallowing in my "very bad day." To distract myself, I decided to head to the grocery store. By the time I returned home, I felt better, helped by a short drive under brilliant blue skies, a dose of fresh air, and the fact that I encountered not a single fence or destructive snowbank.

*Jesus, it comforts me to remember that you know about bad days. Thank you
for becoming human, for sharing our suffering, and for giving us hope.*

OUCH!

*The lips of the godly speak helpful words, but the mouth
of the wicked speaks perverse words.*

PROVERBS 10:32

Last week I opened the cupboard above the stove and was nearly assaulted by a bottle of Tabasco sauce. As it tumbled out, it missed me and shattered on the ceramic stove top below. Or that's what I thought at first. Closer inspection revealed that the little bottle of hot sauce was still in perfect condition. What had shattered was not the bottle but the ceramic stove top! When I searched the web to see whether it could be replaced, I found this piece of sage advice: "Ceramic stove tops are very fragile. Never store anything above them." Now you tell me! After more research and a couple of phone calls, I discovered that repairing the stove would cost more than it was worth. I couldn't help concluding that the little bottle of Tabasco sauce was the most expensive condiment I had ever purchased.

I have come to realize that most of us, like ceramic stove tops, are far more fragile than we may appear. I have an elderly friend who is slipping into dementia. Invariably kind throughout the years I have known her, she is starting to take on a more belligerent tone. The other day, when I was thinking my hair looked exceptionally nice, she told me that it looked awful—terrible, in fact—assuring me that she was only informing me because it is always important to tell the truth.

A couple of days later, my daughter celebrated her fifteenth birthday. Her big gift was a longish down coat that would keep her warm in subzero temperatures. She and I had gone shopping together, and she selected a coat the same color and cut as mine. When I made the mistake of commenting that we would now look like twins, she blurted out that she didn't want to look so old. Now I was not just a woman with bad hair, but an *old* woman with bad hair! Ouch!

Words can tumble from our mouths much like that Tabasco sauce, doing more damage than we might imagine. I have to wonder how often my own words have landed on someone else's fragile heart, shattering his or her sense of well-being. Today I pray for the grace to choose my words more carefully.

*Father, help me today to think about every word that comes out of my
mouth. Let me speak only what is helpful and leave the rest unsaid.*

WHO DO YOU WORSHIP?

*Happy are those who hear the joyful call to worship, for they
will walk in the light of your presence, LORD.*

PSALM 89:15

The other night I took my daughters to see *Justin Bieber: Never Say Never.* We
made the mistake of arriving five minutes before the movie started, too
late to snag anything but seats in the front two rows of the theater. But that
was just the start of my punishment. Having misread the showtimes, I was
stuck purchasing tickets to the 3-D version. There would be no place to hide
from Bieber's famous mop of hair, swirling just millimeters from my face.

Surrounded by an ocean of girls, I spotted only two males in atten-
dance—a clueless dad and a hapless boy, no doubt dragged to the theater by
enthusiastic family members. Speaking of enthusiasm, I was shocked by how
loud a couple hundred teenagers can scream. We faced the double assault
of girls screaming on the big screen as well as in the theater itself. It was a
deafening but hilarious experience to hear all these kids so worked up over
a sixteen-year-old boy, all the more amusing because it so vividly recalled a
Beatles movie I had seen in prehistoric times. I remember sitting in the back
of the theater feeling annoyed by all the girls up front who were bouncing
up and down, waving their hands in front of the screen and screaming at the
top of their lungs. I liked the Beatles, but I couldn't understand the frenzy of
passion they were able to create in many of my friends' hearts.

My brush with Bieber-mania reminds me that our sense of peace is
directly influenced by what or whom we worship. I have yet to meet a single
person who will admit to feeling more peaceful due to adulation of a super-
star. But canvass a roomful of Christians, and you will be hard put to find
someone who hasn't experienced God's presence and peace in worship.

Today let us worship him.

*Lord, let my heart be filled with passion as I think about your beauty, grace,
and strength. Fill me with the knowledge of your presence, I pray.*

February 5
POWER UP

The Kingdom of God is not just a lot of talk; it is living by God's power.

1 CORINTHIANS 4:20

Several years ago I invested in a whole-house generator. Because my office is in my home and because the power goes out a couple of times a year, I didn't want to lose work time during an outage. There's just one little problem. Each time we've had an outage, the generator has failed. Because of a glitch in the system, it won't go on until an electrician comes to the rescue.

Without power it's hard to accomplish much. The same is true in our spiritual lives. Many of us feel weaker than we should because our lives lack the power that comes from God. There is a glitch in our spiritual systems.

In his book *Spirit Rising*, Jim Cymbala makes a similar point. "I love," he says, "to look at the buildings of Manhattan, especially at night when the lights are all on. . . . However, regardless of how influential New York City and its people can be, if you take away the electrical power—which happens occasionally during a blackout—the whole thing shuts down. . . . Without power, all that potential is wasted.

"The same is true for us believers. If we don't have access to spiritual power, how can we accomplish what needs to be done? Power to overcome sin. Power to overcome spiritual enemies that attack us. Power to endure hardship and affliction. Power to witness. Power to speak. Power to pray. Isn't more spiritual power probably the greatest need we have today?"[3]

If you have felt powerless, overcome by weakness, assailed on all sides by frustration, put a stop to it today by refocusing your life on God's purposes—recommitting yourself to doing his will by spreading the gospel and serving those who are lost and hurting. Ask God to glorify himself in you despite your weakness, and he will.

Father, I am tired of being beaten up by troubles and surrounded by difficulties. I need your power to overcome sin in my life and to do your will with boldness and confidence. I want to recommit my life to you. Forgive me for being more interested in building my kingdom than yours. Empower me to do your will, and fill me with your Holy Spirit, I pray.

STOP HIDING

Oh, what joy for those whose disobedience is forgiven, whose sin is put out of sight!
Yes, what joy for those whose record the LORD has cleared of
guilt, whose lives are lived in complete honesty!

PSALM 32:1-2

One thing God never does is build on a weak foundation. If you are serious about knowing more peace in your life, you will have to be honest—with God, yourself, and others. It may be painful at times. But it will also be freeing and life giving, because honesty can open a door to God's grace that may well transform your life. That's what happened to a man by the name of John Van Sloten. Here's how his story begins: "For the most part [I] thought I understood the whole God thing: be good, attend services, learn your catechism, help out a bit, and most important, hide your dark side. . . .

"I was living a developer's life—in the worst sense of the word. I was a nasty, arrogant deal maker. . . . Once, I was told, I was so hard on an electrical engineer that he ended up having a mental breakdown. This was what a developer needed to be, I thought.

"My mind," he confesses, "was constantly engrossed with my net worth. All I ever thought about was the next deal, the next car, the next house, and, sadly, even the next wife."

Then came a moment of extraordinary honesty in which he told a pastor friend everything that was going on in his heart. Instead of feeling ashamed and crushed by his guilt, he felt strangely exhilarated, realizing that someone was looking straight through him, aware of everything he had done, and yet not holding it against him. "I felt completely judged and convicted," he says, "and at the same time forgiven and freed. . . . The love that I felt in that moment was so beautifully merciful, so powerfully gracious, so numinously beyond anything I had ever known."[4]

Van Sloten's choice of words is interesting. He said that once he was honest about his failings, he began to feel whole and reintegrated. The meaning of *shalom*, of course, is "wholeness"—God putting back together what has been ripped apart by sin. The first step is confession. The next step is peace.

Lord, I want to stop hiding and let my life be exposed to the light of your
presence. Heal me and help me and make me whole, I pray.

Looking at the man, Jesus felt genuine love for him. "There is still one thing you haven't done," he told him. "Go and sell all your possessions and give the money to the poor, and you will have treasure in heaven. Then come, follow me."

MARK 10:21

Author Francis Chan points out that when people give their lives to Christ simply because they are looking for a get-out-of-hell-free card or because they want Jesus to "join" them on their journey through life, there is often little or no evidence of change. Why? Because they haven't yet repented, haven't yet grasped the enormity of what is required. Instead of allowing Christ to save and define them, they have simply added a little bit of Jesus, hoping that will "spiritualize" their lives. In their hearts, they want God to follow them around, helping them get wherever it is they want to go, rather than the other way around.

To put it another way, trying to add a little bit of Jesus to your life is like adding salt and pepper to a diet of rice and beans. At the end of the day, your food may taste a little better, but the truth is you are still dining on rice and beans.

Repentance, Chan says, is more like what happened when he met his wife. "When I use the word *repent*," he says, "I think about the time I was in a dating relationship, until one day a girl named Lisa came to my church as a guest soloist and caught my attention. After getting to know her, I knew she was the one I wanted to be with. I didn't consider it an option to ask Lisa if she wanted to date me also. I knew I had to break off the other relationship if I wanted to begin one with Lisa.

"In a sense, this is what repentance is like when we meet Jesus: We totally change direction."[5]

If we want God's *shalom* to characterize our lives, we can't simply try sprinkling a little more peace on top of the status quo. Instead, we have to turn our backs on whatever is holding us back, setting our hearts on the one who calls us forward. That's the recipe for repentance—and for peace.

Lord, help me realize that I am following you and that you are not following me. Forgive me for my attachments to sin. Help me to sever them so I can turn to you wholeheartedly.

HOPE FLOATS

I pray that God, the source of hope, will fill you completely with joy and peace because you trust in him. Then you will overflow with confident hope through the power of the Holy Spirit.

ROMANS 15:13

Ahh . . . February in Michigan. A time for basking in dreams of blue water and summer sunshine, despite the mounds of snow outside. Though icicles hang like sparkling daggers from every roof, the annual boat show reminds us of the inevitability of spring. Sooner or later it will spread like a soft, green carpet over the land, and hibernating Michiganders will emerge sleepy-eyed and hungry for a taste of summer.

After a long, hard winter, it helps to grab hold of any sign that points to winter's end. For me, it's the boat show, full of gleaming white yachts and powerboats that remind me of longer, lighter days ahead. Sometimes our lives can feel much like a Michigan winter—cold, dark, and never-ending. In the midst of these seasons, we often feel isolated and alone. Our faith can even seem to hibernate. At such times we need to grab hold of the promises God has made about what our future holds. Promises like these:

There will be no more death or sorrow or crying or pain.
REVELATION 21:4

They will see his face, and his name will be written on their foreheads. And there will be no night there—no need for lamps or sun—for the Lord God will shine on them.
REVELATION 22:4-5

The Lamb on the throne will be their Shepherd. He will lead them to springs of life-giving water. And God will wipe every tear from their eyes.
REVELATION 7:17

If the fulfillment of God's promises still seems a long way off, remember the words of Birdee Pruitt, a character in a 1998 film starring Sandra Bullock: "Just give hope a chance to float up. And it will, too."

Father, help me to give hope a chance to float up by remembering how everything will end, when the old world and all its evils will be gone forever.

February 9

SPEND IT!

Your heavenly Father already knows all your needs. Seek the Kingdom of God above all else, and live righteously, and he will give you everything you need.

MATTHEW 6:32-33

In difficult economic times, many people are riddled with fear. But a select few are actually having the time of their lives. Why? Because a down economy provides opportunities that don't exist in a healthy economy. In such economies, "cash is king." With money in hand, you can find the bargains of a lifetime—property that sells for pennies on the dollar, blue-chip stocks that are sharply undervalued. If you have cash and the wisdom to spend it well, you can prosper even in the worst of times.

No matter what the state of your personal finances, whether you feel flush or broke right now, you still have treasure to spend that can yield an enormous return. What am I talking about? Something I call "the cash of the gospel," and there is no better way to invest it than in people who are open to seeing their need for God.

Think about how successful investing works. The biggest rewards come when you perceive a stock's upside potential before it becomes obvious to other investors. So you buy oil when it's at $35 a barrel, not when it rockets to $150. In a way, it's the same with people: that irritable boss, the colleague who drinks too much, the neighbor whose children are running amok, the people who rub you the wrong way. On the outside, such people may not appear destined for greatness. They're not people you care to spend time with. But what if God gives you his heart for them so that you begin to see below the surface and start to envision the plan he has for them? What if he invites you to become part of his plan by forging a relationship with them and sharing your most precious resource—your faith—as he leads? Often we're so focused on our own needs, our own challenges, our own fears, that we fail to see the spiritual opportunities that are right in front of us. Taking the focus off ourselves and putting it back on God will yield enormous dividends, not only for us but also for others.

Lord, give me the peace that comes from serving you rather than myself. Help me to trust that as I seek first your Kingdom, you will provide what I really need.

WAITING FOR PEACE TO ARRIVE

You didn't choose me. I chose you. I appointed you to go and produce lasting fruit.
JOHN 15:16

Nobody learns to ride a bicycle by simply poring over instruction manuals. At some point you've got to climb onto the contraption, strap on your helmet, and start pedaling, risking a few spills along the way. But once you get the hang of it, there's nothing like wheeling down the road and feeling the sun caressing your shoulders and the wind blowing through your hair. Similarly, if you want to forge a life of greater peace, you can't just read about it or hear other people talk about it. You have to do something about it.

Catherine Whitmire is an author who is committed to making peace in the world around her. Several years ago she became exhausted as she fought hard against various social evils like poverty and violence. She longed, she said, "to feel truly alive," explaining that she "was tired of waiting for others to create the culture of peace I had been envisioning." So Whitmire decided to try living as if the peace she longed for had already arrived. Because she was intent on forming relationships with people who were not a carbon copy of herself, she decided to move to a more diverse neighborhood than the one she had been living in. She also expanded her garden, opened her home for community singing parties, took walks with friends, and hosted annual celebrations with neighbors, including welcoming the first flower each spring.

As Whitmire began living the life she had imagined, she started to feel physically, spiritually, and emotionally restored, renewed in her desire to work for greater peace in the world. "I had been waiting for peace to arrive," she explains, "but what I discovered is that it is more likely to appear when we begin living it."[6]

What about you? Are you waiting for peace to arrive, expecting God to hand it to you on a silver platter? Why not, instead, take time to think and pray about the kind of life you want to live? Once you have an idea of what that might look like, ask God to help you make wise decisions so you can start living it.

Father, I want to live the best life possible—one that will produce fruit that lasts. Give me the wisdom to know what changes I need to make in order to fulfill your purpose for my life.

ETERNITY AMNESIA

Think back on those early days when you first learned about Christ. Remember how you remained faithful even though it meant terrible suffering.

HEBREWS 10:32

Remember the character Dory from the movie *Finding Nemo*? She was a lovable, ditzy fish with severe memory loss, unable to remember anything for even five seconds. A lot of the movie's humor is sparked by her character as she swims cluelessly through the action. Though she's one of my favorite characters, it's clear that life without a memory is not much of a life.

That's Paul Tripp's point in his book *Forever*. Without keeping in mind what God has in store for us, it will be impossible to live the lives we're called to. According to Tripp, believers who suffer from what he calls "eternity amnesia" are holding on to a disillusioned and miserable form of Christianity. As belief in an afterlife declines, so does our ability to live a life of robust faith now.

Are you unhappy? Make more money. Having difficulty in your marriage? Find a better spouse. Bored? Buy something. Invited to serve? You're far too busy. These are the values of people who have little hope and no peace, who have only this life to live for.

If you suspect you are suffering from a case of "eternity amnesia," take some time today to meditate on words that Jesus spoke to his disciples the night before his death: "Don't let your hearts be troubled," he told them. "Trust in God, and trust also in me. There is more than enough room in my Father's home. If this were not so, would I have told you that I am going to prepare a place for you? When everything is ready, I will come and get you, so that you will always be with me where I am" (John 14:1-3).

Jesus, if you had died merely to improve life in this world, you would have achieved a small good. But you died so that we might have life everlasting. Today I ask for the grace to make all my decisions with the apostle Paul's words: "We know that when this earthly tent we live in is taken down (that is, when we die and leave this earthly body), we will have a house in heaven, an eternal body made for us by God himself and not by human hands" (2 Corinthians 5:1).

You can't say that our bodies were made for sexual immorality. They were made for the Lord, and the Lord cares about our bodies.

1 CORINTHIANS 6:13

Mark Regnerus is a sociologist with some provocative things to say about sex and marriage. Among many other fascinating observations, he points out what many of us instinctively know: most women desire marriage more than most men and there is a woeful imbalance between the number of Christian men and women in the marriage market. The result is that women are more likely to compromise their moral standards in hopes of finding a mate.[7]

Sex used to be one of the primary motivating factors that prompted men to commit to marriage. But when women give in to the pressure to have sex without the protective benefits of marriage, many men, even Christian men, refuse to commit. Additionally, sex bonds a couple together in a way that makes it nearly impossible to make wise decisions regarding the future of the relationship. No wonder many women remain in relationships that are going nowhere or even in abusive, destructive relationships in which it is difficult to experience God's peace.

If you have had sex with someone you're not married to or you are currently in such a relationship, ask God to help you become chaste. Tell him you want to value yourself more highly in the future. Confide in mature Christians who can help you take the necessary steps to either end the relationship or revise it in light of God's commandments. Sexual purity may not be easy, but it is possible. Without it, you will never know the peace God promises.

Father, help us to resist the temptation of letting another human being occupy the central, holy place in our hearts that belongs only to Jesus. Give us the grace to put Christ first and not second, to do what is right and trust him for the results.

HIDDEN SNARES

*When you enter the land the LORD your God is giving you, be very careful not
to imitate the detestable customs of the nations living there. For example, never
sacrifice your son or daughter as a burnt offering. And do not let your people practice
fortune-telling, or use sorcery, or interpret omens, or engage in witchcraft, or cast
spells, or function as mediums or psychics, or call forth the spirits of the dead.*

DEUTERONOMY 18:9-11

Have you ever dabbled in the occult—playing with Ouija boards, looking at tarot cards, having your fortune read, attending a séance? Many
women experiment with the occult, particularly in their teenage years. The
trouble is, these things can deliver an unexpected payload, leaving us suscep-
tible to the power of evil. If we want to know more of God's peace, we need
to be aware of these hidden dangers, not brushing them off as harmless fun
or youthful games but dealing with them seriously and with the help of other
Christians.

Remember that the Hebrew word *shalom* entails the notion of safety.
By assuring us of his peace, God is extending a promise of spiritual security.
But how can we be secure if we have aligned ourselves with spiritual forces of
darkness, whether knowingly or unknowingly? Failing to heed God's warning
against the occult is similar to acting like an impulsive toddler who breaks
free of her mother in order to run out into the road. Even a little involvement in occult practices can be dangerous because it can open a door to the
supernatural world that ought to remain shut.

What should you do if you have been involved in any kind of occult
practices? Begin by asking for God's forgiveness and protection. If you have
any objects that are connected with the occult, such as Ouija boards, horo-
scopes, or satanic music, symbols, or books, get rid of them. Throw them in
the trash and be done with them. Then ask some mature Christians to pray
with you. Tell God you renounce Satan, and ask for Christ's protection. He
will give it.

*Father, forgive me for any way I have knowingly or unknowingly opened myself to
snares by dabbling or being involved in the occult. I want nothing to do with Satan
or any of his works. Surround me with your care and protect me, I pray.*

GOD WON'T WASTE
YOUR STRUGGLES

We know that God causes everything to work together for the good of those
who love God and are called according to his purpose for them.

ROMANS 8:28

A surprise favorite for Best Picture Oscar, *The King's Speech* is a movie about the stammering King of England, George VI, and his struggle to find his voice prior to World War II. Though the movie far exceeded box office hopes, what most people don't know is that the man who wrote the screenplay didn't overcome his own stuttering problem until the age of sixteen.

Born in Britain just seven months after George VI was crowned king, David Seidler explains what it was like to stammer: "Adolescence had hit," he says. "Hormones were raging. I couldn't ask girls out for a date, and even if I could and even if they said yes, what was the point? I couldn't talk to them on a date."[8]

In the early 1980s, Seidler wrote to the king's elderly widow, telling her of his desire to write about her husband's struggles. But she replied, "Please, Mr. Seidler, not during my lifetime." Thinking he wouldn't have long to wait, he set the project aside. But the Queen Mother surprised him by living to be 101. Seidler began writing the story in 2005.

Tom Hooper, the movie's director, has praised Seidler, saying, "It's clearly the best script of his life. He's really writing about his own childhood experiences through the guise of these two characters."[9]

What does this popular movie's backstory have to do with experiencing more of God's peace? It highlights the link that exists between human weakness and human triumph, a link that usually takes time to emerge. Often it's the struggles we dislike most that have the greatest potential to produce something good in the future.

Whatever your weakness or difficulty, ask God to do what only he can, turning it toward a good purpose. Trusting him daily to make sense out of the story you are living will bring you a deeper measure of the peace he promises.

God, I trust you to make something good out of my struggles. Thank
you for loving me and using your power on my behalf.

*Those who look to him for help will be radiant with joy;
no shadow of shame will darken their faces.*

PSALM 34:5

Peace comes in three main varieties—vertical, horizontal, and internal. Vertical peace has to do with our relationship with God. Horizontal peace concerns our relationships with others. Internal peace has to do with our relationship with ourselves. If you are experiencing internal conflict or conflict with others, it's tempting to focus entirely on the internal or horizontal aspects of peace. You may expend a lot of energy trying to resolve these areas of your life. But you will make little headway if you fail to address the most important kind of peace there is, which is peace with the God who made you.

When it comes to marital discord, for instance, author Paul Tripp makes an insightful comment. "I have become more and more persuaded that marriages are fixed vertically before they are ever fixed horizontally," he says.[10] Regardless of what is troubling a marriage—money, sex, poor communication, woundedness—these issues and others will never be resolved without addressing the vertical issue.

According to Tripp, a good marriage isn't rooted in romance but in worship. But what does that mean? Tripp isn't talking about going to church or singing hymns together, though these practices may be good for a marriage, but about the fundamental purpose of your life. Each of us, he points out, is digging for some kind of treasure, looking for something of immense value toward which to aim our lives. The Bible makes this truth clear, saying, "Wherever your treasure is, there the desires of your heart will also be" (Matthew 6:21).

The problem comes when your heart settles for a treasure less than God. When your purpose in life is defined by having the perfect relationship, a comfortable life, money, power, health, or pleasure, you will never find the peace you're looking for. Regardless of whether you are married, single, widowed, or divorced, let your response to life's challenges be driven by an overwhelming desire to know God and live for him. If you get vertical peace right, horizontal and internal peace will follow.

*Lord, let my troubles turn me not to false treasures but to the treasure
of knowing you more deeply. May I know the joy that comes from
looking to you for help and trusting that you will bring it.*

If you love me, obey my commandments.

JOHN 14:15

So much of the life of faith is counterintuitive. We are told that in order to have life, we need to surrender our lives; that the first shall be last and the last first; that the greatest of all will be the servant of all; that happiness consists of giving and not getting; that if someone strikes one cheek, we should turn the other cheek for the next blow. The gospel contradicts our most basic instincts, our notions of how the world should work. And so we resist and rationalize and delay our obedience, wondering why God's peace eludes us.

But we have our moments—times when we do make the sacrifices God asks. Philip Yancey describes such times in his own life, saying, "I have learned that when I choose to follow Jesus, in ways large or small, what seems like a sacrifice actually turns into a benefit: *I* am the one who benefits. When I swallow my pride and apologize to someone I've wronged, I feel a flood of relief. When I give anonymously, as Jesus commanded, I experience more satisfaction. When I resist temptation and invest instead in the hard work of marriage, I gain. As [Thomas] Merton expressed it, 'The gift of ourselves in total submission to God is a sacrifice in which, far from losing anything, we gain everything and recover, in a more perfect mode of possession, even what we seem to have lost. For at the very moment when we give ourselves to God, God gives Himself to us.'"[11]

Trusting God enough to obey him opens up a space for more of his presence within us, and that presence brings us the peace we long for. Today let us seek that peace by first seeking to do God's will, regardless of what he asks.

Father, open my eyes to the places in my heart that still resist you. Forgive me for all the decisions I make that are based on assuming that my ways are better than yours. Help me to love you enough to obey you, embracing the example of your Son, my Lord, Jesus Christ.

PEACE COMES FROM KNOWING WHO YOU ARE

[Jesus]said, "My grace is all you need. My power works best in weakness." So now I am glad to boast about my weaknesses, so that the power of Christ can work through me.

2 CORINTHIANS 12:9

I have a confession to make: I'm not perfect. Not only am I not perfect, I'm sometimes downright difficult to be around. Just ask my children. I also make mistakes—plenty of them—big ones and small ones. I'll probably make some today.

I have another confession: I'm no longer all that surprised or ashamed by my bad behavior or my many mistakes, though I do grieve over them. The reason I'm not surprised is that I've come to realize who I am: a sinner, broken and weak, but loved and cherished by a God who forgives me. Knowing who I am and who God is has given me the ability to face myself more honestly and with greater peace. I know the bottom won't fall out if I do something wrong. I also know that more depends on God than it does on me.

I'm not trying to dodge responsibility for my actions, but I have come to realize that God has always helped me far more than I've been able to help myself. The best way for me to grow, then, is by responding to God's grace initiatives rather than embarking on my own program of self-improvement.

A friend of mine used to say, "Never let your trying be greater than your trusting." He wasn't saying we shouldn't try; he meant that in the Christian life, trust should always trump effort.

One sure sign that we haven't come to terms with who we are is defensiveness about our weaknesses. We can't admit we are not the women we should be. Nor do we believe God is big enough or kind enough to love us. The opposite reaction—beating ourselves up over our many failures—often signals the same problem.

If you are not yet at peace in your identity as a sinful woman saved by grace, ask God today to reveal two things to you: his great mercy and your great need of it. That's a combination that will make for peace.

Jesus, you knew exactly the kind of people you were dying for—sinful people. I'm one of them. Thank you for saving, loving, and forgiving me. Please help me trust you today as I face things in me that need to change.

AT PEACE IN THE STORM

God is our refuge and strength, always ready to help in times of trouble. So we will not fear when earthquakes come and the mountains crumble into the sea. Let the oceans roar and foam. Let the mountains tremble as the waters surge!

PSALM 46:1-3

I magine that you have just fallen overboard into stormy seas. Fortunately, a strong swimmer is nearby to rescue you. But if you flail about in a panic, trying to grab hold of the rescuer, you will only make his job worse. This is how Hannah Whitall Smith pictures the person who finds it difficult to trust God in the midst of personal battles. Instead of turning to God, this person becomes fearful, making it more difficult to receive the help God wants to send.

Smith points out that a great deal of what we call spiritual conflict might more accurately be labeled spiritual rebellion. "We fight," she says, "but it is not a fight of faith, but a fight of unbelief. Our spiritual 'wrestling,' of which we are often so proud, is really a wrestling, not for God against his enemies, but against him on the side of his enemies. We allow ourselves to indulge in doubts and fears, and as a consequence we are plunged into darkness, and turmoil, and wrestlings of spirit."[12]

The next time you are faced with a challenge that makes your knees shake and your heart lurch, think of yourself as a person in stormy seas. Picture Christ coming to you, taking hold of you, and carrying you safely to land. As you calm yourself in his presence, ask for his guidance so you will know how to meet the challenge at hand.

While you pray, remind yourself that the spiritual struggles you face probably won't be overcome in an instant. Instead, they require that you continually surrender, trust Christ for all that troubles you, and stand in the faith he gives you.

God, you promise to be our refuge no matter what. Help me to call upon you and trust in your saving help whenever I am afraid.

February 19

BC

Purify me from my sins, and I will be clean; wash me, and I will be whiter than snow.

PSALM 51:7

I recently purchased a new stove complete with bells and whistles my old, defunct stove didn't have. But before the new stove could be installed, I had to deal with an appalling amount of dirt and grime that lay hidden behind the old one. Holding my nose to ward off the smell of caked-on grease, I was only too happy to get down on hands and knees, scrubbing the surface in preparation for my spanking new appliance.

As I cleaned, I thought about my heart BC—that is, my heart before it "Belonged to Christ." I wasn't a murderer or an armed robber or even a cat burglar. I was just your ordinary, run-of-the-mill sinner, going my own way. Despite trying to be a "good person," I had already broken many of God's commandments during my twenty-one years on earth. Since I didn't even know whether God existed, I allowed myself to pick and choose which of his commandments I would observe. "You shall have no other gods before me." Well, I was pretty much my own god, doing what I wanted. "Honor your father and mother." Okay, as long as they acted in a way that commanded my respect. "You shall not take the name of the Lord your God in vain." I didn't see anything wrong with using a bit of colorful language from time to time. What was the big deal?

As you can see, I had only a surface understanding of what God was asking. When Christ became real to me, all that changed. I wanted to live a different life. Eager to prepare my heart for the God whose goodness I had begun to suspect, I was only too happy to get down on my knees and invite Christ in. Immediately I felt his presence. All the sin and grime that lay hidden in my heart was flushed to the surface and washed away. My apprehension about the present and the future fled as I felt the perfect peace of God sweep over me.

Christ's peace comes when we turn to God, admitting our sins and surrendering our lives. Don't waste this chance to know his peace.

Jesus, thank you for living in me by the power of your Spirit. Give me the grace to repent of anything that displeases you. Wash me, and I will be whiter than snow.

BE QUIET

I said to myself, "I will watch what I do and not sin in what I say. I will hold my tongue."

PSALM 39:1

I felt like I was going to burst, as though I could no longer hold in the retort that was trying so hard to push its way past pursed lips and clenched teeth. For the past five minutes, I'd been subjected to a political tirade delivered by an elderly relative. Those blankety-blank politicians were a bunch of crooks. All they cared about was lining their pockets. Not only was their position on any given issue dead wrong, but it was evil and would lead the country to ruin. The words were spoken with such contempt that it was painful to listen. But I couldn't just walk away. After all, we were in the car heading down the expressway.

The person who was spouting off has a habit of mistaking forcefulness with persuasion. But his extreme statements usually have the reverse effect, making me want to argue on behalf of politicians with whom I disagree. This time I decided not to take the bait. Instead of arguing or trying to point out the extreme nature of what he was saying, I decided to hold my tongue and change the subject.

It worked! As we spoke of other things, the tension in the car began to dissipate, and I congratulated myself for not making a harsh reply to harsh comments.

Later I marveled at how hard it had been for me to keep quiet. I enjoy saying exactly what I think. But doing so isn't always helpful. Clearly, I need to develop my self-control muscles so that keeping silent when it is wisest to do so doesn't seem like such a superhuman task. According to the Bible, this kind of self-control can pay dividends. Here's how Proverbs puts it: "Even fools are thought wise when they keep silent; with their mouths shut, they seem intelligent" (17:28).

What about you? If you make a habit of getting dragged into senseless arguments, particularly with family members, join me in taking the first step toward self-control—decide to be quiet the next time you are tempted to be drawn into a verbal tug-of-war.

Father, give me the grace to know when to speak up and when to stay silent. Help me to look for opportunities to grow in self-control.

WHAT ABOUT THE KIDS?

The love of the LORD remains forever with those who fear him.
His salvation extends to the children's children.

PSALM 103:17

Let's be honest. Though children are a blessing from the Lord, they some-times subtract from, rather than add to, our sense of peace. We worry about a thousand and one things—their health, their faith, their relation-ships. You name it, and we can worry. You've heard the saying, "If Mama ain't happy, ain't nobody happy"? For most of us it would be truer to say, "If the children ain't happy, Mama ain't happy either."

Hannah Whitall Smith points out that many of us have a tendency to take refuge in God without bringing our children into that place of refuge. What she means is that we entrust our own lives to God without entrusting our children to God's care. It's as though we've packed up our belongings and moved into a new home without bringing our children with us. "Every anx-ious thought which we indulge about our children," she says, "proves that we have not really taken them with us into the dwelling place of God."

Smith goes on to say that "if we trust for ourselves, we must trust for our loved ones also, especially our children. God is more truly their Father than their earthly fathers are. If they are dear to us, they are far dearer to him. We cannot do anything better for them than to trust them into his care and hardly anything worse than try to keep them in our own."[13]

To trust our children into the capable hands of a loving God is not to become passive. Rather, it's to let God get out in front, taking our cues from him as we do our best to be the mothers he wants us to be.

Today, as you ask for more of his peace, close your eyes and picture each of your children walking toward God. Even if they seem infinitely far from him, try to imagine them in his presence, because they are. Then tell the Lord that you trust him to care for your children far better than you are able to care for them yourself.

Father, help me to realize that I can't save the people I love. Only you can do that. Give
me the grace today, tomorrow, and the next day to entrust their futures to you.

GET OUT OF JAIL FREE

Forgive others, and you will be forgiven.
LUKE 6:37

Remember the much-desired "Get out of Jail Free" card in the game Monopoly? When you're stuck in jail, you can't buy property on which to build houses and hotels, and ultimately you can't win the game. So it pays to get released from jail.

Some of us need our own "Get out of Jail Free" card when it comes to being locked up in a prison of bitterness and unforgiveness. It is simply impossible to experience God's peace if we haven't forgiven people who have hurt us.

Author Joanna Weaver points out that "hurt and disappointment left to fester will eventually become resentment. Resentment unchecked will harden into bitterness. And bitterness destroys. As someone once put it, 'Bitterness is like drinking poison and waiting for the other person to die.'"

She goes on to say that refusing to forgive those who've wronged us means that we are playing "the role of judge, jury, and executioner. After a brief trial—one-sided, of course!—we march them down to the dark caverns of our hearts and lock them in the dungeon of our resentment. We slam the door shut and rattle it for good measure so they know just how imprisoned they are. Then we clip the key to our belt, pull up a chair, and settle in for a long wait.

"For you see, it is impossible to keep people jailed in unforgiveness without being enslaved to it ourselves," she observes. "The sad part about all of this is that most of the people who've caused us pain are completely oblivious to the fact that they are imprisoned. They may never feel one lash of our inquisitor whip or lose any sleep tossing and turning on the straw mat we've laid for them on the cold, concrete floor of our heart. They won't grow weak and pale from the constant diet of angry gruel and bitter mush. But there's a good chance we will."[14]

What about you? If you've locked anyone into the dungeon of your resentment, open up the door by forgiving that person, whether or not he or she has asked for pardon. Then walk on out to freedom, a spacious place where you can enjoy more of God's peace.

Lord, I want to be free of every shred of bitterness and resentment. Give me the grace to forgive those who have hurt me, just as you forgave those who hurt you.

LIVING IN A MESSY WORLD

It was our weaknesses he carried; it was our sorrows that weighed him down. And we thought his troubles were a punishment from God, a punishment for his own sins!

ISAIAH 53:4

One reason we can trust the veracity of the Bible is because of the terrible stories it tells. Think about it. If you were only interested in promoting the merits of your religion, would you include so many messy stories that cast their protagonists in a negative light? There's Abraham lying about his wife to save his skin. Jacob's boys selling their brother into slavery. Samson acting like a thug. And what about David lusting after Bathsheba? On and on, human weakness is on display throughout the pages of the Bible.

Paul Tripp points out how helpful these stories can be for us because they show us our need for God and for his grace. "The Bible . . . will shock you with its honesty about what happens in the broken world in which we live. From the sibling homicide of Cain to the money-driven betrayal of Judas, the blood and guts of a broken world are strewn across every page. The honesty of God about the address where we all live is itself an act of love and grace. He sticks our head through the biblical peephole so we will be forced to see the world as it really is, not as we fantasize it to be. He does this so we will be realistic in our expectations, then humbly reach out for the help that he alone is able to give us."[15]

To use Tripp's imagery, all of us live at an unsavory address, a place where people do bad things to each other. Experiencing God's peace is not about escaping the neighborhood but about accessing God's grace in the midst of it. Furthermore, one of Jesus' names is *Immanuel*, a name that means "God with us." Instead of removing himself to a celestial gated community so he could be oblivious to our problems, he indwells us through the power of his Spirit, providing everything we need to grow in the peace he offers.

Lord, thank you for not abandoning us and instead becoming one of us. By doing so, you have indeed carried our weaknesses and taken on our sorrows, bringing us peace because of what you were willing to endure for our sake.

February 24

DON'T TAKE IT PERSONALLY

If you do good only to those who do good to you, why should
you get credit? Even sinners do that much!

LUKE 6:33

Here's a news flash: You are a sinful person surrounded by other sinful people.

"That's hardly breaking news," you might say. But if that is so, why do you and I tend to be surprised when someone mistreats us, lashes out at us, and hurts our feelings? Your husband comes home from a bad day at work and takes his anger out on you. Your child is drowning in homework and slams the door in your face when you ask how his day went. Your boss gets on your case for something that wasn't your fault. Husbands, wives, bosses, sons, daughters, colleagues, friends, neighbors, pastors, parishioners—we are part of a great chain of sinful people whose actions can create reactions in the space of a split second.

I remember how hurt I felt the first time one of my children said she hated me. I made the mistake of bursting into tears, thereby empowering my four-year-old. Here was this child I'd poured so much into, telling me what a wretched mother I was because I wouldn't let her do something she shouldn't.

Paul Tripp, speaking of married couples, puts his finger on a problem that can mar any relationship. He says that most of us "tend to personalize what is not personal." He goes on to say that "at the end of his bad day at work, your husband doesn't say to himself, 'I know what I'll do. I'll take my bad day out on my wife so that her day gets as wrecked as mine.' . . . You are living with a sinner, so you will experience his sin.

"Now when you personalize what is not personal," Tripp says, "you tend to be adversarial in your response. When that happens, what motivates you is not the spiritual need in your spouse that God has revealed but your spouse's offense against you, your schedule, your peace, etc. So, your response is not a 'for him' response but an 'against him' response."[16]

Perhaps the first step toward experiencing peace in any relationship is the ability to stop taking another's sin personally so we can see opportunities for ministering to that person instead.

Father, help me to find a better way to fight against sin in the lives of those closest to
me. Enable me to take a step back so I can act for others rather than against them.

GOD'S PLAN A

"I know the plans I have for you," says the LORD. "They are plans for
good and not for disaster, to give you a future and a hope."

JEREMIAH 29:11

Marie Carlson grew up thinking that God had a clear-cut system for dealing with good and bad behaviors. "It went something like this," she says. "God always had an 'A' plan. If you did the right thing and didn't mess up that plan by sinning, you got to enjoy the corresponding 'A' outcome and rewards. However, any major sin altered the 'A' plan—God's best—forever. If you failed, the best you could hope for was the 'B' or even the 'C' plan— God's second or third best. It all made perfect sense . . . as long as you were, in fact, perfect."

Then came the news that turned her self-perception upside down. When Marie was in her early teens, she discovered that her parents had conceived her out of wedlock. "It was hard enough to accept that my parents hadn't wanted me," she says. "The realization that God hadn't wanted me either wounded me beyond articulation. I felt I'd been stamped defective and knocked out of the loop of grace."

Marie struggled with feelings of anger and inadequacy. Then one night she was reading the story of Joseph, who had been sold into slavery by his older brothers. She stopped when she read his gracious response to them years later: "Don't be afraid. Am I in the place of God? You intended to harm me, but God intended it for good to accomplish what is now being done, the saving of many lives" (Genesis 50:19-20, NIV).

Those words, she said, "slapped me stone still. I read them again and felt something inside begin to crumble. All the anger and resentment I'd harbored against God for rejecting me as a 'B-plan' child came flooding back. Encircling the Bible with my arms, I buried my head on the open pages and wept."[17]

Like Marie, many of us feel wounded and inadequate. No matter what you've done or what's been done to you, God says today that you are his "A-plan" child who will enjoy his best forever.

Father, help me know and celebrate what it means to be your beloved
daughter, protected and blessed, honored and esteemed.

SILVER AND GOLD

What do I see flying like clouds to Israel, like doves to their nests? They are ships from the ends of the earth, from lands that trust in me, led by the great ships of Tarshish. They are bringing the people of Israel home from far away, carrying their silver and gold.

ISAIAH 60:8-9

A few months ago a reader wrote to tell me how devastated she'd been by the breakup of her marriage. One day her husband simply told her he no longer loved her and wasn't interested in working things out. The marriage was over.

At times her pain was physical. She felt as though she were having a heart attack. But through the pain and chaos, she refused to doubt God, telling him she knew he was faithful and good. During the months that followed, this heartbroken woman kept seeking him, yielding her life again and again.

Now a year later, after living through what she describes as the darkest time of her life, she speaks about healing and a new freedom to love God that she never imagined possible. Her hope is palpable as she tells of her confidence that the best is yet to come.

Her story illustrates how God works in the lives of those who trust him. Though times of darkness can produce tremendous pain, they can also produce lasting treasure. Like the Israelites returning home after their long exile laden with silver and gold, we come through our own times of difficulty bearing treasures.

The funny thing is, these riches are plundered from the enemy. Often the very things we thought would destroy us end up blessing us and giving us what we need to live with greater joy and freedom.

One of the hardest parts of suffering is feeling that it might never end. When you feel that way, remember this woman's story and the wonderful verse from Isaiah that speaks of God bringing his people home, not beaten and crushed as one might expect, but laden with silver and gold.

Father, thank you for not letting me come through my hard times empty handed. In the midst of darkness, help me to trust.

*You have six days each week for your ordinary work, but on the seventh day
you must stop working, even during the seasons of plowing and harvest.*

EXODUS 34:21

Sometimes I feel like a pot of water simmering on a stove. Turn up the heat just a little bit higher, and I'll start boiling over. Or at least that's what I'm tempted to do when I feel pressured by life's demands. Too many responsibilities, too many obstacles, and not enough energy or patience to make it through the day. Now multiply me by millions of others who are feeling similarly stressed, and it's a wonder the world doesn't spontaneously explode!

I wonder how much of the frustration and anger we feel would disappear if we were able to build regular times of rest into our lives. What if we designated one day a week to cease from our labor so our bodies and souls had time to be renewed? We could spend the day celebrating God's love, expressing our trust in his provision as we enjoyed a meal shared with family or friends. We could do the things that bring us peace, such as taking a walk, playing games, reading, soaking in the bath—whatever rejuvenates us rather than depletes us.

Building Sabbath times into our lives takes commitment. As Wayne Muller observes, "Sabbath is not dependent upon our readiness to stop. We do not stop when we are finished. We do not stop when we complete our phone calls, finish our project, get through this stack of messages, or get out this report that is due tomorrow. We stop because it is time to stop.

"Sabbath requires surrender," he says. "If we only stop when we are finished with all our work, then we will never stop—because our work is never completely done."[18]

This week, why not give yourself a taste of Sabbath rest by reserving a day or an evening to reflect on God's faithfulness and enjoy his blessings.

*Father, give me the grace to stop and rest. Help me trust in your
goodness, basking in your peace and presence.*

WHERE HAPPINESS IS FOUND

Make me walk along the path of your commands, for that is where my happiness is found.

PSALM 119:35

Have you ever wondered why God found it necessary to inscribe the Ten Commandments in stone? Why couldn't he simply have communicated his expectations to Moses and then let him broadcast the message? Perhaps because he wanted to stress the timelessness of his commands, and perhaps also because he knew how good we are at twisting words to suit our fancy.

"Do not commit adultery" could morph into "Don't sleep with anyone unless you're in love." "Do not worship any other gods besides me" could morph into "Go to church once a week, and then live however you please." "Do not make idols of any kind" could morph into "Don't worship statues, but feel free to dedicate your life to money, sex, or power."

Many of us think of the Ten Commandments primarily in negative terms. Don't do this; don't do that. But listen to how God prefaces the giving of the Law on Sinai. He says to Moses, "I am the LORD your God, who rescued you from the land of Egypt, the place of your slavery" (Exodus 20:2). His people are to obey him not because he's a cruel taskmaster but because he has rescued them from cruel taskmasters. Not wanting them to fall into bondage again, he tells them how to live a life that will be marked by his presence and peace.

Ignoring God in order to pursue our own desires will never yield the peace we seek. Doing so may make us happy for a moment, but a pattern of disobedience will eventually lead us into bondage.

Pray today for the grace to believe that the way to life lies not in having your own way but in following God's way. Tell him you need his strength to live the life he wants for you—a life full of freedom and joy.

Father, forgive me for going my own way and ignoring your clear commandments. Help me to embrace your laws, knowing they will lead to a life of greater freedom and peace.

Your unfailing love, O LORD, is as vast as the heavens;
your faithfulness reaches beyond the clouds.

PSALM 36:5

I f I could paint a Michigan winter, there would be plenty of gray in my palette. Much of the time we see very little sunlight, a consequence of living on a peninsula. Billowy snowdrifts, tall pines decked out in layers of white, lakes glazed with ice—these become incredibly beautiful on a rare sunny day in the middle of winter.

Sometimes our spiritual lives seem to be painted with a palette of gray as well. Nothing moves us. Nothing excites us. Everything seems bland and colorless. There are no discoveries, no words from God, no sense of his presence. Like the sun in winter, God seems to be hiding behind impenetrable clouds. On our worst days, the clouds turn from shades of grey to thick black, and we begin to wonder if God still cares for us or even knows what we are going through.

Though we may dislike them, clouds are necessary. They have a purpose. We're grateful for snow that replenishes the groundwater and for spring rains that refresh the earth.

Spiritual clouds also have their purpose. Oswald Chambers says this about clouds: "It is not true to say that God wants to teach us something in our trials. Through every cloud He brings our way, He wants us to unlearn something. His purpose in using the cloud is to simplify our beliefs until our relationship with Him is exactly like that of a child. . . . Until we come face to face with the deepest, darkest fact of life without damaging our view of God's character, we do not yet know Him."[19]

What do you need to unlearn about God today? That he won't help you find a way out of your present difficulty? That he is fickle—here today and gone tomorrow? That he will abandon you when life gets tough or when you make a mistake? That he didn't mean it when he said he was your Father? Whatever untruths your heart is harboring, ask God to use the cloudy seasons in your life to simplify your relationship with him so your view of him as your loving Father becomes stronger.

Father, I don't like it when you seem far away and I feel all alone. Help
me during such seasons to seek you through prayer, spiritual reading,
conversations with friends, fasting, and humble trust.

March 1

LET'S BE HONEST

Since our friendship with God was restored by the death of his Son while we were still his enemies, we will certainly be saved through the life of his Son. So now we can rejoice in our wonderful new relationship with God because our Lord Jesus Christ has made us friends of God.

ROMANS 5:10-11

Have you ever noticed how some preachers mangle the word *God*, transforming it into a two-syllable word that sounds something like "Gawd"? I mean no disrespect, but it rankles me every time I hear it because it strikes me as pretentious. We would do better to use simple, honest words.

Speaking of honesty, let's stop trying to put on a front, hoping others will think we're better than we are. Doing so rarely fools anyone. The main problem with facades is that they discourage the work of the Spirit in us. God builds on truth, not falsehood. If we want to experience more of his grace, we need to lay our struggles and sins before him without pretension.

John Ortberg, in his book *The Life You've Always Wanted*, shares his own struggle with pretension. "I am disappointed with myself," he confesses. "I am disappointed not so much with particular things I have done as with aspects of who I have become. I have a nagging sense that all is not as it should be. . . .

"I attend a high school reunion and can't choke back the desire to stand out by looking more attractive or having achieved more impressive accomplishments than my classmates. I speak to someone with whom I want to be charming, and my words come out awkward and pedestrian. I am disappointed in my ordinariness. I want to be, in the words of Garrison Keillor, named 'Sun-God, King of America, Idol of Millions, Bringer of Fire, the Great Haji, Thun-Dar the Boy Giant.'"[1]

What pretensions have you been holding on to in your relationship with God and others? Queen of America, Thun-Dar the Girl Giant, Idol of Millions? Whatever they are, have the humility and the humor to let go of them in God's presence, trusting that as you do, he will build on the truth of who you are in Christ—Sinner Saved by Grace, Daughter of God, Beloved of the Lord.

Father, help me to become secure enough in your love and forgiveness that I don't have to pretend to be someone I'm not. As I do that, let your life mature in me so I can become the woman you've made me to be.

WHAT DO YOU NEED?

Don't love money; be satisfied with what you have. For God has said, "I will never fail you. I will never abandon you." So we can say with confidence, "The LORD is my helper, so I will have no fear. What can mere people do to me?"

HEBREWS 13:5-6

I was driving down the highway last night when a luxury car whizzed past. I noticed a streak of gleaming white and something else that caught my attention. Emblazoned on its license plate was one simple word: *needy.* I laughed out loud, appreciating the humor and audacity of such a self-designation. That car made me think about the enormous spread between what we think will make us happy (things like luxury cars) and what really does make us happy.

It's no secret that human beings are wired for pleasure. It's what fuels our materialistic instincts. We get a quick rush from buying things. A friend of mine sells expensive laboratory equipment to hospitals. At the end of the day, she says, the purchasing decision is always an emotional one. Hospital employees, it seems, get a kick out of buying the latest, greatest gadgets and machines for labs and operating rooms.

Though it's natural to enjoy buying things, we all know that such pleasures can become addictive. To keep the rush going, we have to keep buying more stuff. Doing so can empty our souls as well as our wallets, making us dependent on shallow pleasures.

If you doubt this, spend a little time taking inventory of all you own. Maybe your vice is shoes or clothes. Or maybe it's being up on the latest in technology. Or maybe you think a new car or new decor for your home will make you feel good. But let's be honest: how many of your possessions have given you anything resembling the peace your heart desires?

Father, thank you for blessing me with more than enough. Please guard my heart against the seductive pleasure of things. Help me to give generously to others, placing my focus where it belongs—on seeking first your Kingdom and not mine.

WHEN YOU DON'T FEEL PEACEFUL

*Come to me with your ears wide open. Listen, and you will find life. . . .
Seek the LORD while you can find him. Call on him now while he is
near. . . . Yes, turn to our God, for he will forgive generously.*

ISAIAH 55:3, 6-7

Like life itself, the journey toward peace rarely proceeds along a predictable path. Sometimes it may even seem as though you have taken one step forward and two steps back. What do you do then?

One thing you can do is begin to think about where you want to go and how you are going to get there. Just as you wouldn't start driving from New York to Florida by heading north to Canada, it would be foolish to set the wrong course on your journey toward peace. Progress can only be made if you continue heading in the right direction, which means, of course, that you are heading in God's direction.

When it comes to navigating the journey, think of repentance as a spiritual GPS that will keep you on course. The Greek word for "repentance" is *metanoia*, which suggests a radical turning away from sin in order to turn back to God. Without such a turning, all our efforts to become women at peace will fail. As Christians, we know that repentance is more than a one-time event. It's something we need to do daily, making necessary course corrections whenever we falter.

Our lack of peace may or may not be attributed to our own sins. But sin is certainly a major obstacle in our quest to experience more of God's peace. However you are feeling today, ask the Lord for grace to recognize the things in your life that are off kilter. As you admit your failings, imagine yourself turning from them and toward God, confident that he will abundantly pardon.

Lord, my journey toward peace is really a journey toward you. Help me to admit and forsake my sinful habits, so that I may run toward you and your forgiveness.

DECISION MAKING AND GOD'S PEACE

The LORD directs the steps of the godly. He delights in every detail of their lives.
Though they stumble, they will never fall, for the LORD holds them by the hand.

PSALM 37:23-24

M any of us feel confused and anxious when it comes to making major life decisions. How should we spend our money? Who should we marry? Where should we live? What job should we take? These and countless other questions can be difficult to sort out. How can we experience God's peace in the midst of such life-altering choices?

The best advice I have encountered on this topic comes from a man who surrendered his life to Christ in the early part of the sixteenth century, Ignatius of Loyola. Based on his own experience, Ignatius wrote what would become a spiritual classic. *The Spiritual Exercises* is a book that offers uniquely helpful guidance on discerning God's will for your life.

In *The Spiritual Exercises*, Ignatius reminds us that we should make every decision with the proper end in mind. For a Christian, that end or purpose is to deepen our life with God. Embracing that principle reduces our anxiety because we realize that any decision we make is merely a means to that end. And why would God not want to help us when he has already told us, "I will guide you along the best pathway for your life. I will advise you and watch over you" (Psalm 32:8)?

As we pray, seeking God's will for our lives, Ignatius tells us to notice how we are feeling. Pay attention, he says, to feelings of "spiritual consolation" (every increase in hope, faith, and charity) and to feelings of "spiritual desolation" (feelings of darkness, disturbance, temptation, and disquiet). Ignatius advises us to make the decision that moves our hearts toward spiritual consolation rather than desolation.

Of course, we should also seek the counsel of mature Christians who know us well and who can confirm or question a direction we are considering. Decision making doesn't have to be fraught with confusion and anxiety. Instead, we can experience God's peace as we seek his will.

Father, thank you for promising to take hold of my hand and direct my
steps. Help me to remember that as I seek to do your will.

BENDY CHICK

A peaceful heart leads to a healthy body.

PROVERBS 14:30

My daughter Katie attended elementary school with another Chinese adoptee by the name of Maggie. Though the two girls look nothing alike, people have always gotten them mixed up. This happened recently when a boy greeted Maggie by saying, "Aren't you that bendy chick?" I laughed when I heard about it, because Katie is the bendy one, able to twist her wrists in a complete circle or bend her fingers straight back until they touch her hand. She's the most flexible person I know.

When it comes to having peace, flexibility is an asset. I'm not talking about moral flexibility, of course—changing our values to fit the environment we're in. What I'm talking about is finding ways to keep the big things big and the small things small.

So much of our stress comes from how we react to little things, like a messy house, a slow driver, a disappointing holiday. Unreasonably high expectations can wreak havoc on our sense of peace. But sometimes peace comes when we learn to lower our expectations, as long as doing so harms no one.

To find out how bendy you are, take note of the things that bother you this week. Consider making a daily list. At the end of the week, place a check next to the big things and a circle next to the small ones. Try to see if there's a pattern in your response to the little things that bothered you—a need for control, an inability to tolerate loose ends, a streak of perfectionism. Then cross out everything with a circle beside it and consider how much better your week might have been had you responded to the little things more flexibly. In the days ahead, do your best to become a bendy chick, a woman who is able to major on the majors and minor on the minors.

Father, your Word says that peace leads to health. You know how easy it is for me to lose peace and perspective, especially when little annoyances pile up. Help me to become more aware of how small things can destroy my peace. Give me the grace to respond more flexibly and gently to the obstacles I face.

March 6
U-TURNS

He is our God forever and ever, and he will guide us until we die.

PSALM 48:14

At the risk of boasting, I have to admit that I'm pretty good at the video game Mario Kart. True, my children beat me more than I beat them, but often not by more than a whisker. When I do lose, it's often because my character got turned around on the track and is driving full speed in the wrong direction. At that point a big, red U-turn arrow pops up on the screen to get my attention.

Sometimes we need a big U-turn arrow to pop up in our own lives. We need it when we're heading down a self-destructive path—drinking too much, involving ourselves emotionally with someone who's married, cutting corners at work, or getting stuck in negative emotional habits. At other times there's nothing intrinsically wrong with the road we're on, but it's just not the right one for us. We may be pursuing a job that won't suit us, a relationship that won't work, a plan for our lives that will keep us from serving God as he wants. At such times, the U-turn arrow might take various forms—circumstances that block the path ahead, a nagging feeling that something isn't right, a Bible passage that keeps coming to mind, a word from friends. If we heed the signs and turn around, we will likely save ourselves and others a lot of grief. We will also become happier and more peaceful because we will be better aligned with God's will for our lives.

If you feel your life has gotten off track in some way, take heart. God does allow U-turns, chances to make a course correction when doing so will lead you closer to him.

Lord, thank you for not hiding your will from me. Please make me aware of the signs when something is wrong. Help me to have open ears and an open heart, that I might hear your voice and do your will.

FEELING GUILTY?

The trouble is not with the law, for it is spiritual and good. The trouble is with me, for I am all too human, a slave to sin. I don't really understand myself, for I want to do what is right, but I don't do it. Instead, I do what I hate. But if I know that what I am doing is wrong, this shows that I agree that the law is good. So I am not the one doing wrong; it is sin living in me that does it.

ROMANS 7:14-17

It's hard to feel peaceful when you have a nagging sense that something in your life is off kilter. Philip Yancey points out that what psychologists call "cognitive dissonance," behaving in ways that contradict your beliefs, is often a euphemism for guilt.[2] You want to adopt a healthy lifestyle, yet you binge on brownies. Although you believe in the sanctity of marriage, you have a habit of flirting with married men. You value generosity, yet you hold tightly to every penny.

Too often, pop culture still dishes out the tired advice that if it feels good, we should do it. Lots of things feel good while we're doing them but make us feel bad later on. That bad feeling is called guilt. And guilt is meant to call us to repentance so we can turn to God and ask him to heal the rift that sin has created in our hearts.

Remember that *shalom* means wholeness. Sin splits us on the inside, so that instead of doing the things we want to, we end up doing the things we hate. If you want to know more of God's peace, don't ignore your guilty feelings. Don't wallow in them, but do pay attention to them, letting them turn you back to God so you can experience the healing power of his forgiveness.

Lord, forgive me for allowing sin to open a rift in my heart and for doing the things I should not do. Help me to seek your forgiveness when I sin, knowing that you love me still.

THE WRONG YARDSTICK

God loved the world so much that he gave his one and only Son, so that everyone who believes in him will not perish but have eternal life.

JOHN 3:16

It's half a yardstick, a mere eighteen inches, yet it can seem an infinite distance, this space between the head and the heart. God tells us so many wonderful things—that he shaped us in the womb, that he chose us as his own, that we are his daughters, that he will never fail or forsake us, that we are forgiven and loved. Yet we doubt.

Joanna Weaver gave her life to Christ as a child. But she could never quite believe God loved her. Instead, she measured herself by the yardstick of God's law and found herself falling short. "I was almost thirty," she says, "before the message of grace finally made the trip from my head to my heart, setting me 'free from the law of sin and death' (Romans 8:2). As the light of the good news finally penetrated the darkness of my self-condemning mind, the 'perfect love' I John 4:18 speaks of finally drove out my insecurity, which had always been rooted in fear of punishment.

"When I finally . . . admitted that in myself I would never be—could never be—enough, I experienced a breakthrough that has radically changed my life. For as I surrendered my yardstick—the tool of comparison that had caused so much mental torment and a sense of separation from God—Jesus took it from my hands. Then, with a look of great love, He broke it over His knee and turned it into a cross, reminding me that He died so I wouldn't have to."[3]

Joanna's story points to Good Friday and to Easter, but it also reminds me of Christmas, because it calls to mind the lyrics of the hymn "O Holy Night":

Long lay the world in sin and error pining,
Till He appeared and the soul felt its worth.

It is Christ's appearing—his birth, his life on earth, and his death and resurrection—that speaks of God's immeasurable love and power, enabling our souls to finally and forever know their worth.

Lord, I want to measure myself by looking at who you are and what you've done for me rather than by looking at myself. As I grow stronger in your love, may I also grow stronger in your peace.

UNNECESSARY BURDENS

Jesus said, "Come to me, all of you who are weary and carry heavy burdens, and I will give you rest. Take my yoke upon you. Let me teach you, because I am humble and gentle at heart, and you will find rest for your souls. For my yoke is easy to bear, and the burden I give you is light."

MATTHEW 11:28-30

My daughter Katie's backpack weighs almost as much as she does. If I had to carry that thing around all day, I'm sure I would end up in the hospital. It makes me long for the day when the digital revolution will finally overtake textbooks, enabling children to transport them on a lightweight electronic device.

Katie's two-ton backpack reminds me of what it feels like to carry burdens that are not my own. Instead of an aching back, they produce an aching heart, robbing me of the peace God has promised. It wasn't long ago that worrying about a situation I can't even remember kept me up most of the night. Then I ran across this quote from Mary Crowley, a single mother, who rose to prominence as the head of a multimillion-dollar company: "Every evening I turn my worries over to God. He's going to be up all night anyway."

Crowley's words remind me of the wisdom of novelist George MacDonald, who once remarked that "no man ever sank under the burden of the day. It is when tomorrow's burden is added to the burden of today that the weight is more than a man can bear." Where did MacDonald's wisdom come from? Most likely from the lips of the Lord himself, who told his disciples, "Don't worry about tomorrow, for tomorrow will bring its own worries. Today's trouble is enough for today" (Matthew 6:34).

We can't off-load our worries onto some kind of digital device. But we have something far better—a promise from Christ that his yoke is easy to bear and that the burden he gives is light.

Lord, help me not to get weighed down by burdens that I shouldn't be carrying alone. When I begin to do that, remind me that your burden is light and that you have promised to provide rest to those who are weary.

GOD WILL PROTECT YOU

*The sun will not harm you by day, nor the moon at night. The LORD
keeps you from all harm and watches over your life.*

PSALM 121:6-7

On March 11, 2011, Japan was rocked by the largest earthquake in its history. Like millions of others throughout the world, I spent time praying
for the Japanese people in the days following the tragedy. But faith is daunt-
ing during such troubling times. How can we feel secure when the planet
we live on is constantly shifting and changing? Earthquakes, tsunamis, hurricanes—we've seen the devastating pictures as they scroll across the screen,
feeling as though we're watching the Apocalypse unfold.

Despite enormous technological advances, human ignorance and vul-
nerability are painfully obvious at such times. We are surprised by how bad
things can get. Again and again we are shocked by the force of nature, surprised that the cities we have built in coastal areas and over seismic faults can
sustain so much damage. It is heartbreaking—and terrifying.

Even those of us who never have to endure such disasters will inevitably face our own personal disasters. A child may die, a spouse may leave, the
world as we know it may change in an instant, flooding us with sorrow. The
Bible, of course, makes no promise of protection from suffering. "What it
does promise," Eugene Peterson declares, "is preservation from all the evil"
in whatever difficulty we face. According to Peterson, that's how Jews and
Christians have always read Psalm 121. No injury, no wound, no disaster will
ever overtake us with its evil power, separating us from God's good purposes
for our lives.[4] On that we can rely.

Today, as you pray for others who are facing disasters large and small,
ask God to draw them to Christ, the one who will preserve them from
all evil.

*Father, I grieve at all the suffering in the world, and I cling to your promise
that you will protect from evil all who belong to you. Help those who are in
great difficulty today to come to know the saving power of Christ.*

March 11

FEELING PEACEFUL

You will keep in perfect peace all who trust in you, all whose thoughts are fixed on you!
ISAIAH 26:3

Is it possible to experience emotional peace regardless of what is going on around you? The answer to that is yes, sometimes it is possible. But should that be our ultimate goal? Though Paul told the Philippians that he had learned to be content regardless of circumstances (see Philippians 4:11), I don't think he was claiming to be immune to episodes of fear, distress, or sorrow. Paul was still human. He still had an emotional life.

The same is true of Jesus. Though he maintained an incredible calm during his trial and imprisonment, we don't know what he was feeling inside as he made his way to the cross. We do, of course, know that he confided in his disciples the night before his death, saying, "My soul is crushed with grief to the point of death" (Matthew 26:38). We know, too, that he had been angry about the way the Temple had become a marketplace and that he was grieved over the death of his friend Lazarus. Clearly Jesus had a rich emotional life, but his emotional responses were entirely appropriate to the circumstances he faced.

When it comes to feelings, it may be that the kind of peace God promises has more to do with reordering our emotional life so that we, too, can respond appropriately to the difficulties we face. That makes sense if we remember that *shalom* contains within it the idea of enjoying good health. Today as you seek more of God, ask him to work his peace into you, like a baker kneading yeast into dough. As you pray, take time to think about any negative emotional patterns that may have developed in your life. Bring these to the Lord, asking him to heal and change you.

Father, thank you for all you have done and all you will yet do. Help me keep my eyes on you, trusting that you will make me into a woman whose life is marked by your shalom.

SURROUNDED BY GOD

Those who trust in the LORD are as secure as Mount Zion; they will not be defeated but will endure forever. Just as the mountains surround Jerusalem, so the LORD surrounds his people, both now and forever.

PSALM 125:1-2

How much would you pay for a device that would instantly transform your emotional life so you never experienced an ounce of emotional pain? What if you could set the device to protect you from feelings of anxiety, sorrow, anger, and frustration? Wouldn't that be great?

Well, maybe not. It might turn you into some kind of bizarre automaton, responding to life like one of those statues of a happy Buddha, sitting cross-legged with a smile on his face. As troublesome as our emotions can sometimes be, they are gifts given by the God who made us. But emotions can be confusing, sometimes leading us to the wrong conclusions, especially in our relationship with God.

"My feelings," says Eugene Peterson, "are important for many things. They are essential and valuable. They keep me aware of much that is true and real. But they tell me next to nothing about God or my relation to God. My security comes from who God is, not from how I feel." Peterson goes on to cite Psalm 125. "'As the mountains are round about Jerusalem, so the LORD is round about his people.'" The image that announces the dependable, unchanging, safe, secure existence of God's people, he says, "comes from geology, not psychology."⁵

Feeling especially calm and peaceful today? Thank God for your sense of tranquility. Feeling troubled and anxious? Don't let it worry you too much. Feeling somewhere in between? God can handle that, too. The Lord's love always encircles you, no matter what is going on in your life.

Father, thank you that you are bigger than any emotion I might have. When I feel tossed about by emotional storms, help me to calm myself by envisioning your faithful love as a mountain surrounding and protecting me. Thank you for your unchanging, rock-solid faithfulness.

DIFFICULTY

How can I know all the sins lurking in my heart? Cleanse me from these hidden faults. Keep your servant from deliberate sins! Don't let them control me. Then I will be free of guilt and innocent of great sin. May the words of my mouth and the meditation of my heart be pleasing to you, O LORD, my rock and my redeemer.

PSALM 19:12-14

Sometimes life is more challenging than it needs to be. Work seems difficult. We get sick. Our children misbehave. There's not enough money to pay the bills. Everywhere we turn, trouble and disappointment assail us. At such times in my own life, I cling to what has become a favorite proverb: "This too shall pass." Though not drawn from Scripture, it's a saying that packs a lot of wisdom, reminding us that life is seasonal. Things will eventually improve.

Sometimes, however, more is needed in our response to life's difficulties. At times we will need to have the courage to ask ourselves an important question, one with searing implications: "Have I brought any of my troubles on myself? Do I bear any responsibility (even slightly) for what I am going through?"

Our decisions have real-life implications. If I cut corners at work, I may lose my job. If I eat too much, I will become unhealthy. If I spend too much, I will fall into debt. Sin has real-life implications, too. Tolerating it can lead to all kinds of difficulties. If I'm self-righteous, I will push people away. If I lie to my friend, I may lose her friendship.

At first sin can seem like the path of least resistance. But in the end, it's the hardest path of all, leading to a life bereft of peace and joy. The silver lining in the "sin cloud" is that once we admit our failings to God, we no longer have to live under sin's power. As we ask God's forgiveness, we are once again open to receiving the help we need to live a better life.

Lord, because I know you love me, I am not afraid to face my failings. Show me my hidden faults and help me turn toward you and receive your forgiveness.

MAKING SENSE OF SUFFERING

Show mercy and kindness to one another.

ZECHARIAH 7:9

To be human is to suffer. It's also human to wonder why we have to. Though there are no simple answers to this difficult question, it is nearly always true that our suffering becomes less painful if we can find meaning in it.

This truth came home to me after undergoing a recent foot surgery. True, the surgery was minor, but it was painful and inconvenient. It would be three months before I could walk again on my own two feet. A few days after the surgery, my next-door neighbors, Bob and Kathy, surprised me with a visit and the gift of a home-cooked meal for my family. Both had suffered through their own share of foot surgeries, and as we compared notes, I felt buoyed by people who knew exactly what I was going through.

We all expressed how easy it had been to take our two functioning feet for granted prior to surgery. The experience had made us more grateful for the blessing of being able to walk without help. Then Kathy commented that, although she was grateful for two feet, she was certainly glad she didn't have three. I understood her point, implying that in her case, three feet would probably have amounted to three separate surgeries!

After they left, I couldn't help but think about how suffering can carve a larger space in our hearts, helping us empathize with others. That was certainly the case with Bob and Kathy, who were quick to offer practical help and encouragement to someone who was suffering as they had been.

My own difficulties also bore witness to another dynamic at work in those who suffer. Though I usually pride myself on being self-reliant, my surgery opened my eyes to the goodness of others, because there were so many people who offered their help.

We know that suffering does not always improve a person's character. Nor does it necessarily reveal the goodness of others. Sometimes the reverse is true. But we do know that God is the only one creative and powerful enough to take the hard things and make them into good things for those who love him.

Father, thank you for being with me in my suffering. Open my eyes to the ways you are working.

March 15

YES!

Jesus Christ, the Son of God, does not waver between "Yes" and "No." He is the one whom Silas, Timothy, and I preached to you, and as God's ultimate "Yes," he always does what he says. For all of God's promises have been fulfilled in Christ with a resounding "Yes!" And through Christ, our "Amen" (which means "Yes") ascends to God for his glory.

2 CORINTHIANS 1:19-20

The release of the iPad sparked a buying frenzy. Long lines snaked outside Apple stores as customers waited for hours for the chance to snag one. Because of shortages, it wasn't unusual for people to wait in vain, only to be told when they reached the front of the line that the store had no more in stock.

One man, lucky enough to snag one, wasn't so lucky when he arrived home with his purchase in hand. A few days later, Apple received his iPad in the mail, bearing this simple note: "Wife said no."

Apple workers got a chuckle from that message, and it wasn't long before executives in the company caught wind of it. Instead of just chuckling, they refunded the man's money and sent him a new iPad bearing this simple note: "Apple says yes." I am guessing that they made two people quite happy that day—the husband who got his beloved iPad back and the wife who realized he hadn't spent a penny for it.

I love the story because it reminds me that *yes* is one of the most popular words in the English language. Do you love me? Will I get that job? Will my children be okay? Will I ever lose weight? These and a thousand other questions, spoken and unspoken, beg for the answer yes. But so often the answer we hear is no. No, you aren't that pretty. No, you aren't that smart. No, you aren't that thin. No, you aren't that rich.

The world has so many ways of saying no to us. But when God sent his only Son, he said the biggest yes of all. Yes to a future full of hope. Yes to peace with God. Yes to living a life of purpose and meaning. Yes to eternal life. Today try counting all the yeses God has already said in your life, thanking him for each one.

Father, I know that sometimes you do say no. But I believe your nos are given in love, designed to lead me to the biggest yes of all: living forever with you.

March 16

BIG GOD

When I look at the night sky and see the work of your fingers—the moon and the stars you set in place—what are mere mortals that you should think about them, human beings that you should care for them?

PSALM 8:3-4

What is the most surprising thing you've learned about God? Here's what I would say if you asked me: "That God is so much bigger and better than I thought he was." The longer I have been a Christian, the more the bigness and the betterness of God keeps growing.

Truth be told, God was big when I first encountered him as a twenty-one-year-old. He was big enough to catch me as I stepped off a cliff and into his arms. At least that's what it felt like when I surrendered my life to him. In that moment, God was not only big enough to catch me when I stepped over the edge but loving enough to flood me with a sense of his presence and peace. I felt safe, happy as never before. The years that followed brought many tangible signs of his goodness. He blessed my work in surprising ways, he freed my father from alcoholism, he led members of my family to him, he restored relationships, he blessed me with children.

To say that God has revealed himself as bigger and better than I first imagined is an understatement. But it is also true that I have attempted to shrink him down to size at times, to imagine, for instance, that he could not possibly forgive me if I couldn't forgive myself, to pray as though he were my servant rather than I his, to doubt that he really cared about me at times when life seemed unbearably difficult.

I like what Chuck DeGroat, a pastor at City Church in San Francisco, has to say about the bigness of God: "Let's face it: if you have a big God, you have to deal with big Mystery."[6] Perhaps that's key when it comes to experiencing more of God. We have to deal with "big Mystery," forgoing the temptation to shrink God. There is too much we do not understand. Too much we cannot comprehend. Faith is an adventure, a hard but joyful journey toward the God who is more powerful and loving than we have any right to expect.

Father, who am I that you should think of me? Yet you have called me by name and invited me to know you. May I know you in the deepest ways possible.

March 17

DISAGREEING

Wise words are more valuable than much gold and many rubies.

PROVERBS 20:15

Okay, I admit it. I dislike conflict. But that doesn't mean I always avoid it. For some reason, I am nearly always surrounded by friends of a fairly different political persuasion than my own. I find that difficult, especially in election years. When do I stand up for things I believe in, and when do I keep silent? How much are my friends willing to learn from me, and how much am I willing to learn from them? Such questions become critical in the midst of a highly charged political environment in which politicians and political parties are often demonized by those on the other side. Can I disagree in a way that is respectful and calm rather than judgmental and angry? These are things I struggle with.

Recently, a well-known Christian author published a book that was attacked by many in the Christian community and celebrated by many on the outside. I haven't read it yet, though I am familiar with the author's work. I suspect the book gets many things right and some things wrong. What troubles me is not so much the mischief that such a book might do but the mischief that Christians do to each other whenever we fail to remember that we are brothers and sisters in Christ. Of course, it's important to stand up for the truths we believe in, but we contradict those truths whenever we do so in a mean-spirited, judgmental way.

I heard a story a few years ago about a Christian publisher who received a bullet in the mail from a supposed Christian with a note that said he deserved to be shot for publishing a translation of the Bible that the writer disagreed with. Admittedly, that was an extreme case. But most of us have seen how vindictive people can be when cherished beliefs come under attack.

By all means, let's contend for the faith. But let's judge *ideas* rather than judging each other. Whether we are discussing a controversial new book or responding to a conflict at church or at home, let's ask for the grace to express our differences in ways that don't contradict the truths we hold dear.

Father, you alone see into the human heart, judging wisely. Help me to disagree with others without judging their motivations. And let your truth prevail.

REMEMBERING

Look, I now teach you these decrees and regulations just as the LORD my God commanded me,
so that you may obey them in the land you are about to enter and occupy. . . . But watch out!
Be careful never to forget what you yourself have seen. Do not let these memories escape from
your mind as long as you live! And be sure to pass them on to your children and grandchildren.

DEUTERONOMY 4:5, 9

High dwellings are the peace and harmony of our descendants. Remember the calamity of the great tsunamis. Do not build any homes below this point."[7] The centuries-old stone tablet bearing this warning stands in the hamlet of Aneyoshi, one of hundreds of such markers planted up and down the coastline of Japan. Fortunately the people of this area heeded the warning of their ancestors, building their homes above the marker and avoiding the fate of the thousands who perished during the 2011 tsunami.

Although many coastal towns had markers bearing similar warnings, many citizens failed to heed them and perished. "People had this crucial knowledge, but they were busy with their lives and jobs, and many forgot," said Yotaru Hatamura, a scholar who has studied the tablets. "It takes about three generations for people to forget. Those that experience the disaster themselves pass it to their children and their grandchildren, but then the memory fades."[8]

How did the people of Aneyoshi hold on to this memory? A twelve-year-old boy by the name of Yuto Kimura explains, "Everybody here knows about the markers. We studied them in school."[9]

Like the Japanese people who heeded the warning, we need to realize that remembering is vital to our well-being. Forgetting what God has done and said will lead to devastation. Remembering will lead to peace. Passing on the sacred memory will enable others to experience the *shalom* God has for them.

Father, help me to remember all you have done and all you have said.
May I cherish your commands and help others to do the same.

PEACE IN THE MIDDLE OF THE FIGHT

Stand your ground, putting on the belt of truth and the body armor of God's righteousness. For shoes, put on the peace that comes from the Good News so that you will be fully prepared.

EPHESIANS 6:14-15

I confess that I have never been in a fight—well, maybe a bit of pushing and pulling in my childhood with my siblings, but nothing along the order of a full-blown brawl. Yet Paul warned the Christians of Ephesus that they would find themselves in the mother of all battles. They would, he assured them, be assailed by the "evil rulers and authorities of the unseen world" (Ephesians 6:12). Urging the Ephesians to stand firm in the Lord, Paul told them not once but three times to put on all the armor of God. Of course, the emphasis on *all* makes sense because missing even a single item of armor would make them vulnerable to the thrusts and jabs of the enemy.

Hailing from the second-largest city in the Roman Empire, the Ephesians would have been familiar with Roman armor. In addition to speaking of a "belt of truth," a "shield of faith," "salvation as your helmet," and "the sword of the Spirit" in Ephesians 6, Paul also speaks of putting on peace as though it were shoes that will prepare us to spread the gospel of peace. One commentator argues that Paul was talking about the Roman *caliga*, a leather half-boot that left the toes free, enabling a soldier to move quickly with a firm grip.

Here's how Eugene Peterson paraphrases Paul's words in *The Message*: "This is no afternoon athletic contest that we'll walk away from and forget about in a couple of hours. This is for keeps, a life-or-death fight to the finish against the Devil and all his angels. Be prepared. You're up against far more than you can handle on your own. Take all the help you can get, every weapon God has issued, so that when it's all over but the shouting you'll still be on your feet. Truth, righteousness, peace, faith, and salvation are more than words. Learn how to apply them. You'll need them throughout your life" (Ephesians 6:12-17).

Today, let's thank God for providing us with everything we need to enter into battle. And let's remember to put on every piece of armor he has so graciously supplied.

Lord, show me how to stand firm, applying the peace you give so I can fight the good fight of faith in the strength that you give.

ANXIOUS PRAYERS

I look up to the mountains—does my help come from there? My help comes from the
LORD, who made heaven and earth! He will not let you stumble; the one who watches over
you will not slumber. Indeed, he who watches over Israel never slumbers or sleeps. The
LORD himself watches over you! The LORD stands beside you as your protective shade.

PSALM 121:1-5

Oddly, instead of helping us grow in faith, prayer can sometimes become an excuse for allowing anxiety to churn in our hearts. Rather than directing our thoughts to God, we direct them to whatever is troubling us. It's no surprise, then, that we come away still feeling fearful.

That's what happened when Pastor Charles Stanley began to pray with a woman whose husband was undergoing surgery. As the woman prayed, Stanley realized that her prayers were becoming more frantic by the second. "Her total focus," he noted, "was on her husband and the operation—none of her focus was truly on God as the Great Physician. . . . I interrupted her prayer and said, 'Ma'am. We need to focus on what God can do in that operating room. We need to focus on who He is and what He is capable of doing.'"

So Stanley began to pray. "I praised God," he says, "for His great love of her husband and of her, of His absolute authority over everything in that hospital, of His wisdom that could manifest itself in every move the surgeon made . . . and when I said 'amen,' I saw in her eyes the peace of God, rather than the sheer panic that had been there just minutes before."[10]

No wonder we need to pray for each other. Often another believer will have the faith we lack. Whether we are praying alone or with others, fear should be an impetus—rather than an obstacle—to prayer. If we let fear take the lead, it will only produce more fear. Instead, we should raise our eyes to God and to his Word, praising and thanking him for his faithfulness, reminding ourselves of who he is and how he loves us. Then we can bring him our requests.

Father, I lift my eyes to you because you are the source of my life. Thank you for all the
ways you have loved me so faithfully, providing for me and hearing my prayers. You are
good and kind and powerful, the Lord of heaven and earth, and I entrust my life to you.

WHAT'S IN YOUR BUCKET?

Whatever is in your heart determines what you say.

MATTHEW 12:34

If we want to bring more peace to our lives and to the lives of others, a good place to begin is by taking an inventory of our hearts. As the Amplified Bible puts it, it's out of the heart's overflow that the mouth speaks. Try picturing a bucket of dirty water. Now imagine putting a brick in the bucket and watching as the dirty water overflows. It's the same with our hearts. Think of the brick as the input we get—the way others treat us, the circumstances we face, the opportunities that present themselves. What comes out of our mouths is strictly a function of what is already in the bucket.

If love, joy, peace, patience, kindness, goodness, faithfulness, gentleness, and self-control, what Paul calls the fruit of the Spirit, are in your bucket, your words will bear witness. But if your words are often tinged with anger, self-pity, hostility, jealousy, or complaining, then something is amiss. Chronic negative speech is a symptom of a heart problem, not a speech problem.

Fixing it requires that we admit we have a problem and that we ask God and others for forgiveness. But that's not all. In Paul's letter to the Galatians (chapter 5), he says that when their lives are controlled by the Holy Spirit, they will exhibit the fruit of the Spirit. If we want our words to produce good things for ourselves and others, we have to learn to yield to God's Spirit, seeking to put every area of our lives under his control and guidance. All of us are guilty of negative speech at times, but the more we ask God to fill us with his Spirit, the more we will find that our tongues become instruments of blessing rather than of hurt.

Father, forgive me for the times I've offended you and others by the way I've spoken. Please cleanse my heart through the power of your Spirit. Pour out your grace and your truth and let me live with greater hope as I daily yield to the power of your Spirit at work within me.

TRAINING AT THRESHOLD

*Train yourself to be godly. "Physical training is good, but training for godliness
is much better, promising benefits in this life and in the life to come."*

1 TIMOTHY 4:7-8

You've probably heard about "training at threshold," a practice that
helps you get the most possible benefit from whatever exercise you do.
Training above or below the threshold will reap positive results, but training
regularly at threshold will get you the most bang for your buck. But how do
you know what your threshold is? Experts in the field of sports physiology say
that the minimum heart rate required to benefit significantly from aerobic
training is in the neighborhood of 60 percent of your maximum heart rate.
Maximum heart rate per minute equals 220 beats minus your age in years. So
if you are twenty years old, your optimum heart rate while training is 120. If
you're fifty, your optimum rate is 102. If you're one hundred and still training,
forget about your heart rate and report directly to Guinness World Records.

Spiritual disciplines can help us train at threshold in our spiritual lives.
Doing so can yield dividends like greater peace and strength as we meet the
challenges of daily life. To refresh your memory of some of the classic disciplines that Christians have practiced over the centuries, here's a short list:

prayer	solitude
fasting	confession
study (spiritual books or Bible study)	Scripture memorization
	service
worship	simplicity[11]
silence	

Why not take a few moments right now to ask God if there are particular spiritual disciplines that you should begin? Ask the Holy Spirit to help
you get started and keep going, giving you the grace to grow stronger as you
seek to live for Christ.

*Father, I want to grow in the likeness of Jesus. Please show me which spiritual disciplines
will help me the most right now, and give me the grace to begin doing them regularly.*

RESET

God loved the world so much that he gave his one and only Son, so that
everyone who believes in him will not perish but have eternal life.

JOHN 3:16

I am not a computer whiz. In fact, one of the most difficult things about starting my own business was leaving behind the help desk—all those smart people who come to your aid whenever you have a computer problem without making you feel like a fool.

The other day my e-mail suddenly went haywire. When I clicked on the inbox, up popped an entirely different screen than the one I was used to seeing. Messages were not arranged by date but by some kind of helter-skelter system I could not decipher. Suddenly and without warning, my most recent e-mails had vanished.

If you're better at computers than I am, you probably know that I simply had to click on the "View" menu, select "Arrange By," "Customize View," "Reset Current View," and then click on "OK" when a box popped up asking me, "Are you sure you want to reset the view 'Messages' to its original settings?" It only took me about an hour to figure out what a help desk could have fixed in about sixty seconds.

When it comes to our spiritual lives, there may be times when we need to push the reset button. If you've been a Christian for any length of time, you probably realize that it's possible to get sidetracked when it comes to our faith. We can fall into negative habits that lead us away from faith, like doubting that God loves us. Like eating everything in sight. Like focusing too much on money. Like thinking everything depends on us rather than on God. At such times, pushing the reset button involves repenting and returning to the foundational truths of our faith, truths like John 3:16 or Matthew 22:37-39, where Jesus lays out the two great commandments that should characterize our lives: "You must love the LORD your God with all your heart, all your soul, and all your mind. . . . Love your neighbor as yourself."

In the end, pushing the reset button means admitting you're not a spiritual whiz and then turning to the one who loves you and is able to help you get back on track.

Lord, keep me on the path that leads to life. Direct my steps and I will not fall.

PEACE IN YOUR RELATIONSHIPS

*The wolf and the lamb will feed together. The lion will eat hay like a
cow. But the snakes will eat dust. In those days no one will be hurt or
destroyed on my holy mountain. I, the LORD, have spoken!*

ISAIAH 65:25

Birds and cats are not normally best friends. That's why the video I
watched surprised me. A couple had documented the relationship of a
crow and a stray kitten for a period of eight months. For several hours each
day, the crow and the kitten could be seen playing together. Whenever the
kitten began to cross the road, the crow would start squawking at it or hop
around, pushing it back toward safety. The crow would also feed the kitten
with its own preferred cuisine—a diet of worms and bugs—no doubt saving
its life. Now that's one nice crow and one fortunate kitty!

Watching that video of the two unlikely friends reminded me of God's
promise that one day the lamb would have nothing to fear from the wolf
because every creature in the world would reflect God's peace. It made me
think, too, of Paul's words to the Romans: "We know that all creation has
been groaning as in the pains of childbirth right up to the present time. And
we believers also groan, even though we have the Holy Spirit within us as a
foretaste of future glory, for we long for our bodies to be released from sin
and suffering" (8:22-23).

Some of the pain and suffering we endure comes from the strife we
experience in relationships, broken and twisted by sin. We find it hard to get
along with certain people at home, at work, and at church. Because of what
Jesus has done for us and because his Spirit lives in us, nothing is impossible
for the God who is able to heal even our most fractured relationships.

Don't wait for the Second Coming to begin to pray about your own
difficult relationships. Ask God for grace and wisdom for yourself and the
people you find difficult. Who knows what unlikely friendships you may be
able to forge as a result of God's peace at work within and through you.

*Father, help me to be ruthlessly honest about ways I have contributed to problems in
my relationships. Help me to repent and to be willing to do whatever it takes to respond
to the grace you will give me as I seek greater peace in the way I relate to others.*

GOD'S PROTECTION

The LORD says, "I will rescue those who love me. I will protect those who trust in my name."
PSALM 91:14

I magine that you and I are walking down the street together when a storm suddenly breaks out. You kindly offer to share the overlarge umbrella you brought with you. But to your surprise, I refuse the offer and just keep walking, veering off in my own direction. When I finally arrive at my destination, soaked from head to toe, I complain to anyone who would listen that even though you had an umbrella, you refused to keep me covered. Wouldn't that be a little crazy?

That's a picture of what happens when we remove ourselves from God's protection by going our own way, living according to our own desires, following our own plans. Consider the woman who has committed her life to Christ and yet thinks she can do whatever she wants as long as she doesn't hurt anyone. So she parties a lot or sleeps with her boyfriend or has an affair with someone at work. But then something bad happens. She gets pregnant or contracts an infection or becomes depressed. Why, she wonders, is her life so miserable? Why does she feel so worthless? Why hasn't God protected her? Doesn't he care what happens to her?

Or what about the woman who spends too freely and wonders why she has fallen into debt? Or the one who makes cutting remarks and wonders why she has so few friends? Or the one who takes a job without consulting God and then wonders why she hates it? Why isn't God helping her? Why hasn't he protected her?

Not everything we suffer is a result of our failure to follow God and keep ourselves within the circle of his protection. But certainly some things are.

If you recognize yourself in any of these examples, ask the Lord's forgiveness. Remember that he is not in the business of running after people with his protective umbrella, covering them regardless of how they choose to live.

Lord, forgive me for going my own way and then expecting you to bless my plans. I want to let go of my plans so I can take hold of yours. Keep me close to you, I pray.

March 26
IT'S THE LITTLE THINGS
THAT GET YOU

*The Holy Spirit produces this kind of fruit in our lives: love, joy, peace,
patience, kindness, goodness, faithfulness, gentleness, and self-control.*

GALATIANS 5:22-23

Last night I picked my daughter up at a friend's house. She'd had a great time and was in a good mood.

But when we arrived home, her mood deteriorated after a quick succession of negatives—like being asked to carry something large and awkward from the trunk to the front door and then ringing the doorbell and no one answering and then watching me fumble for my key without finding it and then words with her sister when she finally answered the door and then nothing interesting to eat in the kitchen and then being told that it was late and she had to get to bed right now. In rapid succession, the incidents piled on, helping to morph my cheerful child into a whiny, angry one.

As I tucked her in and we said goodnight, I talked to her about her frustration, trying to help her identify the incidents that had made her so upset. I did this because I have found that understanding the causes of my own emotional reactions often helps me calm down and handle life better. Taken one by one, little challenges seem more manageable.

Some of us are moving so fast that we simply react without fully understanding what has set us off. Most of the time it's small things piling up. Someone hogging the remote. Children not doing chores. A husband's insensitive comments. A driver cutting us off. We've all heard about the straw that finally breaks the camel's back. I like the way an Amish proverb puts it: "It isn't the mountains that wear you out, it's the grain of sand in your shoe."[12]

The next time you feel frustrated, whiny, or angry, take a moment to review what's transpired in the last few hours. Are little things piling on? If so, try to unpack them one by one, asking God to help you deal with them in a way that displays his wisdom and grace.

Father, help me to understand myself better so that I can gain more self-control—not the kind that comes from rigidly repressing my feelings, but the kind that comes as a fruit of being filled with your Spirit.

WORRY

Give all your worries and cares to God, for he cares about you.

1 PETER 5:7

Robert Sapolsky is professor of biology and neurology at Stanford University and the author of *Why Zebras Don't Get Ulcers*. In this intriguingly titled book, he explains why humans suffer from stress-related illnesses.

When an animal in the wild faces danger it has two options—fight or flight. After fighting or fleeing, assuming it has survived the threat, the animal's nervous system quickly calms down. Not so with us *Homo sapiens*. Though our physiological system is adapted for a fight-or-flight response, it can be activated by anxiety and chronically activated by chronic anxiety. As Sapolsky observes, "How many hippos worry about whether Social Security is going to last as long as they will, or what they are going to say on a first date?"[13] Such worries overload the system, wreaking havoc on our bodies, pushing them into fight-or-flight mode when neither will solve the problem at hand. It's like dialing 911 over and over, activating an emergency response though none is required.

Is it possible to deal with stress in a way that doesn't activate a highly charged response? Fortunately the answer is yes. There are practical ways to keep anxiety at bay. Certainly for Christians, the most practical thing we can do is to follow Peter's advice to give all our worries and cares to God. Some translations say that we should cast all our cares on God. I like that word *cast*, especially in connection with Peter, because he was a fisherman who knew what it was like to draw nourishment from casting his nets on the water.

The next time you feel anxiety rising in your heart, try this little exercise. Imagine yourself in a boat or standing on a pier, fishing pole in hand. Now bait the line with whatever is bothering you. Put the passage from 1 Peter 5:7 in your own words, perhaps something like this: *Father, I want to cast this problem on you because I know that you care about what happens to me.* Then picture yourself casting out your line, watching as it is swallowed up in the sea of God's love.

Lord, I want to stop worrying and start trusting. Help me break the habit of worry by replacing it with a habit of prayer.

March 28

SPICE UP YOUR FAITH

I tell you the truth, if you had faith even as small as a mustard seed, you could say to this mountain, "Move from here to there," and it would move. Nothing would be impossible.

MATTHEW 17:20

Jesus said that even mustard-seed-size faith can move mountains. Think about that. You don't have to have big, big faith to achieve big, big results. You only have to have a little bit of faith because faith is like a seed that is genetically programmed for growth. Growth will happen as long as it's planted in favorable soil.

The mustard tree that Jesus referred to is probably black mustard, growing from a tiny seed that produces a huge bush, sprouting yellow flowers, and climbing to a height of up to eight feet.

I like how one source put it when describing where to plant black mustard: "Disturbed areas are preferred." Though I knew the phrase had a technical definition, I couldn't help but laugh when I read it because our own faith needs to be planted right in the middle of life's disturbances. After all, why would we need faith if everything was already perfect and if everybody already belonged to God?

Of course, faith is far different than wishful thinking. Wishing is simply wanting something badly enough to hope we will get it. The focus is on *what we want.* Faith, on the other hand, is not focused on us or our wants but on *what God wants* for us. It's a Spirit-inspired gift that we put to work in tandem with God's promises. For instance, in Matthew 6:30, Jesus said that the God who cares so wonderfully for flowers that are here today and gone tomorrow will surely care for us. So we can count on it. God's promised provision frees us from chronic worry so we can focus our energy on seeking first his Kingdom rather than ours, placing ourselves in the center of his will.

Father, faith requires taking risks. Help me to take the risks you require. Let me risk believing that you are who you say you are and that you will do what you say you will.

WHAT THE HEART BELIEVES

We walk by faith, not by sight.

2 CORINTHIANS 5:7, KJV

Numerous clinical studies have shown a strong brain-body connection, indicating that what our brains think can significantly impact our health. A few years ago, an experiment was conducted in which professional actors spent a day working on one of two scenes—either an upbeat one or a depressing one. At the end of the day, researchers measured the actors' immune responsiveness. Guess what? Actors who spent the day working on the uplifting scene showed increased immune responsiveness, while actors assigned to the sad scene showed decreased responsiveness.[14]

It strikes me that faith has a similar power to influence our spiritual health. By making the comparison, I am not implying that faith is merely a matter of positive thinking. It's not. Faith is a divine gift that enables us to perceive the truth and respond accordingly. It gives meaning and purpose to the universe and our place in it. As Paul says, those who belong to Christ walk by faith and not by sight. It is faith that enables us to take hold of the truest and most important story in the world—the one that God is telling. Faith puts us smack-dab in the middle of the narrative because we are part of Christ's body and the story of salvation is still unfolding.

Of course, the life of faith has its share of anguish and difficulty. Exercising our faith does not always feel uplifting. But ultimately, faith is what fuels our hope and enables us to perceive what God is doing in the world. It is also what gives meaning to our struggles and confers value on our obedience. In the end, what our hearts believe is what will most significantly impact our sense of God's peace.

Lord, thank you for the gift of faith. When I am tempted to walk by sight and not by faith, remind me that my life only makes sense within the context of the story you are telling. Help me to make the connection.

FAITH WILL TAKE YOU PLACES

*Since we are surrounded by such a huge crowd of witnesses to the life of faith,
let us strip off every weight that slows us down, especially the sin that so easily
trips us up. And let us run with endurance the race God has set before us.*

HEBREWS 12:1

The life of faith is meant to be active, dynamic, and adventurous, not dull, suffocating, and restrictive. Some people say that faith is a verb. I like to think of it as a bike with large, sturdy wheels. As with most bikes, this one only works when you climb on and start pedaling. In other words, you have to do something with the faith you've been given if you want it to take you where God is leading.

Scripture tells us that we have to *stand firm* in faith, *live by* faith, *receive by* faith, *continue in* faith, *contend for* the faith, *put on* faith, *hold on to* faith, *keep* faith, *share* faith, and *conquer through* faith. You get the picture. In order to be the kind of people God wants us to be, do the kinds of things he wants us to do, and live the kind of life he created us for, we need to act on the faith we have. Yes, there are times when we need to be still, when we need to wait patiently for God's direction. But even then, faith goes into action, enabling us to trust that God will speak to us as we come to him in prayer and that he will lead us when we seek his guidance.

Do you want to live a fruitful life? Do you want to experience God? Do you want to become more like the Jesus you love? Then say good-bye to comfort and ease and safety and doing everything your way, and say hello to a life of faith and adventure. Tell the Lord you're tired of straddling the fence and living like everyone around you, caught up with worldly cares and concerns. Tell him you can't go on without a living, vital faith. Ask him today to help you respond in faith to whatever he asks. Then put your faith into action by believing he will answer that prayer.

*Lord, life is short. Help me not to waste it looking for safety, comfort, and security.
Teach me what it means to put my faith into action in the midst of my life right now.*

JUST SO

The LORD grants wisdom! From his mouth come knowledge and understanding. He grants a treasure of common sense to the honest. He is a shield to those who walk with integrity.

PROVERBS 2:6-7

It's easy to think that peace comes from having everything just so. A clean house. Clean children. Everything and everyone in their proper place. Consider a couple of postings on a blog entitled *I Am Neurotic*:

> Every file, folder, song, picture, etc., must be alphabetized and spelled correctly before I can open the file. If I find them uncorrected I will spend the rest of my free time assorting and respelling every file in the computer's hard drive.[15]

> Ever since I started school at 5 years old I have had an obsession with the teacher erasing the chalkboard entirely. Most would rub the eraser around but leave stray lines and continue writing. I would stare at the stray lines and it would drive me crazy the remainder of the class. I would get hot and get headaches. I am 22 years old and in college and nothing has changed.[16]

If you know anyone who suffers from obsessive-compulsive disorder, you know that his or her life is far from peaceful. But what does any of this have to do with the ordinary, run-of-the-mill perfectionist? Only this—that our search for peace will never bear fruit if we insist on trying to control all the unruly bits and pieces of our lives.

If you are frustrated because of all the things you can't control, try bringing them one by one into the presence of the Lord. Ask him to help you sort through the pile, deciding which ones to let go and which ones to hold on to. He can give you wisdom and grace to deal with the things in your life that are threatening your peace.

Father, help me to let go of things I cannot possibly control. Give me wisdom about the situations you want me to be involved with, and show me how to deal with them in your peace.

April 1

PLAY YOUR PART

Our bodies have many parts, and God has put each part just where he wants it.

1 CORINTHIANS 12:18

Any thespian worth her salt knows about the importance of preparation. You begin by memorizing your lines, imagining the scene, acting it out. Once you've done that, you're ready for the first rehearsal. But when you make your entrance, everything goes haywire—apparently you've memorized the wrong part! The director stops the play to inquire just who you think you are and what you think you are saying. The whole thing is confusing, embarrassing, and frustrating. You've worked so hard and only succeeded in messing things up.

That's a very rough analogy to convey what can happen in our own lives when we get our part of the story wrong, taking on a role God never asked us to play. When we come into relationship with Christ, we realize he is the main character in the story of salvation. That means he is also at the center of our personal stories. With the knowledge that we belong to Christ, we forsake the deep selfishness that once characterized us.

Even so, a funny thing can happen over the course of time. Some of us begin to lose our grip on the story we believe in. Forgetting who the Hero is, we begin to act and think as though everything depends on us and very little on God. Instead of rehearsing what Christ has done for us by committing his promises to memory, for instance, we begin to rehearse all the wrong lines—"I've got to do whatever it takes to get that promotion" or "God couldn't possibly save my marriage" or "God must not love me because he hasn't answered my prayers the way I asked him to." Lines like these will cause us to mess up.

The good news about messing up, of course, is that doing so may help us wake up to the fact that we've forgotten the big story that should guide our lives. If you've nudged Jesus into a minor role in your life, ask God's forgiveness, telling him you want the show to go on—but this time with Christ in the lead.

Father, please help me place my own story within the context of the big story you are telling, and then help me play the role that you assign me.

BLESSING THE DARKNESS

I could ask the darkness to hide me and the light around me to become night—but even in darkness I cannot hide from you.

PSALM 139:11-12

Larry Crabb says that we find God only when we need him. Simple words, but true. It's like looking for the light switch in a dark room. No one goes searching for it until the sunlight has gone. Similarly, darkness can impel our search for God.

Several years ago I met the last survivor pulled from the wreckage after the destruction of the World Trade Center in 2001. During our time together, Genelle Guzman-McMillan told me a story about flirting with faith but choosing to live without it. Then, on September 11, her world fell apart and she found herself in complete darkness, buried alive under a mountain of rubble.

"God, you've got to help me!" she prayed, lying beneath a stairwell. "You've got to show me a sign, show me a miracle, give me a second chance. Please save my life . . . and I promise I will do your will."[1]

What shocked me most about Genelle's story was not that she managed to survive after the North Tower collapsed on top of her but how she reflected on that experience. She told me she thanked God for it because it was a wake-up call. In the midst of impenetrable darkness, she discovered his light.

We, too, have found the light that is our salvation. Even so, there are times when we hit patches of darkness, when we don't know what to do, when we feel challenged beyond our strength. Difficult as it can be to navigate our way through the darkness, it is precisely in the midst of it that we can find God.

Rather than giving in to the gloom that threatens us or those we love, let's allow it to press us toward God, believing that he is near, whether or not we sense his presence. As Larry Crabb points out, "When we seek him with a stronger passion than we seek anything else (such as solutions or relief), we will find him. . . . After a long fall through darkness, we will land on the truth of his eternal, almighty, and loving character, and will believe he is always up to something good."[2]

Father, I thank you that even the darkness is not dark to you. In the midst of unimaginable difficulty, you are always up to something good in the lives of those who love you.

THE PLACES THAT SCARE YOU

*Don't let your hearts be troubled. Trust in God, and trust also in me. There is
more than enough room in my Father's home. If this were not so, would I have
told you that I am going to prepare a place for you? When everything is ready,
I will come and get you, so that you will always be with me where I am.*

JOHN 14:1-3

Pema Chodron is the author of *The Places That Scare You*. An American
Buddhist, she writes about the things that frighten us most, offering
an Eastern take on how to deal with these. "We know that all is imperma-
nent, we know that everything wears out," she says. "We don't like it that
we age. We are afraid of wrinkles and sagging skin."[3] Instead of denying the
truth about the impermanence of life, she suggests that we "relax gradually
and wholeheartedly into the ordinary and obvious truth of change."[4] While
there's some merit in what she says, ultimately Buddhism doesn't offer much
consolation in the face of our own mortality.

How can we find true peace in the midst of our fears? As Christians,
we can "relax into" the obvious truth of change because we have a Savior who
will never abandon us. Instead of leaving us alone, he will show us the way
through the places that scare us. But just how does he do that? Remember
that Jesus is called the Word of God. He's God's message about what is real,
true, and good. That means everything about him—his words, his actions,
his reactions, his miracles, and his parables—communicates God and his plan
to us. As the one who is also called the "pioneer and perfecter" of our faith
(Hebrews 12:2, NIV), Jesus blazes the way ahead, showing us both how to live
and how to die.

In the end, we find courage not because we have discovered a method
of dealing with our fears but because we have found a person who can help us
overcome them. He's the one who will lead us, wrinkles and all, safely home.

*Lord, when I am afraid, help me to face my fears by bringing them honestly and hopefully
into your presence. Let me listen for your Word, and may your truth give me courage.*

PRAYING FOR PEACE

*I pray that God, the source of hope, will fill you completely
with joy and peace because you trust in him.*

ROMANS 15:13

Streams in the Desert is a classic devotional, still going strong after more than eighty years. Perhaps one of the reasons for its popularity is that each day speaks words of encouragement to people who are distressed or suffering. Take this entry, for example, which addresses the topic of seemingly unanswered prayers. "Often it is simply the answer to our prayers that cause many of the difficulties in the Christian life. . . . We pray to the Lord, as His apostles did, saying, 'Increase our faith!' (Luke 17:5). Then our money seems to take wings and fly away; our children become critically ill; an employee becomes careless, slow, and wasteful; or some other new trial comes upon us, requiring more faith than we have ever before experienced."[5]

It's enough to make a person stop praying! When I wrote a book entitled *The Peace God Promises*, I should have known better. As I told friends afterward, I wrote the book in what became the least peaceful season of my life. One after the other, the crises kept mounting. Pleading for God's help, I couldn't help wondering whether he was pulling some kind of celestial joke on me.

If I could have set the tone for those months of "promised peace," I would have been sitting on a beach somewhere enjoying perfect serenity. But in that setting, would I have had to wrestle so hard with the promises of peace that God has made to his people? Would I have been so keenly aware of my own need as I sat down to write every day? If God's promises are real, if his truths are robust, then surely they should help me in my time of need. In fact, they did, though perhaps not always as soon as I wanted them to nor exactly how I had expected them to.

In the months that have followed, God's peace has become more tangible to me than ever, though I can't trace exactly how this happened. That's why I would urge you not to give up, even if you have been seeking God's peace and finding only turmoil. It may be God is answering your prayers in the only way that will yield more peace in your life in the years ahead.

Lord, you promise shalom to those who love you. I love you. Give me more of your peace, I pray.

April 5
THE GUILT TRAIN

The LORD is slow to anger and filled with unfailing love,
forgiving every kind of sin and rebellion.

NUMBERS 14:18

Several years ago I took the train from Grand Rapids to Chicago to enjoy a day of shopping. A trip that would have taken three hours by car stretched into a five-and-a-half-hour journey. Mile after agonizing mile, we crawled along, watching cars whiz past on the highway. I felt disappointed, knowing that my time in Chicago would be cut short.

Like the slow train to Chicago, the guilt train has its share of passengers. At times we may find ourselves stuck on that train, afraid we will never get off. When that happens, we can remember that guilt is supposed to be a symptom of something wrong inside. Its function is to alert us to the presence of sin so we can take that sin to God and receive his forgiveness. But sometimes we wallow in the guilt, perhaps because we think we need to punish ourselves before God will take us back.

As Philip Yancey points out, "Guilt is not a state to cultivate or a mood you slip into for a few days. It should have directional movement, first pointing backward to the sin and then pointing forward to change. A person who feels no guilt can never find healing. Yet neither can a person who wallows in guilt. The sense of guilt only serves its designed purpose as a symptom if it presses us toward a cure."[6]

Feeling guilty all the time? Ask yourself what's behind those feelings. If you find that you are always feeling guilty about behavior that's not sinful, confide in a mature Christian friend or counselor who may be able to help you break the habit. If you have done something wrong, ask God's forgiveness and make steps toward changing. Whatever you do, remember that a ride on the guilt train isn't supposed to take that long. Make a decision now to get off at the first possible stop.

Father, Scripture says that you are slow to anger, not slow to forgive. Please help me to pay attention to the guilt I feel, not wallowing in it, but letting it press me toward a cure.

April 6

SPIRITUAL PLASTICITY

*I lavish unfailing love for a thousand generations on those
who love me and obey my commands.*

EXODUS 20:6

Until recently, scientists believed that injuries to the brain could not be healed. If you had a stroke, for instance, the common practice was to offer rehabilitative services only on a short-term basis because long-term therapies were thought to offer little hope. Now all that has changed. Research has shown that the brain is not static but plastic, meaning that with the right kind of exercise and stimulation, it has the ability to change and heal itself.

Based on these findings about the brain, a rehabilitation program has been developed that offers great promise for people with brain injuries or learning deficits. In this type of therapy, patients complete a series of finely honed exercises designed to stimulate specific areas of their brains. These exercises are designed to strengthen areas of weakness in their brains. Day after day, by faithfully challenging weaker areas of the brain, the patients form new neural pathways until eventually many of them are able to gain cognitive function. Though the program can be tedious, it's hard to argue with its remarkable results.

Perhaps we need a spiritual version of this kind of brain therapy—one that can help our spirits grow stronger as we seek to follow the Lord. Come to think of it, perhaps we already have something like that. It's called obedience. I have to admit that obedience has never been my favorite word. It's sometimes tedious and often difficult. In many cases I'd much rather do what I want to do instead of what God wants me to do. Obedience challenges me spiritually to become the person God wants me to be. The more I obey, the stronger and more spiritually mature I will become because obedience creates pathways in my soul for God to work.

Like our brains, our spirits are capable of incredible growth and healing. If we want God's *shalom* to characterize our lives, we have to be willing to obey him.

*Lord, forgive me for resisting you at times. Help me to run in the path of
your commands, confident that they will draw me closer to you.*

Work at living in peace with everyone.
HEBREWS 12:14

Recently I asked an acquaintance about the meaning of the word inscribed on her license plate. Mary explained that "Watutu" was not Swahili, as I had guessed, but what her young son had said when he was trying to learn how to say, "I love you." Then she mentioned an uncomfortable encounter she once had regarding her personalized license plate. One day someone she didn't know accosted her in a parking lot and began reaming her out, taking the word *Watutu* for a slur. Mary was taken off guard by the woman's anger, since the word had no other meaning than what her son had accorded it. Perhaps that angry woman had just been itching for a fight.

Shortly after our conversation I was standing in the customer service line at the local grocery store. In front of me was an elderly woman carrying a package of Van de Kamp's frozen fish. When she got to the counter, she pulled out the receipt for her groceries and pointed to the letters "vdk." "I want to return this because it has vodka in it," she informed the clerk. The startled clerk looked at the receipt and then pointed out that "vdk" did not stand for vodka but rather for the brand. After the woman left, I couldn't help speculating. She must have been horrified to think that the store had been hawking vodka-injected fish. Or worse yet, perhaps she'd been buying Van de Kamp's fish for many years, unknowingly imbibing the whole time.

The two incidents reminded me that in our world misunderstandings abound. Sometimes they spice things up by adding a little hilarity, as in the case of the frozen fish, but at other times they subtract from the peace, as in the case of the license plate. Perhaps we would all experience more peace if we were to make a habit of giving others the benefit of the doubt, remembering that *Watutu* simply means, "I love you."

Lord, help me to take myself and others less seriously, learning to be more generous in the way I interpret both people and situations.

April 8

DON'T FORGET

He took some bread and gave thanks to God for it. Then he broke it in pieces and gave it to the disciples, saying, "This is my body, which is given for you. Do this to remember me."

LUKE 22:19

When it comes to forgetfulness, I am the queen. When I was in elementary school, I would remember to go to my music lesson but forget to bring my instrument. Over the years I have apologized myself out of more forgotten appointments than I like to admit. I have double-booked and triple-booked and shown up a day early and a day late. When it comes to remembering, my brain is a ninety-pound weakling, and no amount of coping strategies seems capable of curing me.

Like most problems in my life, I like to blame this one on my mother. You see, while I was writing this devotion, she called to wish my daughter a happy birthday. Only one problem: my daughter's birthday is more than a month away.

Fortunately, even if we can't remember where we've put our purses or stashed our keys, God can help us remember what's most important—things like who he is, what he has done for us, and how much he loves us. That's good, because experiencing more of God's peace has everything to do with cherishing the central memories of our faith.

If you had room in your brain for only two sacred memories, they should be the memory of the Exodus and the memory of Christ's passion, death, and resurrection. Why? Because the central message of salvation is summed up in these memories. Like the ancient Israelites, God has brought each of us out of our own Egypt, freeing us from the slavery of sin and death. Furthermore, Jesus has delivered us by suffering, dying, and being raised from the dead. He has shown us who God is and who we are—people God loves beyond all imagining.

If we want a steady supply of God's peace, we need to nurture these memories because they assure us that we are destined for freedom and joy, not bondage and slavery. Whatever you forget, remember these things.

Lord, you promised the Holy Spirit would remind us of everything you told us. May your Spirit help me remember the truth and live by it always.

*Letting your sinful nature control your mind leads to death. But
letting the Spirit control your mind leads to life and peace.*

ROMANS 8:6

My daughter Luci has a tender heart. When we are watching a movie with a frightening or repulsive scene, she often covers her eyes. To tell you the truth, much of the time I'm right there with her, not wanting to expose myself to ugly or frightening images that will return to haunt me. But sometimes, when it comes to real life, we have to look repulsiveness straight in the face in order to understand something vital.

That's why I want to take a moment to look at one of life's ugliest facts. Imagine a dead animal in the process of rotting. Its guts are spilled onto the ground. Flies are swarming. The smell of decay is overpowering. We gaze with a certain fascination at this spectacle of ruin, looking at something that was once alive but has now fallen into death and corruption, realizing, perhaps, that it is a vision of our own future, a picture of bodily death.

Author Dallas Willard says that "'corruption' or 'coming apart' is the natural end of the flesh."[7] The New Testament speaks of the flesh, using the Greek word *sarx*. In many instances, Paul uses this word to link the flesh with sin, making it a willing accomplice. The flesh, in this use of the word, is not literally a thing of blood and tissue but the principle that inclines us to live according to worldly values. To avoid confusion with other uses of the word, some Bible versions translate *sarx* as "sinful nature."

Whenever we calibrate our lives toward the values of this world, we are buying into a fleshly way of life that may feel good now but will ultimately lead to corruption—a coming apart of our souls. It is this decay, this coming apart, that is the opposite of *shalom*—the peace that brings God's wholeness and healing.

As Willard points out, the only way to gain life is to embrace the call of Jesus, who said, "If you cling to your life, you will lose it; but if you give up your life for me, you will find it" (Matthew 10:39).

Lord, dying to self is hard. But the hardest and most frightening thing of all would be to fail to take hold of the life you offer. Help me today to die to myself that I might live to you.

MY WAY OR THE HIGHWAY?

May the Lord of peace himself give you his peace
at all times and in every situation.

2 THESSALONIANS 3:16

Sometimes I am amazed at how spiritually slow I am. God tells me the truth flat out in his Word, but I am reluctant to embrace it, wondering if it's even possible to live it out. So I compromise, make excuses, lower the bar. But somehow God manages to move my imperfect heart in the right direction despite my hesitation.

That's what I thought the other day, in the wake of news that should have upset me. I wanted something and didn't get it, even though I thought I deserved it. I admit I did have a few moments of pique. But God gave me the grace to turn away from my disappointment, realizing that if this desire had been something he'd wanted for my life, he would have fulfilled it. And if he didn't give it, then ultimately I didn't want it. I didn't need to put my energy into becoming sad or angry or into trying to get my own way. Instead, I ended the day with a prayer of thanksgiving, praising God and telling him the truth, which was that I only wanted what he wanted for my life. I was at peace.

Dallas Willard puts his finger on the central problem that each of us faces: "When Jesus says that those who find their life or soul shall lose it, he is pointing out that those who think they are in control of their life—'I am the master of my fate; I am the captain of my soul,' as the poet William Ernest Henley said—will find that they definitely are not in control: they are totally at the mercy of forces beyond them, and even within them. They are on a sure course to disintegration and powerlessness, of *lostness* both to themselves and to God. They must surrender."[8]

Today let us pray for the grace to surrender, not to the forces of disintegration and powerlessness, but to the God who loves us and calls us forward in our faith. Surrendering our lives to Christ will be the surest and safest way not only to eternal life but to the best life we can possibly have right now.

Lord, thank you for the times you have not given me what I wanted when it would
have led me further from you. I want to embrace your will in everything.

REMEMBERING WRONGS

O LORD, if you heal me, I will be truly healed; if you save me,
I will be truly saved. My praises are for you alone!

JEREMIAH 17:14

Sometimes the sins of others can steal our peace. Perhaps you were abused as a child and cannot shake the sense that this experience still defines you. Or perhaps you were betrayed recently by someone you trusted. What should you do? How can you discover God's peace?

We know what doesn't work—repressing the memory, pretending it never happened. As Miroslav Volf, the author of *The End of Memory*, points out, "An unexpressed traumatic experience is like an invasive pathogen."[9] Left to fester, it will make us sick.

Volf goes on to say that however we have been sinned against, we must remember the offense rightly. Among other things, that means we should neither downplay nor exaggerate what happened. Why? Because truth is the only thing that gives access to the event, the memory of which needs to be healed. Distortions perpetrate the hurt, spreading it to others and enabling it to lodge more deeply in our souls.

This work of remembering is difficult to do alone. It helps greatly if we can confide in a trusted, mature Christian. Ultimately, our memories of abuse or mistreatment need to be placed within the context of the central memory of our faith—the memory of Jesus' death and resurrection. At the foot of the cross we remember that both we and our abusers are sinners. The Resurrection reminds us that we have a good future—one that even our abusers may come to share, provided they repent and seek God's grace.

If this all sounds hard, it is. But what is the alternative? A life less than it should be, hemmed in by bitterness and fear? If you are haunted by sins that have been done against you, ask God to help you take the first step by remembering rightly. Seek him and he will provide a way to heal.

Father, you know everything about me, even the wounds I hide from myself. I pray today for the grace and courage of honesty. Help me to experience your healing power.

PRAYING FOR YOUR CHILDREN

If a man has a hundred sheep and one of them gets lost, what will he do? Won't he leave the ninety-nine others in the wilderness and go to search for the one that is lost until he finds it?

LUKE 15:4

It's hard to feel peaceful when those you love aren't doing well—especially when it comes to your children. Many of us have children who have strayed from the values we taught them. They may have drug or alcohol problems. They may be caught in destructive relationships. They may be sitting in jail. Or they may be comfortably ensconced in a corner office but living a godless existence. Whatever their circumstances, we know they are not in a safe place because they have turned their backs on God. What then? How can we possibly be at peace when our children are not?

Quin Sherrer, the author of *A Mother's Guide to Praying for Your Children*, speaks of a time when she was praying hard for one of her own. "The snow was still a foot deep, following a freak, three-day winter storm," she explains. "As my husband drove cautiously down the icy pavement, I spied a little lost black lamb not far from the roadside, bogged down helplessly in the white blanket [of snow]. 'Look, look!' I shouted moments later as a farmer stomped his way over to the tiny black ball of wool, swooshed him up in his arms and headed toward the nearby barn to return him safely to his fold.

"My sagging spirits lifted. I had been praying about a troublesome situation in the life of one of our precious 'lambs.' God was reminding us once again that Jesus, the Good Shepherd, was out looking for His sheep. He is out looking for yours, too. Within three weeks after that incident, our 'lamb' called late one night and asked to come home and start over again. 'Yes!' we yelled. 'Come home.'"[10] Quin has since reported that this is the child who, years later, has outdistanced her in prayer and Bible study.

If you are praying for your own lost sheep, take heart, remembering that you are not the only one who is on the lookout for that lamb. Keep praying, believing all the while that God loves your children even more than you do.

Lord, you are the Shepherd who has promised to search out your lost sheep. Please find and save the ones I love who are lost. Hold them in your arms and lead them home.

April 13

"IT IS FINISHED!"

[Jesus] said, "It is finished!" Then he bowed his head and released his spirit.

JOHN 19:30

Live your story from the middle with the end in sight. In other words, if you are a believer in Christ, you have the enormous advantage of knowing how the story of salvation ends. And it's a very good ending.

If you read the Bible from the first to the last page, you will realize that the only parts that are completely happy are at the beginning and the end. There's the first two chapters of Genesis, when Adam and Eve stroll with God through the perfect world he has made. And then there's the last part of Revelation, when Jesus comes back, kicks the devil out for good, and establishes his Kingdom, world without end, amen. Everything else is middle. And a lot of the middle is about battle and suffering and confusion—a whole bunch of ups and downs.

Remember the last words of Christ as he hung on the cross: "It is finished." I used to imagine this as a whispered sigh. But what if it was more like a roar? That would fit, wouldn't it? Jesus, the great Lion of Judah, using his last bit of strength to shout out the victory. The devil was confounded, his power broken, his kingdom plundered. It must have been such an unpleasant surprise for Satan, who thought himself the great winner of everything as he watched the Son of God hanging in agony on a Roman cross.

And why start in the middle? Simply because that's where God has placed us—somewhere in the middle of the mess we call life. Like the big story of salvation, our own story is filled with ups and downs. We experience both joy and sorrow. But we also know that in the end, everything will come out right for those who belong to Christ, and that should make our own personal downs more bearable. That's what I mean by living with the end in sight.

What are you facing today—an illness, a divorce, a demotion, a disaster? Whatever your trouble, Christ has already said your life will turn out well because he has finished the mission he came to fulfill.

Lord, thank you for not hiding the future from us. We don't know everything, but we do know something—who wins. You win, and because of that we win too.

OLD DOG, NEW TRICKS

I will be your God throughout your lifetime—until your hair is white with age.
ISAIAH 46:4

My brother, Jim, is a dog whisperer. His work is living proof that you really can teach old dogs new tricks. Take the dog that kept running away or the one that jumped up on people or the one that got into fights or the one that peed every time someone rang the doorbell. Jim has helped these and a host of other dogs overcome behaviors that make it difficult for dogs and owners to live in peace.

Though I don't mean to insult the Holy Spirit by comparing him to a dog whisperer, even if the latter is my brother, I do want to make the point that the Spirit can help us respond to God throughout the course of our lifetime, regardless of how old or young we may be. That means you and I always have the opportunity to grow in peace, not because of any brilliance on our part but because of the brilliant help God is willing to give.

I was reminded of this yesterday. With my earphones plugged in so I wouldn't miss a word of my favorite Masterpiece Theatre program, I couldn't help but notice that my daughters kept coming into the room to talk to me for one reason or another. One was whining about an upcoming dentist appointment. The other wanted to know where the nail polish was. Then the two started arguing. Finally, long past bedtime, my youngest came in triumphantly displaying a tooth she had just pulled and asked if the tooth fairy would please deliver. You get the picture.

Before giving in to the usual temptation to let my irritation mount along with each new interruption, I had a sudden thought. What if all these interruptions were more than they appeared to be? What if they were simple opportunities for me to offer guidance, correction, or in the case of the tooth, celebration? So each time, off came the headphones as I responded to the situation at hand.

It was a small thing, true. But what if I could adopt the approach that every unwanted interruption is an opportunity in disguise? What if I could recognize them as the Holy Spirit whispering to me, inviting me to go deeper into the ways of God?

*Lord, please help me respond to everyday frustrations in a way
that enables me to serve others and draw closer to you.*

April 15

DE-STRESSING

May the words of my mouth and the meditation of my heart be
pleasing to you, O LORD, my rock and my redeemer.

PSALM 19:14

Ever heard of the advice to punch pillows or scream at the top of your lungs behind closed doors when you feel angry? Just let it out, and you're sure to feel better? I don't know about you, but punching pillows just gets me more riled up.

Words can rile us up as well, adding unnecessary stress to our lives. Compare the doctor who, before performing a procedure, tells you to expect some discomfort to the one who tells you it will be painful. Instead of enabling you to deal with the pain, the latter phrasing will likely increase it. Or what about the person who tells you that your future boss is the boss from you-know-where instead of explaining that she has high standards and can be challenging to work with? Listening to the former kind of talk will likely increase your on-the-job stress.

Similarly, our own words can stoke the fires of stress, even if we say them only to ourselves. Thinking we need to vent, we exclaim, "That's unfair!" or "I hate this!" or "That's the dumbest thing I ever heard!" or "What a fool!" or "This always happens to me!" Instead of improving our mood, such statements only make us feel worse because they level a once-and-for-all judgment against people and circumstances. Strong words paint a bleak picture that will be hard to alter. Once we have leveled the charge, it is difficult to back away from our judgments in order to work toward solutions.

Stress is all about perception. If you feel backed into a corner, you likely will be backed into a corner. Knowing this, what should we do? One thing we can do is start tuning in, noticing how we feel whenever we or those around us employ such language. The second thing we can do is to tell ourselves, "Stop" or "Calm down" whenever we are on the verge of making such statements. Finally, we can ask God to help us to moderate our language. Doing so doesn't mean we are ignoring or suppressing the feelings we have. It just means we are doing our best not to inflame them.

Lord, help me today to choose my words wisely, under the guidance of your Spirit.

SEEING

He has not ignored or belittled the suffering of the needy. He has not turned his back on them, but has listened to their cries for help.

PSALM 22:24

He sat in his wheelchair in the corner of the church where there were no pews. I had never noticed the man before. As far as I could tell, he was by himself. *He must,* I thought, *have a strong devotion to the Lord to haul himself into church on a blustery Maundy Thursday.* He seemed surprised when I said hello after the service. Perhaps few people ever talked to him. I saw him again at successive services, always alone.

Why hadn't I noticed him before? Perhaps because I didn't usually sit up front. After my foot surgery, however, it was the only place that could accommodate a knee walker. Having only one working leg, by the way, is no fun. Every night for several weeks after the surgery, I shut the blinds on the stairwell so my neighbors wouldn't be exposed to the spectacle of my crawling like an oversize ten-month-old up the stairs.

Speaking of spectacles, I created one when I invited my elderly mother to an Easter buffet shortly after my surgery. *What was I thinking?* I wondered, as the two of us bumped along the restaurant's tiny aisles on our respective walkers. Since my mother couldn't handle both a walker and a plate of food, I made several wheeled trips to the buffet table on her behalf, none of which were graceful and all of which were noticed by fellow diners, who gave me looks that seemed to say, "What are you doing here, anyway?"

No one was unkind. It's just that, like most of us, they didn't seem to tolerate differences that well. Like them, we may feel uncomfortable, uncertain how to respond—if we even allow ourselves to notice those who are unlike us, that is. Like the man at church whom I had never noticed before. I hope in the coming weeks to get to know him a little—or at least to greet him whenever I see him. Lord, help me to *see* him.

Father, thank you for giving me tiny tastes of what it's like to be disabled. When I am well, help me to remember my experience in a way that enables me to see the needs of others.

April 17
MAKING PEACE WITH THE PAST

When a certain immoral woman from that city heard he was eating there, she brought a beautiful alabaster jar filled with expensive perfume. Then she knelt behind him at his feet, weeping. Her tears fell on his feet, and she wiped them off with her hair. Then she kept kissing his feet and putting perfume on them.

LUKE 7:37-38

It took guts for the woman to push past the men and through the door of Simon's house. She may have recognized a few as clients. But no one was willing to acknowledge her in this more public setting. Inside, only one man turned to look, a smile in his eyes. It was the rabbi from Galilee.

Tears began rolling down her face in a great, purifying stream. Kneeling behind him, she caressed the rabbi's feet, washing them with her tears. Then, as though she were performing the most sacred of acts, she slowly unwound strands of her coal-black hair, drying his feet and kissing them as she did so. With eyes still welling, she opened the bottle of precious perfume and began pouring it over his feet.

You have probably heard this story many times. But have you ever imagined yourself as that immoral woman? Perhaps it is hard to take on the role of someone who was publicly reviled for her sinful life. But is it so hard to remember the life you led before you surrendered it to Christ? For some, that life was marked by great darkness, by failures and sins and patterns of behavior that alienated us from God.

If that is the case in your life, as it was in mine, don't let the memory of the past haunt you, overtaking your sense of God's forgiveness. Søren Kierkegaard got the story exactly right when he said of this woman that "as she wept, she finally forgot what she had wept over at the beginning; the tears of repentance became the tears of adoration."[11] Today, may our own tears of repentance be transformed into tears of adoration.

Lord, how can I thank you for what you have done? As far as the east is from the west, thus far have you removed my sins from me.

JESUS IN DISTRESSING DISGUISE

You are not controlled by your sinful nature. You are controlled by the Spirit if you have the Spirit of God living in you. . . . The Spirit of God, who raised Jesus from the dead, lives in you. And just as God raised Christ Jesus from the dead, he will give life to your mortal bodies by this same Spirit living within you.

ROMANS 8:9, 11

Let's face it, children can bring out the best and the worst in us. Before I became a mother, I lived with certain illusions. I thought, for instance, that I was a better person than I am. Cool under pressure, generous, sympathetic, forgiving, someone whose mouth is normally under control. But then came kids, and along with them, unrelenting challenges and too little time and too much to do and buttons being pushed and my not always responding like the good woman I want to be.

At least there is one thing I've gotten better at since I've become a mother—asking for forgiveness. Having children has made me aware of how much territory God still needs to claim in my heart. I know how much I need his grace. And that is a good thing.

Mother Teresa had a lovely way of talking about difficult people. She called them "Jesus in distressing disguise." I have found that it helps to use her phrase not just to describe others but at times to describe myself, as well. Whenever I disappoint myself by not acting the way I know I should, it can be easy to become self-condemning. To avoid this trap, I remind myself that Jesus still lives in me despite my many faults.

The next time you stumble, whether with family or friends, ask for forgiveness. And as you do, refuse to wallow in guilt about all your failings. Instead, be merciful to yourself, believing that God will help you. Don't forget Paul's counsel to the believers in Rome. Remember that God has given you the same mighty Spirit whose power raised Jesus from the dead. Surely that's more than enough power to keep you on the path toward peace.

Lord, thank you for indwelling all who belong to you—even me. Help me to recognize your presence in my life.

BELOVED ENEMIES

To you who are willing to listen, I say, love your enemies! Do good to those who hate you. Bless those who curse you. Pray for those who hurt you.

Luke 6:27-28

I used to think I had no enemies. No one who hated me. No one lying in wait to trip me up. No one with my worst interests at heart. But then I decided to redefine the word *enemy*. What if, instead of interpreting the word to mean someone who was trying to kill, attack, or take me down, someone who aimed bombs or grenades at me, I also applied it to people who are hard to work with or live with? People who sometimes offend me or who at times drive me crazy by the things they do or don't do? Not wanting to label them as *the Enemy*, I started thinking of them as *the Beloved Enemy*, because often such people are close to my heart.

I imagine that many of those who sin against us most frequently fall into this category. They are husbands, friends, children, coworkers, and members of our churches. These are people we can't get away from even if we want to. And most of the time we don't want to because we care for them. Still, because we live in close contact with them, the offenses can pile up, affecting our relationship. This is particularly true when negative behaviors remain frustratingly the same. The husband who keeps those sarcastic remarks coming. The child who continues to act disrespectfully. The coworker who always jumps in to take the credit.

Precisely because such people are beloved, we owe it to them to tell them the truth about how their behavior affects us. And precisely because they are our "enemies," we have to do our best to treat them as Jesus instructs: doing good to them, even if they aren't doing good to us.

Lord, help me to do good to others, even if they sometimes act more like enemies than friends. Let me see with your eyes and love with your heart.

Your laws are my treasure; they are my heart's delight. I am determined to keep your decrees to the very end. I hate those with divided loyalties, but I love your instructions.

PSALM 119:111-113

Lately corporations seem intent on squeezing more work out of every person on the job. While technology has led to rapid gains, some of the gains have simply come from loading people with more and more responsibility, making them run like mice on a wheel. If you are an employee, there may not be much you can do about it. But some of us bring this kind of pressure on ourselves by the choices we make.

As the pastor of a large church, Jim Cymbala says that he sometimes sees people in his congregation who are working two or three jobs to get ahead. "They are going to expand their business," he says, "make money for a rainy day, or buy a rental property here or a little side business there, and their assets will grow even faster. Yes, it means missing church on Sunday and missing time with their kids, but they use the old saying 'Mama didn't raise no fool, you know.' In a little while, they tell me, their schedule will lighten up so they can give more attention to the Word and prayer, their service for the Lord, their marriage, their child-raising responsibility . . . soon, but not yet. At the moment, they have to virtually kill themselves for the almighty dollar."[12]

Cymbala isn't faulting those of us who have no choice but to work more than one job. He is only pointing out the importance of priorities. Scripture says, "Wherever your treasure is, there the desires of your heart will also be" (Matthew 6:21). A reasonable paraphrase might go like this: "Wherever your treasure is, there your time and money will also be."

To seek and find more of God's peace means we need to be ruthlessly honest with ourselves to discover what we really treasure. If we find that our treasure gauge—our measure of what is most valuable in life—is malfunctioning, we have only to turn to God and ask him to help us reorder our priorities.

Lord, I want you to be first, not second, third, or fourth. First in the way I order my time, money, goals, and desires. Let everything in my life be evidence of my single-hearted intention to live for you.

HOW MUCH IS PEACE WORTH?

I listen carefully to what God the LORD is saying, for he speaks peace to his faithful people. But let them not return to their foolish ways. Surely his salvation is near to those who fear him, so our land will be filled with his glory. Unfailing love and truth have met together. Righteousness and peace have kissed!

PSALM 85:8-10

What would you do for a quarter of a million dollars? Jump out of a plane (with a parachute, of course)? Parade around in a Mickey Mouse suit in hundred-degree weather? Eat a gazillion hotdogs smothered in red-hot chili sauce? Go swimming in Lake Michigan in February?

For that much money most of us would be willing to do any number of unpleasant things, as long as they didn't involve moral compromise or danger to life and limb. But what are you willing to do today in order to live a life of greater peace?

I ask the question because the priceless peace we seek comes only from following the ways of God, which may not always feel easy. Sometimes they will feel downright unpleasant, at least at first. Here are a few examples. The woman filled with bitterness will need to pray for those who have hurt her. The woman in an illicit relationship will need to break it off. The woman who has based her life on money will need to realize that everything she has belongs to God. The woman who is too busy to pray will need to make time in her life for God. The woman who is worried about her children will need to learn how to surrender them to God's care.

So often the way toward peace is counterintuitive, cutting as it does against our instinctive bent toward self-reliance, self-preservation, and self-aggrandizement. But since when does anything good ever come without effort?

If you desire the precious peace of God, decide today to listen for his voice and then do what he asks. Trust him for the results, and you will not be disappointed.

Father, my heart does not always know the way to peace. Please change me so my first thought is to please you and my last thought is to please myself. Guide me in your ways, whether they feel hard or easy, I pray.

LASHON HA-RA

*May the words of my mouth and the meditation of my heart be
pleasing to you, O LORD, my rock and my redeemer.*

PSALM 19:14

My children and I have developed a way to pass the time during a long drive. We take a simple phrase like "Look at that" and then say it with as many different inflections as we can think of in order to bring out various meanings. It's amazing how quickly an innocuous statement can morph into one that communicates humor, threat, shock, disgust, delight, or anger, depending on your tone of voice and the way you say it.

In Jewish ethical teaching, it is considered wrong not only to slander someone but to say something that will lower someone else's esteem in the eyes of others. The Hebrew term for this is *lashon ha-ra.* So, for instance, you wouldn't say something like this: "I feel sorry for Joe. Being out of work for six months seems to have made his depression a lot worse." Or "Too bad about Sarah's breakup. I thought she finally found a guy who could love her despite her weight." There are, of course, notable exceptions. You can express a negative truth when the person you are speaking to needs the information. So if your friend is thinking of consulting a financial adviser you know to be incompetent, you are free to tell him what you know. Otherwise you are obligated to keep silent.

Rabbi Joseph Telushkin explains that even nonverbal communications can violate this law. "Making a face when someone's name is mentioned, rolling one's eyes, winking, or saying sarcastically, 'So-and-so is very smart' are all violations of the law," he says.[13] The same is true when it comes to the use of innuendo—implying something negative without actually saying it.

What if we were to adopt this rule of *lashon ha-ra* for ourselves? Wouldn't it help us learn greater control of our tongues and our attitudes? Today make a promise to yourself to refrain from negativity toward others—in both your verbal and nonverbal communications. It may prove frustrating at first, but in the end, doing so will increase your peace and contribute to the peace of others.

*Father, help me to face truthfully the delight I have taken in exposing the
weaknesses of others. Forgive me for my lack of love, and help me to change.*

STAR PUPIL

*A Gentile woman who lived there came to him, pleading, "Have mercy on me, O Lord,
Son of David! For my daughter is possessed by a demon that torments her severely."*

MATTHEW 15:22

Remember the story of the Gentile woman who begged Jesus to heal her demon-possessed daughter? Instead of casting out the demon, Jesus seemed to ignore the request. (Keep in mind that in Jesus' culture, men did not talk to women they did not know, and Jews did not talk to Gentiles.) Annoyed, the disciples urged Jesus to send her away. He appeared to comply, stating that his mission was to the Jews only. But she would not give up. Then he went further, insulting her by comparing Gentiles to dogs, a common view among his contemporaries. Instead of taking offense, she simply said, "That's true, Lord, but even dogs are allowed to eat the scraps that fall beneath their masters' table" (Matthew 15:27).

We are relieved that Jesus finally heals the woman's daughter, but many of us view the story with unease. It seems to put Jesus in an unflattering light.

But remember that Jesus was a rabbi. And rabbis used various methods to instruct their disciples. Kenneth Bailey, an expert in Middle Eastern New Testament studies, suggests an interesting interpretation. What if Jesus was giving his disciples an object lesson in faith? What if he was testing this woman and in the end commending her as one of his star pupils so his own disciples could learn something, not only from a woman but also from a Gentile?[14]

Here is how Bailey paints the scene, just after Jesus makes the comment about dogs: "Will she reply with a corresponding insult against the haughty Jews who despise and verbally attack Gentiles, even those in pain? Or is her love for her daughter, her faith that Jesus has the power of God to heal, her confidence that he has compassion for Gentiles and her commitment to him as Master/Lord so strong that she will absorb the insult and press on, yet again, with her request?"[15]

We see in this woman's story an encouragement not only to persist in prayer but to continue to believe in God's love and compassion in the midst of circumstances that may cast him in an unflattering light. Today, may her story impel us to continue to pray for those we love.

*Lord, I won't give up. No matter how things might appear, I will
keep praying, believing that you are loving and merciful.*

God made two great lights—the larger one to govern the day, and the smaller one to govern the night. He also made the stars. God set these lights in the sky to light the earth, to govern the day and night, and to separate the light from the darkness. And God saw that it was good.

GENESIS 1:16-18

Ever travel to Amish country? If so, you know what it feels like to be transported to the nineteenth century. In parts of Michigan, not far from where I live, you can see Amish farms dotting the countryside. Most Amish deliberately limit their farms to eighty tillable acres or less since that's the amount of land a family can work. Instead of seeing natural limitations as something to be overcome, the Amish embrace them. In her book *Amish Peace*, Suzanne Woods Fisher tells the story of an Amish man "who joked that if he were meant to plow at night, God would have put a headlight on a horse." The Amish, she says, "respect natural limitations: sunlight and seasons, hunger and fatigue."

This desire to acknowledge, preserve, and live within certain limitations is one aspect of Amish life that most sets them apart. After all, they live smack in the middle of a culture that prides itself on pushing the limits at every opportunity, overcoming barriers to productivity and play by offering a constant array of new and better gadgets and technologies. Computers, video games, cell phones, and other technological wonders take up more and more of our time. We don't think twice about the constant flow of electricity that enables us to get less and less sleep so that we can do more and more. We're like children who don't want to go to bed, lest we miss something.

But we do miss something. We miss the peace that comes from accepting limits on our time and energy. And then we wonder why we feel so stressed. By hailing this Amish tendency to live within limits, I am not urging us to stop using technology, but we ought to learn from how others have chosen to live. By doing so, our lives will not be diminished but enhanced.

Lord, help me recognize ways in which I have bought into the cultural tendency to ignore my natural limitations. Instead of stretching these, help me respect them so I can experience more peace and less stress.

SENSING GOD'S PEACE

The earth is the LORD's, and everything in it. The world and all its people belong to him.

PSALM 24:1

Several years ago a business leader by the name of Michael Hyatt embarked on a three-week pilgrimage to Mount Athos, visiting several Orthodox monasteries. Toward the end of the trip, Hyatt and his companions visited a small monastic community located on the edge of the Aegean Sea. During their visit, one of the monks offered the travelers tea and pastries served up with stimulating spiritual conversation.

When it was time to go, Hyatt stood on the veranda overlooking the brilliant blue sea and remarked to one of the monks, "I hate to leave, Father. It is so peaceful here."

Nodding, the monk remained silent for a few minutes and then replied, "You know, Michael, anywhere can be this peaceful, *if*—he paused for emphasis—"you have God in your heart. But if you don't, then even a place as beautiful as this can be hell."[16]

Most of us can relate to Hyatt's experience. Standing at the edge of a lake, staring up at starry skies, or walking through snowy woods, we sense a peace we wish would go on forever. Perhaps it is no coincidence that the created world has this effect on us, coming as it does from the good hand of God.

Let's enjoy the beauty of nature, savoring the peace we find there without being seduced into thinking that a villa on the beach or a cabin on a mountaintop is what we really need to be happy. Only God, living within us, can give us what our hearts desire.

Jesus, I ask you to come into my heart today in the deepest way possible. I want to belong to you, body and soul, mind and spirit. Forgive the ways I've ignored your law, hurting myself and others. I ask you to lead me and guide me and dwell in me by the great and perfect power of your Spirit from this day on. I surrender my life to you, now and forever.

THE BAD THING ABOUT MORE

You must not covet. . . . You must not covet.

EXODUS 20:17

Having too much is rarely a recipe for peace, though it's tempting to think so. When you have lots of stuff, you need to spend lots of time paying for it and lots of time taking care of it. Our many possessions can tie us down, making it difficult to respond to opportunities God gives. Oddly, having too much often makes us want to have even more.

In his classic book on the Sabbath, Abraham Joshua Heschel points out that when modern people want to emphasize something in print, we often underline or italicize words. The Bible and other forms of ancient literature used a different tactic—repeating words within the text, as if to say, "Listen and listen up!" Deuteronomy 16:20, for instance, says, "Justice, and only justice, you shall pursue, so that you may live and occupy the land that the LORD your God is giving you" (NRSV). Isaiah 40:1 declares, "'Comfort, comfort my people,' says your God."

Heschel points out that only one of the Ten Commandments is proclaimed twice, and that's the last one, which goes like this: "Do not covet your neighbor's house. Do not covet your neighbor's wife, male or female servant, ox or donkey, or anything else your neighbor owns" (Exodus 20:17).[17] By emphasizing the command, God puts a double fence around our tendency to want more, especially if the more that we want belongs to someone else.

You may not feel wealthy compared to those around you, but most of us who are living in the affluent West are rich compared to the rest of the world. No matter how much we have, all of us can fall into the temptation of coveting what we don't have. If you find yourself stressed out by everything you own, ask God for help and wisdom to begin paring things down. Then listen and listen up so you can experience more of God's peace in your life!

Father, I have so many things I don't need and don't even use.
Give me the desire to live a life of greater simplicity.

April 27
ZOOM!

Unless the LORD builds a house, the work of the builders is wasted. Unless the LORD protects a city, guarding it with sentries will do no good. It is useless for you to work so hard from early morning until late at night, anxiously working for food to eat; for God gives rest to his loved ones.

PSALM 127:1-2

If you asked me to use one word to describe the average speed at which most of us live our lives, my answer would not be *warp speed* (because that's two words) but *zoom!*

Zoom to get ready in the morning. Zoom to drop the children off at school. Zoom to get to work. Zoom to make it to the next meeting. Zoom to the doctor's office. Zoom back to work. Zoom to complete the next assignment. Zoom to the grocery store. Zoom home. Zoom to grab dinner. Zoom to soccer practice. Zoom to the drug store. Zoom home again. Zoom to bed. Zoom, zoom, zoom! No wonder we feel so worn out. Some of us even zoom our way through church.

Okay, enough of zoom. What can we do to dial back a bit so we can experience times of refreshing? The first thing we can do is to realize that trading time for money is often a bad bargain. Much of our rush, rush life is powered by a desire for money. We work longer and play less so we can get ahead. A higher salary, a nicer house, more toys. Wayne Muller puts it graphically by saying that money "is the temple to which we are all drawn to worship, bringing our offerings of time, and taking away the blessings of money."[18] Put it that way, and our addiction to speed seems downright sinful.

When it comes to work, we may not always be able to slow things down. But most of us have at least some discretionary time. This week, ask yourself how you can get a better return when it comes to investing the precious resource of your time.

Father, time is your gift. Help me spend it wisely on things that will bring peace to me and my family.

If I ride the wings of the morning, if I dwell by the farthest oceans, even there your
hand will guide me, and your strength will support me. I could ask the darkness to hide
me and the light around me to become night—but even in darkness I cannot hide from
you. To you the night shines as bright as day. Darkness and light are the same to you.

PSALM 139:9-12

Many years ago a friend of mine lost her husband. He didn't die from an illness or an accident. He wasn't a casualty of war or self-inflicted violence. In fact, he didn't die at all. Nor did she lose him to another woman or to drugs. Her husband just closed up inside, spending more and more time on the Internet, searching for God knows what, until he finally vanished from her life, demanding a divorce. My friend was bewildered and hurt, unable to rescue her marriage because she didn't even know what was wrong. She suspected an addiction to pornography, but she couldn't prove it. Her husband wouldn't say. Not a word.

Dietrich Bonhoeffer speaks of the isolating effects of sin and the power of confession to break that isolation: "In confession the break-through to community takes place. Sin demands to have a man by himself. It withdraws him from the community. The more isolated a person is, the more destructive will be the power of sin over him, and the more deeply he becomes involved in it, the more disastrous is his isolation. Sin wants to remain unknown. It shuns the light."[19]

But as soon as the sin is confessed, its grip is broken. As Bonhoeffer says of the repentant sinner, "He is no longer alone with his evil for he has cast off his sin in confession and handed it over to God."[20]

Psalm 139 speaks of God's ability to see through our darkness. Confessing our sins to a trusted sister in Christ can help us enter that place of safety, right in the middle of God's people.

Lord, you know the condition of my heart. Help me to confess
my sin, and bring me into the light of your presence.

COMPARED TO WHOM?

If we have enough food and clothing, let us be content. But people who long to be rich fall into temptation and are trapped by many foolish and harmful desires that plunge them into ruin and destruction.

1 TIMOTHY 6:8-9

Have you ever heard someone remark in surprise at how happy the people they visited in a third-world country seemed despite their poverty?

I noted something similar when I saw the movie *Babies*, a delightful film capturing the first year in the life of four adorable babies on four different continents—Ponijao from Namibia, Mari from Japan, Bayar from Mongolia, and Hattie from the United States. While the babies have many things in common, like their penchant for sucking on toes, in many respects their lives are strikingly different. Ponijao, for instance, is literally "dirt poor," wearing next to nothing and playing happily with rocks, empty cans, and refuse. Mari, on the other hand, enjoys the obvious advantages of being born into a prosperous and sophisticated Japanese family. Despite the fact that these children are at opposite ends of the material spectrum, both seemed reasonably happy.

Of course, temperament can have a significant impact on our sense of happiness. But perhaps there's more to it than that. Robert Sapolsky points out that once you have the basics covered, such as food and shelter, *being* poor isn't as bad for you as *feeling* poor. The trouble is, many people feel poor. "Thanks to urbanization, mobility, and the media," he points out, "something absolutely unprecedented can now occur—we can now be made to feel poor, or poorly about ourselves, by people *we don't even know*. You can feel impoverished . . . by Bill Gates on the evening news, even by a fictional character in a movie."[21]

Though Ponijao and Mari are too young to be affected by this dynamic, it may be that Ponijao will grow up in his isolated village a happy man, unaware of his relative poverty, while Mari will unhappily realize some are better off than she is. When it comes to the Ponijaos and Maris of the world, most of us fit into the Mari category. Knowing that, let's be on guard against comparing ourselves to movie stars and moguls, choosing instead to be content with what we have.

Lord, help me to learn to be content, no matter my circumstances.

April 30
JUST LET IT GO!

He alone is my rock and my salvation, my fortress where I will not be shaken. My victory
and honor come from God alone. He is my refuge, a rock where no enemy can reach me.
O my people, trust in him at all times. Pour out your heart to him, for God is our refuge.

PSALM 62:6-8

A friend of mine enjoys being with elderly people. It's a good thing,
because she spends several hours a week working in a nursing home.
One of her favorite people there is a woman by the name of Mabel. Recently
Mabel was sitting across the table from someone who suffers from dementia.
The poor woman was perseverating, going over and over incidents from the
past that still bothered her. Though her conversation was garbled and hard
to follow, she seemed tormented by her thoughts.

So Mabel went into action. Looking the woman straight in the eye, and
with all the force of her personality, she offered the best advice she could
give: "Just let it go! Let it go!" A little confused herself, Mabel didn't realize
the woman she was talking to no longer had the mental capacity to follow her
sage advice.

But Mabel's words still found their mark. In the days and weeks that
followed, my friend kept remembering the scene. Whenever she faced circumstances she couldn't control, she could almost hear Mabel exhorting her,
"Just let it go! Let it go!"

What is it that you are having trouble letting go of? Is it a situation with
your family? Is it a comment your friend made? Is it a frustrating coworker?
Is it a nagging memory that has you in its grasp? Whatever it is, it's time to
hand it over to God.

Today, let's praise God and thank him that we are still in our right
minds. And let us also ask him to send us his Spirit so we can let go of the
things we cannot control in order to take hold of the help he gives.

Father, I waste so much mental energy worrying. Help me put that
energy into trusting you—with all my heart and all my mind.

May 1

DON'T GIVE UP!

O LORD, hear me as I pray; pay attention to my groaning. Listen to my cry for help, my King and my God, for I pray to no one but you. Listen to my voice in the morning, LORD. Each morning I bring my requests to you and wait expectantly.

PSALM 5:1-3

Last week a friend of mine was going through a tough time. So she asked some of her friends to pray, throwing in the request that perhaps we could also pray for a neighbor whose house and yard were an ever-present eyesore. This week, when I asked how she was doing, she said that the gorgeous spring weather was lifting her mood. Then she added this comment:

> I asked for prayers that our crazy neighbor would clean up her trashed house and yard. This, after almost thirty years of frustration. Well, the day after I asked for prayers, this very neighbor started to rake, trim, and plant new bushes in her yard. It was so unbelievable that my husband and I reasoned she was getting ready to sell. That's when I remembered my prayer request. Wow!

Yesterday my friend's nonbelieving husband remarked, "I don't know what you did to Janine [not her real name], but now she's outside painting her rusty railing!"

Chuckling, my friend told me her neighbor has been up at the crack of dawn every day working on her yard. "I laughed," she said, "as I confessed to my husband that our group has been praying for Janine to clean up her act."

Though my dear friend still struggles with various challenges, it seemed as though God was saying, "Hey, if I can work through your neighbor, I can do anything. Don't give up." I think she got the message.

Father, though there are many things in our lives we can't control, we can do something—we can keep praying. Help us to pray!

May 2

THE "SPEAK WALL"

Pour out your hearts like water to the Lord.
Lift up your hands to him in prayer.

LAMENTATIONS 2:19

"I'm lonelier than you might think."
"My smile hides a lot about me."
"I have attempted suicide."
"All I want is to be loved."

Students at Grand Rapids Christian High School have posted these and other messages on something called the "Speak Wall." Unlike social networking sites such as Facebook, this is a literal wall—a place where they can tack up an anonymous note telling the truth about themselves without anyone knowing who they are. Students can also post notes of encouragement in response to another's gutsy self-disclosure. The story of the eight-hundred-foot wall recently made front-page news in the *Grand Rapids Press*.[1]

But what is so newsworthy about teenage angst? Perhaps the story hit the press because it occurred at a school with the reputation of catering to students who already have it made. The Speak Wall gives voice to the widespread brokenness of even the most privileged among us.

I wonder what would happen were we to construct a Speak Wall in our churches and workplaces. Would we find similar brokenness? I suspect we would. We might even add our own plaintive notes to the wall.

However you are feeling right now, know that you are not the only one who struggles. Join me in crying out to God, letting prayer become your personal Speak Wall. Pray honestly and with hope for yourself and for others. And then do your best to forge connections with other believers so you can say what's on your heart—and listen to what's on theirs.

Father, even without a "Speak Wall," you know exactly what's inside
my heart. Please encourage me today and build up my hope.

DON'T LOSE YOUR MITZVAH

I am praying that you will put into action the generosity that comes from your faith as you understand and experience all the good things we have in Christ.

PHILEMON 1:6

Okay, it's time to learn a little Hebrew. *Mitzvah* is a Hebrew word that is translated "commandment." But unlike the word *commandment*, which may sound onerous to many of us, *mitzvah* has a positive connotation. Rather than being a dreary burden, doing a *mitzvah* is more like an opportunity, a chance to bless God and participate in his work by blessing someone else.

Let's take a look at another Hebrew word: *tzedakah*. It's a specific type of mitzvah. The word *tzedakah* is sometimes translated "charity," but this is somewhat misleading since tzedakah is considered an obligation—something that justice requires—rather than something people do out of the kindness of their hearts. As with many other ethical matters, Jewish rabbis have had countless discussions regarding the importance of tzedakah, identifying eight degrees of giving. The lowest degree is to give grudgingly. The next degree is to give less than you should but cheerfully. The eighth and highest degree is to give in a way that enables others to support themselves.

Many Jewish people have tzedakah boxes in their houses, where they can set money aside to be given to those in need. The rabbis say it's not just giving that's important but *how* you contribute. Give away your time and money with a smile and an attitude of respect, and you will have done a mitzvah. Give it with disdain, and you will have lost your mitzvah.

As Christians, we are called by God to participate in his work by giving to those in need. It's a way of spreading his peace, extending it to others. Perhaps you can remind yourself of this opportunity by obtaining your own tzedakah box, depositing money every week that you intend to give to those in need.

Lord, you call us to be like you. Help me to reflect your generosity by freely, cheerfully, and wisely giving time and money to those who are in need.

CUMBER

Don't you realize that in a race everyone runs, but only one person gets the prize? So run to win! All athletes are disciplined in their training. They do it to win a prize that will fade away, but we do it for an eternal prize. So I run with purpose in every step. I am not just shadowboxing. I discipline my body like an athlete, training it to do what it should.

1 CORINTHIANS 9:24-27

Ever try running when you're overweight? No fun, is it? The same is true when you're running the spiritual race Paul speaks of. Imagine trying to run the Boston Marathon in a fat suit while dragging everything you own along with you, and you will get a sense of what I'm talking about. The problem comes down to what the Quakers call "cumber"—the unnecessary accumulation of material goods that clutter our lives and distract us from the things of God.

I like the way Paul speaks about running straight to the goal and having "purpose in every step." What a way to think about our lives! To be honest, I don't often think that way. I'm guessing you don't either. But I want to.

How can we get rid of things that encumber us, that keep us from focusing more of our time and energy on seeking first the Kingdom of God? We can begin by taking time to identify and deal with the things in our lives that make us feel spiritually flabby and overweight.

Even if you only have time for a tiny step today, take it. Do something small—clean out a drawer, give away some clothes; just begin the process. As you lighten your load, you may find it easier to run the spiritual race. Ask God today to help you aim straight at the goal, with purpose in every step.

Father, show me how to get in shape so I can run the race with the goal always in sight.

May 5

THE GOSPEL IS PEACE

*[Jesus] told them, "Go into all the world and
preach the Good News to everyone."*

MARK 16:15

Most of us live in a world populated by people who don't think like us.
Either they don't believe in Jesus at all or they don't believe in Jesus
the way we do. How can we live at peace with others even when our values
and aspirations are worlds apart?

I like what John Piper has to say about the importance of daily being
"stunned by grace in our lives." As he told the staff at his church one day, "If
we aren't amazed by grace towards us, we will be a finger-pointing church
mainly." According to Piper, the key is to be more amazed that you are saved
than that others are lost.[2]

Though I don't care for finger pointing in general, I think Piper's focus
offers a healthy antidote to the notion that to get along with others in our
multicultural, multitheological world, you have to throw out your brains and
your beliefs in order to pretend that all religions are equally valid.

Because some in the church have been harsh and condemning in their
treatment of people who don't think like they do, it is tempting to conclude
that disagreeing is always wrong. Better to keep peace by skirting the issues,
pretending they don't exist. But that would be foolish. Instead of buying into
an ideal of political correctness, we need to learn how to contend for the
faith in a way that persuades, not merely through the power of our words,
but also through the power of the love we put into those words.

Our goal as Christians is not to win arguments but to spread the gospel
so that others might join us on the side of marveling at the stunning grace
of God.

*Lord, give me wisdom in the way I talk to others about what I believe. May my words and my
actions always add up to what I know to be true—that you are holy and that you are loving.*

May 6

FEER NOT!

Be strong and courageous! Do not be afraid and do not panic before them.
For the LORD your God will personally go ahead of you.
He will neither fail you nor abandon you.

DEUTERONOMY 31:6

What are you afraid of? Your children getting kidnapped? A stock market crash? Public speaking? Spiders? Snakes? Bedbugs? The dentist? Heights? Failure? Flying? Rejection? Crowds? Darkness? Job loss? Illness? Affliction? Old age? Death? Whether our fears are triggered by creepy crawly creatures, being shut up in small spaces, or things that go bump in the night, all of us are afraid of something.

We know, of course, that some fears can be useful. For instance, if you are approaching a precipice, fear will cause you to stay clear of the edge, preventing a headlong fall. Fear of becoming incapacitated in old age may encourage you to adopt a healthy diet and a more active lifestyle. Fear of failing might motivate you to work harder.

Fear is not a problem unless it begins to control us. Being controlled by anything or anyone but God is a miserable, life-destroying experience. It keeps us locked up in our heads, unable to live the life we were meant to live or use the gifts we've been given.

Fortunately, we are not left to battle our fears alone. Pastor Rick Warren points out that there are 365 "Fear nots" in God's Word—one for every day of the year. It seems obvious, he says, that "God is serious about you trusting Him." The next time you feel assaulted by fear or anxiety, don't try to battle it by yourself. Get out your Bible and find one of these verses. Remember that Paul calls God's Word "the sword of the Spirit" (Ephesians 6:17). Take hold of that sword today, and with God's mighty power, stand strong against the fears that threaten your peace.

Lord, every time I am afraid, help me to picture myself, sword in hand, walking behind you. Make me strong and courageous because of your mighty presence in my life.

May 7

GUTSY GUILT

The LORD disciplines those he loves, and he punishes each one he accepts as his child.

HEBREWS 12:6

I yelled at my daughter the other day. Truth be told, it wasn't the first time. Though I want to become a more peaceful mom, I often find my own sin getting in the way. Like me, you may have sinful habits and patterns that get in the way of enjoying the peace God promises. Some of these may plunge you into prolonged periods of guilt. How can you remain confident of God's fatherly love, despite your own frequent failings? John Piper has an interesting take on this problem.

To the fallen saint who knows the darkness is self-inflicted and feels the futility of looking for hope from a frowning judge, the Bible gives a shocking example of gutsy guilt. It pictures God's failed prophet beneath a righteous frown, bearing his chastisement with brokenhearted boldness:

> Rejoice not over me, O my enemy; when I fall, I shall rise; when I sit in darkness, the LORD will be a light to me. I will bear the indignation of the LORD because I have sinned against him, until he pleads my cause and executes judgment for me. He will bring me out to the light.
> MICAH 7:8-9, ESV

This is courageous contrition. Gutsy guilt. The saint has fallen. The darkness of God's indignation is on him. He does not blow it off, but waits. And he throws in the face of his accuser the confidence that his indignant judge will plead his cause and execute justice for (not against) him. This is the application of justification to the fallen saint. Brokenhearted, gutsy guilt.[3]

Join me in admitting that you're not a perfect woman—that you have sins and failings too. As you do that, make a promise to yourself and to God that the next time you stumble, you will not wallow in guilt. Let's accept God's discipline, realizing that he is acting as a good father should. Instead of giving in to the enemy's lies, let's throw them back in his face, trusting in God's unfailing love.

Father, you punish all those you accept as your children. Help me to remain confident of your love even when I am experiencing your discipline.

PERSPECTIVE

*You intended to harm me, but God intended it all for good. He brought
me to this position so I could save the lives of many people.*

GENESIS 50:20

Perhaps you've heard of Bethany Hamilton, the thirteen-year-old surfer who lost her arm in a shark attack in Hawaii. Her story is told in the movie *Soul Surfer*. Early on, we see Bethany attending a youth night at her church. Youth leader Sarah Hill, played by Carrie Underwood, is showing the group a series of zoomed-in photos, challenging them to guess what they're looking at. When the second photo pops up on the screen, one of the boys guesses it's a "dead, rotting brain." While the teens are busy voicing their revulsion, Sarah zooms out, revealing the truth. They hadn't been viewing anything half as gross as a rotting brain. It was merely an ordinary walnut. Sarah's point was that when you're too close to what's happening, it can be tough to have perspective.

Remember the old saying "Time heals"? Time has the power to put distance between us and the circumstances that caused our suffering. Though distance can't erase our suffering, it can help us stand back a bit, enabling us to see a bigger picture. Often the only way to get to that bigger picture is by clinging to God, refusing to believe he has abandoned us. We also get there by listening for his voice, by reading his Word and praying, and by staying in touch with other believers who can support us through it.

When interviewed about the movie, Carrie Underwood later commented on how impressed she was when she met the real Bethany. "She didn't ask, 'Why me?'" Carrie noted, "but 'What for?'"

Anyone who has suffered some kind of tragedy knows that "Why me?" questions aren't off the table. God allows them. But often he doesn't answer them. If you want an answer, the more productive question to ask is "What for?"

Bethany's answer to her own "What for?" question about the shark attack was shaped by the intense media response to her story. To reporters who asked how she could respond so positively to what had happened, she simply replied, "I could never have embraced this many people with two arms."

*Lord, when life is too difficult for me to handle, help me trust you. Give
me the strength to believe that you intend to use my circumstances to bless
and not destroy. Help me to gain perspective as I cling to you.*

May 9

DOUBT YOUR DOUBTS

*The LORD passed in front of Moses, calling out, "Yahweh! The LORD! The God of
compassion and mercy! I am slow to anger and filled with unfailing love and faithfulness."*

EXODUS 34:6

Timothy Keller, pastor of Redeemer Presbyterian Church in New York
City, advises Christians that "faith without some doubts is like a human
body without any antibodies in it." He says, "People who blithely go through
life too busy or indifferent to ask hard questions about why they believe as
they do will find themselves defenseless against either the experience of tragedy or the probing questions of a smart skeptic. . . . It is no longer sufficient
to hold beliefs just because you inherited them."[4]

By saying this, I don't think Keller is saying we should doubt God's
faithfulness whenever we encounter difficulty. This brand of doubting makes
us weak, leading, as it does, to unbelief. Instead, Keller is arguing for a kind
of intellectual honesty that requires us to grapple with hard questions in a
way that will make our faith stronger, not weaker.

Keller has also famously advised skeptics to doubt their doubts about
Christianity. Perhaps it would also be wise to advise the weakest among us
to begin to doubt our doubts about God's character. God says he is a loving
Father, and we act as though we are orphans. God reveals himself as all-
powerful, but we don't think he can help us. God tells us he forgives, and we
cling to our guilt.

The reason for our doubts? Sister Wendy Beckett archly observes that
many who call themselves Christians may well have embraced a false god.
"Sometimes I blush for those who think themselves Christian," she says, "and
yet the God they worship is cruel, suspicious, punitive and watchful. Who
could love such a God?"

She goes on to say, "I have the greatest admiration for atheists, because
by definition they have rejected a false 'God.'"[5] Her point, of course, is not
that atheists are right in rejecting God, but that they are at least right in
rejecting a caricature of God that contains more shadows than light. Though
the God we love will always be mysterious, we can be sure of one thing—in
him there is no darkness at all.

*Lord, there are so many things I don't understand about you.
Help me to know you and then to know you more.*

May 10
PUSH, PUSH, PUSH!

You made the moon to mark the seasons, and the sun knows when to set.

PSALM 104:19

I don't understand the popularity of extreme sports. You will never see me schlepping a pack up K2 or scrambling up Mt. Everest's icy peaks. Nor will you find me bouncing up and down at the end of a bungee cord or climbing into an Indy race car. The most dangerous sport you'll catch me at will probably be Mario Kart. To my way of thinking, life is challenging enough without taking on an activity that could, with one miscalculation, end in death or maiming.

Why do some people find such joy in pushing the limits? Is it the rush they get from flirting with danger? Is it the feeling that they are somehow bigger than life or the belief that ordinary rules don't apply to them?

Though most of us don't engage in extreme sports, many of us have made pushing the limits a habit. We sleep less so we can do more. *Push, push, push* has become an American mantra. Unfortunately, it has also added tremendous stress to our lives.

Wayne Muller points out that "we can work without stopping, faster and faster, electric lights making artificial day so the whole machine can labor without ceasing. But remember: *No living thing lives like this.* There are greater rhythms that govern how life grows . . . seasons and sunsets and great movements of seas and stars. . . . We are part of the creation story, subject to all its laws and rhythms. . . .

"To surrender to the rhythms of seasons and flowerings and dormancies is to savor the secret of life itself."[6]

If you are living a rush, rush life, ask yourself why. Are you willing to pay the cost of regularly ignoring the God-given rhythms by which creation operates? Find a way to slow down and "surrender to the rhythms of seasons and flowerings and dormancies" so that as one of God's creatures you can savor the secret of life.

Father, instead of rebelling against the natural rhythms of life, help me experience more of your peace by surrendering to them.

SABBATH

You must not even light a fire in any of your homes on the Sabbath.

EXODUS 35:3

Susannah Heschel, the daughter of Rabbi Abraham Heschel, says that Friday evening was always the best night of the week in their home. "My mother and I kindled the lights for the Sabbath," she explains, "and all of a sudden I felt transformed, emotionally and even physically."[7] To her, Sabbath was an atmosphere she entered into every week. It was a foretaste of paradise. "The Sabbath," her father said, "comes like a caress, wiping away fear, sorrow and somber memories."[8]

Wouldn't it be great to have one day a week that created this kind of atmosphere in your own home? In addition to special prayers and a wonderful meal, Sabbath in the Jewish tradition is also a time for refraining from work, a time in which a person can simply relish being in the presence of God along with friends and family.

When Susannah was growing up, her father pointed out that just as it was forbidden to light a fire on the Sabbath (because it's considered a form of work), it was also forbidden to kindle the fires of righteous indignation. "In our home," she says, "certain topics were avoided on the Sabbath—politics, the Holocaust, the war in Vietnam—while others were emphasized."[9] Sabbath was not a time for dwelling on all that was wrong in the world but for creating a sense of celebration and restfulness, a taste of the life to come.

Why not consider having your own Sabbath celebration? You can put together a short liturgy of prayer by selecting readings from the Old and New Testaments that speak of God's work of deliverance. Enjoy a festive meal with family or friends. Celebrate God's goodness by remembering what he has already done and what he has promised to do. On this one special day, remember to avoid talking about topics that will kindle a fire of righteous indignation in your heart.[10]

Father, I need sacred space in my life, time to withdraw from the workaday world and be with you. Help me find a way to build times of Sabbath rest into my life.

May 12

ALONE WITH OURSELVES?

Devote yourselves to prayer with an alert mind and a thankful heart.

COLOSSIANS 4:2

Why is it so hard for many of us to carve out a regular time for prayer? I suspect it has something to do with our drive to accomplish things combined with our fear of loneliness. Most of us find it far easier to rush around "getting things done" than to sit still even for a few moments with no other goal in mind than opening our hearts to God. When we do manage to pray, fears we have kept at bay by our constant activity may rush in. A thousand distracting thoughts may take hold. We can feel empty and alone, wondering why God seems elusive. We fill up the silence with constant petitions or chattering thoughts or nonstop spiritual reading, thinking we are the ones who have to control and direct the time.

Prayer, of course, is not meant to be a task we check off our lists but a time for being with the God we love. But what if we are afraid he won't show up, validating our fears that we are unloved, unworthy, and unlistened to? Perhaps the first thing to do is to simply surrender that fear to God, imagining ourselves in his presence. Instead of lingering on our negative feelings or on the distractions that try to take hold, we simply let go of them, gently lifting our hearts to God. It may be helpful to pray through a brief Scripture passage, lingering on God's Word as we pray it back to him.

Spending a few minutes this way each day will increase our appetites for prayer because we will find God is faithful and leads us in surprising ways. As we spend time in his presence, God may give us the courage to face ourselves truthfully, without harshness or condemnation. He may open our minds to his thoughts. He may give us his heart for others. Whatever God does within us and through us will be good, because it will be accomplished in love and for love.

The more we pray in this way, the more surprised we will be to look back on our formerly prayerless lives and discover that it was we, and not God, who had sometimes failed to show up.

Father, thank you for being with me when I pray, whether I know it or not. Help me to sense your presence as I grow in faith and trust.

MOTHER'S DAY

God blesses those who work for peace, for they will be called the children of God.
MATTHEW 5:9

Perhaps you have heard the story of how Julia Ward Howe wrote the lyrics to "The Battle Hymn of the Republic." On November 18, 1861, after reviewing Union troops near Washington, DC, she awoke in the night with the words of the hymn firmly in mind. "So, with a sudden effort," she explained, "I sprang out of bed, and found in the dimness an old stump of a pen which I remembered to have used the day before. I scrawled the verses almost without looking at the paper."

Remember the first verse?

> *Mine eyes have seen the glory of the coming of the Lord;*
> *He is trampling out the vintage where the grapes of wrath are stored;*
> *He hath loosed the fateful lightning of his terrible swift sword;*
> *His truth is marching on.*
> *Glory! Glory! Hallelujah! Glory! Glory! Hallelujah!*
> *Glory! Glory! Hallelujah! His truth is marching on.*

Despite the militancy of that hymn, in 1872 Howe organized a Mother's Day for peace in New York City, which was repeated in Boston for about ten years. She and others across the country wanted to establish a special day each year in which mothers could unite to help prevent future wars. Finally, on May 8, 1914, the US Congress passed a law designating the second Sunday in May as Mother's Day. The next day, President Woodrow Wilson issued a proclamation declaring the first national Mother's Day as a day for Americans to show the flag in honor of those mothers whose sons had died in war.

Today as we consider the many wars that rage throughout the world, let us do what we can through prayer and action to bring peace to our world.

Father, may there be a new openness to the gospel in the most troubled regions of the world. I pray today that you will help our leaders seek peace and pursue it wherever possible.

May 14
TAMING THE JUNGLE

I am the vine; you are the branches. Those who remain in me, and I in them,
will produce much fruit. For apart from me you can do nothing.

JOHN 15:5

Last year I planted a tiny garden in my postage-stamp-sized backyard—cramming in peppers, carrots, red radishes, white radishes, lettuce, strawberries, and tomatoes—lots and lots of tomatoes. So many tomatoes, in fact, that in just a few weeks, my raised garden bed looked like a giant tomato jungle. The plants were so thick that many of the other vegetables failed to thrive, unable to compete for the nutrition and sunshine they needed. Though I had plenty of tomatoes, I mourned the loss of the other plants and decided that I would do better next year, curbing my appetite for tomatoes so our family could enjoy a mix of vegetables.

Just like plants in a garden, there are things in our lives that will only grow if they are given the necessary space and nourishment—things like prayer, faith, rest, spiritual gifts, wisdom, serenity, and joy. Finding balance in life is rarely easy, in part because life is seasonal, always changing. There are times when work or family life makes unavoidable claims on our time and energy. We know that. But we also add things to our lives—even many good things—without giving the matter much thought. As always, having too many good things is not a good thing after all, because a harried schedule can choke out the life of God within us, preventing us from bearing the fruit God desires.

Take some time today to imagine your life as a garden. What does it look like? What plants does it contain? Have you kept up with the weeding? What needs thinning, pruning, or plucking out? Assuming you can do the necessary work to trim whatever needs trimming, is there anything new you would like to plant in your garden? Ask God's Spirit to direct your thoughts, showing you the kind of garden God envisions for your life. Then ask for help to plan and plot the garden according to God's direction. Watch and see what happens as you make the necessary changes in your life.

Lord, help me to be rooted and grounded in you. Make my
life a fruitful garden that will bring you glory.

May 15

DEFLATING YOUR FEARS

You will trample upon lions and cobras; you will crush fierce lions and serpents under your feet!
The LORD says, "I will rescue those who love me. I will protect those who trust in my name."

PSALM 91:13-14

I f you've ever read J. K. Rowling's Harry Potter series, you will be familiar with the fantasy creature called a "boggart." The problem with boggarts is that they have the ability to turn into a person's worst fears. So for
Ron Weasley, it's spiders, while for Harry Potter, it's the notoriously creepy
dementors. In more than one movie, we see Ron and Harry practicing their
self-defense skills against boggarts, so if and when their worst fears do materialize, they are able to survive.

What boggarts are you facing? I used to be squeamish about snakes,
but I can honestly say I've overcome the feeling. How? Simply by facing it.
The fancy term for this technique is "conditioning." The idea is to subject
yourself to small doses of what you fear until you can gradually tolerate larger
doses. Eventually, the fear will be reduced or eliminated.

I dealt with my dislike of snakes by giving in to my daughter's entreaty
for a pet snake. After a year of having Rico in our home, I attended a reptile
expo at the urging of my daughter. This time, the repulsion I had previously
felt was gone, despite the fact that there were more than fifty snakes in the
room. I even found myself admiring the beautiful patterns on some of them.
Believe me, I am still not a snake lover, but at least I am no longer creeped
out by simply seeing one.

Maybe it's time to ratchet up your confidence by overcoming a specific
fear in your life. Ask God to help you face it rather than run from it. Doing
so will weaken it and empower you.

Lord, I am sometimes a coward, shrinking back from things that frighten me. Please
give me the ability to stand against my fears, and as I do, free me from them.

May 16

CONTROL FREAK

Can all your worries add a single moment to your life? And if worry can't accomplish a little thing like that, what's the use of worrying over bigger things?

LUKE 12:25-26

Chances are you know someone who is a control freak—a person determined to micromanage every detail of life at home, at work, and at church. Though mothers aren't the only ones who can fall into the control trap, I think we are more prone to it because of the degree of control we need to exercise when our children are young. Some of us get stuck there, treating grown children as though they are two-year-olds who need to be protected, lest they dart into the path of an oncoming car. Little coincidence, perhaps, that "mother" can be transformed into quite another word simply by adding an *s* at the beginning.

Of course, some amount of control is necessary to every life. But outsize attempts at control are pathological, rooted more in anxiety than in any kind of lust for power. Being a control freak leads only to frustration and difficulty, because even when our attempts at control are successful, we have probably alienated someone in the process. What's more, if we have a controlling style of relating to life, we may reach a point of no return, where the habit gets calcified and is nearly impossible to break.

One of my close friends has a mother who typifies this pattern. Suffering from dementia, she is still trying to control everything, though now she does it through a fog of confusion, without the ability to make sound decisions. This makes the family's efforts to care for her much more difficult.

How do you know if you're the controlling type? Just watch the way people respond to you, particularly members of your close family. They'll let you know. If you find that the label *control freak* does apply, don't brush it off as though it's no big deal. It *is* a big deal. Think, instead, of what you might be missing because your style of responding to life makes it hard for God to care for you. Ask him for the grace to recognize when you are trying to exercise more control than you should. Stop now, before it is too late.

Lord, please show me if I am trying to control too much of my world. Help me, instead, to learn how to rest in your care.

May 17

SEASONS

For everything there is a season, a time for every activity under heaven.

ECCLESIASTES 3:1

When my children were young, I rarely had a moment's peace. I adopted both of my girls when they were babies, and though I loved being their mother, I soon found that being single with children was a recipe for crazy making. Even something simple like mowing the lawn had to be carefully planned to coincide with nap time.

I remember one disastrous morning. I had forgotten to roll the trash can out to the end of the driveway so the garbage truck could empty it. Hurrying outside, I assured my five- and three-year-old children that I would be back in a moment. And I was. But in the space of that moment, a mini-calamity ensued. My youngest (a future basketball player) had a bad habit of throwing her dolly in the air and then catching it. While I was dragging the can to the curb, she threw the cloth doll up in the air, landing it in a pan of hot water simmering on the stove. Attempting to rescue the doll, her older sister, Katie, flipped it neatly out of the pan. As it sailed to freedom, my younger daughter caught it with ease. Only this time, that dolly was hot! Luci was howling with pain as I walked in the door.

Okay, I should not have left a pan of water simmering on the stove, even if it was on a back burner. But, really, who would have guessed that danger lurks everywhere, even in a cuddly, pink doll? If you have children, you have your own stories to tell. Like me, you have probably wondered if you will ever find a moment's peace.

The writer of Ecclesiastes reminds us that life unfolds as seasons. The season you are in now will eventually pass, and another will take its place. In the midst of life's challenges, try to find a few moments to turn your heart to God in prayer. You might listen to an audio recording of Scripture while you're driving, memorize a Bible verse while cooking, or read a psalm before bed. The God of peace will be there to help you, no matter how busy you are.

Lord, even though this season of my life is busy, it only takes a moment to turn to you. Help me remember that in the midst of a hectic day.

THE RABBI AND HIS ADMIRER

God said, "Let us make human beings in our image, to be like us."... So God created human beings in his own image. In the image of God he created them; male and female he created them.

GENESIS 1:26-27

Joseph Telushkin tells a delightful story about a well-known rabbi who wrote several books about the importance of guarding one's tongue and not speaking negatively about others (*lashon ha-ra*). It seems that one day the rabbi, known as the Chaffetz Chayyim, was traveling to a lecture he was supposed to give that evening, when he encountered a man sitting opposite him on the train. When the rabbi inquired where his fellow passenger was headed, the man replied, "I'm going into town to hear the Chaffetz Chayyim speak tonight. After all, he's the greatest sage and saint in the Jewish world today."

Embarrassed by the man's lavish praise, the rabbi responded, "Sometimes people say such things, but it's not true. He's not such a great sage, and he's certainly no saint."

The man shot back, "How dare you disparage such a great man!" Then he slapped the rabbi in the face.

Later that night, when the man arrived at the lecture, he was chagrined to learn of his mistake. After the rabbi's speech, he rushed over to beg forgiveness.

Smiling, the rabbi merely replied, "You have no reason to request forgiveness. It was my honor you were defending. On the contrary, I learned from you an important lesson. For decades, I've been teaching people not to speak *lashon ha-ra* about others. Now I've learned that it's also wrong to speak *lashon ha-ra* about oneself."[11]

The story of the rabbi and his ardent admirer conveys the truth that, just as we don't have God's permission to speak ill of others, neither do we have his permission to speak ill of ourselves. Make a promise today to stop robbing yourself of God's peace by saying disparaging things.

Lord, thank you for treating me with dignity and love. Help me to accept who I am in your eyes, treating myself with the same respect you offer me.

May 19

DIFFICULT PEOPLE

To you who are willing to listen, I say, love your enemies! Do good to those who hate you. Bless those who curse you. Pray for those who hurt you.

LUKE 6:27-28

Want a surefire way to improve your relationships with others, even with those who have a way of rubbing you the wrong way or offending you every time they open their mouths? I'm not going to offer you a seven-step guide, nor am I going to tell you there's a pill you can take that will help you get along with the most abrasive people in your life. My advice is much simpler. I'm sure you've heard it before, but let me remind you.

The best way to deal with the difficult people in your life is to pray for them—regularly. But be careful how you pray. Avoid the temptation of telling God what jerks they are, praying for them to change so you can experience relief. Instead, pray that God will richly bless them. As you do so, ask God to help you see them the way he does.

Every act of intercession is an act of generosity. God honors that generosity, sometimes in powerful ways. When you pray for a person, you bring them with you into the throne room of God. That's where prayers are answered and grace is given. There, in God's presence, you can receive his heart for the people you are praying for. He can show you the best way to pray for them.

Here's what Dietrich Bonhoeffer says about what happens when we pray: "I can no longer condemn or hate a brother for whom I pray, no matter how much trouble he causes me. His face, that hitherto may have been strange and intolerable to me, is transformed in intercession into the countenance of a brother for whom Christ died, the face of a forgiven sinner."[12] Though Bonhoeffer is talking about praying for other Christians, this same transformation can happen as we pray for those who don't yet know Christ.

Who do you find it hard to like, difficult to tolerate, impossible to forgive? Try a little experiment. Decide you will pray for that person every day for the next twenty-one days. You may be surprised what your heart discovers.

Lord, make room in my heart for difficult people. Show me how to pray for them and how to relate to them. Give me your grace, I pray.

SUGAR, SUGAR

Your unfailing love is better than life itself; how I praise you! I will praise
you as long as I live, lifting up my hands to you in prayer. You satisfy me
more than the richest feast. I will praise you with songs of joy.

PSALM 63:3-5

I love sugar—always have, always will. When I was a child, I used to climb up on the kitchen counter when no one was looking. I'd dip a spoon into the sugar bowl and then aim the heaping spoonful of white stuff straight at my mouth. Once I swallowed so much sugar that I managed to give myself a coughing fit, complete with tiny granules bursting through my nose.

The problem with sugar is that it never leaves you feeling satisfied. One bite of a candy bar just makes you start thinking about the next bite, and then the bite after that. Our desires can be like that too—impossible to satisfy.

Wayne Muller believes that most of us try to find happiness through satisfying our desires. But the two are not necessarily linked. "We can feel the difference between happiness—which is often simple and easy, an inner shift toward appreciation and gratefulness for what is before us," he says, "and desire, which is often frantic and relentless, cutting the heart with its sharp and painful demands. If we do not disengage, if we stay on the wheel of desire, if we do not stop and pray and sing and walk, the pattern of our addictive craving is free to escalate without limit."[13]

What kind of sugar are you craving right now? More shopping? An expensive vacation? A relationship to fill the void? Whatever it is, take some time to reclaim your freedom by stopping to take a walk. As you do so, use the time to pray and sing, breaking away from anything that might threaten your peace.

Father, thank you for all the good things in my life. Help me to celebrate your
ordinary blessings without counting on them to satisfy my deepest desires.

May 21

HATING TOO LITTLE?

The LORD of Heaven's Armies will be exalted by his justice. The holiness of God will be displayed by his righteousness.

ISAIAH 5:16

If you were to be completely honest, telling me exactly who or what you hate, I would know something very important about you. The information you disclosed would tell me where you are on your spiritual journey. Or, to use another metaphor, it would act like a spiritual gauge, measuring the condition of your soul.

If you are like me, you may have a hard time admitting to hatred of any kind. But what if I were to tell you that God allows hatred—that he expects it of us? Would you brand me a heretic? Or a lunatic? The Bible, you might say, tells us that God is love, so how can we tolerate even a shred of hatred in our lives?

Perhaps the point is not so much that we never hate but that we have the right target for our hatred, imitating God by hating the things he hates. Paul tells the Romans to "hate what is wrong" (12:9). We know that God hates every form of sin, not just because sin transgresses his laws, but because sin violates *shalom*, breaking the peace. Sin prevents us from living life as it's supposed to be lived.

Like God, we are to hate the sin and not the sinner. But we get confused, finding it difficult to separate the two. Fortunately Christ has done what we can't—separating sin from the sinner by virtue of his sacrifice on the cross.

Still, instead of loving the things God loves and hating the things God hates, our disordered and divided hearts often make the mistake of tolerating what he will not tolerate—greed, selfishness, pride, and lust—and then hating what he loves—purity, goodness, humility, and kindness. Our quest as Christians is to let God remake our hearts so we love whatever makes for shalom and hate whatever destroys it.

Father, your laws are neither impulsive nor arbitrary, but are given for our good. Give me the grace of an undivided heart, loving what you love and hating what you hate.

TOGETHER

Two people are better off than one, for they can help each other succeed. If one person falls, the other can reach out and help. But someone who falls alone is in real trouble. . . . A person standing alone can be attacked and defeated, but two can stand back-to-back and conquer. Three are even better, for a triple-braided cord is not easily broken.

ECCLESIASTES 4:9-10, 12

Joe and Viola Byler live on a farm in Lancaster County, Pennsylvania. On the first floor of their two-story Amish home is a kitchen-family room combination, warmed by wood stoves. Author Suzanne Woods Fisher shares a story about the importance of the kitchen-family room in her book *Amish Peace*:

"'It's the only room that's heated,' Viola explains. 'At night, the entire family gathers here. Everyone is together. The kids do their homework, Dad reads, I'll be finishing up something in the kitchen.'

"Wouldn't it be simple to heat the other rooms? Granted, the Amish don't have central heating, but it couldn't be that hard to lug a kerosene heater upstairs so the kids could study quietly. Would it?

"The answer comes swiftly.

"'No!' Viola says, eyes wide. 'We love being together. It's our way. Why, if other rooms were heated, everyone would . . . well, they would scatter!' She says it as if it were a sin."[14] Suzanne Woods Fisher tells this story to illustrate the Amish emphasis on community and belonging. Research, she says, indicates that Old Order Amish suffer far lower rates of major depression and heart disease than the general population. Perhaps, she says, it is this emphasis on togetherness that contributes to their emotional and physical strength.

The point of this story is not to get you to turn off the heat to all but the kitchen and family room but to say that when it comes to experiencing good health—an aspect of *shalom*—we have important choices to make. How can we keep our families from becoming fragmented and scattered? How can we connect to others in vital Christian community? Ask God today to help you to make wise choices so you can experience the peace that comes from belonging to those who love him.

Father, Son, and Holy Spirit—you are a community of love. Help me to be rooted and grounded in a loving community so I might know more of your peace.

May 23

SANDPAPER PEACE

As iron sharpens iron, so a friend sharpens a friend.
PROVERBS 27:17

Have you ever rubbed sandpaper back and forth against a rough piece of wood? It takes a lot of work to produce something solid and silky beneath your fingers, with no rough edges or splinters. That's a picture of how God sometimes works, placing us in community with different kinds of believers, some of whom rub us the wrong way.

In fact, the people who get on our nerves or who see things differently than we do can render a priceless service. Though they can make life difficult at times, they can also be instruments God uses to work peace into our lives. How? By showing us how to speak the truth in love, exercise forbearance, benefit from criticism, handle conflict, show patience, demonstrate Christ's love, and stay accountable. They can help us grow up spiritually and emotionally. And we can do the same for them.

I remember early in my career working with a colleague I'll call Ed. Both of us were editors who wanted to publish books that would build up the church and God's people. But we had very different ideas of how to do that. He wanted to publish books I was convinced no one wanted to read. And I wanted to publish books that failed to interest him. The tension between us made working together difficult, and I was tempted to conclude that Ed was both stubborn and clueless. Likely he thought the same of me.

Eventually Ed left the company. But it wasn't long before we found ourselves working together again. Both of us had helped launch a ministry to disadvantaged women. This time, the Ed I saw in action was quite effective, using his skills to grow the ministry. A gifted writer, Ed composed letters to donors and kept the organization afloat financially. As we worked together in this new setting, the tension that had characterized our earlier relationship vanished and we began to forge a genuine friendship.

Over the years, Ed and I had worked on each other's personalities like sandpaper, smoothing out the rough edges. To echo the words of Parker Palmer: "Community will teach us that our grip on truth is fragile and incomplete, that we need many ears to hear the fullness of God's word for our lives."[15]

Lord, please help me to develop the kind of community that will continue to smooth out my rough edges so I might grow in both peacefulness and usefulness.

THE PEACE OF "HEARING" GOD

"Today when you hear his voice, don't harden your hearts as Israel did when they rebelled, when they tested me in the wilderness." . . . Be careful then, dear brothers and sisters. Make sure that your own hearts are not evil and unbelieving, turning you away from the living God.

HEBREWS 3:7-8, 12

The Hebrew word *shema* is translated "listen" or "hear," as in "Listen, O Israel! The LORD is our God, the LORD alone. And you must love the LORD your God with all your heart, all your soul, and all your strength" (Deuteronomy 6:4-5). As is often the case, this Hebrew word packs more punch than its English equivalent. Instead of merely referring to perceiving sound through our ears, it also means perceiving sound through our hearts. But what does that mean? Simply that the word *shema* contains within it the idea that we have to understand and respond appropriately to the words our ears perceive.

Long story short, what this passage from Deuteronomy and many others in the Bible are saying when they use the word *hear* is "listen and obey."[16] This is the winning combination that will bring more peace to our lives, even if what God asks is difficult. By living out this deeper meaning of *shema*, we will remain in God's will, which is always the safest place to be.

Interestingly, this connection between hearing and obeying is also borne out in Latin. Wayne Muller tells of learning about this from his friend Henri Nouwen. "Henri," he says, "insisted that the noise of our lives made us deaf, unable to hear when we are called, or from which direction. Henri said our lives have become absurd—because in the word *absurd* we find the Latin word *surdus*, which means *deaf*. In our spiritual life we need to listen to the God who constantly speaks but whom we seldom hear in our hurried deafness."

Muller goes on to say, "Henri was fond of reminding me that the word *obedient* comes from the Latin word *audire*, which means 'to listen.' Henri believed that a spiritual life was a pilgrimage from absurdity to obedience—from deafness to listening."[17]

Lord, open my ears to hear your voice and my heart to do your will.

TOUCHING

He had healed many people that day, so all the sick people eagerly pushed forward to touch him.

MARK 3:10

My daughter kept pestering me for the pet of her dreams—a snake. Ugh! The last thing I wanted in the house was a slimy, slithery snake. "But snakes aren't slimy," Katie insisted. "They're cute." She kept showing me photos of snakes in a hopeless quest to convince me of their attractiveness.

For several years the dialogue went something like this:

"Mom, can I get a snake?"

"Yes, as soon as you move into your own apartment." (She was six when we first began the conversation.)

"But, Mom, snakes make great pets, and I really want one."

"Yes, and think how great it will be to have your very first snake in your very own apartment."

Since one of Katie's virtues is not giving up, we had the same conversation several times each year. Last year I finally caved. We visited a local pet store with a large inventory of Katie's dream pets. I was looking for the smallest and most mild-mannered. Did they have anything that would grow no longer than three to five inches with a short life span? No, came the reply. Think more in the three- to five-foot range with a life span of ten to fifteen years. Bad news! Still, I could hope that my daughter would soon tire of the snake. With that in mind, I asked the clerk, "Any market for used snakes?"

"Maybe," he said. "Some people will take a full-grown snake, but nobody wants a snake that hasn't been handled. If your daughter is serious about getting a snake, she'll need to spend time with it." Apparently snakes that are never touched become ornery, prone to biting.

A few days later, we took home a tiny red corn snake that Katie promptly christened Rico. Since then, Rico has fit into the family fairly well. He's actually kind of cute and not a bit slimy.

My experience with Rico reminds me of the importance of touching and being touched. If even snakes need regular handling to calm them down and keep them civilized, how much more do we need the touch of another human being in order to maintain our own sense of calm and well-being?

Lord, help me to be sensitive in the way I make contact with others. Teach me to reach out in a way that conveys your love and grace.

May 26
TAKE OFF THE MASK

I was born a sinner—yes, from the moment my mother conceived me.

PSALM 51:5

John Ortberg makes the point that many of us are afraid to reveal who we really are, especially in church. The very place that should be a refuge for us, a safe place to reveal ourselves, is too often the place where we put on masks. But even the most carefully constructed mask will eventually slip. Ortberg tells of being in a store one day with one of his children who was pestering him for a toy. Finally, in exasperation, he responded, "No, I'm not going to get you that toy. I'm not going to get it for you today. I'm not going to get it for you tomorrow. I'm not going to get it next month or next year. I am *never* going to get it for you! Do you understand? *When you're seventy and I'm a hundred years old, I'm still not going to get it for you!*"

Just then the clerk looked at him and said, "You look awfully familiar. Do you teach at Willow Creek Community Church?"

Ortberg recounts what happened next: "I said, 'Yes, my name is Bill Hybels.' I didn't really say that, but I wanted to. I wanted to hide. It was awful."[18]

The problem with hiding is that we miss out on the benefits that come from true community. Why? Because God doesn't build on falsehoods. Neither will he build up a congregation where everyone is intent on projecting a false self. As Ortberg observes, "It's possible for people to attend the same church . . . year after year, without anyone ever knowing them. . . . Nobody knows their marriage is crumbling, their heart is breaking. Nobody knows they are involved in a secret pattern of sin that is destroying their soul. This is not God's plan. It's a mockery of community."[19] Church is meant to be a place where people are healed. It's a hospital, not a set for filming a major motion picture.

You needn't reveal your deepest secrets to everyone you meet in church. But you should have at least a few people who know you well and one or two you can talk to about your trials, temptations, and failings.

Lord, you knew the truth about me from the beginning, and yet you loved me then and love me still. Help me relax into that truth so I don't have to hide from others. Make me open to your grace, I pray.

GRATITUDE, SHARP AND SWEET

Praise him, sun and moon! Praise him, all you twinkling stars! Praise him, skies above! Praise him, vapors high above the clouds! Let every created thing give praise to the LORD, for he issued his command, and they came into being. He set them in place forever and ever. His decree will never be revoked.

PSALM 148:3-6

If you live in a northern climate, you know there are few joys as sharp and sweet as spring, unfolding slowly into lush abundance at the end of a long, harsh winter. The sunshine, the colors, the smells—everything conspires to make you glad.

Sometimes we don't know what we have until we've lost it for a time, like the woman who walked into her doctor's office complaining of a pain and walked out knowing something might be seriously wrong. "I walked out feeling stunned," she said. "Yet I walked out into the street and it shone like the New Jerusalem. . . . Houses, shops, pavements, bare winter trees, were all incredibly beautiful to me that morning. Everything was transfigured. Even the fishmonger's smile, when he handed us two cod fillets, seemed beautiful and very precious, as if it was a gift. In fact everything seemed to be an astonishing gift on that bleak morning when I wondered whether I was being asked to give it back again."[20]

Life can bring such joy and pain, a contrast of light and darkness. If we let them, the losses we suffer can be a filter through which we see the ordinary gifts of life in sharper relief—the ability to breathe, walk, hear, sing, pray, hold another's hand. All these can be occasions for gratitude, even when life is difficult.

Today, let us focus not on our losses but on all we have been given. Let us live with eyes wide open to God's many blessings.

Lord, thank you for blessing me not just once in a while but daily. Open my eyes to your goodness so I may sing your praise.

A MISSION FOR YOUR MOUTH

*Whatever is in your heart determines what you say. A good person
produces good things from the treasury of a good heart, and an evil
person produces evil things from the treasury of an evil heart.*

MATTHEW 12:34-35

S top it!" I screamed, threatening violence if she did it again. An instant
earlier, my mouth had been munching contentedly on a peanut butter
cookie. Now it was launching ballistic missiles. What happened? I had been
standing in the kitchen, balancing precariously on crutches after a recent foot
surgery, when one of my children snuck up behind me and began tickling me.
Not what I needed! But, really, did I have to threaten violence, overreacting
to her little prank?

Our mouths can get us into so much trouble, propelled by emotions
that move at lightning speed, unleashing primal urges. Why is it that most of
us can control every muscle in our bodies but one? No wonder James likens
the tongue to a flame of fire or a dangerous poison (see 3:6-8). According to
Jesus, the tongue is unique because it is connected to the heart. Of course,
when the Bible speaks of the heart, it is not talking about muscle tissue but
about the very core or center of human beings.

The only remedy, then, for dealing with a tongue problem is to attend
to the heart problem. We need more of God's Spirit transforming us on the
inside so that what comes out of our mouths will build up and not tear down.

In his book *War of Words: Getting to the Heart of Your Communication Struggles*,
Paul Tripp makes the vital point that we are Christ's ambassadors, his primary representatives on earth. Because of that, he says, we need to understand that God has a mission for our mouths.

What is the mission God has for your mouth today? Ask the Holy
Spirit to shape your heart with his presence so your words will fulfill his
purpose.

*Lord, forgive me for speaking harshly in anger. Please show me what it means to
become a woman who is not controlled by selfishness, but by your Spirit.*

BLESS THE LORD, O MY SOUL

Those who live in the shelter of the Most High will find rest in the shadow of the Almighty. . . .
Do not be afraid of the terrors of the night, nor the arrow that flies in the day.

PSALM 91:1, 5

Perhaps you know that observant Jews pray at least one hundred prayers every single day. Called *berakah*, these prayers offer continual thanks to God for his many blessings. There's a blessing to say when you get dressed, before you eat, after you eat, when you survive danger or illness, when you hear thunder, when you see a rainbow, and even when you encounter a particularly beautiful person. I especially like the blessing you say when you wake up in the morning. It's one of the first prayers a Jewish child is taught. Here's how it goes:

> I am grateful before you, living and eternal King for returning my soul to me with compassion.
> You are faithful beyond measure.

Imagine praying this simple prayer with intention every day for seventy, eighty, or even ninety years. Wouldn't that shape the course of your life, helping you to be mindful of God, aware that he is the Keeper of your soul, the Creator who calls you to rise up and enjoy another day of life?

Perhaps you think praying all these prayers would be tiresome. But what if such prayers trained you to always be looking in the right direction, proclaiming God's faithfulness throughout the day? What if they prevented you from acting as though everything depended on you and nothing depended on God? What if they made you realize you are never alone?

As Christians, we could benefit from adopting a similar practice. Our prayers don't have to be long, but they do have to be intentional, peppered with praise and thanksgiving. This week, why not consider praying the *Modeh Ani*, the Hebrew name for the prayer above, before you even step one foot out of bed? As you pray, remember that one day you will awake to pray it with a resurrected body that will never be touched by illness or death.

Father, thank you for giving me life and breath and strength. You are faithful beyond measure.

PRAY CONTINUALLY

*Pray in the Spirit at all times and on every occasion. Stay alert and
be persistent in your prayers for all believers everywhere.*

EPHESIANS 6:18

The apostle Paul was constantly urging believers to pray. He exhorted the
Ephesians to "pray in the Spirit at all times and on every occasion." To
the Thessalonians, he said, "Pray continually" (1 Thessalonians 5:17, NIV).
Perhaps Paul was thinking of the Jewish practice of blessing God throughout
the day, from the moment you wake up until the moment you close your eyes
to go to sleep. Here are a few blessings to say at bedtime:

Blessed are thou, LORD our God, Master of the Universe, whose
Word brings on the evening. May the living and eternal God rule over
us always and forever. Blessed are Thou, LORD, who brings on the
evening.

Blessed are you, O LORD our God, King of the Universe, who created
day and night. You roll away the light from before the darkness, and
the darkness from before the light. Blessed are you LORD, who creates
the evening twilight.

Blessed are You, LORD our God, King of the Universe, who makes the
bands of sleep fall upon my eyes, and slumber upon my eyelids.

May it be your will, O LORD my God, and the God of my fathers, to
let me lie down in peace, and to let me rise up again in peace.

Tonight as you close your eyes, remember that one day you will open
them to find that you have passed from death into life, enjoying the gift of
God's forever peace.

*Lord, as I close my eyes, help me to close my heart to all that does not bring me closer
to you—fear, unbelief, and anger. Instead, may I rest in your presence, I pray.*

May 31

THE PEACE OF DELIVERANCE

They arrived at the other side of the lake, in the region of the Gerasenes. When Jesus climbed out of the boat, a man possessed by an evil spirit came out from a cemetery to meet him. This man lived among the burial caves and could no longer be restrained, even with a chain. Whenever he was put into chains and shackles—as he often was—he snapped the chains from his wrists and smashed the shackles. No one was strong enough to subdue him.

MARK 5:1-4

I was praying for a friend's brother the other day, a man unable to break his addiction to alcohol. As I prayed, this passage from Mark's Gospel came to mind. It felt as though the Holy Spirit was highlighting it so I would know how to pray. The man I was praying for isn't psychotic, nor is he living in a cemetery. But like the demon-possessed man described in Mark's Gospel, he is incredibly isolated, having little contact with family or friends.

Instead of being alarmed by the story, I felt encouraged. Why? Because I know that what Jesus did for the man in the Bible can still happen today. It was precisely in a place of isolation, bondage, and death that Christ reached out and delivered a man no one else could help. The devil must have thought he had a lock on this guy's life. But then Jesus showed up and changed everything.

As I prayed, I could almost hear the Spirit saying, "See what I am capable of! I can reach the most unreachable person, changing a place of death into a place of life." That's how I am praying for my friend's brother.

Chances are you have a few hopeless cases on your own prayer list, people whose lives seem to be hurtling toward physical and spiritual death. If that is the case, read Mark 5:1-20 and let the Holy Spirit build your faith, shaping the way you pray.

Lord, come with your power. Come with your love. Drive out the darkness and bring your light—a light that the darkness cannot overcome.

June 1

PRAYING FOR YOUR CHILDREN

The children of your people will live in security. Their
children's children will thrive in your presence.

PSALM 102:28

Because of her many books on the topic, Stormie Omartian has become
well known for her confidence in the power of prayer. But what many
people don't know is that as a young girl she was physically and emotionally
abused by a mother who was mentally ill. Her book *Stormie* is the account not
only of the pain she suffered but of the gracious God who reached through
her brokenness and brought healing to her life.

Because of the abuse she suffered, she was terrified that she, too, might
become an abusive mother. When her first child was born, she developed
tremendous fears for his physical and emotional safety. Though never abusive, she was always anxious, filled with fear that something might happen to
her son. One day she cried out to God, saying, "Lord, this is too much for me.
I can't keep a twenty-four-hours-a-day, moment-by-moment watch on my
son. How can I ever have peace?"[1] One of the answers to her agonized plea
was a sense that she and her husband should cover their son in prayer.

Since that time, she has experienced countless answers to prayer
and has taught thousands of people to pray, one of whom is her daughter,
Amanda. Here's what Amanda had to say when she was just thirteen years
old about how prayer made a difference in her life:

"At my school, I had a classmate who was very mean and I never wanted
to go near her because she scared me. When I told my mom, she decided we
should pray together for this girl. I thought that was a good idea and so we
prayed nearly every day until school was out and through the summer too.
The following school year, a miracle happened and that girl changed completely, and she became one of my best friends. It affected my life and it was
one of the greatest things that ever happened to me."[2]

What a privilege it is to be able to pray for and pass on the practice of
prayer to the next generation. Prayer reminds us that, though we have a role
to play, our burdens ultimately belong to God, who graciously listens as we
cry out to him.

Father, help me to pray consistently and with faith for the children in my life.

June 2

GIVE IT A REST

The LORD is my strength and shield. I trust him with all my heart.
PSALM 28:7

Last night, despite the fact that the temperatures were soaring, my daughter was wearing her favorite pair of winter pajamas. "Honey," I suggested, "why don't you change into something cooler? You're going to be so hot tonight." It was unsolicited advice that I had offered previously.

Instead of changing into more sensible pajamas, as I had advised, Luci simply rolled her eyes and said, "Mom!" drawing out the word as though it had three syllables. I got the message. Luci is a teenager now. I need to back off and let her make more of her own decisions—like what to wear to bed. She doesn't need me micromanaging her life, treating her like she's a toddler.

But old habits die hard, and I find myself slipping back into my controlling mother role more than I should. Of course, the odd thing about being controlling is that it never produces what we long for—an end to our anxiety. Instead, our effort to control things and people simply adds more stress to our relationships. Attempts at control set us up for repeated failures, since no one can completely control their own lives, let alone the lives of others.

Think about it like this. Imagine you've just stepped onto an Airbus A380. Instead of trying to force your way into the cockpit so you can fly the plane, you merely proceed down the aisle until you find your seat, believing that the pilot will deliver you safely to your destination. After all, he has the necessary skills to fly the world's largest airliner. Storming the cockpit would be an act of madness—and suicide.

Similarly, navigating life in this world takes the kind of complex skills that only God possesses. Trying to wrest control of our lives from him would be an act of madness—even suicide. Though God doesn't want us to be passive spectators, neither does he want us to try to control the things that are best left in his care. If you want to reduce your anxiety, resist the temptation to try to control everything. Recognize it for what it is—a crazy attempt to do the impossible. Instead, ask the Lord to show you how to step back and find rest, knowing he is in control.

Lord, help me to learn how to rest in you. Enable me to surrender
more of my life into your capable and powerful hands.

June 3

THE ACID TEST

The Holy Spirit produces this kind of fruit in our lives: love, joy, peace, patience, kindness, goodness, faithfulness, gentleness, and self-control. There is no law against these things!

GALATIANS 5:22-23

Suppose you inherited a necklace from your great-aunt. You've admired it all your life, but you're uncertain of its value. It looks like gold, but you're not sure. How can you tell if you've got the real thing? You could try this simple test—placing a drop of nitric acid on it. If the acid starts bubbling or fizzing when it hits the surface, too bad, because it's not gold. If the metal is unaffected, then it's the real deal. This little procedure is known as the "acid test."

Let's try another acid test. This time it's about you, not a piece of jewelry. But don't worry—we're not going to use nitric acid on you. We aren't going to test for gold either, but for the precious presence of the Holy Spirit in your life.

Paul Tripp points out that what we say and how we say it tell a great deal about what's controlling us. "Words are spoken," he says, "that should never have been uttered. They are spoken at the wrong time, in the wrong place, or with emotions that are raging out of control. Words are spoken when silence would have been a more godly, loving choice. They are more driven by personal desire and demand than the purposes of God or the needs of others."[3]

We know that self-control is one of the fruits of the Spirit. It's an indicator of how much we are being controlled by the Holy Spirit. So out-of-control speech problems are a kind of acid test that reveals who or what is driving us. As Tripp points out, "If my words don't flow out of a heart that rests in his [the Holy Spirit's] control, then they come out of a heart that seeks control."[4] It's as simple as that.

When it comes to the way we speak, not one of us is perfect. But all of us are being perfected, assuming, of course, that we are daily submitting our lives to Christ. Join me today in praying for one of the most forgotten fruits of the Holy Spirit—the quality of self-control.

Father, I can't be a woman at peace without having self-control. Help me to develop this fruit by living in the power of your Spirit.

June 4

NO PRAYER, NO PEACE

May the LORD show you his favor and give you his peace.
NUMBERS 6:26

Have you ever tried brewing coffee without water or driving a car without an engine or working on a computer without a screen? I didn't think so. Trying to become more peaceful without spending time with God in prayer is the same thing—a logical impossibility. Only regular times of prayer can provide the essential foundation for our search for greater peace.

The reasons for this are obvious. Peace comes from being in vital communion with God, who is the source of all peace. But you can't be in communion with him if you never talk to him, praise him, listen to him, confide in him, confess to him, or thank him. Just as you wouldn't (I hope) refuse to talk to your spouse or a close friend, it's foolish to refrain from talking to God and then pretend that you want to have an intimate relationship with him.

The problem, of course, is that there are so many obstacles to prayer. We are surrounded by people who need us, things we need to do, and things we want to do. Everything seems urgent; many things seem enticing. They all shout for our attention. But God rarely shouts. Instead, he waits patiently, despite the 1,001 things we put before our relationship with him. I'm not trying to send you on a guilt trip but motivating you to make prayer one of your highest priorities. As you pray, resist the temptation to make prayer all about you—your needs, your concerns, your petitions. Of course there is a place for you in prayer, but put praise and thanksgiving and listening first, because these will help you keep God first in your heart.

As you make prayer a more regular part of your life, consider Mark Buchanan's advice. "Prayer, before it's talking," he says, "ought to be listening. Before it's petition, it should be audition. Before it calls for eloquence, it requires attention. God speaks. We listen. Prayer's best posture is ears cupped, head tilted toward that Voice."[5]

Lord, give me ears to hear your voice. Help me to make space in my life to listen and to pray.

DON'T BRING IT IN THE BOAT

My father taught me, "Take my words to heart. Follow my commands, and you will live. Get wisdom; develop good judgment. Don't forget my words or turn away from them. Don't turn your back on wisdom, for she will protect you. Love her, and she will guard you."

PROVERBS 4:4-6

I love to fish, though I rarely get the chance. On a recent evening while vacationing in Florida, my daughter and I joined several people on a drift boat to try our luck. While others were hauling in yellowtail snappers, I caught a grunt, a bait fish, and an eel—nothing to brag about. The eel gave the most fight, wrapping its body around the line in a frenzied attempt at escape. As soon as the crew realized what I was hauling out of the ocean, they started shouting, "Don't bring it in the boat! Don't bring it in the boat!" I assure you I had no intention of hauling that ugly sucker inside the boat. I knew enough about eels to be cautious, realizing their razor-like teeth can inflict severe injuries. The crew simply cut the line, and it was over.

My encounter with that hapless eel made me think of the crew's warning: *Don't bring it in the boat!* What if instead of an eel I had caught something dangerous that *looked* like a trophy fish? Would I have recognized the risk, or would I have kept reeling in the line?

The more I thought about it, the more I wondered about the things we haul into our own lives: certain relationships, habits, and ways of thinking. Some of these might not seem so dangerous at first. An innocent flirtation with a married man. A habit of doubting God's goodness. Taking too much prescription medicine. Patterns of bitterness or complaining. An addiction to buying things. All these can inflict incredible damage, stealing our joy and peace. The best way to avoid damage is to simply cut the line. Don't even bring it in the boat.

Ask the Lord today if there's anything you've been bringing into your boat that doesn't belong there. If there is, ask him to give you the grace to cut the line and make an end of it, keeping you out of harm's way.

Father, sometimes I don't know what's good for me. But you do. Help me recognize danger before I even get close to it. Keep me safe, I pray.

CONFRONTING EVIL

Put on all of God's armor so that you will be able to stand firm against all strategies of the devil. For we are not fighting against flesh-and-blood enemies, but against evil rulers and authorities of the unseen world, against mighty powers in this dark world, and against evil spirits in the heavenly places. Therefore, put on every piece of God's armor so you will be able to resist the enemy in the time of evil. Then after the battle you will still be standing firm.

EPHESIANS 6:11-13

Peace doesn't come from pretending there's no such thing as evil. Even though it can never destroy the soul of someone who belongs to God, evil can do plenty of damage in this world. Have you ever been somewhere and sensed the presence of evil? Charles Stanley tells of traveling with a group from his church to do mission work in Haiti. While there, he had an experience that frightened him.

He and others were watching a man perform a dance. "As he danced and whirled his machete in our direction," Stanley says, "I suddenly felt a horrible presence of evil all around us. Momentarily, I was filled with fear for my physical safety and the safety of the people with me. My immediate response to this fear was anger, and out of that anger I began to pray and intercede for our safety.

"This fear," he explains, "was rooted in the *spirit* realm. It was a fear I've come to recognize as a fear that any Christian *should* feel in the face of pure evil. Why do I say it is a good thing to feel fear of evil? Because that fear can and should drive you to pray, to trust God to deliver you from the power of evil, and to get as far away from evil as possible."[6]

Both fear and anger can be helpful emotions, especially if they motivate us to work against and pray against evil. At times, fear is like the gauge on a thermostat, registering the spiritual temperature around us.

Lord, help me not to be naive about the power of evil. Equip me with the belt of truth, the body armor of righteousness, the shoes of peace, the shield of faith, the helmet of salvation, and the sword of the Spirit, which is the Word of God.

TREASURES OUT OF DARKNESS

*What do I see flying like clouds to Israel, like doves to their nests? They are ships from the
ends of the earth, from lands that trust in me, led by the great ships of Tarshish. They are
bringing the people of Israel home from far away, carrying their silver and gold. They will
honor the LORD your God, the Holy One of Israel, for he has filled you with splendor.*

ISAIAH 60:8-9

If you know your biblical history, you will remember that Isaiah lived in
Jerusalem and played a prophetic role from 742 to 686 BC. One of the
greatest of the Old Testament prophets, Isaiah warned of the suffering that
would ensue if God's people failed to repent. But he also foretold a time
when their suffering would end and they would enjoy the Lord's blessings.

This passage from Isaiah pictures the Jewish people returning from
exile, not as a raggedy band of beat-up captives, but as wealthy people
escorted home on ships. I like to think that this is a picture of how God
works through our own hard times. We don't come through them defeated
and dejected but with treasures in hand, because God causes everything to
work together for the good of those who love him (see Romans 8:28). And
everything includes our suffering.

This principle also appears in Exodus, when the Israelites were set free
after years of captivity. After the last of the plagues, the Egyptians couldn't
wait to get rid of their former slaves, loading them down with silver and gold.
Instead of running away from Egypt like a dejected band of captives, God's
people left like a victorious army, plundering the people who had seemed
so strong and who had afflicted them for four hundred years (see Exodus
12:31-36).

What suffering are you enduring right now? Ask God to bring you out
with treasures of wisdom and faith, so that like the Israelites, you can attest
to his faithful love.

*Father, you know how trouble assails me. Hear my cry and come to my rescue.
Deliver me and bless me, and I will proclaim your faithfulness.*

TOO MANY WORDS

*Let everything you say be good and helpful, so that your words
will be an encouragement to those who hear them.*

EPHESIANS 4:29

"M om, no offense, but sometimes you talk too much." Katie had asked a question, and I must have delivered an answer that seemed either boring or belabored. I made a mental note to try to get to the point more quickly the next time she asked me something.

A story is told about Benjamin Disraeli, the nineteenth-century British prime minister. A junior member of parliament once solicited his advice about whether he should speak up about a controversial issue.

"Do you have anything to say that has not already been said?" Disraeli asked him.

"No," the man conceded. "I just want the people whom I represent and the members of Parliament to know that I participated in the debate."

Disraeli answered, "It is better to remain silent and have people say, 'I wonder what he's thinking,' than to speak up and have people say, 'I wonder why he spoke.'"[7]

If each of us were to follow Disraeli's advice, think of how much more peace there would be in the world. No more endless meetings in which people talk simply to hear the sound of their voices. No more nonstop media chatter. No more senseless blogs and tweets.

Have you ever wondered about the endless stream of opinion surveys that populate our world? Eager pollsters solicit our thoughts on issues ranging from the best brand of diapers to the secret of world peace. Then come the results: 51 percent say one thing, while 48 percent say the opposite and one percent respond in the "other" category. Why don't the pollsters give you the option of saying, "I don't know" or "I don't care" or "I'm not going to offer my opinion on foreign policy because I am not qualified to judge the issues at hand"?

Sometimes we talk too much and ponder too little, with the result that our world is full of clamor and stress. Let's get comfortable with the phrase "I don't know" and then start learning to practice the discipline that is called "keeping our peace."

*Lord, I know there is wisdom in cultivating silence. Help me to keep silent
at times when I am tempted to talk just for the sake of talking.*

WHEN CHURCH IS THE PROBLEM

*How foolish can you be? After starting your Christian lives in the Spirit,
why are you now trying to become perfect by your own human effort?*

GALATIANS 3:3

Sometimes, sad to say, our lack of peace comes from going to church. For many of us, church is our most important source of community. It's a place where our spiritual lives are invigorated and our relationships strengthened. Being part of a healthy church enables us to grow as Christians. But what if church is contributing to our lack of peace?

For plenty of women, it's extremely difficult to utter a certain two-letter word, *no*, especially when someone at church asks for their help. So they say yes to every committee, every good cause, every Bible study, every opportunity to serve. While some have taken on the heart of Christ in their service, others have just plain worn themselves out. If you recognize yourself in the latter category, ask God to help you know when to say yes and when to say no. Put a little distance between the request and your answer, giving yourself time to take the matter to Christ, expecting him to guide you.

Church can also deplete our peace if the community of Christians we belong to is characterized by legalism. All variety of churches have been guilty of morphing the gospel into a religion that depends primarily on effort rather than grace. Of course, it takes effort to live as Christians, but if we find little joy and peace in doing so, it may be that we are living a distorted form of Christianity.

What's the best way to deal with legalism in a church community? The place to begin is in your own heart. Recognize it as a serious distortion of the gospel, admitting to yourself and to God your continued desperate need for grace. Live that prayer daily, and you will find your faith becoming more passionate and your life becoming more peaceful.

Lord, I want to lean forward into the gospel, living by its truth, growing into your likeness. Help me to learn how to depend on you more than I depend on myself.

HEALING PRESENCE

Jesus traveled throughout the region of Galilee, teaching in the synagogues and announcing the Good News about the Kingdom. And he healed every kind of disease and illness.

MATTHEW 4:23

I am afraid many of us have succumbed to what I call Christian phobias. We've developed unnatural fears about things that are meant to characterize the Christian life. I'm thinking of things like prayer, evangelism, and healing. Yes, we know prayer is important, but many of us are afraid of the empty space between God and us. Even if we manage to carve out the time to pray, how will we fill up that space? So we read books *about* prayer rather than actually spending time *in* prayer. And when it comes to sharing our faith, many of us run for the hills. We're too afraid of offending someone. And then there's the problem of healing, which we would much rather leave to the professionals.

Pastor Jim Cymbala speaks of the church as being a "Holy Ghost Hospital." I like that metaphor because it reminds us that God's Spirit, living within us, is in the business of healing and restoration. As God's people, we are to be a healing community, a place where sick people get well.

Larry Crabb, a Christian psychologist, poses an important question: "Could it be that training in counseling has become so necessary and valued because few Christians know what it means to release the energy of Christ from within them into the souls of others?" He goes on to ask, "If the battle is against soul disease, and if the real disease is disconnection caused by sin that leaves the person starving for life, isn't it our calling to supply life to one another, at least a taste of it that drives us to run to the source?"[8]

I am not knocking professional therapists and psychiatrists. I have great respect for what they do, and some situations call for professional intervention. But we also, as Crabb says, "need folks who can talk to us wisely and sensitively and meaningfully about our deepest battles, our most painful memories, and our secret sins." Let's ask Christ to fill us with his energy so we can continue to touch others with his healing presence.

Lord, by myself I can do nothing. But with you, anything is possible. Teach me how to release not my energy but yours so others may experience your healing presence.

IN THE DESERT

*Do not forget that he [God] led you through the great and terrifying wilderness
with its poisonous snakes and scorpions, where it was so hot and dry. He gave you
water from the rock! He fed you with manna in the wilderness, a food unknown
to your ancestors. He did this to humble you and test you for your own good.*

DEUTERONOMY 8:15-16

Remember when Adam and Eve got shoved out of the Garden of Eden after taking that fatal bite of fruit? In the Bible, the opposite of this garden paradise is the wilderness, the desert. A harsh place without the ability to sustain life, the desert is described in Deuteronomy 8:15 as a "great and terrifying wilderness." It's a waterless place filled with venomous snakes and scorpions. So it seems an odd spot for a loving God to send his people or to send his beloved Son, which he did prior to his public ministry.

As the opposite of Eden, the desert is a harsh place where human beings are forced to face the effects of sin, which has withered and destroyed the peace of the whole world. It's where Jesus battled Satan, conquering the temptations that plague us all. But the desert is also portrayed as a place of opportunity—a place to meet with God and learn to trust him as he cares for us in Earth's most inhospitable place. In the Israelites' journey to the Promised Land and Jesus' journey to his public ministry, Scripture portrays the desert as a bridge to something far better. Get through the desert with your faith intact, and you will know how great God is and how greatly he wants to bless and use you.

As human beings whose hearts are roiled with the strife that sin brings, we no longer live in Eden, where perfect peace reigns. Thrust into the wilderness, we are not abandoned there but led by the Spirit to learn the lessons that only the desert can teach us. Today, let us remember that Jesus has led the way both into and out of the wilderness, beckoning us to endure such times with faith, believing that as we do, he will help us grow in trust and fruitfulness.

*Father, sometimes life seems rich and full. At other times it seems
barren and harsh. Help me to find the peace that comes from learning
to trust you to care for me during the difficult seasons of life.*

HIS HELP WILL SURELY COME

All glory to God, who is able, through his mighty power at work within us, to accomplish infinitely more than we might ask or think.

EPHESIANS 3:20

I once had the privilege of attending a meeting of Alcoholics Anonymous with a family member who needed help. In that small circle of broken, honest people, I felt the tangible presence of God. These men and women had come to the end of themselves and the beginning of faith, so desperate for help that they were willing to admit the truth about themselves.

It struck me then that this was a model for my own life—to present myself to God as I truly am, broken and desperate for his grace. The truth is, no matter how much God heals and restores us, none of us can survive for even a moment without his help.

But it is easy to forget this, to fool ourselves into thinking we are in charge of our lives and we can handle our problems our way. So we build strategies, consciously or unconsciously, for handling life's challenges in ways that depend more on us than they do on God. Perhaps the strategies work well enough on small problems, but what happens when we encounter something bigger—a real disaster or tragedy? What then? Do we try and try and try, beating our heads against a wall, or do we come to realize anew, to use the language of Alcoholics Anonymous, that our lives have "become unmanageable" and that only a "Power greater than ourselves" can help us?

If you are feeling powerless in the midst of life's difficulties, don't give in to discouragement. Your weakness, faced with honesty and hope, can be the very pathway God will use to display his strength. Wait for his help, which will surely come.

Lord, I come before you today to admit my brokenness and need. I don't have the wisdom, the patience, or the courage to deal with the challenges in my life on my own. Please turn my weakness into your strength. I will make sure you get all the glory.

NON-ANXIOUS PRESENCE

All praise to God, the Father of our Lord Jesus Christ. God is our merciful Father and the source of all comfort. He comforts us in all our troubles so that we can comfort others. When they are troubled, we will be able to give them the same comfort God has given us.

2 CORINTHIANS 1:3-4

Remember the actor Gregory Peck in the classic film *To Kill a Mockingbird?* As Atticus Finch, the lawyer who defends Tom Robinson, a black man falsely convicted of rape, he is the epitome of cool. I don't mean the kind of cool that comes from being the most popular person in town. In fact, he is vilified for representing a black man in his small Southern town. Atticus's kind of cool comes from an inner stability that radiates outward, with the potential to transform the situation.

This kind of stability is what would-be pastors learn about in seminary—the ability to maintain a "non-anxious presence" in the midst of a conflict. I like that phrase because it highlights an ideal I'm still striving for. When my children are arguing, I'd like to help them calm down by maintaining my own sense of inner peace. When my mother has surgery, I'd like to be able to help her by staying calm myself. When I disagree with someone, I'd like to do so in a way that builds peace rather than destroys it.

To say that I want to learn how to maintain a non-anxious presence is simply another way of saying I want to be more like Christ. Think about all the times he radiated peace when others around him were falling apart. He told a group of mourners that the little girl who died was only asleep, and then he brought her back to life (see Mark 5:38-42). He quieted a storm at sea while his disciples were panicking (see Matthew 8:24-26). He reassured his disciples of his gift of peace shortly before his death (see John 14:27-30).

I wish I could tell you I have learned how to stay cool no matter what happens, but that would not be true. Yet if God is the one who comforts us in all our troubles, surely he can express that comfort through imperfect people like you and me.

Father, I want to look more like Jesus—to respond as he would and to think the way he does. Change me by recreating the life of Christ within me through the power of your Spirit.

June 14

POWER

You will receive power when the Holy Spirit comes upon you. And you will be my witnesses, telling people about me everywhere—in Jerusalem, throughout Judea, in Samaria, and to the ends of the earth.

ACTS 1:8

Though I know very little about how electricity works, I know the power we use in our homes and workplaces has to be transformed before we can access it. Energy that travels over long distances, for instance, can only be transmitted if it is transformed into high voltage. If the voltage is too low, it will never reach us. To bring the power to us, step-up transformers are used to convert the energy. But delivering that high-voltage energy to our homes is only the first step. Once it arrives, it can't simply be blasted into our houses. Step-down transformers are employed in order to decrease the voltage so the energy can be used safely.

It's important to note that though transformers deliver the power, they don't create it. They simply convert energy so it can be safely and profitably used. When it comes to spiritual power, I like to think that we are all called to become transformers, conveying God's power to those around us. On our own, we have no power to bring peace to this world. But God, who is the Source of all power, can work through us, using us as conduits to convey his peace, grace, and healing power to those around us.

Ask God today to help you to open up to the work of the Holy Spirit in your life. Tell him you want to receive all the power he offers, not just so you can be transformed but so you can be a person he uses to transform the lives of others. Without God's power, there will be no peace. With it, nothing is impossible for those who love him.

Lord, I want to receive everything you have for me. Please fill me with your Spirit. Guide me and use me in a way that brings glory to your name, I pray.

June 15

SENSELESS?

You watched me as I was being formed in utter seclusion, as I was woven together in the dark of the womb. You saw me before I was born. Every day of my life was recorded in your book. Every moment was laid out before a single day had passed.

PSALM 139:15-16

One of the most painful memories from my pre-Christian days is the hollowed-out feeling that came from believing life had no meaning. Without meaning, nothing matters—not beauty nor bravery nor joy; not suffering nor sadness nor love. There is nothing to strive for, plan for, hope for. To live in a world without meaning is to live as a lonely atom in a vast universe of nothingness.

But that picture of the universe changed the moment I began to suspect the old story I had learned as a child—the one about God making the world and then sending his Son to save it—might actually be true. It was shocking, the idea that God felt impelled by love to come to earth and die for my sins. That he subverted death by his powerful sacrifice. Suddenly I had a big story to believe in, one that gave meaning to my life.

Sometimes we lose our peace because we lose our place in the big story God is writing. Perhaps we once saw ourselves right in the center of it, knowing he loved us, believing he had called us to serve him. But then disasters unfolded. Disappointments happened. Suffering ensued. What then?

Miroslav Volf points out that inner healing is advanced "by integrating remembered wrongdoing into our life-story. . . . We integrate events into our life-story by giving them positive *meaning* within that story."⁹ So the woman who has been abused may discover insights that will later assuage the suffering of others. Or the abandoned wife may find strength in her relationship with God that she hadn't thought possible. Finding meaning in what we have suffered is not something that can be engineered or controlled. Rather it is something that God can do in us and for us as we wait for his healing grace.

Lord, you are the only one who knows the whole story—past, present, and future. Open my soul to your grace, and send me your healing power.

BREATHE

*You made all the delicate, inner parts of my body and knit me together in
my mother's womb. Thank you for making me so wonderfully complex!
Your workmanship is marvelous—how well I know it.*

PSALM 139:13-14

Over the years I've learned a couple of simple tricks to reduce my stress
level. One of these is to practice deep-breathing techniques. You
needn't be a Buddhist to recognize that the right kind of breathing exercises
can help you feel more peaceful. The reason for this calming effect is based
on the way God designed our bodies.

Let me explain. Whenever you're faced with an emergency, your sympathetic nervous system kicks in. Your muscles tense up, your heart beats
faster, your blood pressure increases, and adrenaline begins coursing through
your body. The body's 911 system is preparing you for an explosive burst of
energy to enable you to make a fight-or-flight response. Though the system
is superbly adapted for dealing with immediate dangers, such as fending off a
mugger or escaping from a house on fire, the sympathetic nervous system will
wreak havoc on your body and your mind if it becomes chronically activated,
which is exactly what happens when you're under constant stress.

By contrast, the parasympathetic system lowers your heart rate,
decreases your blood pressure, and enables you to rest. Deep breathing acti-
vates the parasympathetic system, increasing your sense of calm.

Here's how to do one breathing exercise. Begin by sitting up straight.
Then exhale fully through your mouth. Breathe in deeply through your nose
and into your abdomen, letting it fill with air. Hold your breath for two to
five counts and then exhale slowly through your nose. Try doing this for five
to ten minutes on a regular basis. To enrich the time, begin by imagining
yourself in God's presence, thanking him for how fearfully and wonderfully
he has made you.

*Father, thank you for making my body the way you have. Help me to learn practical
ways to take care of myself so I will begin to live with more peace and less stress.*

June 17

HEALTHY IN BODY AND SOUL

*Dear friend, I hope all is well with you and that you are as
healthy in body as you are strong in spirit.*

3 JOHN 1:2

My dog is the calmest creature I know. But sometimes even she can get a little squirrely. The other day I took her with me to explore a local art fair. Normally Kallie loves to be in the middle of a crowd. But as we were walking along, she suddenly made a beeline for the opposite side of the street, dragging me behind her. Her body spoke the language of fear—back hunched, head down, and tail pinned tightly between her legs.

Wondering what had frightened her, I looked around, expecting to see a hulking dog, barely concealing its rage through bared teeth. But there was nothing—only a pleasant crowd milling about. And then I spotted it: a metal grate surrounding a tree in the sidewalk. To test my theory, I started walking toward it. Sure enough, as soon as we got near, Kallie started pulling with all her might in the opposite direction.

When I described this phenomenon to my brother, the family dog whisperer, I wondered aloud if perhaps she had developed this neurosis after catching her foot in a grate, though I couldn't remember her ever having done so. "Well, maybe," he said. "But you have to understand that if a dog like Kallie isn't exercised regularly, she's going to start developing some problem behaviors. You need to make sure she stays in good shape. That will head off a lot of trouble."

His advice made sense because I realize how much regular habits of exercise can help me to head off a lot of my own problem behaviors—things like crankiness, complaining, and depression. Being a couch potato makes it easy for me both to gain weight and to lose perspective. In our search for more of God's peace, let's not overspiritualize everything, ignoring obvious ways in which we can grow stronger and become less stressed.

Father, help me do what I need to in order to make time for regular exercise. I want to take better care of my body so I can function effectively in the ways you want me to.

GRACE + GRACE + TRUTH = GOD'S LOVE

*Grace, mercy, and peace, which come from God the Father and from Jesus Christ—
the Son of the Father—will continue to be with us who live in truth and love.*

2 JOHN 1:3

We know the Bible is God's Word. All of it—even the messy, gory, challenging parts of the Old Testament that we find hard to decipher. But as important as Scripture is, God wanted to communicate himself even more clearly, so in an ultimate act of grace, he sent his Son.

John's Gospel describes this momentous gift by saying, "The Word became flesh and made his dwelling among us. We have seen his glory, the glory of the one and only Son, who came from the Father, full of grace and truth" (John 1:14, NIV). It's interesting that John describes Jesus as the Word and also as the one who came from the Father, full of grace and truth. All aspects of Jesus—what he said, the miracles he performed, the way he lived and died—are a message from God, a revelation of his character. John goes on to say, "The law was given through Moses; grace and truth came through Jesus Christ" (1:17, NIV).

Mart De Haan, of RBC Ministries, points out that most of us have either a grace default or a truth default. Those oriented toward grace, for instance, are always willing to give the benefit of the doubt. They will do almost anything to smooth things over, even if that means disregarding the truth at times.

On the other hand, those who are oriented toward truth can sometimes be harsh and insensitive. But Jesus was perfectly balanced, oriented toward both grace and truth. De Haan goes on to remind us that just as adding two parts hydrogen to one part oxygen yields water, the life of Jesus would seem to indicate that two parts grace plus one part truth yields the love of God. That is the divine equation that should characterize our lives as followers of Jesus Christ.[10]

Let's ask God to help us remember this formula as we encounter people who disagree with our most cherished beliefs. Let's also remember this formula for God's love when it comes to relating to those closest to us.

Lord, please make me more like you today, adding two measures of grace to every one measure of truth so I can reflect your love and peace to others.

June 19

PEACE WITH THE QUESTION MARKS

In the beginning God created the heavens and the earth.

GENESIS 1:1

Fascinated by the most minute details of Scripture, Jewish sages have paid special attention to the very first word of the Bible, *beresheet*, which means "in the beginning." Drilling down on the first letter of this word, *bet* ב, they pointed out that this is the second letter of the Hebrew alphabet. Why, the sages wondered, did the Bible begin with the second letter of the alphabet, rather than the first?

In her book *Walking in the Dust of Rabbi Jesus*, Lois Tverberg provides their fascinating answer: "To show that the Scriptures do not answer every question, and not all knowledge is accessible to man, but some is reserved for God himself."[11]

Even for those of us who believe in Christ, life is full of question marks. Why did my child get ill? Why did my marriage fail? Why did my job evaporate? What is going to happen to me? How will I get through this? What if I don't? Countless questions surround us, as they do every person. At times, God provides answers. But there are many times he does not. What do we do then? Do we become frustrated, angry, fearful? Or do we decide to keep trusting him in the middle of all the question marks?

I think the Jewish sages were onto something. God both reveals and conceals. Some things he simply keeps to himself. And that is all right because he is God. He knows what we need to know and what we don't.

What are the question marks in your life right now? Take a few moments to lift them up to God, trusting that he knows the answers, though you may not. Tell him you are confident that he is big enough and good enough and wise enough to deal with each one in a way that displays his faithfulness and care. Then leave the questions right where they belong—in his capable hands.

Lord, you know how much I like things to be clear, to be lined up and buttoned up. But everything is not clear. In the midst of unanswered questions and uncertain times, help me continue to place my trust in you.

## June 20

HOW TO BE WHOLE

Let the peace that comes from Christ rule in your hearts. For as members of one body you are called to live in peace.

COLOSSIANS 3:15

Is wholeness just a buzzword, something to describe a therapeutic goal or a proclivity toward health, as in Whole Foods Market or whole-body workouts? Or is there more to it than that? Remember that the Hebrew word *shalom*, often translated "peace" in English translations of the Bible, can also be translated as "wholeness." But what does it mean to be whole?

Perhaps we could get an idea of what wholeness means by looking at the polar opposite. Let's go back to the story of the man whose mind and soul were so devastated that he was living in the hills and among the tombs along the shores of the Sea of Galilee, a constant danger to himself. Here's how Mark's Gospel describes the scene. Jesus has just arrived with his disciples. Intent on delivering the man, he commands the demon to identify itself, and he gets this reply: "Legion, because there are many of us inside this man" (5:9). A multitude of demons infesting the man, each vying for space inside him, fragmenting his soul and shattering his mind.

To be whole is to be the opposite of this ruined man. It is to be complete, unbroken, sound in body, soul, and spirit. It is to be as God intended you to be before sin came and wrecked everything—including you.

We know that Christ restored this man to his right mind. If he was able to do that for such an extreme case, why do we doubt he can help us? Scripture tells us the peace of Christ rules in our hearts when the word of Christ richly dwells within us (see Colossians 3:16, NIV). The word *richly* implies fullness, abundance. If Jesus is not richly dwelling within us, something else will be—conflict, worry, strife, bitterness, anxiety, greed, guilt, envy, anger, lust. A thousand things can fill us, crowding out the life of God and creating divisions within our souls. No heart is perfectly unbroken in this broken world. But we can be confident that the heart set on Christ, committed to living by his Word, is being restored to his likeness and kept in his peace.

Lord, teach me what it means to be steeped in your Word—reading, remembering, believing, and living by it. As I do that, may your peace rule in my heart.

TWO-WAY PROMISES

A wonderful future awaits those who love peace.

PSALM 37:37

"There is no peace for the wicked," says my God.

ISAIAH 57:21

Though most of us think of God's promises in positive terms, as we should, Scripture is full of promises that sound frighteningly negative. These reverse promises serve as warnings for those who show little regard for God and his ways.

The first promise for today, from Psalms, is one you can build on. It's like bedrock for those who belong to Christ and pursue his ways. But what if you are doing just that and feeling anything but peaceful? Notice that Psalm 37 promises a wonderful future but not necessarily a wonderful present. Every life holds challenges and sorrows that must be endured with faith and trust. At such times we can cling to this promise from Romans: "We know that God causes everything to work together for the good of those who love God and are called according to his purpose for them" (8:28). We will all know times of peace and times of difficulty because we are not yet inhabiting the future God has promised.

But for the wicked, Isaiah proclaims, there will be no true peace. How could there be, since peace comes from knowing God and from trusting him enough to obey him? A life in perpetual rebellion is a life in perpetual turbulence. Though things may look peaceful on the outside for a time, on the inside things tend to fall apart because there is no central core to hold us together.

The peace we long for depends not only on God's promise but on our obedience. Step by step, as we place our trust in Christ, doing what we know he wants us to do, we can be confident that we are moving closer to the wonderful future God has promised for all those who love peace.

Lord, regardless of whether your ways seem hard or easy, help me to embrace them, trusting that they will draw me closer to you.

STORMS WILL COME

The fears of the wicked will be fulfilled; the hopes of the godly will be granted. When the storms of life come, the wicked are whirled away, but the godly have a lasting foundation.

PROVERBS 10:24-25

We know the havoc hurricanes can wreak on human life and property. But what about the damage to sea life? Though countless fish may perish in any given storm, some have an uncanny ability to survive. Researchers in Florida have followed the progress of tagged sharks that swam into deeper water just prior to the onslaught of a hurricane. How the sharks knew what was coming is uncertain, but scientists believe they may have sensed changes in barometric pressure, which in turn affects hydrostatic pressure. Some sixth sense enabled them to swim to open waters to avoid the worst of the storm.

This strategy of moving into the deep when storms approach suggests a spiritual strategy for our own lives. We need to deepen our lives with God when we face challenges of various kinds.

Longfellow once famously wrote that "into each life some rain must fall." But anyone who has lived for more than a few years will recognize this as a terrific understatement. For many of us, the storms that come, whether emotional or physical, will be prolonged and difficult, testing the limits of our strength. At such times, it makes sense to flee to safety, to the deeper waters of Scripture, prayer, obedience, and fellowship with other believers.

Seasoned fishermen have repeatedly noted that some fish seem to feed more aggressively just before a storm, as though they sense that food will soon become scarce. If we live our lives in preparation, feeding on God's Word and living in alignment with it, God will enable us to survive whatever storms may threaten our peace.

Lord, I know that difficulty will come. Help me to prepare for it by deepening my life in Christ, not neglecting the things that make for peace.

WHAT DO YOU BELIEVE?

What is the price of five sparrows—two copper coins? Yet God does not forget a single one of them. And the very hairs on your head are all numbered. So don't be afraid; you are more valuable to God than a whole flock of sparrows.

LUKE 12:6-7

Joan Didion's memoir *The Year of Magical Thinking* chronicles her grief in the year following the unexpected death of her husband, fellow writer John Gregory Dunne. Perhaps the bleakest moment in that chronicle is when she quotes her late husband, stating with hopeless finality that "no eye is on the sparrow."

Though she probably didn't intend it as an insult, the words jumped off the page at me like a slap. It was such a blatant contradiction of everything I believe to be true. Later, it occurred to me that Didion's statement sums up our own struggle as people of faith. When life is bleak beyond imagining, what do we really believe? What do we think is going on? Either God's eye is on the sparrow or it is not. Either God really has counted every hair on every head or he has not. Either Jesus knew exactly what he was talking about when he spoke of God as a loving and forgiving Father or he did not. It's as simple and as hard as that.

When life is going well, it's easy to assert the truths of the gospel. But when we are overtaken by crushing sorrows or mounting difficulties, what do our hearts tell us then?

Most of us can remember times when God came through for us in the midst of great difficulty. Let's not forget the evidence of his faithfulness when new challenges arise, giving in to fear rather than drawing on faith to sustain us. Let's let times of suffering strengthen us rather than weaken us, trusting that God knows how to get us through.

Father, I want to be a woman who lives by faith and not by sight.
Give me eyes to perceive your faithfulness, I pray.

DOUBLE, DOUBLE TOIL AND TROUBLE

In their time of trouble they cried to you, and you heard them from heaven.

NEHEMIAH 9:27

Two weeks ago I felt like a magnet for trouble. A series of problems with a vacation property I own were conspiring to turn one family's stay into "the worst family vacation ever." As a part-time landlady, I enjoy creating memorable vacation experiences for people. This just wasn't the kind of memorable I had envisioned. I cringed at the thought that the story of their week at my place might enter their family lore as the worst vacation ever. To ease the sting, at the end of their stay I gave them a check for half the rent, thereby turning the most profitable week of summer into a sizable loss for me. Ouch!

Then a problem cropped up with one of my children, and I wasn't sure how to handle it. Then my elderly mother started having difficulties. Then something happened with my other daughter. On and on it went—a great, rolling tumbleweed of trouble heading my way.

One thing about nonstop trouble is that it can help you put life's difficulties into proper perspective. Yes, I felt bad that my renters thought they were renting a three-bedroom condo when it was only a two-bedroom condo, and that a previous renter had walked off with the pots and pans, and that the maids forgot to leave the sheets, and that the toilets backed up, and that the plumber was expensive, and that I had to make two sixty-mile round-trips to the property, and that I didn't get any writing done that week. But at least the sun was shining the whole week and the pool worked and the beach was lovely and nobody died. After a while, you learn how to find a little brightness in the cloudiest of skies.

What troubles are you facing right now? Join me in asking God to help you see at least a little bit of light in the midst of them—not the kind that emanates from an oncoming train, but the kind that comes from perceiving the daylight on the other side of the tunnel.

Lord, please break the cycle of difficulties that are harassing me right now, and give me hope in the midst of them. Grant me wisdom to know how to respond to them.

June 25

DON'T SHRINK BACK

We do not belong to those who shrink back and are destroyed,
but to those who have faith and are saved.

HEBREWS 10:39, NIV

Sometimes I feel like the incredible shrinking woman. Some big, hairy problem comes stomping onto the scene, and I feel too tiny to stand up to it. Instead of holding my ground, confident that God is with me and will never abandon me, I start looking for the exits. But often there are none. And I, little person that I am, have to stay in place and learn how to trust God in the midst of my difficulties.

When it comes to facing up to trouble, many of us are experienced escape artists. But when escape is not an option, we may be tempted to try other strategies, taking refuge in things that promise to soothe or counter our pain. Here are a few of my own favorite strategies: eating, buying, blaming, complaining. Funny that none of these ever bring me real peace. Sure, brownies are soothing, but they don't stop me from worrying. Buying things works for a little while, until the novelty of the latest purchase wears off. And blaming and complaining just spread the misery.

So what does help? Here are a few simple things from my list: (1) having a regular prayer time; (2) talking things over with friends and asking for prayer; (3) interceding for others, which takes my mind off myself; (4) using the wisdom God gives to deal with the problem at hand; (5) time, since some problems can only be dealt with by outlasting them; (6) doing everything with as much faith as I can muster.

Even if you have only a little faith, decide to put it to work. To grow strong, faith needs exercise, much like a muscle that grows larger when it's challenged. The next time a big, hairy problem comes stomping onto the scene, resist the temptation to run. Instead, face it with the faith you have, asking God to reveal his power through you.

Father, it's true that I am weak, but it's also true that you are strong. Help
me to access your strength by exercising the faith you've given me.

DEFENDING THE PEACE

People who wink at wrong cause trouble, but a bold reproof promotes peace.

PROVERBS 10:10

In October 1941, in the midst of World War II, Winston Churchill famously advised students in Harrow, England: "Never give in—never, never, never, never, in nothing great or small, large or petty, never give in except to convictions of honour and good sense."[12]

The previous year, in June 1940, Churchill had rallied his people in a radio broadcast: "We shall not flag or fail. We shall go on to the end. We shall fight in France, we shall fight on the seas and the oceans, we shall fight with growing confidence and growing strength in the air, we shall defend our island, whatever the cost may be. We shall fight on the beaches, we shall fight on the landing grounds, we shall fight in the fields and in the streets, we shall fight in the hills; we shall never surrender." Then he added a postscript, heard only by the aide to whom he whispered it: "And we shall fight with the butt end of broken beer bottles because that's bloody well all we've got."

Fortunately for England and the world, the great tide of evil was pushed back, the Germans were defeated, and peace was restored. Had Churchill and others not stood in the breach and refused to give up despite the odds, much of the world would have fallen to Nazi domination.

Oddly, peace is something you can't have without a willingness to fight for it. That's true whether we are fighting through obstacles that keep us from experiencing God's peace, or whether we are defending the rights of others. Trying to maintain the peace by avoiding conflict at all costs will only erode it. We need to value peace enough to be willing to defend it when necessary. How do we do that? One important way is by heeding the words of the prophet Micah: "What does the LORD require of you? To act justly and to love mercy and to walk humbly with your God" (6:8, NIV).

Lord, help me to stand up for what is right regardless of the odds, to defend myself and others against encroaching evil. Teach me to act justly, to love mercy, and to walk humbly with you.

WHAT'S IMPORTANT?

As Jesus and the disciples continued on their way to Jerusalem, they came to a certain village where a woman named Martha welcomed him into her home. Her sister, Mary, sat at the Lord's feet, listening to what he taught. But Martha was distracted by the big dinner she was preparing.

LUKE 10:38-40

Remember the story of Martha and Mary? Jesus had brought a boatload of disciples to their home in Bethany, and Martha was irritated because her sister wasn't helping with all the work involved in entertaining guests. But when she tried to get Jesus to take her side, he surprised her by saying, "My dear Martha, you are worried and upset over all these details! There is only one thing worth being concerned about. Mary has discovered it, and it will not be taken away from her" (Luke 10:41-42).

If I had been Martha, living in that day and age, I might have been tempted to conclude that Jesus was like most men, clueless about how much work it took to feed and provide for guests. But that interpretation doesn't really wash, because Jesus was no hidebound first-century male. So what else might be at work in the story?

Here's how Augustine interpreted it, imagining what he would have said to Martha if given the chance. "But you, Martha, if I may say so, are blessed for your good service, and for your labors you seek the reward of peace. Now you are much occupied in nourishing the body, admittedly a holy one. But when you come to the heavenly homeland will you find a traveler to welcome, someone hungry to feed, or thirsty to whom you may give drink, someone ill whom you could visit, or quarrelling whom you could reconcile, or dead whom you could bury?

"No, there will be none of these tasks there. What you will find there is what Mary chose. There we shall not feed others, we ourselves shall be fed. Thus what Mary chose in this life will be realized there in all its fullness; she was gathering fragments from that rich banquet, the Word of God. Do you wish to know what we will have there? The Lord himself tells us when he says of his servants, *Amen, I say to you, he will make them recline and passing he will serve them.*"[13]

Lord, you are the Bread of Life. Let me accept your invitation
to sit down at your table and feast on your Word.

June 28
WHEN YOU FEEL INADEQUATE

I can do everything through Christ, who gives me strength.

PHILIPPIANS 4:13

I've been writing books for many years. Despite what you might think, it doesn't get any easier as time goes on. What hampers me most is my lack of faith. Face-to-face with a blank computer screen, I have a mini crisis of faith each morning, certain that I haven't got a thing to say that's worth reading. I'll send e-mails, make phone calls, walk the dog, pay bills, eat a banana—anything as long as I don't have to start writing. Finally, when I can't dodge it anymore, I'll open up the latest file, see where I left off, and ask God to help me. After a while, the writing usually begins to flow.

For most of us, life is full of such miniature faith crises. We doubt we can do what God has called us to do—to show patience to our children, understanding to our husbands, skill in our work, wisdom in times of trouble. And we're right. We don't have enough of what we need. So we stall and make excuses and try to dodge our responsibility, which only increases our anxiety.

To be human is to be inadequate. It is to be limited. It is to be weak in many respects. When we look at our deficiencies, there's ample cause for concern. But instead of training our eyes on our weakness, we need to train our eyes on God's strength and on his promises to love and provide. So today, as always, we come before his throne, asking him to fill our emptiness with his fullness and to trade our weakness for his power. Today we take a small step of faith so God can give us his strength.

Father, when small crises of faith come my way, help me to recognize them, remembering that your strength is always available to me. Let me grow in confidence as I grow in prayer and dependence on you, knowing that your power works best in my weakness.

WORRYING OUT LOUD

Do everything without complaining and arguing, so that no one can criticize you. Live clean, innocent lives as children of God, shining like bright lights in a world full of crooked and perverse people.

PHILIPPIANS 2:14-15

Jen burst into the room, tears streaming down her face. "I can't stand my life!" she exclaimed.

Wondering whether her daughter was suffering from hormone overload or something worse, her mother asked what on earth was wrong.

"You!" the daughter shot back.

Probing further, it became clear to my friend that her teenage daughter was in a state of high anxiety. Pouring out her fears, this young girl told her mother that she was worried about school, anxious about a grandparent in failing health, concerned about the family business, wondering whether there would be enough money for college and whether the economy might collapse. She just couldn't handle it anymore.

"But, honey," my friend said, "you don't have to handle it. Don't worry about Grandpa. Your dad and I are taking care of him. And our business is doing well. I promise there will be enough money for college. The economy isn't great, but it's getting better. What made you so upset about all these things?"

"You!" came the emphatic reply, once again. "You're always complaining about the business, about Grandpa's health, and about how terrible the economy is!"

My friend was stunned. She hadn't realized that her words of complaint and concern had been driving a stake of anxiety into her daughter's sensitive heart, causing her to worry about issues that no thirteen-year-old should have to deal with.

When it comes to complaints, none of us have a clean slate. But perhaps we can take this story to heart, realizing the power that words have to erode the peace of those we love. Today, let's ask the Lord to place a guard on our lips, so that whatever comes out of them builds up rather than tears down.

Lord, forgive me for my habit of complaining and for worrying out loud in front of other people. Please replace these with habits of gratitude and praise, not papering over my concerns but recalling your faithfulness in the midst of them.

June 30
GET ME OUT OF HERE!

Give all your worries and cares to God, for he cares about you.

1 PETER 5:7

I love the scene in the movie *Young Frankenstein* in which the young Dr. Frederick Frankenstein, played by Gene Wilder, is about to enter a room where the monster he has created is held. Here's how the scene unfolds:

> Dr. Frankenstein: Love is the only thing that can save this poor creature, and I am going to convince him that he is loved even at the cost of my own life. No matter what you hear in there, no matter how cruelly I beg you, no matter how terribly I may scream, do not open this door or you will undo everything I have worked for. Do you understand? Do not open this door.
>
> Inga: Yes, Doctor. . . .
>
> [Dr. Frankenstein goes into the room with the monster. The monster wakes up.]
>
> Dr. Frankenstein: Let me out of here. . . . What's the matter with you people? I was joking! Don't you know a joke when you hear one? [14]

Why include this crazy scene in a book about peace? Think of it like this: each of us has made decisions that we believe are blessed and directed by God. The choice to follow Jesus no matter what. The decision to become involved in a particular ministry. Often we make these decisions in the midst of experiencing God in an almost tangible way. But then we come down from the mountain to live out daily life. For some of us, the choices we made may eventually lead us into monstrous troubles. What then? Do we rush for the door, determined to get out no matter what? Or do we take our problems to the throne of grace, trusting that God will lead us? Today, let's gather up every trouble or care that has come as a result of doing what we said we would do and bring each of them straight to God, laying them at his feet and asking for his help.

Father, by myself I can't handle the problems that have come my way from trying to do your will. Please lead me and help me, Lord, I pray.

July 1
THE BEST ANTIDEPRESSANT

The word of the LORD holds true, and we can trust everything he does. He loves whatever is just and good; the unfailing love of the LORD fills the earth.

PSALM 33:4-5

This morning a reader contacted me to tell me how one of my books had encouraged her. After reading her note, I was the one who felt encouraged. Despite suffering severe economic hardship, she seemed buoyed by the way God kept speaking to her. She cited Psalm 91:14: "The LORD says, 'I will rescue those who love me. I will protect those who trust in my name.'" Then she went on to cite Psalm 3:3: "You, O LORD, are a shield around me; you are my glory, the one who holds my head high." Holding on to this one passage from the Bible, she said, had done more to keep her anxiety at bay than the most powerful antidepressant.

For two years her husband has been without work. Her own income has also been drastically depleted as a result of the recession. Together, they have been barely scraping by. Despite their struggles, she says she is excited to see what God has in store for them not *after* their trials but *through* their trials.

Her words buoyed me because I happened to be in a funk this morning, anxious about what was happening in the life of someone I love. She reminded me that God has made a promise we can count on. He will indeed rescue us. He will be a shield around us to protect us from the enemy.

No matter how hard life gets, keep resisting the devil, who will try to bring you down by whispering faithless, fearful words into your ears. Stop listening to him, but keep listening to the Lord, whose Word holds true no matter what or who is pulling you down.

Father, thank you for your timely, powerful Word. Help me to hold on to it, like a life raft in stormy seas, believing that you will use it to bring me safely ashore.

HIDING

How can I know all the sins lurking in my heart? Cleanse me from these hidden faults. Keep your servant from deliberate sins! Don't let them control me.

PSALM 19:12-13

If you're looking for peace, you might want to think twice about buying a rental property. I purchased a lovely (or so I thought) piece of real estate a few years ago. I was certain it would be a good investment. But there was one problem—my beautifully decorated, upscale condo smelled. The odor would come and go, and it was hard to pin down exactly where the smell was coming from. I hired plumbers to check out P-traps and toilet seals, furnace repair technicians to look for dead animals or improperly installed equipment. At one point, I was certain I had fixed the problem only to discover that the smell had returned full force. No amount of household deodorizer could cover it.

Everything visible had been checked. So the problem, I reasoned, must be lurking behind walls or beneath the floor. My youngest daughter suggested with a hint of a smile that perhaps a bad fairy was hiding somewhere, cutting wind. Hmmm . . . I hadn't thought of that.

Finally a plumber sent smoke bombs through the pipes and, lo and behold, smoke started billowing from the walls of the closet in the utility room. When the closet was ripped out, the plumber found the culprit—a pipe that had been improperly installed. Amazingly, it had escaped the notice of the builder and the city inspectors who signed off on the new construction. For four years it lay hidden behind the walls, spreading a noxious smell through the vents.

What's the point of this smelly story? Simply that hidden problems can steal our peace. When we allow sin and weakness to lurk in our hearts, they will sooner or later make their presence known. It's far better to deal with them openly and honestly. Otherwise, the Lord may need to lob a few smoke bombs our way in order to reveal the source of the problem so we can finally face it with his grace.

Father, you see through to the heart of every person. I ask you to reveal any hidden sins or weaknesses in my life. Help me to face these honestly and with hope, confident that you will stand by me and help me to change.

PEACE TAKES PRACTICE

He must become greater and greater, and I must become less and less. He has come from above and is greater than anyone else. We are of the earth, and we speak of earthly things, but he has come from heaven and is greater than anyone else.

JOHN 3:30-31

My daughter was playing tennis with friends. I watched as she and another player volleyed. Each was paired with a teammate who had rarely played before. In addition to missing balls, these beginners would make the usual mistakes, hitting at the wrong angle or with too much or too little force. Like many sports, tennis is all about controlling the ball, a skill that increases with practice.

The Christian life is like that sometimes. Many of us come to Christ unpracticed in the virtues that characterize the Lord we love. Then God calls us into the game, asking us to abide by the rules he put into play when he created the universe. At first our attempts to be like Jesus may feel awkward and difficult. Perhaps we've developed habits like cursing or feeling sorry for ourselves or telling half-truths or gossiping or giving in to feelings of rage and anger. Sometimes we stumble. But if we pick ourselves up and keep going, God's Spirit will work in us to unwind these problem behaviors and give us the grace to change. The more we practice the virtues, the more virtuous our lives may become.

As with the beginners in my daughter's foursome, it can help to be friends with those who are more experienced than we are. Mature Christians can become our mentors, encouraging and showing us what a life of virtue looks like. Ultimately, becoming more like Christ means enjoying more of the *shalom* he offers—healing, wholeness, and the blessing of good relationships. All are part of the peace he promises.

Lord, help me to become like Jesus so that with each year his likeness will increase in me. And as he becomes greater and greater and I become less and less, may his peace characterize my life.

THE PEACE OF CHASTITY

*Run from sexual sin! No other sin so clearly affects the body as this
one does. For sexual immorality is a sin against your own body. Don't
you realize that your body is the temple of the Holy Spirit?*

1 CORINTHIANS 6:18-19

Before committing his life to Christ, Saint Augustine once famously said,
"Give me chastity and continency, only not yet."[1] Though his honesty
may surprise us, few of us know what chastity really means. Contrary to popular belief, chastity is not synonymous with abstinence or celibacy. Like courage and kindness, chastity is a virtue. The chaste person is able to take his or
her sexual desires and order them according to the demands of love rather
than lust, which is chastity's opposite.

Writer Ronald Rolheiser explains it like this: "To be chaste is to experience people, things, places, entertainment, the phases of one's life, life's
opportunities, and sex in a way that does not violate them or ourselves.
Chastity means to experience things reverently, so that the experience of
them leaves both them and ourselves more, not less, integrated."[2] Because
each of us has been created in the image of Christ, we should respect and
revere ourselves and others. To treat people as objects for our pleasure is to
diminish and demean them. And to allow others to treat us that way is to
allow ourselves to be degraded.

Under this definition, married couples who are faithful to each other
can have sex and be chaste. Single people, on the other hand, are chaste
when they abstain from sex because that is appropriate to their state in life.
Chastity allows them to treat themselves and others with the dignity and
respect that Christ's love demands.

To put it in simpler terms, chastity is like a governor on an engine that
regulates its speed. Without it, the engine could accelerate to the point that
it is destroyed. Though chastity might sound odd and old-fashioned in our
sex-saturated society, it's a virtue that will restore God's peace in our lives.

*Lord, help me not to be controlled by my sexual desires but to
control them with the help of your Holy Spirit.*

July 5
TEMPERANCE

Do you like honey? Don't eat too much, or it will make you sick!
PROVERBS 25:16

If chastity is out of fashion, so is its cousin, temperance. If you're like me, the word *temperance* conjures visions of the temperance movement in the late-nineteenth and early-twentieth centuries. Though the movement was well intentioned, who can forget hatchet-wielding Carrie Nation, who was repeatedly arrested and fined for her habit of marching into saloons and smashing them up? The resourceful Carrie financed her activities by giving lectures to the public at which she sold souvenir hatchets for twenty-five cents apiece. Believing she was on a holy crusade, she described herself as "a bulldog running along at the feet of Jesus, barking at what He doesn't like."[3] Of course, not everyone appreciated her nonstop barking, as evidenced by the popular barroom slogan: "All Nations Welcome but Carrie."

Doesn't sound very peaceful, does it? Of course, that's not what I mean by temperance. Like chastity, temperance is often mistakenly linked with prudishness and narrow-mindedness. But in reality, temperance is a mark of strength. While chastity involves the ability to control one's sexual appetite, temperance involves the ability to control one's appetite for food and drink. Just as lust is the opposite of chastity, gluttony and drunkenness are the opposites of temperance. Who but a strong person is able to control her appetite?

This week I had dinner with family friends. One of the children ordered a meal large enough to feed four big-time wrestlers for four days straight (slight exaggeration). These supersized portions have become the norm at restaurants across the country. What are we to do? Stop going out to eat? Go on yet another diet? Have weight-loss surgery? One thing we can do is to ask God to help us grow in the old-fashioned virtue of temperance, which will produce in us not only greater health but more peace, because we will no longer be slaves to our appetites.

Lord, I want to enjoy life's blessings without overdoing it. Help me to be in charge of my appetite rather than letting it be in charge of me.

July 6
PEACE NEEDS A STRONG FOUNDATION

The LORD examines both the righteous and the wicked. He hates those who love violence. . . . The righteous LORD loves justice. The virtuous will see his face.

PSALM 11:5, 7

For peace to flourish, evil must be resisted. But how you resist can make all the difference. Take the temperance movement. Thankfully, not everyone adopted crusader Carrie Nation's rambunctious methodology. Many others chose peaceful ways to advance the fight against drunkenness and its attendant evils.

Concerned about the women and children who were impoverished by their husbands' drinking habits, one person chose a more thoughtful approach. Many saloons promoted free lunches for their patrons, counting on the fact that the cost of the food would be more than offset by the resulting alcohol sales. But what they didn't count on was a woman by the name of Amanda Way, an abolitionist and reformer who hailed from Kansas. Amanda had the temerity to organize poor families, making sure they showed up at the saloon at lunchtime. Taking their seats at the bar, they would eat up all the food.

Face-to-face with a group of hungry women and children, the saloon keepers could no longer ignore the way they were affecting their neighborhoods. Nor could the men who spent their paychecks at the bar enjoy themselves with impunity. Now they at least had to wonder whether they might encounter their own wives and children in the next lunch crew.[4]

Real peace is built on foundations of justice, and justice can be a costly struggle. As Christians, we are called to pursue it, not to shrink back or ignore the wrongs we see. We can't fight all the world's wrongs, of course, but we can do something. Securing the peace by establishing and maintaining justice takes thoughtfulness, persistence, wisdom, courage, generosity, and prayer. If we're serious about peace, we need to open our hearts to God, asking him what he wants us to do to uphold justice.

Father, give me a heart that loves justice and pursues peace. May there be just a little more peace in this world because of me.

PEACE IN SERVING

*Even the Son of Man came not to be served but to serve
others and to give his life as a ransom for many.*

MATTHEW 20:28

Sometimes we're clueless about what's good for us. We may, for instance, resist saving money when we think we have too little or refrain from exercising when we feel tired. But spending every last penny or making a habit of surrendering ourselves to the couch doesn't usually produce positive results. Similarly, we can be tempted to spin a little cocoon around ourselves whenever we become depressed, anxious, or sad. Though it's good to examine the issues that are troubling us, we can't allow them to suck us into a whirlpool of self-concern.

Several years ago Nancy Guthrie was approaching Mother's Day with the distressing realization that it would be the only one she would ever celebrate with her five-month-old baby, Hope, who suffered from a rare metabolic disorder. Determined to focus on the gift of her child rather than the sorrow she felt that her baby would not live long, Nancy began thinking of all the people she knew who had lost their mothers or their children, or who had never even been able to have children. And then she did something incredible:

"I made a list and went to the store to buy Mother's Day cards. . . . It is not easy to find a big selection of cards for men who've lost their mothers or mothers who've lost children, so I had to improvise. But I sent out a big stack of cards. . . . Early Mother's Day morning, I called a woman in my church who had buried her mother who died of breast cancer the month before. . . . Then at church that morning, I looked over and saw a woman with four small children whose husband had recently left her. I walked over and wished her happy Mother's Day, telling her that I thought she was an incredible mother to her children. It seemed to matter. There's something good that happens to me when I'm able to get my eyes off of my own pain and minister out of it to other people who are hurting."[5]

Taking the focus off ourselves when we are feeling down requires strength and grace. But doing so releases the power of love in us, a power that can bring peace even in the midst of the most difficult circumstances.

*Lord, help me to be sensitive to the sufferings of others. Give me the
grace to help even when I feel like I'm the one who needs help.*

FINANCIAL PEACE

*Let all that I am wait quietly before God, for my hope is in him. He alone
is my rock and my salvation, my fortress where I will not be shaken.*

PSALM 62:5-6

The Dow Jones Industrial Average just fell off a cliff again. Investors are panicking, wondering where to take refuge in these uncertain times. (When are they ever certain?) I'm sending up a prayer, asking the Lord to watch over my savings. No doubt millions of similar prayers are ascending to his throne along with mine.

The last time this happened, nearly three years ago, I, too, was in a panic. But having survived the worst of that downturn, I feel a bit calmer, determined not to head over the cliff along with all the other lemmings. Looking back at the last panic, it's clear that all my sleepless nights and anxious days failed to produce even one positive idea or outcome. None of it made my life any better. In fact, it made it much worse. It was only God in his good timing who made things better, helping me to get through.

Now, with the economy faltering again, I may have a chance for a do-over. How will I respond this time? News analysts say that people are still shell shocked by the last recession, making them more likely to panic and sell everything. But what if you experienced God caring for you and your family despite your losses? Wouldn't that make you even more likely to trust him this time around?

It's fine to pray that God will preserve our savings. But while we do that, let's also pray that, no matter what happens, we will remember this truth: God alone is our rock and our salvation. He is our fortress where we will not be shaken. Whether you're facing a financial panic or another kind of personal crisis in your life, remember this, and you will not be disappointed.

*Father, thank you for showing me your faithfulness. Help me
in this uncertain time to place my trust in you.*

TASTING THE PEACE GOD PROMISES

The wolf and the lamb will feed together. The lion will eat hay like a cow. But the snakes will eat dust. In those days no one will be hurt or destroyed on my holy mountain. I, the LORD, have spoken!

ISAIAH 65:25

A few weeks ago my children and I attended a church in which a photo of a lion and a lamb sitting peacefully together was projected onto a large screen at the front. Of course, the image had been Photoshopped, because no self-respecting lamb would be crazy enough to cozy up to a lion. But this image, which on the face of things seems absurd, captures one of God's greatest promises, when he will, he says, create peace between natural enemies, between those who eat and those who get eaten, between the haves and have-nots of this world.

As I looked at the image, I thought about my children, who had recently been fighting. What would life be like if they were always at peace? And what about their schools? What if there were no distinction between the "cool" kids and everybody else? Or what about their city? What if the folks from the "good" neighborhoods started partying with the folks from the "bad" neighborhoods? What if we all became friends? What would life feel like then?

And what about me? What about my own internal divisions? What would it be like to always be at peace with myself? No self-doubt, no recrimination, no regret, no saying one thing and doing another. My life would be peaceful because it would always align with God's ways.

For that matter, what would the whole world be like if it were perfectly at peace? God has promised to create a world we can barely imagine, a new heaven and a new earth. But imagine it we should. And long for it and pray for it as well. While we are doing that, let us continue to find joy in the peace that is already ours by virtue of what Christ has done for us.

Father, help me to taste the peace that you promise to create in the new heaven and the new earth. Give me zeal for your Kingdom and the courage and strength to do the things that promote peace.

July 10

REPAIRING THE WORLD

All nations will come to your light; mighty kings will come to see your radiance.

ISAIAH 60:3

We know that Jesus was a Jew, but how often do we reflect on the fact that our own faith springs from Jewish roots? Even a little familiarity with Judaism can yield rich insights. Take the Hebrew phrase *tikkun olam*, a rabbinic concept that has been around since at least the second century. It can be translated "repairing the world." But how does one go about repairing the world?

The Jewish people speak of being called "to perfect the world under God's sovereignty." Looking at their contributions to history, you would have to admit they have gone some way toward doing that. Many of the big ideas on which our own culture is founded are Jewish ideas—the sanctity of human life, absolute morality, the equality of all persons before the law, and many more.

"We were the people," Rabbi Jonathan Sacks says, "who were born in slavery to teach the world the meaning of freedom. We were the people who suffered homelessness to teach humanity the importance of every people having a home. We were the people who were the quintessential strangers to teach humanity that 'Thou shall not oppress the stranger' (Exodus 23:9). We were the people who walked through the valley of the shadow of death to teach humanity the sanctity of life. We were the people who were always small but yet survived to teach the world a people does not survive by might nor by strength but by My spirit, says G-d (Zechariah 4:6)."[6]

In terms of the Jewish duty to "repair the world," Sacks goes on to say that in our relativistic age, we must "teach people once again to hear the objective 'Thou shalt' and 'Thou shalt not.'"[7] And we must, he says, also teach them that *shalom* is found in God himself, the mighty one who is able to turn an enemy into a friend.

As Christians, we, too, are called to be repairers of the world, believing that our efforts will not be in vain but will come to fruition when Christ comes again.

Lord, your world has been ruptured by sin and marred by disobedience. Help us to repair it by heeding your call to spread the gospel and by remembering the command to act justly, to love mercy, and to walk humbly with you.

The LORD passed by, and a mighty windstorm hit the mountain. It was such a terrible blast that the rocks were torn loose, but the LORD was not in the wind. After the wind there was an earthquake, but the LORD was not in the earthquake. And after the earthquake there was a fire, but the LORD was not in the fire. And after the fire there was the sound of a gentle whisper. When Elijah heard it, he wrapped his face in his cloak and went out and stood at the entrance of the cave.

1 KINGS 19:11-13

We live in a house with four floors of living and office space. Though running up and down stairs is great for the body, sometimes the body just doesn't want to be bothered with them. So instead we shout up the stairs: "Time for homework." "Mom, I'm leaving." "Dinner is ready." "Can I take the dog for a walk?" You get the idea. Without an intercom, my children and I sometimes resort to hollering at each other in order to communicate.

But God rarely hollers. Take prayer. When is the last time God shouted at you to sit down and pray right now—or else? Even though prayer is essential to living a vital Christian faith, it may also be the first thing to slip from your schedule. Everything else seems more urgent. The children are late for school. Your husband is sick. The toilet overflowed again. Your boss wants that report right now. And it's only eight o'clock in the morning. In the midst of a hectic life, how can you drop everything and pray? One thing you can do is learn how to pray continually, as Paul advised, saying, "Never stop praying. Be thankful in all circumstances, for this is God's will for you who belong to Christ Jesus" (1 Thessalonians 5:17-18).

Even if you don't have time to sit down and pray for a half hour each morning, you can pray on the go: "Lord, please heal my husband." "Let me be your servant today." "Give me wisdom for handling that report." "Thank you for blue skies and a family that loves me." Simple prayers can help orient you to the Father who loves you rather than to your troubles. Once the clamor finally subsides, consider what you can do to streamline your life so you can find time to read God's Word and listen for his voice.

Lord, I want to spend time growing in my relationship with you. Please help me to make prayer a significant and regular part of my life.

PEACE EVERYWHERE

The eyes of the LORD search the whole earth in order to strengthen those whose hearts are fully committed to him.

2 CHRONICLES 16:9

I noticed him as I was waiting in the checkout line, trying to quell my impatience—the cashier on the right. At first glance, he seemed ordinary—a young man working behind the register at an electronics store. But then I saw his lips slide back, not in a smile but in a grimace. It happened again. And then another time. Realizing this was not some fit of pique but a glitch in physiology, I looked away. Then I sent up a quick prayer, asking God to bless him. When it was time for me to step up to the register, I saw something else. The man's body was disproportionate. From the chest up he was of average size, but his legs looked like Humpty Dumpty's. Whether he had lost weight through dieting, surgery, or illness, I wasn't sure. I just kept praying, asking God to help and heal him. And then, purchase completed, I walked out of the store.

God offers us the opportunity to see others—to recognize their pain, their happiness, their need. But so often I am preoccupied by my own concerns, wondering, for instance, how long I will have to wait in line and whether I will have time for one more errand. Consequently I miss the opportunity God gives to share his peace with others.

As women, we need to remember that we are created in the image of the God whom Isaiah called *Sar Shalom*, or "Prince of Peace" (9:6). We have the extraordinary privilege of being his ambassadors in the world, reflecting his character to those we meet through kind words, listening ears, and continual prayer.

Join me today in asking God to open your heart to the opportunities he brings. Pray for the grace to take your eyes off yourself so your eyes can be on others. And remember that God is searching the whole earth for a woman like you whose heart is fully committed to him. That's the woman he will strengthen and bless.

Lord, help me to notice others and to listen as your Spirit guides my response to them. Let me be an ambassador of peace, I pray.

July 13
DEALING WITH CONFLICT

A servant of the Lord must not quarrel but must be kind to everyone.
2 TIMOTHY 2:24

How should we handle the conflicts that come our way? You've probably heard the business buzzword "best practices," a phrase used to describe the best methods for accomplishing any given task. Are there best practices when it comes to dealing with the inevitable conflicts that arise in our lives?

Let me begin by describing a couple of worst practices. The first is to duck out and pretend there's no problem. All of us have preferred escape routes: eating, shopping, engaging in social media, taking a walk. Some are helpful as cool-off strategies that can help us calm down and gain perspective. But as formulas for resolving conflicts, they fail miserably. In the end, escapism is all about me. It does nothing to solve the problem.

Another worst practice is blaming others, putting them on the defense for their faults and weaknesses. Afraid, angry, or frustrated, we lash out, escalating the conflict in the process. If we can't bring ourselves to confront the person directly, we may displace the blame by kicking the cat (or the dog), yelling at the children, or even castigating ourselves, because somebody has got to take the blame. Like escapism, blame is also all about me.

The most effective strategy for bringing peace to a personal conflict is neither to escape nor to attack but to stand still in the midst of it and allow ourselves to feel the pain. The point is to feel not only our own pain but also the pain or perspective of the other person. This takes grit. But with practice and grace and prayer, we can begin to imagine what the other person might be thinking and feeling. We can also consider the effect our words and actions may have. We don't have to conclude the other person is right and we are wrong, but we do have to be open to his or her perspective. This best-practice strategy puts the focus on *us* rather than on *me*.

If two people in a conflict can learn to do this for each other, it will be far easier to resolve the conflict. Even if you are the only one who is willing to face things in this way, you will find it can be a transformative process, allowing you to experience more of God's peace.

Lord, help me to step back and consider the other person's point of view. Keep me from giving in to the temptation of casting him or her in the most negative light possible and help me to see the other person as you do.

July 14

THE GOOD THING ABOUT CONFLICT

*All of us who have had that veil removed can see and reflect the glory
of the Lord. And the Lord—who is the Spirit—makes us more and
more like him as we are changed into his glorious image.*

2 CORINTHIANS 3:18

The other day, my thin-as-a-rail daughter yelled in alarm, "Mom, I'm fat!"
When I turned to look, I saw that she was standing in front of glass sliders, looking at her reflected image. I walked over and stood beside her. Sure enough, the glass compressed my image, making me appear a foot shorter and fifty pounds heavier. I stepped away in relief, feeling as though I had just looked at myself in a fun-house mirror.

Although most of us are familiar with how certain kinds of mirrors can create false images, I wonder how many of us are aware that the image we project to ourselves about ourselves can also be false. Sometimes, instead of creating negative images, our inner mirrors can create images that are all too flattering, hiding personality defects or weaknesses from the very person who most needs to see them.

What do I mean by that? Before I had children, I thought I was a nicer, kinder, wiser, gentler person than I really am. It wasn't hard to be nice when I wasn't under the pressure of caring for little ones who often did not want to do what their mother thought they should. Plus there was the added pressure of protecting and providing for them. Being a mother has given me a more accurate picture of my spiritual maturity, or lack of it.

Ken Sande, the author of *The Peacemaker*, makes a similar point by saying that "God may also use conflict to expose sinful attitudes and habits in your life. Conflict is especially effective in breaking down appearances and revealing stubborn pride, a bitter and unforgiving heart, or a critical tongue."[8] Though it's not much fun to see ourselves, warts and all, it's an essential part of following Christ. Why? Because he doesn't just barge in and make us perfect once we belong to him. He requires our permission to continue to shape and mold us. If we want to be women whose lives reflect the beauty and peace of God, we have to be willing to reflect his character as well.

*Lord, thank you for loving me despite my many imperfections. Because
of your love, I have the courage and confidence to face my weaknesses,
believing you are shaping me toward glory and not toward defeat.*

TAKING SIDES

"I pray that they will all be one, just as you and I are one—as you are in me, Father, and I am in you. And may they be in us so that the world will believe you sent me.

JOHN 17:21

When I was in graduate school, I joined a Christian community filled with people who were passionate about their faith. Though I learned a great deal, there were inevitable difficulties. One thing my experience of community life taught me was how fallible even the best-intentioned Christians can be.

I recall one of the leaders making the point that whenever there's a disagreement, it's important not to adopt another person's offense. In other words, if Sarah and Lisa disagree on something and begin arguing, don't line up behind Sarah and then feel stung by anything Lisa might say to Sarah. Let them have their disagreement, but don't get sucked in. Sadly, that is exactly what happened to the community. Two of the leaders began to see things quite differently. Or perhaps their disagreements had been there all along and had finally bubbled to the surface. What had started out as a tug-of-war between two individuals quickly morphed into a great, long conga line of people pulling and tugging on the rope until there was so much disagreement that the community finally split apart. Ironically, one of the hallmarks of the community had been its commitment to work toward greater Christian unity.

This dynamic of divisiveness is not uncommon in churches, in the workplace, and with families and friends. Two people argue, and others are drawn into the conflict. A married couple divorces, and friends and family take sides. Siblings stop speaking to each other, and the family is torn.

Of course, there are times when we have to take sides—when something of crucial importance is at stake. But there are many other situations in which adding our two cents to an argument that is already underway will only make things worse.

Someone once said that even Jesus had one prayer that remained unanswered. It was his prayer for unity. Let's do what we can to help that prayer be realized by refusing to spread the division that comes from getting sucked into someone else's argument.

Lord, give me the wisdom to know how to handle myself in the midst of a disagreement, mindful of your prayer that we would all be one even as you and the Father are one.

THE DEVIL, YOU SAY!

We are not fighting against flesh-and-blood enemies, but against evil rulers and authorities of the unseen world, against mighty powers in this dark world, and against evil spirits in the heavenly places.

EPHESIANS 6:12

A few years ago I was in the midst of negotiating a deal for a client regarding a children's book she wanted to write. We made the deal, and she began writing. Once the contract was signed, the publisher began looking for an illustrator. The trouble was, the illustrator they picked would have ruined the project, at least in our judgment. His drawings were dark and depressing, not the thing for communicating God's love to children. But the publisher wasn't willing to budge. I won't bore you with the details of how we resolved the issue, but I will tell you the way to a solution was long and difficult and at one point, things got a bit acrimonious.

As the process unfolded, I noticed a lot of distrust seeping into the relationships of those involved. It happened so regularly and with such force that I began to wonder if something more was afoot. Sensing that this particular book had the potential to transform the lives of countless children, I began to wonder whether Satan might be trying to derail it.

I shared my suspicions with the people I was working with, and we began to pray that God would protect the discussions that were going on in order to resolve the issue. Eventually another artist was assigned to the project, and the publication moved forward. There were more disruptions along the way. But when the book finally came out, it was an instant bestseller, adopted by churches across the country and around the world, making its way into the hearts of children and the parents who read it to them.

Though I don't believe demons are squatting behind every bush, I do think they are more active than some of us might imagine, intent on subverting God's work in the world. Let's not be naive to their influence. Instead, let us seek God for his wisdom, power, and discernment to do the things he's asked us to do.

God, when I encounter trouble, please give me the discernment to know who the real enemy is. Give me wisdom and strength to engage in spiritual battle when necessary.

LITTLE JUDGMENTS

Do not judge others.

MATTHEW 7:1

I was delighted to note that there were a couple of open parking spots in the small lot behind the medical building. Swinging the steering wheel to position the car for the closest spot, I realized the space was partially blocked. A heavyset woman was standing by the adjacent van with the driver's door wide open. She didn't look like she was going anywhere soon, so I put the car into reverse, thinking to myself how thoughtless some people can be, just standing there taking up space when other people are trying to park.

After parking the car in another spot, I walked into the building to pick up my daughter from her appointment and then came back out to the lot. The woman was still standing by her car. Before we left, I glanced in her direction again. Something didn't look right. When I asked if she needed help, I realized she was close to tears. She had been trying—God knows how long—to climb into her van, but her right hip was full of bursitis and she couldn't lift her leg high enough to get her bulky frame into the driver's seat. She had been too embarrassed to ask for help even though she was distressed and in a lot of pain. How, she wondered, was she ever going to get into her car and get home? Then she mentioned that she had just seen her doctor, whose office was in the medical building I had just left. With her permission, I alerted his nurses and they came out to help.

I felt sorry for her, aware of how distressing her situation must be. But I was glad that I had been able to render a small service. Afterward, I reflected on how quickly I had concluded that the woman was rude when she had actually been afraid and in pain. What if I had just driven off with my original judgment intact?

My experience that day made me wonder how often I make snap judgments that bear no resemblance to reality. Such judgments prevent us from noticing the troubles of others. They can create a cloud of negativity rather than an environment where peace can flourish.

Lord, help me to become aware of all the little judgments I make throughout the day. When I am tempted to draw negative conclusions, put a check on my spirit. Help me to ask myself if I really know everything I need to know about people— like what's on their minds and in their hearts—to see them accurately.

The thief's purpose is to steal. . . . My purpose is to give them a rich and satisfying life.

JOHN 10:10

I'm not much of a gardener, but I do have a few tomato plants in the backyard. Trouble is, my luscious tomatoes have been disappearing at an alarming rate. I finally realized who the culprit was when, one day, the thief stepped brazenly into our yard. I watched as he reached out a greedy hand, grabbed a single, ripe tomato and then turned quickly to make an escape. Yelling at him to "drop that right now!" made no difference whatsoever. He simply scampered up the nearest tree with his treasure intact. If he could have managed it, I'm sure he would have turned around, stuck out his tongue, given me the raspberries, and then chortled out a victory cry.

Searching for a solution online, I found that this kind of thievery is common among the mischievous creatures we call squirrels. The problem was what to do about it. Here's what one fed-up gardener had to say: "I've tried the water bowl, cayenne pepper on the ground, garlic and pepper sprayed on tomatoes, CDs tied to supports, and even hot sauce injected into tomatoes. They really enjoyed the injected ones, thought it was salsa."[9]

Those thieving squirrels remind me of how easy it is to lose many of the other things we value—things like peace, which can be snatched from us in an instant. Perhaps it's time we took a stand against the most common culprits, especially those we *can* do something about. Here's my list:

Filling my schedule too full
Buying too much stuff (lots of stuff takes lots of time to care for it)
Not exercising
Not praying
Listening to the lies of the enemy

The last, of course, is the most insidious. Satan has a gift for telling plausible lies, which will fill you with doubt and anxiety if you listen to them. Though you can't stop him from lying, you have the power to reduce his audience by one. Whatever you do today, refuse to give in to his deceptions. Listen instead to the voice of the Lord who loves you.

Father, I know what I need to do. Give me the grace to do it.

God said, "Let us make human beings in our image, to be like us. They
will reign over the fish in the sea, the birds in the sky, the livestock,
all the wild animals on the earth, and the small animals."

GENESIS 1:26

Michael Fishbach loves photographing whales. So it seems fitting that he spent Valentine's Day with family and friends whale watching in the beautiful Sea of Cortez. The adventure began when he spotted what appeared to be a dead humpback whale floating in the water. Coming in for a closer look, he realized it was entangled in a nylon gill net. Suddenly the whale exhaled, loud and clear, through its blowhole. Deciding to investigate, Michael jumped into the water. "As I swam alongside the animal," he said, "our eyes met. There were no words we could share, but I wanted to let the whale know that we were there to help. . . . The sight of this large and beautiful creature trapped and so close to death was almost overwhelming," he said.[10] Though it was dangerous to be close to a young whale in distress, Michael and two friends spent the next hour cutting away at the net with a small knife, hoping to free the animal before it drowned.

Finally, with one last slash of the net, the whale slipped free, and everyone in the boat cheered. Then, for a full hour, the whale provided them with a nonstop display of joy. Michael watched in awe, counting at least forty breaches as well as several tail lobs, tail slaps, and pectoral fin slaps.

The whole experience was captured on video. As the whale performs her incredible display, a young girl can be heard saying, "I know what she is doing. She is showing us that she is free."

To that a woman replies, "I think she is showing us a thank you dance."[11]

Whether the whale was saying thank you or simply celebrating being alive, God's promise of peace is meant for all of creation. I have often wondered whether we underrate the feelings and intelligence of other animals. Perhaps doing so makes it easier to disregard their sufferings. But God has given us the incredible privilege of being stewards of his creation. Let's fulfill that role reverently and with wisdom. As we do, we can be confident that God's peace will spread throughout the world he has made.

Lord, thank you for the gift of creation and for the privilege of being your
steward. Help me to exercise my responsibility wisely and well.

July 20
STANDING FIRM

If you want me to protect you, you must learn to believe what I say.
ISAIAH 7:9 (TLB)

Imagine that you are sound asleep, when suddenly you're woken by a large blast. You rush outside, thinking that a neighboring house has just exploded. But everyone insists that the noise came from inside your house. Rushing back in, you discover the source. A hole thirty-two inches wide and forty feet deep has just opened up in the floor. A little bigger, and your body might be lying mangled at the bottom of it, because the gaping hole happens to be located beneath your bed!

Sound unlikely? It happened to Innocenta Hernandez, who lives in a neighborhood just north of Guatemala City.[12] Built on volcanic deposits, this area of the country is particularly prone to sinkholes. In 2010, a giant sinkhole swallowed a three-story building and a nearby home. The trouble with sinkholes, of course, is that although they often form gradually, they can open up suddenly, with disastrous results.

Listen to what God said more than 2,500 years ago to a man who was standing over a spiritual sinkhole, though he didn't know it. The prophet Isaiah delivered this word to King Ahaz of Judah: "If you do not stand firm in your faith, you will not stand at all" (7:9, NIV). A few sentences earlier, Isaiah noted that "the hearts of the king and his people trembled with fear, like trees shaking in a storm" (7:2). But Isaiah went on to assure the king that he had nothing to fear from his enemies because God would soon act. Unfortunately, Ahaz spurned the message, allying himself not to God but to a foreign power, which eventually led to disastrous consequences for his people.

Like Ahaz, each of us will face challenges that seem too big to handle. Confronted by them, we may even begin to tremble like trees in a storm. When that happens, let's move away from the sinkhole of fear and doubt and take our stand on firmer ground.

Lord, when I am afraid, remind me that your Word is true and that you are the rock on which I stand. Help me to stand firm because my faith is grounded in you.

July 21

UP CLOSE

Give, and you will receive. Your gift will return to you in full—pressed down, shaken together to make room for more, running over, and poured into your lap.

LUKE 6:38

People were packed tight, elbowing for a place on the truck headed to Port-au-Prince. Chickens and bags of produce were crammed in alongside the human cargo. Yet another hurricane had struck Haiti, and people were talking about the worst-hit area, a city called Gonaïves, where two thousand people had died.

"I'm from Gonaïves," a young man spoke up. All eyes turned quickly to him, taking in the ragged shirt, the hair embedded with straw. He spoke of broken bodies lying in the street and of the struggle to find food and water. There were people still stranded on rooftops, homes filled with nothing but mud. "These clothes," he said, "I've been wearing them since last Saturday" (eight days previous).

As he talked, a middle-aged man reached into a plastic bag and handed him a white polo shirt. Then someone else gave him a T-shirt. Then another person offered a pair of green shorts, and another gave a comb, and someone else handed him a bar of soap. Then a woman held out a crumpled ten-goud bill (about 25 cents) and started saying, "Just give what you can. Five goud, ten goud, fifty goud, anything you can give to help him out." She soon had a fist full of bills to hand to the young man, who by then was crying.

Before he could find the words to respond, they told him not to worry. "You didn't even ask for anything; we just want to give. We're all Gonaïvians now."[13]

Everyone on that truck was poor. Kent Annan, author of *Following Jesus through the Eye of the Needle*, observes, "Each person in the back of this truck must in some way battle, throw elbows, squeeze for what she or he needs. From a distance via the news, you wonder how anybody makes it. Up close you wonder too, but less so because you see the little things. You see the person beside you pass along ten gouds, a shirt, a bar of soap."[14]

The story makes me think of my own "up close" moments. What are the needs of the people around me? I want to notice them and give what I can. For it's often in the up-close spaces where God can most reveal his love.

Father, I want to spread your shalom. Help me to show others your peace today.

DON'T LET EVIL GET THE BEST OF YOU

Don't let evil conquer you, but conquer evil by doing good.

ROMANS 12:21

Luci is really strong!" My daughter's karate instructor sounded surprised, perhaps because with her slight frame and sweet demeanor, Luci is nobody's idea of a bruiser.

Once we were in the car, Luci turned to me and said, "Mom, Lisa thinks I'm strong. Do you think I am?"

"Yes, honey. Remember when we were playing around in the kitchen last night and I was trying to fake some karate moves and you broke my hold? I couldn't believe how strong you were." She laughed, joyous at learning this new fact about herself.

I think we can make the same mistake in reverse when it comes to the biggest disrupter of peace in the world—the power of evil. I don't mean to imply that evil isn't powerful, only that it is not as strong as we think it is. Paul told the Romans, who would soon suffer persecution, that they could not merely *resist* evil but *overcome* it. How? By doing good.

Miroslav Volf comments that "to triumph fully, evil needs two victories, not one. The first victory happens when an evil deed is perpetrated; the second victory, when evil is returned. After the first victory, evil would die if the second victory did not infuse it with new life."[15] In the world, we see this when one tribe or group of people commits an atrocity and the victims respond with retribution. The same cycle happens on an individual level, close to home. A husband lashes out, and his wife gives it back to him in spades. A child is disrespectful, and her mother goes on a rant about how vile and worthless her daughter is.

It takes strength to refrain from responding to evil with evil, but even greater strength to respond to it by doing good. If we want to enjoy God's peace, we need to consider how we respond to the sins of others. Today let's determine that instead of granting evil a second victory, we will deal it a decisive defeat.

Lord, give me your strength to do what might otherwise be impossible for me—responding to those who hurt me by doing good and not evil.

CIRCUIT BREAKERS

Don't you realize that your body is the temple of the Holy Spirit, who lives in you and was given to you by God?... You must honor God with your body.

1 CORINTHIANS 6:19-20

Several years ago, when I was having the attic remodeled into an office, the carpenter doing the work discovered two inscriptions. One was on the brick chimney that transects the space. The other was on two-by-fours that had been hidden behind a wall of bead board. While the second one was signed by the builder, both inscriptions indicated that construction on the house had begun in July 1925.

Old houses are famous for their charm, even though living in them is not always a charming experience. Sometimes simple activities remind you of just how old they are. Take ironing, for instance. Whenever I forget to turn off the TV or the ceiling fan when plugging in the iron in an upstairs bedroom, the circuit breaker trips, shutting off the power. Though I think of it as an inconvenient interruption, the circuit breakers are providing an invaluable service, preventing me from overloading the electrical system, risking fire or even electrocution.

Likewise, in our own lives, God has placed natural circuit breakers that can alert us to the fact that we are on overload. Say, for instance, you are trying to get ahead at work and putting in loads of overtime. Or say you can't give no for an answer when anyone asks you to do something. Or say you are spending every minute ferrying your children to activities so they won't miss out. Eventually, your body will attempt to get you to slow down. Natural circuit breakers come in many forms, including headaches, fatigue, irritability, illness, and weight gain. When these things begin to manifest, resist the temptation to brush them off as inconvenient interruptions. Instead, take the time to examine your life prayerfully, asking God to show you if your priorities are his priorities. If you sense the need to make course corrections, don't delay. Your peace depends on paying attention to the natural circuit breakers that operate in every human life.

Lord, help me to recognize and live by my limitations. I don't want to be swept along by busyness just because the world I live in is so frantic. Instead, help me to order my life according to your priorities.

UMPIRES

*Let the peace that comes from Christ rule in your hearts. For as
members of one body you are called to live in peace.*

Colossians 3:15

If first words have anything to do with a child's destiny, then my youngest
daughter, Luci, is destined for a career in sports. Despite my eagerness to
hear her baby lips finally form the word *mama*, what came out first was the
word *ball*. To this day Luci is fascinated by balls. Footballs, basketballs, soft-
balls, baseballs, volleyballs, soccer balls. If it bounces, she wants it.

Last year, Luci played on her middle-school basketball team for the
first time. I loved watching the players improve as the season progressed.
Though most of the games were marked by good sportsmanship, there was
an occasional lapse. During one of the games, a player on the opposing team
couldn't keep her hands off her opponents. I watched in consternation as she
pushed, shoved, and elbowed my daughter at every opportunity. Surprisingly,
the referees never called it. After the game, Luci's coach promised to file a
complaint against the referees who had worked the game. Because of their
inaction, a game that should have been safe and fun was anything but.

Though I am not a dyed-in-the-wool sports fan, I know enough
to realize that a good referee or umpire can help make or break a game.
With that in mind, let's consider the umpire that Paul chose to speak of in
Colossians 3:15. Reminding the early Christians of the importance of maintaining unity, he said, "Let the peace that comes from Christ rule in your
hearts." The word *rule* in this verse comes from the Greek word *brabeuo*, which
refers not to the rule of a king but to the work an umpire does at a game.
With that in mind, you could paraphrase the verse like this: "Let the peace
that comes from Christ act as an umpire in your hearts." In other words, let
it make the call so that whenever you have a difference with another believer,
Christ's peace will have the last, definitive word.

*Lord, I want your peace to characterize all my relationships, especially with
those who belong to you. When there are disagreements, help me find a way
through them in a way that does not destroy the peace but preserves it.*

July 25
HIDING THE WORD

I have hidden your word in my heart, that I might not sin against you.

PSALM 119:11

Several years ago I picked up an all-weather jacket at a local thrift shop. The coat was in great condition. Before washing it, however, I went through all the pockets to make certain the previous owner hadn't left anything behind. The search yielded a five-dollar bill tucked away in an inside zippered pocket. Since I had only paid two dollars for the jacket, my thrift-shop purchase had netted a 150 percent profit.

Like the money tucked into the pocket of my jacket, God's Word hidden in your heart can net an enormous return on investment. But how exactly do you hide his Word? One way is through simple memorization. If you're like me, however, you might find that a challenge. I recall how amazed I was to learn that a friend had committed entire books of the Bible to memory while I struggled to memorize one short psalm. Once I made the mistake of remarking to an elderly woman that I was too old to memorize Scripture. "Nonsense!" she shot back. "I didn't start memorizing Bible passages until I was sixty-five!" Since she knew an awful lot of them by heart, my handy excuse was quickly demolished.

Surely, even the least mnemonically gifted among us (that's me) can memorize a few Scripture passages. Here are a couple from Psalms to get you started. Think of them as little bullet prayers to put in your arsenal. Commit them to memory, and then start shooting them whenever you feel assailed by anxious, doubting thoughts.

The LORD is my strength and shield. I trust him with all my heart. He helps me, and my heart is filled with joy. (28:7)

Many sorrows come to the wicked, but unfailing love surrounds those who trust the LORD. (32:10)

If you stock your heart with the Word of God, you will find yourself netting great dividends, both now and in the future, helping you to experience more of his peace.

Lord, your Word is alive. Help me to hide it in my heart so that I might be guided by it.

WHY LIVING IN THE FUTURE
DOESN'T WORK

*Don't worry about tomorrow, for tomorrow will bring its own
worries. Today's trouble is enough for today.*

MATTHEW 6:34

Have you ever tried living in the future? I have, and I can tell you it's a flat-out failure. As a strategy for escaping or even resolving present problems, it simply doesn't work.

Audrey Niffenegger is the author of a fascinating love story, entitled *The Time Traveler's Wife*. Like all good love stories, the main characters, Henry and Clare, have to prove their love despite all obstacles. In their case, the most nettlesome obstacle is Henry's odd habit of slipping in and out of time. To complicate matters, this strange phenomenon occurs without warning and without his permission. Though such a condition would be obstacle enough for any relationship, things are made more difficult by the quirky fact that whenever Henry time travels, he does so without clothes. Whenever he arrives in his new time zone, which may be many years in the future, he has to find a way to adjust to his altered circumstances while looking for creative ways to clothe and provide for himself. (Remember, naked men don't carry wallets.) Over and over, he arrives at his destination totally unprepared to deal with it.

This wonderfully strange story is a great parable for understanding why living in the future simply doesn't work. We don't have the resources for dealing with it. For one thing, we're not yet the people we will be. Even if we had the ability to time travel, we might be unnerved by future events, little realizing that God intends to use the intervening years to make us into the kind of people who can handle them.

Plus, unlike Henry, our anxiety about what might happen will propel us into a false future, one that likely will never happen. That leaves us tilting at windmills, wasting precious energy that could better be spent on living fully in the present moment, which may indeed provide us with a better future.

By making the case that we can't live in the future, I'm not saying we shouldn't plan for the future in practical ways. I am only making the point that we can't spend our best energies on worrying about what might or might not happen. That's a recipe not for peace but for insomnia.

Lord, help me to greet the present with faith and trust. Thank you for giving me enough strength to deal with today's troubles. Give me the grace to entrust the future to you.

July 27

A MERRY HEART

A cheerful heart is good medicine, but a broken spirit saps a person's strength.

PROVERBS 17:22

My friend Leslie is a school social worker. On a recent visit to a gift shop, she picked up a tongue-in-cheek guide to self-therapy, printed on a pad of tear sheets. The idea is to use each sheet to record clinical notes during a do-it-yourself therapy session. The first heading is "Psycho Drama of the Moment." Underneath it are lines to record your notes. Then comes the heading "How Do I Feel about It?" followed by "How Do I Really Feel about It?" The next heading is "This Problem Likely Stems From":

mother	early weaning
father	original sin
sex	basic unlovability
no sex	bad luck

I love the part about "Psycho Drama of the Moment" because if I'm not having one, it seems that one of my children is. That's when emotions can really fly. At times, all of us find ourselves with people who are reacting in ways that are anything but peaceful. How can we keep our own emotions in check and avoid becoming part of a great big chain reaction of emotional instability?

In chemistry, a stabilizer is a chemical that inhibits a reaction that would otherwise occur between two or more chemicals. I like to think that humor can sometimes act as an emotional stabilizer, helping to restore a sense of equilibrium. No doubt all of us will experience our share of psycho dramas, many of which will not look half as bad in retrospect. With that in mind, let's not miss the opportunity to step back and laugh at ourselves whenever the opportunity arises, mindful of Proverbs 17:22, which says in the King James Version, "A merry heart doeth good like a medicine: but a broken spirit drieth the bones." Let's resolve today not to allow doom and gloom scenarios, our own or others', to break our spirits and dry up our bones.

Lord, help me to lighten up and stop taking myself and others so seriously. Give me the perspective that comes from cultivating a cheerful heart.

IMAGE IS EVERYTHING

So God created human beings in his own image. In the image of God
he created them; male and female he created them.

GENESIS 1:27

The year 1960 was a watershed for political campaigns because it was the year radio lost out to television. In what has become known as the Great Debate, Vice President Richard Nixon's deep, strong voice carried well over radio. Listeners were sure he had won. But the majority of the seventy million people who had watched the first-ever televised presidential debate named Senator John Kennedy of Massachusetts the hands-down winner. Why the difference?

Nixon had entered the debate exhausted and underweight after a two-week stay in the hospital for a serious knee injury and a hectic campaign schedule to make up for lost time. Arriving at the debate in an ill-fitting shirt tucked into grey suit pants and a jacket, he appeared bland and sickly against the gray background. He also made the mistake of refusing makeup, with the result that he looked sweaty and unshaven on camera. It didn't help that viewers could see him wiping the sweat from his forehead.

By contrast, Kennedy's navy suit looked crisp against the gray backdrop. Well-rested, tanned, and perfectly groomed, wearing makeup to cover up any imperfections, he appeared the picture of health and vitality. The influence of that one debate on the election was enormous. From then on, candidates and their campaigns have paid enormous attention to the image they project.

As Christians, we, too, should be concerned about our image. I'm not saying we should spend time and energy making superficial changes in order to impress people. On the contrary. The kind of changes we are called to make go much deeper and take more personal investment. They can only be made as we cooperate with the work of the Holy Spirit. Remember that *shalom* means wholeness. As we become like Christ, we become whole. No longer suffering from as many interior and exterior divisions, we can more readily reflect God's image in the world around us. Instead of being Christians whose woundedness and sinfulness alienate others, we can become people whose peace and wholeness draw others to Christ.

Father, make me whole, not just for my sake but so I can complete the mission you have for me—representing you here on earth in a way that brings you glory and not disgrace.

IF IT DOESN'T WORK, STOP IT!

Let God transform you into a new person by changing the way you think.
ROMANS 12:2

I magine that you have made it your goal to get butterflies to fly in forma-tion. How beautiful it would be if they could fly together like a flock of birds. You begin modestly, attempting to get one butterfly to fly in a straight line. Enticing it with nectar seems to work, so you try it with a few more butterflies. You pick the most successful of these and attempt to get them to fly in a straight line together. But as soon as you release your star pupils, everything devolves into chaos, with butterflies flying in every direction. Still, you're not willing to give up because you can envision how great it would be if they could only learn what you're trying to teach them. Every day you perform the same trials with the same frustrating results. After a while, you find yourself disliking the creatures you once cherished because these pesky insects won't do what you want them to no matter how hard you try.

The point of this far-fetched example is that our efforts to control cir-cumstances and people are often as misguided as the scenario I've outlined. We want children to behave perfectly, employees to perform flawlessly, and circumstances to unfold as we think they should. But our oversized efforts at control produce the same frustrating results. Perhaps it's time to realize that if something is not working, it may be time to stop doing it.

According to Edwin Friedman, who is associated with family sys-tems therapy, the most effective leaders focus on managing themselves in the group rather than on focusing on how to manage the group itself. Such leaders strengthen the organization by staying connected to others without allowing themselves to be sucked into the anxious, emotional processes that often swirl around them. By doing this, they are able to lead from the inside rather than by trying to coerce others from the outside.

If you feel chronically frustrated at home or at work, ask yourself whether you may be trying to exert a level of control that is unhealthy and unwise. If the answer is maybe or yes, try redirecting your energy, asking God to show you how to manage yourself in the midst of challenging people.

*Lord, help me to stop doing things that don't work. Instead, give me
the grace to grow in maturity so I can also grow in peace.*

THE NEED TO BE LOVED

May the God of peace . . . equip you with all you need for doing his will. May he produce in you, through the power of Jesus Christ, every good thing that is pleasing to him.

HEBREWS 13:20-21

One reason dogs make such great pets is that they have a no-holds-barred approach to love. Whenever I come home, my dog, Kallie, greets me as though I'm the best thing that's ever happened to her. A more grateful, adoring dog you will not meet. She follows me around the house and insists on sleeping under my bed at night, just to be close to me. If dogs were capable of sinning, I'm sure their most common failing, more common even than shredding slippers or chasing cats, would be the sin of idol worship.

Of course, dogs don't worship people because we're so wonderful but because we have purposely bred traits of affection and loyalty into them. While that kind of relationship works well between dogs and humans, it's a little over the top in our relationships with people. And most of us don't expect or want that.

But some of us fall into the trap of craving the kind of universal love and acceptance that only exists between a boy and his dog. We can't stand the thought that someone might not like us, so we do everything in our power to be accepted, wearing masks and telling half-truths when whole truths are required. Not wanting to rock the boat, we do our best to avoid conflict. But such behaviors don't guarantee smooth sailing. Motivated by fear and not love, they lack the creative energy that is needed for finding real solutions to real problems.

Jesus was never one to smooth things over. Read the Gospels carefully and you will find the one we call the Prince of Peace more often disturbed the peace, speaking the truth when truth was called for. He did this because he had not come to bring a superficial brand of peace; he came to bring true *shalom*. As women who belong to him, we are called to have integrity, doing what is right regardless of what others may think. We need to aim at real peace, not the counterfeit kind that keeps us from experiencing all that God has for us.

Lord, give me the courage to be who you are calling me to be.
I want to please you first in everything I do.

July 31
TAKE CARE OF YOURSELF

I myself will tend my sheep and give them a place to lie down in peace.

EZEKIEL 34:15

What sinister condition can be responsible for the following disorders: high blood pressure, irritability, confusion, headache, memory lapse, fatigue, weight gain, aching muscles, hallucinations, depression, and death? If you guessed sleep deprivation, you would be right. Sleep is a need as basic as food and water. Getting by on less and less is a recipe for sickness, stress, and unhappiness. Why, then, do so few of us put a high enough priority on getting the sleep we need?

I have a friend who frequently nods off during social events. She isn't bored and doesn't suffer from narcolepsy. It's just that she has a habit of packing too many good things into her life. I'm guessing many of us are like that. We cram our schedules to the max.

On average our brains constitute 3 percent of body weight and consume about 25 percent of body energy. Just as we wouldn't expect cell phones or laptops to work without charging their batteries, we shouldn't expect our brains to continue to work without the chance to recharge.

The good news is that unless you suffer from a sleep disorder, it may be fairly easy to solve the sleep problem. Try these simple tips to get your sleep:

Go to bed and get up at the same time every day.
Exercise, but do it in the morning or afternoon.
Avoid watching television or using a computer thirty minutes before bedtime.
Take a closer look at your daily schedule. Can anything be eliminated to afford more time for sleep?
Drink a glass of warm milk or chamomile tea.
Take a relaxing bath before bedtime.

Consider moving sleep up on your priority list. If you continue to neglect this basic need, you can't expect God to make up the difference by zapping you with peace.

Father, help me to accept my limitations and to be content with the number of hours in a day. Help me to take care of myself by making sleep a higher priority.

PEACE IN THE DARKNESS

Seek the Kingdom of God above all else, and he will give you everything you need.

LUKE 12:31

In addition to working with orphans, Katherine Welch has an international ministry to victims of human trafficking. Her work takes her into parts of the world that most of us can't imagine. It's in the midst of the darkness that she struggles to find God's peace. Listen to her reflections on a recent trip.

"I know what I'm gonna face when I do certain things and go certain places, and it is always uncomfortable. I've learned to recognize the lies and understand the darkness that I feel, but that doesn't mean I have any magic words to make it go away. It takes training to endure and press on and in and go ahead.

"Sometimes it is discouragement and I question my being there. I often suffer from sleeplessness and sometimes I get uncharacteristically anxious about a lot of different things not even related to the work at hand. I just press into the Father, as hard as I can; and understand that these thoughts are unbidden, these anxieties are not truth, these feelings are false. I plead for and receive peace, joy, and strength."[1]

Katherine's ministry takes her onto the front lines of the battle with evil. The enemy would like nothing better than to drive her out or neutralize her by planting seeds of anxiety and doubt. But Katherine has learned to endure, to plead for and receive the peace and perspective she needs.

Her experience reminds me a little of those commercials in which the effectiveness of a particular laundry detergent is proven by its ability to clean the worst kinds of stains. Viewers are treated to a before and after view, noting how the dirtiest clothes come out spotless after being washed. Likewise, Katherine's experience tells us that God's peace works no matter where we are or what we are confronting. God can transform a heart that is anxious and doubtful into one that is full of joy and strength.

As you press into the Father today, take a few moments to pray for Katherine, asking God to keep her in his peace. Pray, too, for the countless women and children she is serving throughout the world, asking God to free them from slavery and bring them into relationship with himself.

Father, help Katherine and others like her to press on. Protect them from evil and from discouragement. Give them grace, peace, wisdom, and power for the fight ahead.

August 2

ONE AND DONE

*He does not punish us for all our sins; he does not deal harshly with us, as we deserve.
For his unfailing love toward those who fear him is as great as the height of the
heavens above the earth. He has removed our sins as far from us as the east is from
the west. The LORD is like a father to his children, tender and compassionate to those
who fear him. For he knows how weak we are; he remembers we are only dust.*

PSALM 103:10-14

Usain Bolt is the world's fastest man. In 2008 he broke the world record for the one hundred meter run three months before the Beijing Olympics. Since then he's dominated every competition. But that didn't prevent the six-foot-five Jamaican from being disqualified at the recent world track and field championships held in Daegu, South Korea. Crouching at the line for the one hundred meter final, Bolt jumped the blocks early, which disqualified him from the race.

Fellow runners were stunned. Bolt was the latest to fall victim to a new rule referred to as "one and done." One false start, and the favored athlete was erased from the competition. The rule was adopted to accommodate television broadcast schedules and fans who disliked waiting through countless false starts for races to begin. Prior to that, each runner had been allowed a second chance.

Fortunately for us, God doesn't have a "one and done" rule. If he did, who on the planet would be left to run the race spoken of in Hebrews: "Since we are surrounded by such a huge crowd of witnesses to the life of faith, let us strip off every weight that slows us down, especially the sin that so easily trips us up. And let us run with endurance the race God has set before us" (12:1).

The truth is, God is even more familiar with our failings than we are. And still he loves us. That's the miracle, the good news that's worth celebrating every single day of our lives. If you've fallen prey to the lie that God couldn't possibly forgive you for what you've done or how many times you've done it, decide today to reject it. Don't dignify it by giving it a hearing in your heart. Instead, find a way to show God you are sincerely sorry. Commit to making amends. But rest in this truth and let it shape the race ahead: as far as the east is from the west, so far has he removed your sins from you.

*Lord, you are a merciful Father who loves his children.
Help me to accept this truth with gratitude.*

August 3

GRIEVING

When Mary arrived and saw Jesus, she fell at his feet and said, "Lord, if only you had been here, my brother would not have died." . . . "Where have you put him?" he asked them. They told him, "Lord, come and see." Then Jesus wept.

JOHN 11:32, 34-35

Several years ago a friend I hadn't seen for some time told me her mother had died. Wendy's loss was made worse by the feeling that few people understood what she was going through. More than one insensitive friend seemed surprised that she was still grieving a few weeks after her mother's death. Why the insensitivity?

I don't think it was a matter of callousness. Wendy has good friends. But perhaps few of them had experienced the death of a loved one. They simply lacked the imagination to understand the depth of her loss.

Listen to how Leslie Allen, the author of *A Liturgy of Grief*, reflects on his own experience of losing his mother: "Sixty years ago, after my mother died, I recall the drapes kept firmly closed at the front windows in the daytime, my older brothers wearing black armbands on their coats, and a black tie replacing my school tie for a long time. Now a funeral service may be reduced to an ostensibly more healthy form of a celebration of life. In general, church services can be uncomfortable and unsatisfying for the one who grieves, for these services may reflect an aversion to sorrow that takes no account of the somber realities of life."[2]

Perhaps our cultural aversion to grief explains why funerals no longer have dirges—somber songs that give vent to our sorrow and mourning. In his book, a commentary on the book of Lamentations, Allen remarks that the dirge "gave permission for broken piece after broken piece to be picked up and wept over."[3] Perhaps it is time to bring back the dirge, to give ourselves permission to look at the broken pieces of what has happened, weeping over them as we pray and trust God for the peace we seek.

Lord, you know the grief of losing a person you love. Give me the grace to weep and to mourn and yet to have hope for what you have promised to do. Help me to be sensitive to others as they grieve too.

STOIC

*You keep track of all my sorrows. You have collected all my tears in
your bottle. You have recorded each one in your book.*

PSALM 56:8

The year was 387. A small group of Africans were leaving Italy to return
to their homeland. Among them were a mother and son. The two had
developed a close bond over the years, the mother praying ceaselessly until
her son's conversion, which had occurred the previous year. Now they were
staying in the seaport town of Ostia, awaiting transportation to their home
in North Africa. One day as the two were conversing, the mother turned the
conversation in a surprising direction.

"My son," she confided, "I no longer find any personal pleasure in a
longer life here. I really don't know why I remain here. The great hope of
my life has been fulfilled." She went on to tell him that "God has more than
answered my prayers since I now see that you have turned your back on
worldly values and have dedicated yourself completely to him. So, what am I
doing here?"[4]

Within five days, she developed a fever. A few days later, at the age of
fifty-six, she was dead. Though the mother accepted her death peacefully,
her son did not. "A huge wave of sorrow," he says, "washed over my heart, a
rushing torrent that threatened to pour from me as tears. And yet my eyes
were dry, held tight by the stern command of my will. The tension tore me
apart. . . . Like a fool, I was upset because I was human and so affected by the
death of a human being."[5]

Gradually the son was able to express his sorrow, saying, "Finally, alone
with you, my God, I was able to weep, to weep about her and for her, to weep
about myself and for myself. With relief I was able to let go the tears I had
been holding back, letting them flow as fully as they wished, spreading them
out as a soft pillow for my heart. My heart came to peace resting on those
velvet tears, tears that were seen by you alone."[6]

The story of Monica and her famous son Augustine is told in
Augustine's autobiography, *Confessions*. Through it we discover that even this
great man had to learn that peace sometimes comes only through our tears.

*Lord, help me to weep freely in your presence when I need to. And let
the tears that are seen by you alone help my heart find peace.*

God blesses those who mourn, for they will be comforted.

MATTHEW 5:4

Nicholas Wolterstorff lost his twenty-five-year-old son, Eric, in a mountain climbing accident in Austria. In the classic memoir *Lament for a Son,* he points out that part of the pain grief entails is the profound loneliness it produces.

"I have been daily grateful," he says, "for the friend who remarked that grief isolates. He did not mean only that I, grieving, am isolated from you, happy. He meant also that *shared* grief isolates the sharers from each other. Though united in that we are grieving, we grieve differently. As each death has its own character, so too each grief over a death has its own character—its own inscape. The dynamics of each person's sorrow must be allowed to work themselves out without judgment. . . .

"There's something more: I must struggle so hard to regain life that I cannot reach out to you. Nor you to me. The one not grieving must touch us both."[7]

I remember losing my sixteen-year-old sister many years ago. She died instantly in an automobile crash. I realize now that neither my parents nor my brothers were able to comfort me because they were crushed by the burden of their own grief. What helped me most were friends who came alongside, offering small gifts, invitations to go out, and ears to listen when I felt ready to speak.

If you have suffered a traumatic loss, whether a death, an illness, or the loss of your livelihood, be patient with those around you who are also grieving, realizing that their way of dealing with loss may be different from yours.

If you know someone who is suffering right now, ask God to show you how to be the "one not grieving" who is able to touch them in a way that brings his peace.

Lord, make me a woman who can come alongside others in their grief. Show me how to bring even a little bit of shalom to those who suffer.

SEEING THROUGH DARKNESS

[God] comforts us in all our troubles so that we can comfort others.
2 CORINTHIANS 1:4

O ne of the conditions of childhood, at least my childhood, was to envy the animal kingdom for powers I did not possess. Wings were a particular object of my longing. If only I could soar like a hawk through the sky, then I would be happy. One of my daughters suffered the same malady. Her condition, however, manifested itself as feline envy. She wondered why God hadn't enabled her to see in the dark like a cat. Now, thanks to modern technology, she no longer needs to accept her biological limitations. Instead, she can purchase a reasonably priced night vision scope, one that relies on starlight, moonlight, and infrared light to pierce the darkness in front of her. Such scopes are great for warfare, hunting rabbits, spotting boats on the water, observing wildlife, or in my daughter's case, satisfying whatever random curiosity she might have about what is lurking in the dark. I imagine it would have come in handy for Tarzan and Jane, surrounded as they were by all those jungle creatures.

When it comes to seeing through the darkness, there are additional possibilities. In his book *Lament for a Son*, Nicholas Wolterstorff processes his grief by observing: "Our culture says that men must be strong and that the strength of a man in sorrow is to be seen in his tearless face. . . .

"But why celebrate stoic tearlessness? Why insist on never outwarding the inward when the inward is bleeding? Does enduring while crying not require as much strength as never crying? May we not sometimes allow people to see and enter it?" He goes on to say, "I shall look at the world through tears. Perhaps I shall see things that dry-eyed I could not see."[8]

Could it be that by letting others see the crushing burden in his heart, Wolterstorff became more open to seeing theirs? Opening ourselves to the pain of others is not necessarily a path to peace. But it can be. Particularly when doing so makes us sensitive to suffering in a way we had not been previously. That's when we can sit down beside someone and ease his or her burden simply by acknowledging that it exists.

Lord, I don't want to deny pain as though I can ignore it away. Help me allow myself to feel it without becoming mired in it. As I do, open my eyes wide so that I might see others as you do.

FANTASIES

*"I know the plans I have for you," says the LORD. "They are plans for
good and not for disaster, to give you a future and a hope."*

JEREMIAH 29:11

I remember my first trip to Disneyland. My friends and I were so enthralled with Fantasyland that we spent most of the day there. We were having such a good time that we nearly forgot to visit the other attractions in the park, places like Adventureland, Frontierland, and Tomorrowland. That's not really so different from what happens when some of us get lost in our personal fantasies.

We fantasize about a relationship, hoping that a certain person will one day fall in love with us. Or we fantasize about an improbable career, like becoming a famous artist, actress, or movie star. And who hasn't fantasized about winning the lottery? There's nothing wrong with having dreams, of course. But fantasies are unhealthy because by definition they are based solely on our imaginations, untethered to reality.

If fantasies are so unrealistic, why do we cling to them? One reason is that they can produce a kind of sham peace. Unsatisfied with life right now, I can distract myself by imagining a beautiful future. The problem with fantasies, of course, is that they can be instantly demolished by the pinprick of harsh reality. While fantasies may calm and console us for a time, they will eventually come to an end. The person we are fantasizing about falls in love with someone else. We grow into middle age no closer to becoming a rock star. We hit retirement with precious little money in the bank. That's when the pseudopeace we've derived from our fantasies quickly dissolves, leaving us deflated and depressed.

Feeding on fantasies is like eating cotton candy for breakfast, lunch, and dinner. If we make a habit of it, we will suffer from spiritual and emotional malnutrition because falsehoods don't have the power to nourish. Instead, they steal our attention and energy away from the grace God gives us to live in the present, helping us to build a better future.

What fantasies are you harboring? Ask the Holy Spirit to reveal them to you. Then ask for grace to let go of them so you can take hold of the good life God has for you.

*Lord, I am not afraid of facing the truth as long as you are with me when I do. Give me courage
to deal with my disappointments and faith to believe you will help me build a better future.*

PEACE TAKES TIME

God blesses those whose hearts are pure, for they will see God.

MATTHEW 5:8

Last weekend I purchased a new watch. I'd done my homework, trolling the Internet in search of the best price. Then I decided to check out Macy's to see if they had it in stock. They did! Better yet, they could size the watchband on the spot so I could wear it instantly. I decided to pay a few more dollars rather than ordering it online and waiting for it to arrive. Like most people, I enjoy getting what I want when I want it.

The other night I was talking to one of my daughters about a behavior issue. "Why don't you ever apologize when you're wrong?" I asked her.

"But I do," she countered.

"Yes, you say you're sorry, but your tone of voice makes it clear you don't mean it."

"That's because you always make me apologize right away. I might be sorrier if I had a little more time to calm down and think about things."

Her observation made perfect sense. Now she has a little more space before she is expected to take responsibility for what she's said or done.

It strikes me that my hurry for her to make peace (with her sister, in this case) was misguided. Like anything good in life, peace takes time. But most of us want it right here, right now. And no wonder. It doesn't feel good to lack peace. Being without it when we think we need it most can tempt us toward hopelessness, making us doubt we will ever experience the peace God promises. But our journey toward peace will deepen as we make God the goal of our lives, living for him, trusting him, seeking to please him. If we do that, we will one day turn around, surprised to find his peace has been worked into our hearts, even though we don't know how.

Father, help me to keep my eyes on the goal: more of you. I want to know you and serve you and live in your presence daily. Give me the grace to stay the course.

*Thank you for making me so wonderfully complex! Your
workmanship is marvelous—how well I know it.*

PSALM 139:14

Imagine that you are subjected to a series of mild shocks, equivalent to the
static shocks that come from rubbing your foot across the carpet. As the
shocks keep coming, you feel more and more stressed. Now imagine that
your next-door neighbor experiences the exact same series of shocks. The
only difference is that she is allowed to run over to a candy bar sitting on her
dining room table and begin chewing it after each shock. Some time later,
you develop an ulcer while your neighbor does not. If you think that the
candy bar made the vital difference, you would probably be right.

Sound far-fetched? A physiologist by the name of Jay Weiss performed
a similar experiment on rats. He let one rat run over to a piece of wood and
gnaw on it after each shock. That rat was far less likely to develop an ulcer
than the one that experienced a series of shocks with no relief. A masochistic
variation on Weiss's experiment delivered a series of shocks and then allowed
the stressed rat to run across the cage and bite another rat to its heart's
content. Guess what? All that biting worked wonders! It seems victimizing
others is a great stress reducer.[9]

So what's the takeaway for us? Should we all be eating more chocolate
bars or beating up on others whenever we feel frustrated? Of course not. The
point is that our stress has to go somewhere. Unless we find positive ways
to release it, either our bodies will absorb the stress or we will find harmful
ways to release it.

One of the best stress relievers known to humankind is exercise. We
know that psychological stress can activate the body for a fight-or-flight
response even when none is needed. Exercise uses up the energy that the body
is prepared to expend, thereby relieving the stress we feel. Other strategies,
like talking to a friend or distracting yourself with an activity you enjoy or
even imagining that you are doing something pleasant, can also offer relief.
Whatever you do, don't make the mistake of ignoring stress. Instead, look for
practical ways to relieve it so you can experience more peace in your life.

*Father, help me to find positive ways to deal with stress. Show me how to
take charge of my health in a way that brings me greater peace.*

BLAME

*Do you know the laws of the universe? Can you use them to regulate
the earth? Can you shout to the clouds and make it rain?*

JOB 38:33-34

Temple Grandin was diagnosed with autism in 1950, at a time when little was known about this neurological disorder. Remarkably, she became a renowned animal scientist, an author, and a professor at Colorado State University. In a particularly poignant scene from the HBO film that was made about her life, the doctor who diagnosed her condition callously explained to her mother that autism was caused by a mother's coldness to her child.

At around the same time, another nonscientific theory was circulating in psychiatric literature about the cause of schizophrenia. This theory was so popular that someone invented a fancy adjective to identify the supposed culprit. Schizophrenia, it was asserted, was caused by "schizophrenogenic" mothers. Of course, later research debunked the notion that anyone— including mothers—had the power to cause schizophrenia in their offspring. Instead, it was linked to a neurochemical problem.

Because we mothers are good at blaming ourselves for everything under the sun, I hardly think we need the assistance of the medical community to make us feel guiltier than we already do. As Erma Bombeck once famously quipped, "Guilt is the gift that keeps on giving." It's also the thing that keeps on stealing—our peace.

So how can we get free of the guilt? Studies have shown that those who have a strong internal sense of control—people who think their actions cause much of what happens around them—have far greater stress responses in the midst of uncontrollable events than those who do not. So if you are a person who feels in charge of your life, you are at risk for greater stress because you will have a tendency to take responsibility for things outside your control.

Let's stop accepting blame for things we haven't a hope of controlling. While we're at it, let's stop kidding ourselves that we are in charge of the universe. Instead, let's remember who is, calling on his name and trusting in his care.

*Lord, I am tired of taking the blame for things I cannot control. Help me to entrust my
life to you more deeply. Teach me what it means to be controlled by your Holy Spirit.*

WHIRLED PEAS

They offer superficial treatments for my people's mortal wound.
They give assurances of peace when there is no peace.

JEREMIAH 6:14

Have you ever seen the bumper sticker that says, "Visualize Whirled Peas"? I admit I got a chuckle out of it the first time I saw it. It's such a refreshing alternative to slogans like "Embrace Peace," "Give Peace a Chance," "Peace and Love," or even "Girly Girls for Peace." I'm tired of brightly colored bumper stickers and cheerful slogans implying that our search for peace is easier than it is. Such slogans seem rooted in the belief that peace is primarily a matter of willpower, something we can achieve if we all get together and try a little harder. While I'm all for togetherness and trying hard, I don't think these can ultimately produce the peace we long for.

Here's why. Peace is something only God can give. Here's how Rick Warren, pastor of Saddleback Church, puts it: "There will never be peace in the world until there is peace in nations. There will never be peace in nations until there is peace in communities. There will never be peace in communities until there is peace in families. There will never be peace in families until there is peace in individuals. And there will never be peace in individuals until we invite the Prince of Peace to reign in our hearts."[10]

If you want to visualize world peace, imagine yourself holding one of those Russian nesting dolls, only yours is shaped like a globe with progressively smaller globes inside. Start opening the globes. When it's time to pull out the last and smallest one, you will find the hidden heart of peace. It's not a globe but a small figurine that looks a lot like you—a woman in whom Christ's Spirit lives. He is the one we call the Lord and giver of peace.

Lord, thank you for making peace through your sacrifice. Help me to spread your peace by living out the gospel in my life so that more people might come to know you.

HAVE SOME FUN!

*It is useless for you to work so hard from early morning until late at night,
anxiously working for food to eat; for God gives rest to his loved ones.*

PSALM 127:2

"Adults never have any fun," proclaimed my oldest daughter with the 100 percent certainty common to teenagers. This time I had to admit she was right, at least when it came to my life. I couldn't remember the last time I'd really had fun. Was it on my trip to the grocery store or when I was paying bills or taking the dog to the vet or hurrying to meet a writing deadline or rushing to pick up a child from karate class or cooking dinner or meeting with teachers at my children's schools or shopping for back-to-school clothes or arranging for home care for my elderly mother? Like yours, my days are packed, but not usually with things I love to do. As I reflected on my daughter's remark, I started wondering if I would even recognize fun if it landed on my doorstep. Had I completely forgotten how to play? I hoped not.

I decided to break out of my routine and do something a little out of the ordinary. Unsure of what to do, I began by making a list of things I had done in the past that were genuinely fun:

crabbing	attending a baseball game
shelling	playing laser tag
snorkeling	shooting pool with friends
waterskiing	drift fishing
surf fishing	kayaking
swimming in Lake Michigan	

Noticing that the most frequent theme threading its way through my fun list was water, I decided to rent a stand-up paddleboard and try my luck on Lake Michigan. Last weekend my children and I shared the board with hilarious results.

Why not consider adding a little fun to your own life? If you can't remember how to play, try making a list of the most memorable fun you've had. Let it spark ideas for the present. Remember, one aspect of *shalom* is well-being. Perhaps a little burst of play is all that's needed to put your world back into balance.

Lord, you've placed me in a beautiful world. Help me find ways to enjoy it.

GUARDRAILS

Don't worry about anything; instead, pray about everything. Tell God what you need, and thank him for all he has done. Then you will experience God's peace, which exceeds anything we can understand. His peace will guard your hearts and minds as you live in Christ Jesus.

PHILIPPIANS 4:6-7

My daughter had a habit of falling out of bed when she was a toddler. Fortunately she slept in a bed that was fairly low to the ground, and when she fell, it was onto soft carpet. Still, no sense taking a fall in the middle of the night if you don't have to. The problem was solved when I found a railing that fit snugly under the mattress, keeping her sound asleep and safely in bed until her "holy rolling" days were over.

Though I'm not sure why, I am also more prone to rolling off the edge at night—not onto the floor, but into thoughts full of doubt and anxiety. Somehow darkness magnifies the troublesome issues that crop up in the daytime. If you're like me, you may find yourself trying to solve your most nettlesome problems in the middle of the night. I can assure you it's a strategy that rarely works.

So how can you counter this problem? One thing you can do is simply to remind yourself that night is always a terrible time to solve anything. To reinforce the thought, try conjuring an image of a hamster running endlessly on a wheel. Then promise yourself you'll deal with the issue that's bothering you, but not until morning. Write it down if you have to. After that, roll over and go back to sleep. If sleep still eludes you, try doing what Paul urged the Philippians to do—pray about everything, and thank God for all he has done. Don't pray anxiously and endlessly; pray simply and with as much faith as you can muster. Then thank God for all that is good in your life, making sure your prayer of thanksgiving is at least as long as your prayer of petition. After you've done that, imagine the Father standing at the edge of your bed, placing a guardrail of peace around it to keep you safe.

Lord, you give your beloved sleep. Help me to find rest as I place my trust in you.

MORNING AND EVENING

*Every day of my life was recorded in your book. Every moment
was laid out before a single day had passed.*

PSALM 139:16

Maybe it was the title of the blog that fascinated me. What woman wouldn't want to sneak a look at a blog entitled "The Art of Manliness"? In a recent post, Brett and Kate McKay talk about the importance of morning and evening routines for building a successful life. Citing examples from the lives of men like Theodore Roosevelt, William Blake, and John Quincy Adams, they offer models of how men can lead lives of greater significance by paying attention to their daily routines.

"Imagine," they say, "a string with a series of beads on it. The beads represent your goals, relationships, and priorities. Tip the string this way or that way, and the beads easily slide off and onto the floor. But tie a knot on each end of the string, and the beads stay put. Those knots are your morning and evening routines. They keep the priorities of your life from falling apart and thus help you progress and become a better man."[11]

I agree with their philosophy, and I would contend that their advice applies to women as well. I can't tell you how many times my well-intentioned plans for the day have fallen short, leaving me with a sense of frustration and guilt. At times the shortfall can be attributed to a poor start or a late finish. What do I mean by a poor start? For me it means that I am consuming too much media in the morning—watching or reading the news. Doing so gobbles up my time for prayer and Scripture reading. Late finishes can be blamed on a similar culprit—too much media, either movies, books, or news.

What are your time wasters? How might your life look if you could carve out sensible, disciplined goals for your morning and evening routines? If you and I were to put first things first in our routines, we could experience more of the peace that comes from a job well done or a life well lived. Join me this week in thinking about the goals you have for your life and how you might achieve them. Do so prayerfully, asking God to help you shape your day by paying more attention to how you begin and end it.

Lord, you order the day and the night. Help me to order my day in a way that is pleasing to you.

August 15

IF I WERE A SQUIRREL

Using a dull ax requires great strength, so sharpen the blade.
That's the value of wisdom; it helps you succeed.

ECCLESIASTES 10:10

Squirrels are famously persistent, a trait that often gets them what they want but sometimes gets them killed. They get into trouble when they persist in a strategy that simply doesn't work. Ever notice how many roadkill victims are squirrels? Perhaps that's because they have only one strategy for what to do when they are trying to cross the road and encounter oncoming traffic—scurry back to the side of the road they started from.

We look at the squirrel and scoff, wondering why they don't adopt a more flexible strategy for evading oncoming traffic. As human beings, we realize that we have the cognitive ability to change course as needed. But if this is so, why do we so often return to failed strategies for coping with stress, trying the same unsuccessful solutions over and over with little effect?

Let me give you an example. Say you work with someone who annoys you. Despite your prayers for patience and for her to change, her annoying habits persist. So you redouble your prayers. While prayer is always a great strategy, you may need to add something to it—like taking action. It might, for example, be advisable to speak kindly but directly with your coworker about whatever is causing the difficulty. You might say something like this: "When you interrupt me, it makes me feel as though what I have to say is unimportant." The conversation may be uncomfortable, but it's likely to yield better results than a strategy that encourages passivity and ends in pique.

Prayer is always good. But prayer that is never accompanied by action may simply be a passive and ineffective way of dealing with problems that are stealing your peace. Ask God today for wisdom in changing your strategies for dealing with stress.

Father, you've given me a brain. Help me to use it. Give me the flexibility
to consider new ways for dealing with the everyday stresses I feel.

August 16

COOL

God chose things despised by the world, things counted as nothing at all, and used them to bring to nothing what the world considers important. As a result, no one can ever boast in the presence of God. God has united you with Christ Jesus. For our benefit God made him to be wisdom itself. Christ made us right with God; he made us pure and holy, and he freed us from sin.

1 CORINTHIANS 1:28-30

The other day my daughter started unpacking the social dynamics of her middle-school class, listing who was in the cool group and who wasn't. I found it interesting that most of the girls I liked best were in the latter category. Stick with them, I advised. Among them were girls who were funny, kind, fun, modest, intelligent, and sensitive. Girls who would make great friends, I thought.

Though I remember from my own middle-school days how appealing cool can be, I also remember the pressures on kids who did everything they could to be part of the "in" group, sometimes throwing their values—as well as their friends—under the bus if that's what it took.

For many of us, the pressure to be cool still persists, though it's not as obvious. Our kind of cool might require having the right kind of house or car. Or it might mean dressing in a particular way or having the right relationship or having children who excel at everything. It might even mean going to the right kind of church. Our need for cool stems from insecurity. Uncertain and uncomfortable about who we are, we define ourselves by what others think of us. But a lifetime of being cool won't deliver what we want—the sense that at the core we are acceptable and lovable. That only comes as we sink our roots into God.

If the need to be cool still lingers in your life, be honest about it, asking the Lord to help you grow beyond it. Tell him you want the kind of security that comes from knowing how deeply he loves you. As you grow in that knowledge, let his Spirit release you from the constraints you have placed upon your life so you can become the wonderful, unique woman God intended you to be.

Father, release me from the fear of what others think of me. Help me to grow in confidence so I can be the woman you want me to be.

August 17

EMBEZZLING

Wealth is treacherous, and the arrogant are never at rest.

HABAKKUK 2:5

Who or what is stealing your peace? We know the usual suspects—the things that add worry, strife, and difficulty to our lives. But what if the robber-in-chief is an invisible culprit, operating behind the scenes to slowly but steadily drain peace from our lives without us noticing? What then?

Abraham Joshua Heschel's classic work on the Sabbath stresses the importance of attitude when it comes to celebrating Sabbath. "He who wants to enter the holiness of the day," he says, "must first lay down the profanity of clattering commerce, of being yoked to toil. He must go away from the screech of dissonant days, from the nervousness and fury of acquisitiveness and the betrayal in embezzling his own life."[12]

What a striking phrase—the one about embezzling from your own life. Heschel is saying that greed causes us to betray ourselves, to do something that's both foolish and immoral, filching riches that are meant to characterize our lives. Riches like trusting that we belong to a Father who will provide. Riches like being at peace because God is in charge. Riches like enjoying life's simple and most satisfying pleasures.

So often we don't recognize greed for what it is. Because so many of us have bought into a lifestyle that requires amassing more and more wealth, we may mistake greed for industriousness or even prudence, little realizing how costly our greed has become.

Like a receding tide exposing what lies beneath the surface, the recent economic downturn has shown many of us how flimsy and fragile the things we depend on really are. If you suspect that greed has been embezzling your peace, tell God you want it to stop, and ask him for the grace to change.

Lord, forgive me for spending so much time and energy acquiring things I thought would make me happy. I want your riches to characterize my life. Help me to seek first your Kingdom and your glory, confident that you will provide.

BE CURIOUS

You must all be quick to listen, slow to speak, and slow to get angry.
Human anger does not produce the righteousness God desires.

JAMES 1:19-20

My daughter has the gift of intellectual curiosity. Remember those rapid-fire machine guns that always showed up in the old movies about gangsters? That's how fast Katie can spit out questions that are too hard for her mother to answer. Because of her penchant for seeking answers to life's many mysteries, she loves the saying about curiosity killing the cat but satisfaction bringing it back.

When it comes to curiosity, most of us would benefit from becoming a little more curious about our own emotional reactions. Take anger. What is really powering it? Frustration, fear, sadness, hurt? In her book *Walking in the Dust of Rabbi Jesus*, Lois Tverberg points out that being angry often indicates that we have made a negative judgment about someone.

The stranger who cut me off in traffic: he's a jerk. The surly clerk behind the counter: she should be fired. The teacher who gave my child a failing grade: he's incompetent. On and on the judgments go, powering our anger despite the fact that there may be a thousand explanations for why people do what they do. Maybe the stranger who cut us off was heading to the hospital with chest pains. Perhaps the clerk was going through a divorce. Maybe the teacher who failed our child is simply telling the truth. The point is that we can never fathom another person's heart.

Tverberg points out that Jesus warned his followers against calling anyone a fool because to do so was to render "the final verdict on the *person*. . . . A person who is ignorant can learn, but for a 'fool' there is no hope," she says.[13]

I don't think Jesus was telling us to throw out our brains when he told us not to judge. He wasn't urging us to paper over sin or act as if nothing was wrong. But he was saying we are not equipped to judge another person's heart. Only God knows people well enough to do that. To judge others is to be guilty of arrogance because it means usurping God's power and authority.

The next time you discover you have rendered an angry judgment against someone, ask God's forgiveness. If you're angry at yourself, remember that God is the only wise judge, even of your own heart.

Lord, when I am angry, help me not to sin. Let me leave
judgment in your hands, where it belongs.

BE KIND TO YOURSELF

Thank you for making me so wonderfully complex! Your workmanship is marvelous.
PSALM 139:14

I magine your heart as a garden. As the plants grow, enriched by sun and rain, other things begin to grow as well. Tiny seeds, once dormant, have begun to sprout. Now imagine that the gardener comes along and is surprised by what she sees. The garden she once envisioned has been replaced by one that includes several strange plants, already deeply rooted.

Disheartened, she could simply throw up her hands and walk away, leaving the garden to fend for itself. Or, disliking the invaders, she could try tearing them out, risking damage to the other plants. Or she could approach the situation more calmly, deciding to become familiar with each new plant so she can tend the garden more effectively.

In the garden of your heart, emotions like joy, happiness, awe, and compassion spring up. But other emotions grow there as well—anger, shame, fear, disappointment, jealousy. Like the gardener who is surprised by what's growing in her garden, we can be taken off guard by our emotional reactions. Disliking what we see, some of us respond like the disheartened gardener, thinking nothing can be done about our most deeply rooted feelings. So we let them run riot, allowing them to overrun the rest of the garden. Others of us are like the gardener who is so distressed by what she discovers that she destroys the garden in her haste to rip out the unwanted plants. We do that when we treat ourselves harshly, with self-condemnation, trying to suppress or destroy feelings we would rather not have.

Like gardens, our hearts won't flourish under harsh or neglectful treatment. Far better to treat ourselves with kindness and compassion as we learn to handle feelings we'd rather not have.

The next time you feel angry, disappointed, hurt, anxious, or ashamed, don't rush to bury the feeling and don't scold yourself for having it. Allow yourself instead to experience the feeling and think about what caused it. Remember that emotions are neither good nor bad. What matters is how you respond to them. Taking a more accepting approach to unpleasant emotions will keep them from controlling you, enabling you to experience greater peace and emotional healing as you begin to understand yourself better.

Father, please help me to respect how fearfully and wonderfully you have made me.

TRIGGERS

The LORD rules over the floodwaters. The LORD reigns as king forever.
The LORD gives his people strength. The LORD blesses them with peace.

PSALM 29:10-11

I am a self-confessed news junkie. Last month, however, I hardly tuned in to television news, preferring to get my fix through print media instead. As news reports of a double-dip recession kept pouring in, I surprised myself by remaining calm. Then I made the mistake of turning on the television, with very different results. Though the news was identical to what I had previously read, my response was notably different. As I watched commentators speculating on every possible scenario, I could almost see my anxiety rising like the red line on a thermometer. The takeaway was clear: watching televised news tends to trigger my anxiety. If I want to remain peaceful, I need to find a way to limit my exposure.

What are your triggers—the things that ramp up your anxiety, making it difficult for you to remain peaceful? Maybe it's talking to friends who have a tendency to look at negatives more than positives. Perhaps it's pressuring yourself to be perfect or comparing yourself to others or checking the stock market too often or packing too many things into a day or making a habit of asking, "What if, what if, what if?" We all have triggers that rob us of the peace we desire, draining our energy and making it difficult to live positive, productive lives. Avoiding these makes practical sense.

In the next few days, ask God to help you identify the unconscious triggers that threaten your peace. Then seek him for the wisdom to know how to handle them.

Father, sometimes I feel like a rabbit that is startled by the slightest movement.
The reports about the world around me—and the world itself—can rob
me of peace. Help me experience your continued care, and give me greater
wisdom about how to deal with the things that make me anxious.

BROKEN

You have allowed me to suffer much hardship, but you will restore me to life again and lift me up from the depths of the earth. You will restore me to even greater honor and comfort me once again. Then I will praise you with music on the harp, because you are faithful to your promises, O my God. I will sing praises to you with a lyre, O Holy One of Israel.

PSALM 71:20-22

In the gripping novel *Sister*, a character by the name of Beatrice writes to her younger sister, Tess, about uncovering the roots of her own pervasive insecurity. The final abandonment came, she says, when her mother packed her off to boarding school. That was when her younger brother's death and her father's desertion coalesced into the overarching message that she was unwanted and alone. But now, as an adult, she has discovered a surprising truth. Rather than rejecting her, her mother had been trying to protect her by sending her away. Yet her essential problem remains: she is still broken, even if that brokenness is based on a misunderstanding.

"The problem was," she says, "knowing the reason I was insecure didn't help me to undo the damage that had been done. Something in me had been broken, and I now knew it was well intentioned—a duster knocking the ornament onto the tiled floor rather than its being smashed deliberately— but broken just the same."[14]

Like Beatrice, we may suffer from unintentional wounds inflicted during childhood. While greater self-understanding can be helpful to the healing process, understanding alone cannot put us back together because broken is still broken. But unlike characters in a novel, we have access to a Healer who is able to transform us, using the hurt we have suffered for a purpose yet to be revealed.

Today as you seek the Lord, who is our healer, ask him for a deeper understanding of the roots of your brokenness. Then pray that he will touch you with his healing and redeeming power.

Lord, you alone can mend what's broken and shattered in me. Help me to be open to the work of your Spirit so I can live in a way that brings you glory.

GOT MILK?

My lover said to me, "Rise up, my darling! Come away with me, my fair one!"
SONG OF SONGS 2:10

Last week I received a note from my daughter's school informing me that though the school year is nearly over, Luci's milk account still has more than forty-five dollars. Further investigation revealed the not-too-surprising news that my daughter has not been drinking her milk. So I sat her down for yet another lecture, trying to convey the importance of establishing enough bone mass when she's young so that when she reaches my age and beyond, she won't suffer from fractures that could have been avoided. As you might imagine, my lecture didn't convince.

Luci's aversion to milk reminds me of a point Mark Buchanan makes in his book *The Rest of God*. "God," he says, "gave us the gift of Sabbath—not just as a day, but as an orientation, a way of seeing and knowing. Sabbath-keeping is a form of mending. It's mortar in the joints. Keep Sabbath, or else break too easily and oversoon."

Mark goes on to say that "Sabbath imparts the rest of God—actual physical, mental, spiritual rest, but also the *rest* of God—the things of God's nature and presence we miss in our busyness."

I remember working for a man who was a workaholic. Joe would spend hours at work every night. Though he was devoted to his work, he never seemed to stay on top of things. The more time he put in at work, the less productive he was. Or to say it more colloquially, the harder he worked, the behinder he got. At least that's how his employees saw it.

Just because we devote boatloads of time and energy to something doesn't guarantee a good return. Because time is such a precious commodity, let's give some of it to God, who is able to transform the time we spend with him into mortar for our joints, ensuring that we will break neither too easily nor oversoon.

Father, help me to mark out a Sabbath time in my week. As I do,
I pray that you will reveal yourself and replenish my strength.

PRACTICAL PEACE

He lets me rest in green meadows; he leads me beside peaceful streams.

PSALM 23:2

A re there practical ways to build more peace into our lives—things we can do to alleviate the stress and tension we feel? Happily, there are. You have probably considered several of these ideas already. If so, take this opportunity to review the options and then try a few.

Don't bottle up your concerns. Instead, connect with friends who are able to provide a listening ear.

Limit your caffeine and sugar consumption.

Soothe yourself with a cup of tea. Green tea and black tea contain theanine, a substance that may have a calming effect.

Distract yourself by cooking a nice meal.

Drink a warm glass of milk. Milk contains tryptophan, a substance that can calm you.

Eat a little dark chocolate.

Hire help.

Take a bike ride.

Play with a pet.

Go outside for a few minutes every day.

Take a bath with lavender bath salts or oil.

Watch a funny movie.

Dedicate one evening a week to do something simply because you enjoy it.

Lie down and begin tensing and then relaxing your muscles, starting with your toes and working your way up to your neck and head. Tense each muscle group for five seconds and then relax for thirty.

None of this is rocket science. That's the advantage. The psalmist's vision of green meadows and peaceful streams isn't just about heaven. We can begin to taste God's rest right now. Adopting a few simple practices may be what you need to ratchet down your stress levels.

*Lord, help me to find simple ways to eliminate stress so
I can experience more peace on a daily basis.*

WHAT IF?

Give all your worries and cares to God, for he cares about you.

1 PETER 5:7

Besides adding joy to one's life, children can add plenty of anxiety. When you love a person, especially someone as vulnerable as a child, you can begin to feel a lot more fear.

I was voicing my own fears recently when a good friend opened his heart, telling me not to waste my energy. He went on to say that he had spent years worrying about one of his two sons. "Max," he said, "was always my greatest concern. When he was five, he tested positive for a rare disorder that could eventually debilitate him. The doctors told my wife and me he would probably start showing symptoms by the time he was a teenager, maybe sooner. I was so afraid for him that I couldn't sleep at night, worrying about what to do.

"But I never thought twice about Josh. He had always been so healthy. He was smart, well-liked, funny. I knew he was going to be successful in whatever he did. Then, suddenly, his life went into a tailspin during his senior year in high school. We found out that he suffers from bipolar disorder. Sadly my fun-loving, capable kid has vanished. Josh's case is so severe that he has been in and out of psych wards for the last several years and he can't hold down a job.

"The odd thing is that all those sleepless nights spent worrying about Max were completely off track. It's been twenty years since we heard about the likelihood of his developing that disorder, but he hasn't exhibited a single symptom, and the doctors now say he probably won't."

My friend's point, of course, is that worrying about what *might* happen is a waste of precious energy because it means we are preparing for eventualities that will probably never materialize. As Mark Twain once quipped, "I am an old man and have known a great many troubles, but most of them never happened." Or as a Swedish proverb puts it: "Worry often gives a small thing a big shadow." If your life is overshadowed right now by anxiety, ask God to bring you out of that shadow and into the light of his presence, enabling you to trust him for whatever is troubling you.

Father, I can't see even one minute into the future, so help me stop trying to do so. Instead, teach me to live in this present moment, casting all my cares on you.

SMOOTH SAILING?

Peace I leave with you; my peace I give you.

JOHN 14:27, NIV

What comes to mind when you hear the word *peace*? For me it's the cliché of a pond in perfect stillness or a sea with just enough breeze to allow for smooth sailing. Turbulent water is nowhere in the picture. All is quiet and serene. But the truth is, if I possessed that kind of peace all the time, I would probably go crazy. I would certainly become fat, sleepy, and bored. Surely that can't be what God intends when he offers us his peace.

I like what Charles Spurgeon, the great nineteenth-century preacher, had to say about the blessings of trouble. He is talking about how not to raise a son, but the same advice would apply, of course, to raising a daughter. "If you want to ruin your son," Spurgeon says, "never let him know a hardship. When he is a child carry him in your arms, when he becomes a youth still dandle him, and when he becomes a man still dry-nurse him, and you will succeed in producing an arrant fool. If you want to prevent his being made useful in the world, guard him from every kind of toil. Do not suffer him to struggle. Wipe the sweat from his dainty brow and say, 'Dear child, thou shalt never have another task so arduous.' Pity him when he ought to be punished; supply all his wishes, avert all disappointments, prevent all troubles, and you will surely tutor him to be a reprobate and to break your heart. But put him where he must work, expose him to difficulties, purposely throw him into peril, and in this way you shall make him a man, and when he comes to do man's work and to bear man's trial, he shall be fit for either."[15]

Could it be the trials that often throw us into such confusion and cause us to question God's love are in the end meant not to rob us of peace but to make us women who are filled with *shalom*—whole, healed, confident, safe, prosperous, complete—able to hold our heads high not because life is easy but because we belong to a Father who loves us and teaches us how to live?

Father, forgive me for doubting you every time life is difficult. Remind me that you can use the trials I face to make me more like you.

WHO'S YOUR DADDY?

Keep me safe, O God, for I have come to you for refuge.
PSALM 16:1

Walter Mosley is the author of a series of bestselling mystery novels featuring Easy Rawlins, a hard-boiled private investigator living in the Watts neighborhood of Los Angeles. During the course of a recent interview, the sixty-year-old writer touched on the influence of his father, a black man who had grown up in the racially charged South. One day Mosley's father sat him down and told him about every person he had ever seen die. "And it was just amazing," Mosley remarked. "Little children killing each other . . . black people killing white people, white people killing black people . . . people being hung, people dying because there was no protection on their jobs."

When asked whether his father's encounter with violence in the segregated South had made Mosley expect the same kind of violence in his own life, he responded, "Not at all. One of the things my father did was he made me feel extraordinarily safe. He made me feel that 'I've taken care of it. Nothing's going to happen to you.' And I always felt like that. Now things did happen. I got stopped by police and they would pull guns on me and do all kinds of things but all through that I was never really worried because my father said, 'You're going to be safe,' and I believed my father. And on the whole it's been true."[16]

Contrast Mosley's experience of his father's protective influence with that of Diane Bartholomew, writing from the York Correctional Institute in Connecticut. Bartholomew's father raped her when she was a young girl and later tried to run over her and her sister with the family car. After his death she described her feelings as she approached his casket: "Hello, Dad, and good-bye. Good riddance. The others are sad, sobbing. Why? Have they forgotten all the things you did to us? I stand here feeling nothing, unless you count relief." She was so hurt and frightened by her father that she wanted to make certain he was really dead. "Then," she says, "I'll know you can't hurt us anymore, Dad. Then I'll know I'm safe."[17]

Two different fathers. Two different children. Two completely different ideas of what constitutes safety. However your father made you feel, I pray that you will know God as the Father who keeps you safe.

Lord, this world is not safe, but you are safe. Help me to find refuge in the shadow of your wings.

August 27

I'LL FLY AWAY

Our days may come to seventy years, or eighty, if our strength endures; yet the best of them are but trouble and sorrow, for they quickly pass, and we fly away.

PSALM 90:10, NIV

Good News for Ann Spangler!" That was the headline on a postcard I recently received, indicating that some generous company stood ready to fork out $14,480 for my funeral expenses. Plus, this company would give me a free Walmart gift card. All I had to do was sign up for a special insurance plan. I can't tell you how excited I was! I thought about what I might buy with that gift card—maybe a beautiful floral arrangement for my casket or perhaps a new outfit to wear when they laid me out. So many possibilities.

When it comes to news that is genuinely good, you can't beat the best news of all, which is that anyone who belongs to Christ will live forever. How exactly this works, no one but God knows. But I like to imagine it something like this: say your deepest desire is to travel to the outer reaches of the universe. Amazingly you find a spaceship that is capable of taking you there. Under your own power, you know you will never get there. But as a passenger on that powerful ship, you will make it.

I think something like that happens in our relationship with Christ. Say he is your deepest desire. Wherever he is, you want to be. United to his power, you push past the limits of your mortality, contradicting the usual expectations.

The psalmist says, "Our days may come to seventy years, or eighty, if our strength endures; yet the best of them are but trouble and sorrow, for they quickly pass, and we fly away" (Psalm 90:10, NIV). And he was right as far as the usual course of things. But our life expectancy goes from eighty to infinity with the coming of Christ, whom the Bible calls "the pioneer and perfecter of faith" (Hebrews 12:2, NIV). What does that mean? Among other things, it means he does everything first and then we follow. Like him, we will die. And like him, we will rise again. United to the Source of life, we are destined to live forever.

Now that's good news, even without a free gift card to Walmart!

Lord, thank you that as the old spiritual says, someday "I'll fly away, oh glory, I'll fly away. When I die, hallelujah, by and by, I'll fly away."

August 28

EXTREME PEACE

God blesses those who work for peace, for they will be called the children of God.
MATTHEW 5:9

M ildred Lisette Norman was seventy-two when she started walking across the country for the seventh time. Possessing nothing but the clothes on her back, she wore her trademark blue tunic emblazoned with the words "Peace Pilgrim," the name she had come to be known by. This silver-haired woman began walking when the Korean War was underway and kept walking right on through the conflict in Vietnam. Remarkably, she managed to live on the road without money, never once asking for food and shelter but receiving what she needed. Wherever she went, she spoke to people not only about the need for peace among nations and peoples but of the need we all have for inner peace. The following are among her many memorable quotes:

This is the way of peace: Overcome evil with good, falsehood with truth, and hatred with love. There is nothing new about this message, except the practice of it.

You have much more power when you are working for the right thing than when you are working against the wrong thing.

Only outer peace can be had through law. The way to inner peace is through love.

Since steps toward spiritual advancement are taken in such varied order, most of us can teach one another.[18]

Peace Pilgrim lived what many of us would consider an extreme life. She was forty-four when she undertook her first pilgrimage and seventy-two when she died in an accident while being driven to a speaking engagement. She lived prayerfully and with faith, desiring to tell others the vital truths she had learned about peace. Whether she was a Christian or merely a Deist I am uncertain, but I am sure she knew something important about peace.

Lord, we are all at different stages on our journey toward peace. Help me to be willing to teach others and to learn from them.

LIVE WHAT YOU BELIEVE

Today I am giving you the choice between a blessing and a curse! You will be blessed if you obey the commands of the LORD your God that I am giving you today. But you will be cursed if you reject the commands of the LORD your God and turn away from him and worship gods you have not known before.

DEUTERONOMY 11:26-28

Peace Pilgrim embraced a life of voluntary simplicity, gradually paring down her possessions and attachments over a period of fifteen years. Looking back on her life, she referred to a mountaintop experience in which she experienced what she called "the first glimpse of what the life of inner peace was like." That experience set the course for the rest of her journey.

She came to realize that peace was impossible for people whose lives are not in harmony with the laws that govern the universe. "Insofar as we disobey these laws," she remarked, "we create difficulties for ourselves by our disobedience. We are our own worst enemies. If we are out of harmony through ignorance, we suffer somewhat; but if we know better and are still out of harmony, then we suffer a great deal.

"So," she explained, "I got busy on a very interesting project. This was to live all the good things I believed in. I did not confuse myself by trying to take them all at once, but rather, if I was doing something that I knew I should not be doing, I stopped doing it, and I always made a quick relinquishment. You see, that's the easy way. Tapering off is long and hard. And if I was not doing something that I knew I should be doing, I got busy on that. It took the living quite a while to catch up with the believing, but of course it can, and now if I believe something, I live it."[19]

Wish you could say the same? I know I do. Why take the long, hard way to peace when we have it in our power to do the things we should and not do the things we shouldn't? Let's ask God right now for the grace to embrace a very interesting project—to start living what we believe.

Lord, you must be tired of all my excuses. I certainly am. I want to know the peace that you alone can give. Help me today to be willing to pay the price.

ENEMIES

*Stay alert! Watch out for your great enemy, the devil. He prowls
around like a roaring lion, looking for someone to devour.*

1 PETER 5:8

In the spring of 1943, the body of a British soldier washed up on the shores of Spain. A briefcase containing secret documents spelling out a planned invasion of southern Europe was still attached to the man's wrist. Snagging the documents before the British could retrieve them, the head of German intelligence in Spain delivered them to Berlin. As soon as the Nazis discovered that the Allies had been planning a simultaneous invasion in the Balkans and Sardinia, they deployed their troops accordingly. When Allied forces landed in Sicily on July 9, the Germans were taken by surprise. It took them two weeks to realize the dead soldier had been a ruse.

The body, it turns out, had not been that of a soldier, but of a Welsh vagrant who had died from swallowing rat poison and whose corpse had been carefully packed in ice until the secret plan was ready to unfold. The plot itself was cooked up by the British spy agency MI5.[20] Clever deceptions like this one helped the Allies defeat a terrible enemy.

Though we can be glad for the Allies' decisive victory, the story holds a lesson for us because we, too, are engaged in a battle with a powerful enemy. Only this time, the bad guy is the one who is the master of deceit. His name, of course, is Satan. If he cannot succeed in demoralizing us to the point that we forsake our faith, he will try to neutralize us by making us miserable. He does so by feeding us a constant stream of plausible lies about ourselves, others, and God.

One way to guard against such lies is to make obedience a cherished habit. Disobedience makes us vulnerable to all manner of evil. Another way is to pray and read Scripture so that when you hear a lie that contradicts God's Word, you will recognize it for what it is. A third way is to stay in touch with other Christians. Voicing our doubts and fears to such friends can expose lies that might otherwise flourish inside our minds. Today, ask yourself what is making you fearful, angry, anxious, or doubtful. If you find you have unknowingly been harboring a lie, reject it, asking God to help you embrace the truth with faith and peace.

*Lord, may your Spirit dwell in me, transforming my mind and
making me quick to recognize the truth and reject the lie.*

WHY FORGIVE?

If you forgive those who sin against you, your heavenly Father will forgive you.
MATTHEW 6:14

I magine that your head is an inch below the water line. You can see the sky, but you can't break through the surface. Your foot has become entangled in an old log that has settled to the bottom of the river, and you are struggling to free yourself. Your lungs feel like they're ready to give out. Finally, with one last wrenching attempt, you get your leg loose and break through the surface, gasping for air. That's a rather dramatic picture of what it can feel like when we are finally able to forgive someone who has wronged us deeply.

Donald Miller points out that there are several practical reasons why we need to forgive. "The first," he says, "is because, believe it or not, forgiveness is a pleasurable experience. No kidding, it feels much better than anger or hate. . . .

"The second reason for you to forgive is that it removes you from being entangled in the rather dark thing that hurt you in the first place. . . . Forgiveness gives you a taste of what it feels like to be God, and it's a terrific feeling. God forgave us because it gave Him pleasure to do so. He was happy to do so. Love forgives, and so does God, and so can you.

"The third reason to forgive is that you open yourself up to amazing possibilities for a happy life. When you don't forgive, you draw the curtains in your soul and your life gets dark. When you forgive you let the light in again, and you go on about your life in peace. And don't you want some peace? Isn't it time for some peace?"[21]

Feeling entangled, embittered, defeated? Isn't it time you came up for air? Isn't it time for some peace?

Lord, you forgave prostitutes and thieves—a whole crowd of people, including self-righteous people who wanted to destroy you. Anyone who came asking was met with forgiveness. I came asking, and you forgave me. Give me the courage to do the same for others, leaving judgment in your hands.

THE TROUBLES YOU
CAN SEE RIGHT NOW

That is why we never give up. Though our bodies are dying, our spirits are being renewed every day. For our present troubles are small and won't last very long. Yet they produce for us a glory that vastly outweighs them and will last forever! So we don't look at the troubles we can see now; rather, we fix our gaze on things that cannot be seen. For the things we see now will soon be gone, but the things we cannot see will last forever.

2 CORINTHIANS 4:16-18

What if you knew you were going to win the lottery, not right now but just in time for retirement? How would that knowledge affect your response to stock market declines, a tough economy, job loss? I'm guessing you would have financial concerns, but not many of the kind that keep you up all night.

Or what if you knew that a child suffering from a debilitating disease was sooner or later going to be completely healed? How would that affect your thinking about his or her future?

Paint the bleakest scenario you like, but then add a happily-ever-after ending and you will begin to see what Christ has promised for us. The apostle Paul believed in happy endings. How else could he have characterized his own prodigious afflictions as small, calling them "light and momentary troubles" (2 Corinthians 4:17, NIV)?

We know the Bible paints a vivid picture of what heaven will be like. Let's try to imagine it with the help of Sally Lloyd-Jones and *The Jesus Storybook Bible*:

Where is the sun? Where is the moon? They aren't needed anymore. God is all the Light people need. No more darkness! No more night! And the King says, "Look! God and his children are together again. No more running away. Or hiding. No more crying or being lonely or afraid. No more being sick or dying. Because all those things are gone. Yes, they're gone forever. Everything sad will come untrue.[1]

Today I challenge you to start living your life by this remarkable truth— that one day soon "everything sad will come untrue." There will be a happy ending.

Heavenly Father, thank you for giving me a glimpse of how the story ends. Help me to look, not at the troubles I can see right now, but at what you have promised for the future.

SQUEEZE

We ourselves are like fragile clay jars containing this great treasure. This makes it clear that our great power is from God, not from ourselves. We are pressed on every side by troubles, but we are not crushed. We are perplexed, but not driven to despair. We are hunted down, but never abandoned by God. We get knocked down, but we are not destroyed. Through suffering, our bodies continue to share in the death of Jesus so that the life of Jesus may also be seen in our bodies.

2 CORINTHIANS 4:7-10

Squeeze an orange and you get juice. Squeeze a horn and you get noise. Squeeze a finger and you get an "ouch!" That's what happened to me the other day when one of my daughters grabbed hold of my ring finger, right where it had been badly bruised beneath the nail. "What's that black mark?" she asked, pressing down.

"Ouch, ouch, ouch! That really hurt!" I squealed. The look on my face sent her spiraling into fits of laughter. Then she apologized.

"Sorry, Mom. I didn't mean to hurt you. I wasn't thinking."

Sometimes trouble is like that. It squeezes us way too hard. That's when we find out what we're made of, what's really inside. Ken Sande, president of Peacemaker Ministries, helps all kinds of people resolve conflicts so they can avoid going to court. Over the years he has come to believe that conflict inevitably shows what we really think about God. "By your actions," he says, "you will show either that you have a big God or that you have a big self and big problems. To put it another way, if you do not focus on God, you will inevitably focus on yourself and your will, or on other people and the threat of their wills."[2]

Ken advises people to focus not on the conflict but on how God wants them to act in the midst of it. To my mind, that means we don't play games, we don't call names, we don't vilify. We don't try to win by whatever means necessary. We do trust God, imitate him, and treat others with respect.

Ken's advice is sound. When the dust settles, and it's time to move on, we will leave the situation with a sense of peace, not because things turned out the way we think they should have, but because we acted the way we know we should.

Lord, I want to magnify you, not the troubles I face. Help me keep you first by seeking your glory today.

"OUR FATHER . . ."

When you pray, don't be like the hypocrites who love to pray publicly on street corners and in the synagogues where everyone can see them. I tell you the truth, that is all the reward they will ever get. But when you pray, go away by yourself, shut the door behind you, and pray to your Father in private. Then your Father, who sees everything, will reward you.

MATTHEW 6:5-6

Over the years, I have engaged in various methods of prayer—Scripture meditation, silent contemplation, thanksgiving, intercessory prayer, and liturgical prayer—and while I've been enriched by each, my favorite way of praying continues to be praying the Lord's Prayer. Far from becoming rote, praying the prayer that Jesus taught his disciples has become deeper with each repetition.

In his book *Jesus Through Middle Eastern Eyes*, Kenneth Bailey tells of meeting a young Latvian woman after the fall of the Soviet Union. Knowing she had grown up under communism, he asked how she had come to faith. Had Christians in her family, perhaps an elderly grandmother, or members of an underground church, influenced her? The answer was an unqualified no. Everyone in her family had been atheists. How then had she come to know Christ? Here's what she told him:

"At funerals we were allowed to recite the Lord's Prayer. As a young child I heard those strange words and had no idea who we were talking to, what the words meant, where they came from or why we were reciting them. When freedom came at last, I had the opportunity to search for their meaning. When you are in total darkness, the tiniest point of light is very bright. For me the Lord's Prayer was that point of light. By the time I found its meaning I was a Christian."[3]

Perhaps you have prayed this prayer for many years or only rarely. Whatever your experience, I would encourage you to pray it slowly, thoughtfully, and reverently at least once a day. From this small act of prayer, a tiny point of light will shine and spread, and the Father, who knows all secrets, will bless you with the peace that comes from belonging completely to him.

Our Father who art in heaven, hallowed be thy name. Thy kingdom come, thy will be done on earth as it is in heaven. Give us this day our daily bread, and forgive us our trespasses as we forgive those who trespass against us. And lead us not into temptation. But deliver us from evil. Amen.

THE PEACE OF NATURE

God looked over all he had made, and he saw that it was very good!
GENESIS 1:31

I remember visiting the home of author Elisabeth Elliot, just north of Boston, right at the edge of the sea. Commenting on the stunning view from her office window, I mentioned that it must be a great place to write. Elisabeth's answer: "Yes, if you can't write here, you can't write anywhere."

Years earlier I had taken a trip west, into the mountains of Colorado. I was in the midst of making a difficult decision. While toiling away at the most stressful job of my life, I received an offer from another company, one that would mean a complete shift of career. My first instinct was to grab it. But I didn't trust myself. I wanted time to think and pray, to see what God had in mind. In the midst of a sixty-hour work week, I had found it difficult to hear anything but my own anxious thoughts buzzing around in my head.

But then I went on vacation, camping in Colorado. I remember hiking out one clear, September morning, in search of a mountain lake. What I found was spectacular—a great mountain, framed by blue skies, reflected on the serene surface of the lake below. As I took in the scene, I sensed the pressure and stress that had characterized my life for months seeping away. It felt as though I were exhaling after a prolonged period of time in which I had been holding my breath. I don't remember how long I looked at that peaceful scene, but I was in no hurry to get away. As time passed, it occurred to me that the world was a far bigger place than I had lately made it. I had been obsessing over my tiny slice of it, forgetting that the world God made is expansive, full of possibilities. I felt a new freedom to step into an unexpected possibility that had recently presented itself. When I returned home, I handed in my notice, eager to begin the next phase of my career.

Visiting that author, sitting by that mountain lake—these are two experiences of many that convince me it is possible to sense God's presence simply by experiencing the wonder of his creation. When was the last time you were able to sense God's presence in the midst of his creation? I encourage you to make time this week to take in the beauty of the world that he has made.

Lord, thank you for creating a world of stunning beauty. Help me to make it a priority to spend time enjoying your creation.

THISTLES AND THORNS

The LORD gives his people strength. The LORD blesses them with peace.
PSALM 29:11

The other day I made a list of things that bug me—little things I can't seem to eradicate from my life. Here they are:

a cluttered house
children who argue
slow cars in the fast lane
long grocery-store lines
clerks who are rude
telemarketers
plugged toilets
computer malfunctions

spam
pop-up windows
calling a helpline and getting
    none
misplacing my keys or phone
people who don't clean up
    after their dogs

Admittedly, none of this is big stuff. But it's often the little stuff that threatens to steal my peace. Listen to what a seventeenth-century spiritual writer by the name of Claude de la Colombière says about the annoyances that plague us: "All our life is sown with tiny thorns that produce in our hearts a thousand involuntary movements of hatred, envy, fear, impatience, a thousand little fleeting disappointments, a thousand slight worries, a thousand disturbances that momentarily alter our peace of soul. For example, a word escapes that should not have been spoken. Or someone says something that offends us. A child inconveniences you. A bore stops you. You don't like the weather. Your work is not going according to plan. A piece of furniture is broken. A dress is torn. I know," he says, "that these are not occasions for practicing very heroic virtue. But they would definitely be enough to acquire it if we really wished to do so."[4]

So what should I do with my list of annoyances? Tear it up? Wish it away? Or let it remind me that God has a tried and true strategy for building up his life in me? Come to think of it, maybe I should take that list and draw lots of thistles and thorns around it, reminding myself that far from stealing my peace, little stuff can increase it.

Lord, help me to stop complaining about the little thorns you allow in my life, because complaining only drives them deeper. Instead, let me trust you to bring good out of them, deepening my peace in the days ahead.

HOT POTATO

Give all your worries and cares to God, for he cares about you.

1 PETER 5:7

Ever played the game Hot Potato? Here's how it works. Begin by designating an item—a potato, a book, a beanbag—as the "hot potato." Form a circle, turn on the music, and then start passing the "hot potato" around. When the music stops, whoever is holding the potato is out, and the game begins again until only one player is left.

Sometimes anxiety functions like that hot potato. We give it to each other. Peter tells us the secret of dealing with it. "Give all your worries and cares to God," he says, "for he cares about you." Listen to how one pastor unpacks this advice:

"Cast all your anxiety. Anxiety is not meant to be held on to. It's not a treasure or a keepsake. Anxiety is not a bosom friend or a comfort toy. Anxiety is an enemy. It's an enemy to a sober mind. It's an enemy to peace. It's an enemy to faith. Anxiety chews at the roots of the plant of faith and life until, having eaten away the root system completely, it leaves us like stalks stuffed into fertile soil but with no way of gathering nourishment and nutrients.

"Dishonest Christians pretend there is no cause for anxiety in life. They 'keep a stiff upper lip' and don plastic masks. Inside they're twisted into a pretzel of worry, but their dishonesty and hypocrisy keeps them from telling others. The text simply assumes that faithful Christians living for the Lord Jesus will know anxiety in this world. All those who live godly lives in Christ Jesus will be persecuted. And that persecution will give rise to anxiety, worry, and fear. But, we are to throw or cast anxiety away."[5]

I might add that plenty of things in addition to persecution will give rise to our anxiety. No matter what's causing anxiety, the point is not to throw it at each other but to cast it on the Lord, who is well able to deal with it.

Father, if there's anything contagious about my life, I pray that it won't be anxiety but the peace that comes from learning to trust you.

WHAT GOOD IS WORRY?

When I am afraid, I will put my trust in you.

PSALM 56:3

I don't think it's possible to eliminate every shred of worry from our lives. Maybe someone on planet Earth has found a way to stop worrying forever, but I have yet to meet the person. Having said this, I think it is both advisable and possible to reduce the amount of worry we feel.

Let's look at why worry is problematic. First, worry transports you away from reality and into your imagination. Though your anxiety may have sprouted from something concrete, it quickly leads to a make-believe world in which the dragons and demons you face will seem far bigger, fiercer, and more numerous than they are.

Second, God deals in reality. Worrying catapults you into a future that may never happen, but it is in the present that you need God's grace.

Third, though worry can instigate a search for solutions, chronic worrying rarely, if ever, results in anything helpful. (Ask yourself whether you have ever felt glad that you worried and fretted about something.)

Fourth, as Chuck Swindoll points out, "We worry when we subtract God's presence from our crises." It's hard to feel peaceful if you think God is absent just when you need him most.

You can probably come up with your own list of reasons why worry is problematic. Perhaps our goal should not be to eliminate every atom of worry from our lives but to use it for a good purpose. In that case, worry could function like an alarm clock, warning us that we need to pray about something or do something in order to address a problem. Just as we wouldn't let an alarm clock keep ringing once it's done the job of prying us out of bed, we shouldn't let the worry alarm keep sounding once it's woken us to the need to take our concerns to the Lord. Instead of letting worry become a way of life, let's think of anxious feelings as a call to prayer and action, based on the wisdom God gives.

Lord, help me to notice anxious thoughts the minute I start thinking them. As I do, help me to turn to you for help and perspective, trusting you will give it in your good time.

September 8

LEAKS

The LORD said to Job, "Do you still want to argue with the Almighty?
You are God's critic, but do you have the answers?"

JOB 40:1-2

Ever had a leaky faucet? If so, you may be aware that ignoring even a small leak can prove costly. When it comes to experiencing God's peace, there's another slow drip that can cost you plenty—a habit of blaming God. Some of us engage in the practice so regularly we barely notice we are doing it. Whenever something goes wrong, we ask why God allowed it.

This question is asked ad nauseam in the media. Shortly after Princess Diana died in an automobile crash, Philip Yancey received a call from a television program. "Can you appear on the show?" the producer asked. "We want you to explain how God could possibly allow such a terrible accident."

Philip had his own questions: "Could it have had something to do with a drunk driver going ninety miles an hour in a narrow tunnel? How, exactly, was God involved?"[6]

Many people have publicly blamed God for mistakes they made. A boxer by the name of Ray "Boom Boom" Mancini made this comment after throwing a punch that killed another boxer: "Sometimes I wonder why God does the things he does." And what about the young woman who wrote to Dr. James Dobson: "Four years ago, I was dating a man and became pregnant. I was devastated! I asked God, 'Why have You allowed this to happen to me?'"[7] Huh? Whatever happened to taking personal responsibility?

You and I may not be guilty of such irrationality, but we may blame God for bad things that happen simply because we live in the midst of a fallen world. Blaming God is a surefire way, not of experiencing more of his peace, but of draining every last drop of it from our lives.

Father, I don't know why you allow certain tragedies to happen. Help
me to stop trying to answer the unanswerable and to focus instead
on how I can respond in the midst of such tragedies.

IS THERE A TERRORIST IN YOUR LIFE?

*LORD, how great is your mercy; let me be revived by following your regulations.
Many persecute and trouble me, yet I have not swerved from your laws. . . . The
very essence of your words is truth; all your just regulations will stand forever.*

PSALM 119:156-157, 160

Some of us live under the rule of terrorists—people who will do their best
to make our lives miserable if we don't do what they want us to (and even
if we do). These kinds of terrorists often start young—think of the toddler
who throws nonstop tantrums or the child who whimpers whenever she's
displeased. Adults, of course, can be the worst terrorists of all. Think of
chronic complainers, whiners, controllers, and "cling-ons," as well as those
who are verbally and physically abusive. Emotionally immature, they create
an atmosphere that can poison the peace of anyone in their orbit.

When such people are at work, sabotaging an organization, Edwin
Friedman calls them pathogens, identifying them as people who

> are invasive of other people's space by nature;
> lack the ability to regulate their emotions and behaviors;
> cannot learn from experience; and
> have lots of stamina.[8]

Dealing with such people can be extremely difficult. If you are in an
abusive situation, you will need outside help to stay safe. But the best way to
deal with the ordinary, run-of-the-mill terrorists is to address their behaviors
by changing yours. Stop allowing yourself to get sucked in every time they
throw a fit. Find ways to create space in the relationship. Set boundaries you
will not allow them to cross without appropriate consequences. Decide that
you will stop overfunctioning so they can stop underfunctioning. And don't
forget to pray for them while you're at it.

Whatever you do, find a way to take care of yourself, realizing that the
healthier you are, the less influence they will have.

*Lord, if I am encouraging and tolerating bad behavior in others by what I am doing or not
doing, please show me what I can change and then give me the power to make the changes.*

INSIDE YOUR HEAD

*Don't worry about anything; instead, pray about everything. Tell
God what you need, and thank him for all he has done.*

PHILIPPIANS 4:6

Consider the following scenario. It's been a great morning. Feeling ener-getic, you've already accomplished several things on your to-do list. Plus your boss complimented you on an important project. And your husband called just to say he loves you. You feel happy and at peace.

Then you notice that you have an e-mail from your child's school, the kind that informs you of his latest grades. Opening it, you note with distress that he's just gotten an F on a test. You get a little jolt of adrenaline. Why didn't he study harder? He never listens. Everything you've tried to do to help him has failed. Last week he got a C- and now it's an F. What if he has to be held back? You doubt he'll ever make it to college. No one will hire him if he doesn't have a degree. He's going to be poor for the rest of his life.

What has just happened? You have gone from zero to sixty in the space of seconds. Starting with a bit of bad news about Johnnie's grades, you now have him living in poverty for the remainder of his earthly life, despite the fact that he's only twelve years old. One of the problems with anxiety is that it accelerates our fears, taking us to places that don't yet exist and presenting us with problems we don't need to solve—like Johnnie's future homelessness.

Picture anxiety as a kind of laminate spreading across your brain and locking you inside your head. Pinging back and forth, your anxious thoughts accelerate, making it hard to focus on anything else. Then picture something else, a word from God forming in your mind: "Do not be anxious about any-thing, but in every situation, by prayer and petition, with thanksgiving, pre-sent your requests to God" (Philippians 4:6, NIV).

So you direct your thoughts away from Johnnie's bleak future and toward the Lord himself, calling to mind the ways he's helped you in the past and thanking him for them. Lingering over God's faithfulness, you then ask for help in dealing with the present situation, trusting in his guidance, which will come in God's good time. That is the way toward peace.

*Lord, plant your Word deep inside my heart and let the Holy
Spirit remind me of it when I most need to hear it.*

September 11

WHAT'S THAT SMELL?

Now [God] uses us to spread the knowledge of Christ everywhere, like a sweet perfume. Our lives are a Christ-like fragrance rising up to God. But this fragrance is perceived differently by those who are being saved and by those who are perishing. To those who are perishing, we are a dreadful smell of death and doom. But to those who are being saved, we are a life-giving perfume.

2 CORINTHIANS 2:14-16

My friend Leslie recently gave thanks for a "nosy" neighbor. Perhaps I should clarify by saying that she was really thanking God for a neighbor with a good nose. Unbeknownst to Leslie a gas leak had formed in the pipeline that entered her home. Fortunately, the pipeline is next to her neighbor's driveway. As soon as he smelled it, he alerted her to the problem and disaster was averted.

Did you know that natural gas is actually both odorless and colorless? As a precaution, the utility company adds an odorant that smells like rotten eggs to help people notice gas leaks. What a good idea!

Perhaps God does something similar—only he does it with his followers who faithfully share the Good News. The apostle Paul spoke of his passion for spreading the gospel wherever he went, saying that by doing so, his life had become a fragrance presented by Christ to God. But he noted a strange phenomenon: not everyone perceived that fragrance the same way. To those who were open to the gospel, Paul smelled like an inviting perfume, but to those who were not, he smelled noxious. Here's how *The Message* puts Paul's words: "Because of Christ, we give off a sweet scent rising to God, which is recognized by those on the way of salvation—an aroma redolent with life. But those on the way to destruction treat us more like the stench from a rotting corpse" (2 Corinthians 2:15).

As we witness about Christ, through our lives and our words, the gospel is either perceived as an invitation or as a premonition, depending on the state of a person's heart. Regardless of that dynamic, we cannot stop sharing, first, because we cannot judge the paths people will eventually take, and second, because that bad smell may be just the warning they need to turn around and embrace the way to salvation and peace.

Lord, like Paul, I want my life to give off the aroma of Christ so that others may know him. Give me courage and grace to be his witness.

Since you have been raised to new life with Christ, set your sights on the realities of heaven, where Christ sits in the place of honor at God's right hand. Think about the things of heaven, not the things of earth. For you died to this life, and your real life is hidden with Christ in God.

<small>COLOSSIANS 3:1-3</small>

Every year my neighborhood hosts a garden tour that is open to the public. One of the most beautiful gardens on the tour belongs to the house directly across the street from mine. From spring through fall, I am treated to stunning, storybook views every time I look out the window. Though my neighbor's home is beautiful, I have often thought my more moderately priced home the better choice simply because of the view it affords.

When real-estate magnate Donald Trump was asked why the units in his buildings were selling while other buildings were not, here's what he said: "Go and look at the windows in their building and then look at mine, and you will know the answer."[9] Paul Tripp cites this story in his book *Forever: Why You Can't Live without It*, pointing out that life is all about windows. Large windows let in the light and add a feeling of spaciousness. If the view outside is lovely and interesting, all the better. If the windows are small and few, then the place will feel cramped and dark.

Tripp points out that all of us look at life through some kind of window. We may, he says, be looking through the window of past hardship or the window of philosophy or psychology or the window of the right-here-right-now. Whatever window we adopt has a profound effect on how we will live our lives.

Without the window of *forever*, Tripp says, peace and joy will be elusive. We will be thrown by circumstances. We will forget where we're going and whom we belong to. But with forever in view, all that will change. Our hope will increase, our confidence will build. We will realize we are on a journey that will someday end in complete fulfillment. Let's remember, as Tripp says, that we haven't yet moved to our final address. Keeping this in mind will enable us, he says, to "face difficulty without wanting to give up and experience pleasure without becoming addicted to it. We live with hope in our heart, eyes to the future, and hands holding this present world loosely."[10]

Lord, I want heaven to fill my thoughts. Help me to listen carefully to what you have promised in your Word, I pray.

DESTINATION

Above all, you must live as citizens of heaven, conducting yourselves in a manner worthy of the Good News about Christ. Then, whether I come and see you again or only hear about you, I will know that you are standing together with one spirit and one purpose, fighting together for the faith, which is the Good News.

PHILIPPIANS 1:27

If you have ever been to London, you have probably ridden on the Tube, the city's subway system. The first time I traveled there on business, I felt intimidated until I learned how easy it is to get around. As in many cities, the various subway lines are color-coded so you have merely to pinpoint your destination on the map and then take the appropriately colored line to reach it. To figure out which way to go, you simply locate the last stop on the route in the direction of your destination. Since each route is labeled according to its final destination, it is easy to avoid hopping a train heading the wrong way. So if you are at Westminster and want to go to Whitechapel, for instance, you have to take the green line labeled Upminster.

As in my experience of traveling by subway, it helps to have our final destination in view, lest we lose our way along the journey. In his first letter, Peter says that all who follow Christ are "temporary residents and foreigners" (1 Peter 2:11). Likewise, Paul reminds us that we are citizens of heaven and not of earth. In practical terms, that means it's a mistake to treat this life as though it's all there is, trying to squeeze from it everything our hearts desire and then letting inevitable disappointments cast shadows on our faith.

Paul Tripp points out that even if we are confused on this point, "God always responds to us with eternity in view."[11] No wonder we don't always get what we ask for. God is using a different timeline, a different end goal, allowing the difficulties and trials we face to shape us toward heaven. Peace comes, in part, from letting go of our limited time horizon in order to grasp hold of the eternity God promises.

Lord, you have promised me heaven. Help me to have a richer understanding of what heaven is and what that means for my life right now, I pray.

IS THAT ALL THERE IS?

We are citizens of heaven, where the Lord Jesus Christ lives. And we are eagerly waiting for him to return as our Savior. He will take our weak mortal bodies and change them into glorious bodies like his own, using the same power with which he will bring everything under his control.

PHILIPPIANS 3:20-21

In the category of "Most Depressing Song in the History of the World" comes Peggy Lee's classic hit, "Is That All There Is?" In case you are too young to remember it, I will offer a recap. Throughout the song, the singer croons about notable life experiences, things like her house burning down, a visit to the circus, falling in love for the first time. After each, she poses the plaintive question: "Is that all there is?" Lamenting over life's many disappointments, she refuses to kill herself lest death itself might also disappoint her. In some ways, she sounds like the pop version of the teacher in Ecclesiastes, who proclaimed, "I came to hate life because everything done here under the sun is so troubling. Everything is meaningless—like chasing the wind" (2:17).

Paul, on the other hand, tells us that though much in our world is broken, it is not meaningless. On the contrary, what meets the eye is not all there is. There is so much more. Reminding us that we belong to heaven more than earth, Paul promises that Christ will one day take our "weak mortal bodies" and transform them into something glorious like his own. Not only that, but the Lord will accomplish this feat by using "the same power with which he will bring everything under his control." One day, we will realize that nothing in this world is outside the overwhelming power of Jesus Christ. Everything—even mental illness, decrepitude, and death—will give way to him. Everything that causes us anguish will be defeated and overturned.

I have a young friend who is autistic. On that day, she will become fully herself. My mother is slipping into dementia. She will be restored. My sister died suddenly, at the age of sixteen. She will be raised up.

What in your life has been disappointing? For whom do you grieve? As you bring each one into view, remember that *everything, everywhere* is going to be conquered by the same mighty power that raised Jesus from the dead and that will surely raise us from death to life. Is that all there is? Not on your life!

Lord, I long for the day when your mighty power will conquer everything, everywhere. Until then, let me grow strong in this hope.

HIDDEN THINGS

Everything that is hidden will eventually be brought into the open.

MARK 4:22

Heather Rowe read these words from Mark's Gospel with the sudden impression that God was about to reveal something important about her husband, Paul. Despite their love for each other, she felt frustrated by her husband's insensitivity, hostility, and social awkwardness. He often withdrew when others were present, preferring to play video games or read. His comments sometimes bordered on cruelty. He never seemed to care how she felt, despite all her attempts to tell him. Feeling guilty about her reactions to her husband's behaviors, she cried out to God, asking him to transform her: "Lord," she pleaded, "my husband's arrogance, his cynicism, his neglect, his hostility are laying heavily on me like a massive weight!"

"Why are you wearing them?" The question came suddenly.

Startled, she realized she had been taking these things on herself by the way she had reacted to him over the years.

"What are you going to do with them?" God asked.

She responded by saying she wanted to nail everything to the cross—all the arrogance, pride, resentment, cynicism, neglect, and hostility.

"What do you have left?" God seemed to say.

"I am seeing a lonely, frightened little boy."

"Do you think you could love him?"

"Oh yes, I could love him. I could take him in my arms and comfort him."

Later, she explained, "God told me to try to see that lonely, frightened little boy every time I looked at my husband. He told me to look beyond all the other rubbish because he took all of that on himself on the cross."[12]

A short time later, Heather discovered that her husband had Asperger's Syndrome, a high-functioning form of autism. No wonder he acted the way he did. Greater understanding has brought with it greater peace, though there are still struggles. By coming before God in prayer and by listening to his Word, Heather has experienced God enabling her to accept and love her husband, despite his challenges.

Like Heather, we cry out to God about our own difficult relationships. Like her, let us trust him to respond.

Father, please teach me how to relate to the difficult people in my life.

TRAVELING MERCIES

I look up to the mountains—does my help come from there? My help comes from the LORD, who made heaven and earth! . . . The sun will not harm you by day, nor the moon at night. The LORD keeps you from all harm and watches over your life. The LORD keeps watch over you as you come and go, both now and forever.

PSALM 121:1-2, 6-8

Psalm 121 is known as a psalm of ascent, one of a group of psalms prayed by Jewish pilgrims on their way to Jerusalem to worship at three annual feasts. The psalmist looks to the mountains, perhaps wondering if thieves and robbers lurk there. Or perhaps he is thinking of the mountains around Jerusalem, longing to worship God in the Temple.

Each verse repeats a theme as if to underline or italicize it, highlighting the truth it affirms. And what is this truth? That on every journey—even on the journey of life—God is our protector.

Last night I was discussing the psalm with friends. Someone asked why the psalmist said that neither the sun nor the moon would hurt you. The phrase sounded strange. One person suggested that the psalmist might be referring to the sun and moon gods of the surrounding peoples. Another remarked on how difficult it is to live in a desert climate, where sunstroke is always a danger. Still another mentioned the link between the words *lunacy* and *moon*, wondering if the pilgrims who prayed the psalms would have linked the moon to mental instability. We concluded that in this case the sun and moon must signify anything that might terrify or threaten you by day or by night. Our discussion wrapped up when one friend attempted a modern paraphrase of verse 6, quipping:

The Dow Jones Industrial will not strike you by day,
    nor the Hang Seng Index by night.

With that we parted. And when it was time to sleep, I did just that.

Lord, though trouble will come, you will protect me from evil, whether it stalks in broad daylight or prowls in the dark. Thank you for watching over my soul.

CALMING YOUR INNER BULLY

Don't copy the behavior and customs of this world, but let God transform you into a new person by changing the way you think.

ROMANS 12:2

Rare is the school without an anti-bullying campaign. We know how easy it is for children at the receiving end of such behaviors to be devastated by them. The same is true for adults. Interacting on a regular basis with people who belittle and malign us is hazardous to our emotional health. Who wants to be around someone who communicates their contempt, with or without words, indicating that they think us boring, bossy, stupid, flaky, weak, inconsiderate, ugly, insensitive, worthless, or a failure?

But what if the bully is you? I'm not implying that you bully other people. But, truth be known, some of us have a habit of bullying ourselves. Here are a few examples of things we might say to ourselves that we wouldn't dream of saying to anyone else:

What an idiot!   Nobody likes me.
Why can't I do anything right?   I look awful.
God hates me.   God won't forgive me.
I'm worthless.

Researchers estimate that we have, on average, seventy thousand thoughts in the course of a single day. It's inevitable that some of them will be negative. But when our negative thoughts greatly outweigh our positive thoughts, we have a problem. Many of these thoughts come to mind unbidden, operating just below the surface of consciousness. Writing them down can help us become more aware of them, forcing them out into the open so we can challenge their accuracy. Once we become aware of these internal dialogues, we can replace them with milder, neutral, or even positive statements that affirm the truth of who we are and what God thinks of us.

Why not spend some time paying attention to your thoughts today? Try writing down the negative ones, and then take each one to God in prayer.

Lord, I don't want to bully myself or anyone else. Help me to recognize the way I pressure and condemn myself, and teach me how to counter such thoughts with truth from your Word.

SEEING THE GLASS AS HALF-FULL

How joyful are those who fear the LORD—all who follow his ways!
PSALM 128:1

Study after study shows that optimists are both happier and healthier than pessimists. Optimists experience less stress and don't give up as easily as pessimists. They even tend to live longer. Unfortunately, I'm a pessimist. The online quiz I took proves it. So what should I do? Conclude that I was born a pessimist and will remain a pessimist? No, that's way too pessimistic!

According to Martin Seligman, a clinical psychologist who has spent more than thirty years studying this topic, pessimists are capable of adopting a more optimistic approach to life. One way to do that is to change the way you explain your successes and failures. Typically, optimists are good at maximizing their successes and minimizing their failures. Say, for instance, someone compliments you for your cooking. You could explain the compliment to yourself positively by thinking, *I have turned out to be a pretty good cook!* Or you could brush it off by thinking, *I guess I got lucky with that recipe.* The first explanatory style takes credit for a job well done, while the second views the success as an isolated incident, not likely to repeat itself.

As Christians, we sometimes hesitate to take credit for our success because we don't want to become proud. But what if taking credit where credit is due helps us to better reflect the joy we have in Christ, who, after all, has given us every reason to be optimistic?

What about our failures? We have to be honest about them as well, but failure doesn't have to be something we get stuck in. Instead it can become a teacher, leading us toward greater insight. I remember traveling by myself for several days in Europe after a business trip. Whenever I got lost, instead of getting upset as I was accustomed to do when traveling on more familiar territory in the United States, I simply told myself, *I don't have to hurry. Anyway, I'm learning my way around.* That little coping mechanism added peace to my adventure, keeping me from feeling frustrated and alone.

If you tend toward pessimism as I do, try a little experiment. Spend the next week trying to maximize your successes and minimize your failures. See if it produces a little more happiness in your life.

Lord, with you as my Savior, I have every reason to be an optimist. Help me to recognize patterns of thinking that keep me from experiencing your hope.

HOW TO REMEMBER

*I recall all you have done, O LORD; I remember your wonderful deeds of long ago. They
are constantly in my thoughts. I cannot stop thinking about your mighty works.*

PSALM 77:11-12

In the movie *Gigi*, Honoré Lachaille, played by Maurice Chevalier, and
Madame Alvarez, played by Hermione Gingold, sing a song commemo-
rating a romantic night spent together many years before. While he recalls
an evening that was lit by a "dazzling April moon," she declares that it was
June and there was no moon. He mentions Friday, but she is certain they
were together on a Monday. He envisions her in gold, but she swears she was
dressed entirely in blue. Their contradictory memories swing back and forth
throughout the song, which is capped by the refrain: "Ah, yes, I remember it
well." The gentle humor of the lyrics points out something we all know—that
people can remember the same event in very different ways.

The same is true when it comes to our ability to remember how God
has acted, both in Scripture and in our own lives. Take the Israelites. After
fleeing from Egypt, they could have built a society that mimicked Egypt's
cruelty toward the weak and defenseless. That's often how things go when
subjected peoples find freedom. The underdogs become the oppressors.
Instead, the Israelites enshrined humane principles in their law regarding the
treatment of slaves coupled with the obligation to welcome foreigners, laws
far in advance of their contemporaries. They did this because their overarching memories pertained not to the evil they suffered but to the good they
experienced from God's delivering hand.

We, too, have been delivered by a loving and redeeming God. Basing
our lives on this memory will free us from the danger of becoming more like
the people who have hurt us rather than the God who has saved us. It will
also free us from the memory of our own sins and failures as we choose to
remember above everything the mercy and love that God has shown us.

*Father, let the memory of your love and mercy surround me,
reshaping me into the image of your Son, Jesus.*

September 20

LIVING FOR THE KINGDOM

*The Kingdom of God is not a matter of what we eat or drink, but of
living a life of goodness and peace and joy in the Holy Spirit.*

ROMANS 14:17

I live in an older home in an older neighborhood. Friends sometimes comment on how much character my house has with its crown moldings, arched doorways, and built-in bookshelves. But as anyone who has ever owned an older home knows, character does not come cheaply. There is always something to fix, patch, improve. No matter how much effort and money I put into it, I know my house will eventually crumble into nothing. That's the truth about most things. They will not last.

But some things will. Our souls will. But that's not all. The work we do *for* Christ and in Christ—that will last too. As N. T. Wright puts it, when it comes to building for God's Kingdom, "You are not oiling the wheels of a machine that's about to roll over a cliff. You are not restoring a great painting that's shortly going to be thrown on the fire. . . . You are—strange though it may seem, almost as hard to believe as the resurrection itself—accomplishing something that will become in due course part of God's new world.

"Every act of love, gratitude, and kindness; every work of art or music inspired by the love of God and delight in the beauty of his creation; every minute spent teaching a severely handicapped child to read or to walk; every act of care and nurture, of comfort and support, for one's fellow human beings and for that matter one's fellow nonhuman creatures; and of course every prayer, all Spirit-led teaching, every deed that spreads the gospel, builds up the church, embraces and embodies holiness rather than corruption, and makes the name of Jesus honored in the world—all of this will find its way, through the resurrecting power of God, into the new creation that God will one day make."[13]

So today let us remember that because of what Christ has done in our lives, we are called, as Paul tells the Romans, to live a life of goodness and peace and joy, seeking first the Kingdom of God.

*Lord, I want to stay on course, using the new life you have given me
to build up your Kingdom, not mine. For the things that are done for
you and in your power—these are the things that will last.*

RUNNING ON EMPTY

*Those who love their life in this world will lose it. Those who care
nothing for their life in this world will keep it for eternity.*

JOHN 12:25

What if you were tethered to a treadmill running at about four miles
an hour? There is no off switch on this treadmill and nobody around
to release you from the tether. Even if you were in great shape, you wouldn't
survive the experience. On and on you would run until your body finally
gave way.

This is a picture of what life can ultimately feel like when you are constantly running after things the world thinks are valuable—money, power,
sex, security, prestige. No matter how hard or how long you run, you will
never be satisfied—the treadmill just keeps going. In the end, your whole-
hearted pursuit of such things will destroy rather than fulfill you.

If this is so, why do we keep pursuing what will not satisfy? One reason
is that we get a temporary sense of well-being. With enough money in the
bank, we feel secure. With children in the best schools, we feel confident
they will succeed. With each new purchase, we get a little hit of pleasure.
There's a lot of positive reinforcement. But the system only works if we keep
on keeping on, finding something else to feed our pleasure machine. The
problem comes, of course, when the system is disrupted and the machine
breaks down. We lose a job, our investments sour, a child strays, we become
ill. When some or all of the things we counted on to make our life feel meaningful, safe, and pleasurable are taken from us, what then?

Such disruptions can be incredibly painful and frightening. They
may throw us into a season of tremendous anxiety. We may for a time feel
exhausted, empty, and lost. But what if they are, in the end, a godsend, an
opportunity to get free from the tether, to stop living on a treadmill and
begin living a life of greater peace and freedom?

If you find that you are spending time on that treadmill, ask God to
free you so you can pursue the peace that comes from having his goals and
desires at the center of your heart.

*Lord, in those empty, anxious times, help me wait on you, believing that
you want to fill me with a love so full that it will satisfy my soul.*

FACING DOWN THE GREAT LIE

I am with you always, even to the end of the age.
MATTHEW 28:20

Adolf Hitler is credited with identifying a deceitful technique called "The Big Lie." The principle is that people will more easily swallow a big lie than a small one. According to Hitler, people do not believe others have the nerve to create big lies, making them more likely to believe a giant falsehood. In order to be believed, one needs a lie that is both big enough and simple enough. Once you have that, you only need to keep repeating it. Eventually, most people will swallow it whole.

Most of us will never have to face down the lies of a figure like Adolf Hitler. But lies will come. The biggest one is this: "God is not with you." That's it. Over and over, Satan will repeat the lie, usually when you are facing some kind of challenge. A child falls ill: "God won't hear your prayers." You've lost your job: "God doesn't care." Your marriage has run into difficulty: "God can't do anything because it's already too far gone." You've committed the same sin once again: "God doesn't want anything to do with you."

Over and over the drumbeat of lies can penetrate our hearts until we begin to believe a lie so big and so obviously at odds with our faith that it chills our hearts, convincing us that God is not who he says he is—*Immanuel*—meaning, "God with us."

Jesus himself had to face down this terrible lie when he was hanging on the cross. The religious leaders who watched him dying flung it at him saying, "He saved others . . . but he can't save himself! So he is the King of Israel, is he? Let him come down from the cross right now, and we will believe in him! He trusted God, so let God rescue him now if he wants him!" (Matthew 27:42-43).

If you have been entertaining falsehoods about God's faithfulness, take a moment to ask for God's forgiveness. Tell him that you are not going to listen to the lies of the enemy. Ask him to arm you with "the sword of the Spirit" (Ephesians 6:17), which is his Word. Then take your stand. Resist the devil, and he *will* flee.

Father, forgive me for letting the enemy into my heart by listening to lies about you. Arm me with the sword of the Spirit, helping me to stand strong, placing my faith and trust in you no matter what happens.

BIZARRO WORLD

I have told you all this so that you may have peace in me. Here on earth you will have many trials and sorrows. But take heart, because I have overcome the world.

JOHN 16:33

S ome of you are probably too young to remember Bizarro World, a fictional place introduced by DC Comics in the 1960s. This strange, cube-shaped planet, also known as Htrae (Earth spelled backward), is populated by Bizarro and his sidekicks, who are weird mutations of Superman and his friends. Their Bizarro Code goes like this: "Us do opposite of all earthly things! Us hate beauty! Us love ugliness! Is big crime to make anything perfect on Bizarro World!" Besides regrettable deficits in the grammar department, Bizarro World also has a rather strange monetary system, as evidenced by the salesman who hawks Bizarro bonds with the catchy slogan: "Guaranteed to lose money for you."

A fan of all things Superman, comedian Jerry Seinfeld is one of several who have helped enshrine Bizarro World in popular culture. In one episode of his sitcom, Seinfeld's character discusses the pilot for a program with executives from NBC. Hoping to up the ante, his friend George Costanza tries to negotiate for more money. But as a result of his bungling, the pilot is canceled and later reinstated for less money. "You don't negotiate to get a lower salary!" Jerry exclaims. "That's negotiation on the Bizarro World!"

What could Bizarro World possibly have to do with a book about biblical peace? Well, look at it this way. When Jesus came, he turned everything upside down. He said the first would be last and the last would be first. He said that when someone strikes you on your cheek, you should turn the other cheek for the next blow. He said if a person takes your shirt, you should offer your coat as well. He said that anyone who wants to be great should humble herself like a little child. Following Jesus as he turns your world upside down is the only way to true peace, strange as that may seem.

Compared to Christ's Kingdom, our world is not that dissimilar to Bizarro World. On planet Earth, life doesn't work the way it was meant to. But fortunately for us, Christ is not content to leave it that way. Instead, he has begun to remake the world one heart at a time, spreading his peace, establishing his love, enabling us to live the life he offers.

Lord, rather than holding on to the values of this broken world,
help me to accept your values and to live by them.

GIRLFRIENDS

A person standing alone can be attacked and defeated, but two can stand back-to-back and conquer. Three are even better, for a triple-braided cord is not easily broken.

ECCLESIASTES 4:12

Are there any mean girls in your past? Though many of us have suffered through our share of difficult relationships with other females, the good news is that many of us have also benefited from having great girlfriends. When a group of women aged 45-55 was recently asked to rate their optimism about the future, 25 percent gave themselves a 10 out of 10 score, indicating that they expect good things in coming years. Only 17 percent of men in this age range were as optimistic. What's the reason for the gender gap? Researchers think it boils down to the fact that women tend to have stronger social circles than men. (By the way, studies also show that religious women tend to live longer than nonreligious ones because of the opportunity for increased social interaction through church.)

"The most optimistic women," reports Gail Sheehy, "spend about six hours a day in social interaction. Some of that time may be with a friend at work, with family, a husband or children, or with a partner, a love interest or neighbors. But girlfriends are the bedrock. The most optimistic women have an inner circle of anywhere from four to a dozen friends who 'have their back' and will drop everything to help in a crisis."[14]

As Sheehy points out, these are not merely Facebook friends or LinkedIn contacts but real flesh-and-blood women who are there for each other. This truth has certainly been borne out in my own life. In fact, I've been blessed not only with girlfriends but sisters in Christ, women who love me and pray for me. I know that I can tell them anything without fear that they will pass along secrets or talk behind my back. Not only that, but my friends make a great sounding board whenever I need advice.

If you have friends like that, give thanks to God today for each one. If not, invest time and energy to start making some, asking God to guide you to other women, remembering, as Francis Bacon remarked, that friends can double your joy and halve your grief.

Lord, thank you for every single girlfriend you have ever given me, especially for my sisters in Christ. Enable me to be as good a friend to them as they are to me. Help me to be open to forging new friendships as you lead.

WHO'S IN CHARGE?

*"Don't sin by letting anger control you." Don't let the sun go down while
you are still angry, for anger gives a foothold to the devil.*

EPHESIANS 4:26-27

Rabbi Joseph Telushkin is the author of a fascinating book entitled *The
Book of Jewish Values: A Day-By-Day Guide to Ethical Living*. In it he offers a particularly useful piece of advice that will help you keep the peace or restore it
once it's been lost. "Restrict the expression of your anger," Telushkin advises,
"to the incident that provoked it. Be as critical or annoyed as you like."[15] But
make sure your words remain focused on the incident that made you angry in
the first place. If you do that, you will probably not say anything permanently
damaging to yourself or others.

Telushkin is not telling us to ignore our anger or to stuff it in a box but
rather to put a leash on it. Similarly, Paul tells the Ephesians "Be angry but do
not sin" (Ephesians 4:26, RSV). Paul assumes we will get angry. The point is
what we do with our anger. Do we control it, or does it control us? Paul also
sets limits to our anger by saying we should never let the sun go down on it.
In other words, don't go to bed angry.

For some of us, anger has always been a problem. Getting it under control is a huge challenge. It's like trying to leash train a dog that's always been
allowed to run wild. At first the dog will strain at the leash, pulling you down
the street and barking at every other dog in sight. But if you're patient and
persistent and know even a little bit about dogs, you will eventually be able to
train it to walk beside you. You can do something similar with your anger.

If you have a hard time putting your anger on a leash, consider getting help, perhaps taking a course in anger management. And don't forget
that another name for the Holy Spirit is the Helper. Ask God to guide you
through the power of the Spirit, helping you to learn how to control your
anger so it no longer controls you.

*Father, forgive me for the ways I have let anger control me. Teach me how to be angry
without sinning. Guide me by the power of your Spirit, and help me to change.*

*Hear my prayer, O LORD; listen to my plea! Answer
me because you are faithful and righteous.*

PSALM 143:1

Last year someone gave me a journal on which these words are printed:
"God, grant me the serenity to accept the things I cannot change."
Though I use the journal regularly, I confess that I've secretly disliked the
prayer printed on the front cover. Why? For one thing, the pages of my
journal are filled with the names of those I am praying for, people who desperately need something to change in their lives. They need healing, peace,
provision, salvation, wisdom, rescue, hope. They are people who are out of
work, who have lost a loved one, who are in jail, who are depressed or dying.
It seems an assault on faith to embrace a prayer that implies that some circumstances will not likely change. For another, this prayer challenges deeply
embedded beliefs about my own ability to change things. After all, I am a
fighter, not someone who gives up. I am active, not passive. Or at least that is
how I like to see myself.

At first I was tempted to give the journal away or consign it to the trash
bin. Instead, I forced myself to use it. I kept it because I suspected that God
was trying to get my attention. After all, this prayer has hit a chord with millions of people who have struggled with various kinds of addiction. Surely
there was something I needed to learn from it.

As I began to unpack the prayer, I considered the obvious—that it
expresses the starting point of faith, which is my own inability to provide for
anyone's deepest needs, including my own. To reach this place is to face reality, to let go of illusions. To stop kidding myself about what I can and cannot do. Though illusions can be comforting, they keep me leaning into my
own limited powers rather than God's all-sufficient power. Contrary to first
impressions, the serenity prayer is not about giving up but about letting go
so God can do what only he can, and that is to bring healing, peace, salvation,
wisdom, rescue, and hope to those who need it. There are of course some
things in life that we can change. That's why the whole prayer goes like this:

*God, grant me the serenity to accept the things I cannot change, courage
to change the things I can, and wisdom to know the difference.*

CONNECTING THE DOTS

"I know the plans I have for you," says the LORD. *"They are plans for good and not for disaster, to give you a future and a hope."*

JEREMIAH 29:11

A few years ago, Steve Jobs gave the commencement speech at Stanford University. He told the audience that his decision to drop out of college years earlier was the best one he'd ever made. Why? In part because dropping out of required courses that bored him made it possible for him to drop in on any courses that interested him. One of these was a course on calligraphy, a class that seemed entirely impractical, focusing as it did on all the minute details that make for great typography.

"None of this," he told the Stanford students, "had even a hope of any practical application in my life. But ten years later, when we were designing the first Macintosh computer, it all came back to me. And we designed it all into the Mac. It was the first computer with beautiful typography. If I had never dropped in on that single course in college, the Mac would have never had multiple typefaces or proportionally spaced fonts. And since Windows just copied the Mac, it's likely that no personal computer would have them. If I had never dropped out, I would have never dropped in on this calligraphy class, and personal computers might not have the wonderful typography that they do. Of course it was impossible to connect the dots looking forward when I was in college. But it was very, very clear looking backward ten years later."

Jobs drove the point home again, saying, "You can't connect the dots looking forward; you can only connect them looking backward. So you have to trust that the dots will somehow connect in your future. You have to trust in something—your gut, destiny, life, karma, whatever. This approach has never let me down, and it has made all the difference in my life."[16]

As Christians, we trust in something far better than our "gut" or "karma." In these uncertain times, it's worth remembering the advice of one of the world's most successful men. No matter how hard we try to peer into the future, we can never connect the dots looking forward. Only God can do that. Even now, God is at work connecting the dots of our personal stories, working out his plan for all those who love him.

Lord, thank you for connecting the dots in my life. Help me to entrust the future to you.

September 28

DEPRESSION

*If I ride the wings of the morning, if I dwell by the farthest oceans, even there
your hand will guide me, and your strength will support me. I could ask the
darkness to hide me and the light around me to become night—but even in
darkness I cannot hide from you. To you the night shines as bright as day.*

PSALM 139:9-12

Kathy Cronkite, daughter of the famed newscaster Walter Cronkite, has
written about her struggles with depression, describing what it felt like:

I walk outside, it's the first day of spring, sun shining, breeze wafting,
birds singing—so what? My baby gives me one of those dazzling
you're-the-only-one-in-the-world smiles—so what? My best friend
calls with good news, my boss gives me a raise, my husband cooks
my favorite meal—so what? None of it touches me, nothing makes
me smile. I'm one beat off, one step removed from all around me. . . .
Although I am no longer suicidal, as I write this the weight is still
on my shoulders, the stone sits in my stomach, my face wears a tight
mask. I don't give in to it. I keep myself moving, the battle invisible
even to those closest to me. But now, at least, I know what's dogging
me. I know this will not last. I am not going to die. I am not going
to feel this way forever. The world is not crumbling. I am not crazy,
or bad, or lacking in faith or in discipline. I have a disease. It's called
depression.[17]

Those of us who have never suffered from clinical depression have little
idea of how dark the darkness must be for those who do. If you suffer from
this disorder, you may wonder how you will ever experience God's peace.
Though I have no easy answers to offer, I can say with confidence that God
has not left you and he will not fail you—ever. Today I pray that he will find
a way to encourage you and give you hope. I pray, too, that you will discover
medical and practical help to ease your suffering.

*Lord, you know the inner workings of the mind better than any psychologist
or psychiatrist. Please bring your healing power to all who suffer from
depression and other mental disorders. Don't let them give up. Instead, hold
them, strengthen them, and put them on the path toward peace.*

HUMILITY

True humility and fear of the LORD *lead to riches, honor, and long life.*
PROVERBS 22:4

Last week I had a chance to meet one of my heroes, a woman by the name of Temple Grandin. Perhaps you have seen the movie that was made about her remarkable life. A successful scientist who happens to be on the autism spectrum, Temple has remarkable humility. She's also very funny. Here's what she said when asked whether it would be a good idea to cure autism if we had the capability: "In an ideal world the scientist should find a method to prevent the most severe forms of autism but allow the milder forms to survive. After all, the really social people did not invent the first stone spear. It was probably invented by an Aspie who chipped away at rocks while the other people socialized around the campfire. Without autism traits we might still be living in caves."[18]

When the movie about her was still in production, she was interviewed by *BEEF* magazine. (She is, after all, an animal scientist.) I loved what she had to say about the perils of impending fame: "I have to remind myself not to get a big head. You know what happens. Just look at statues of famous people; they all have pigeon poop on them." [19]

When it comes to humility, I am reminded of the phrase "gateway drugs." Does that sound strange? Here's the connection. Humility, it would seem, is a kind of "gateway virtue"—the entryway to the rest of the virtues. To use another metaphor, humility provides the soil in which all the virtues can flourish. Sir Thomas More once characterized it as "that low, sweet root, from which all heavenly virtues shoot." The word *humble*, is, in fact, related to the Latin words *humilis* and *humus*, both of which mean "earth."

Pride, on the other hand, has an unyielding quality to it. It's like a slab of cement from which nothing grows but weeds that spring up between the cracks.

Scripture links pride to judgment and destruction, while humility is linked to wisdom and favor. If we long for more of God's *shalom*, we need to embrace the virtues, especially humility.

Lord, pride blinds. Open my eyes to recognize and repent of any arrogance in my life. Teach me what it means to be humble.

STRESSED OUT!

A cheerful heart is good medicine.

PROVERBS 17:22

Want to know the leading cause of stress? Here's what one perceptive observer has concluded: "Reality is the leading cause of stress for those in touch with it." Or how about this: "I try to take one day at a time, but sometimes several days attack me at once." Or this: "Cheer up, the worst is yet to come." Or even: "When I hear somebody sigh, 'Life is hard,' I am always tempted to ask, 'Compared to what?'"[20]

A little humor can help break up the stress we feel, easing the intensity of the moment. Perhaps it can even do more than that. Norman Cousins, former editor of the *New York Evening Post*, famously claimed that nonstop doses of Vitamin C, coupled with a diet of humorous books and movies, healed him of ankylosing spondylitis, an autoimmune disease that causes pain and stiffness, primarily in the spinal joints. Though his claims were never clinically verified, it's clear that all those Marx Brothers movies he watched had a positive effect. "I made the joyous discovery," he said, "that ten minutes of genuine belly laughter had an anesthetic effect and would give me at least two hours of pain-free sleep. When the pain-killing effect of the laughter wore off, we would switch on the motion-picture projector again, and, not infrequently, it would lead to another pain-free sleep interval."[21]

Laughter can at least help put our problems in perspective, breaking the cycle of worry and anxiety. If you're in the market for some good laughs, try a few of these classic films to get you started: *Groundhog Day, Big, Duck Soup, The Pink Panther,* or *The Trouble with Harry.* Even better, make sure you get your fix of babies and toddlers, whose laughter is infectious, even if your "fix" merely includes getting a few good laughs from YouTube.

Lord, help me to stop taking life so seriously. Surround me with people whose joy is infectious so that I can begin to put my trials in proper perspective.

October 1

HEALING

When Jesus saw him and knew he had been ill for a long time,
he asked him, "Would you like to get well?"

JOHN 5:6

The man was lying on a cheap straw mat, propped up on his arms. He felt lucky to get a spot at the pool, where the ill gathered, but not lucky enough to make it into the water as soon as it began to stir. Like many, he was sure the pool's curative powers were activated by a visiting angel who would stir up the water from time to time.

"Would you like to get well?" the rabbi asked, balancing on his heels to look the man in the face. The question startled him. Didn't this teacher realize he had been an invalid for thirty-eight years, almost as long as most healthy men live? Something in the rabbi's tone, however, kept him from giving an angry retort.

Instead, he replied, "I can't, sir . . . for I have no one to put me into the pool when the water bubbles up. Someone else always gets there ahead of me" (John 5:7).

There! That should put a stop to the conversation. Instead came the quick command: "Stand up, pick up your mat, and walk!" (verse 8). The man felt something lift him to his feet. Hardly knowing what he was doing, he bent down to snatch up his mat. To the amazement of all, he simply gave a quizzical look and then began walking.

The odd question—"Would you like to get well?"—may cause us to wonder whether the invalid had wanted to be healed. Commenting on this passage, Mark Buchanan says, "Sickness can actually steal the place of God. It can become the sick person's center, the touchstone by which he defines himself. Illness is a tyrant with huge territorial ambitions. It is a seductress with large designs. It wants not only the sick person's body. It wants his heart and mind also."[1]

Pain, especially when prolonged, can be a vortex that is hard to escape. If you are praying for healing for yourself or others, ask God to restore both body and soul as a sign of his powerful presence and his promised peace.

Lord, heal those who are suffering from chronic illnesses that
threaten to take over their identities. Give them strength and peace,
courage and hope. Raise them up and make them whole.

October 2

SMALL PROBLEMS

Joyful is the person who finds wisdom, the one who gains understanding.
PROVERBS 3:13

I n a hurry as usual, I climbed into the car to drive my daughter to school. When I turned the key in the ignition, nothing happened. I tried twice more with the same result. The battery was dead! We would have to walk. At least it was a pleasant morning and we lived only a few blocks from school.

What, I wondered, had drained the battery? Then I remembered that the interior lights had been on when I parked the car in the driveway the night before. I had meant to investigate but had been too busy carting groceries, getting dinner, and helping the children with homework. If I hadn't overlooked a little problem in the first place, I realized, it wouldn't have grown into a bigger one this morning.

That's how it is with most things. Small problems that are overlooked grow into bigger problems that can threaten the peace. Take my friend Jan. A mother of three, she confided not long ago that she was worried about two of her boys because she had caught them telling lies. It wasn't anything big. They would say they were going to bed when they were really hiding under the covers playing video games. Or they would assure her they had done their homework when they hadn't. Or they would blame someone else for an infraction they had committed themselves.

She was shocked to realize both boys had become inveterate liars. Why hadn't she and her husband noticed the problem earlier? She wasn't quite sure. Maybe their lies had at first seemed inconsequential. Maybe she and her husband had thought it enough to simply chide them. Maybe both parents had been too busy to pay close attention to what their children were telling them. Whatever the case, Jan realized that overlooking the problem had made it grow larger and more entrenched.

Every day a thousand things assail us. Overlooking some of them is probably a good idea. But ignoring the wrong ones means we are asking for bigger trouble later. Ask God today to help you pay attention to what matters so that small problems will stay small rather than crowding out the peace he has for you.

Father, please show me any problems I may be ignoring in myself or others.
Then give me the grace and wisdom to know how to deal with them.

WHEN IT'S GOOD TO PROCRASTINATE

In peace I will lie down and sleep, for you alone, O LORD, will keep me safe.

PSALM 4:8

Most of us procrastinate. We put off doing things we fear or dislike, stretching a dental checkup from six months to twelve, paying the bills at the last minute, cramming the night before a test. Though procrastinating can keep anxiety at bay for a short while, in the long run, it acts as a catalyst for worry because we cannot dodge our responsibilities forever. Putting them off only increases our fear, making it more potent as the deadline draws near. Still, I can think of at least one instance in which procrastination may be an effective strategy.

Try this: At night, whenever you are tempted to worry, say to yourself, "I'll worry about it in the morning." If you are afraid you will forget about it, write it down. Then leave it until the next day. Why? Because our brains have a way of dramatizing situations at night, letting fear grow out of proportion to reality. Worrying in the middle of the night is like stepping onto a bullet train headed to a future that doesn't exist. It will only exaggerate our problems and minimize the list of possible solutions, setting us up for more anxiety.

By contrast, daylight can act as a powerful counterbalance to unbridled worry. It can erase or diminish our anxiety, reducing it to more manageable proportions. In the daytime, our brains are less gullible, decreasing the chance that we will embrace high-anxiety scenarios and increasing the chance that we will find positive ways to cope with our problems.

Tonight as you go to sleep, remember, as Philip Gulley has said, that "fear can keep us up all night long, but faith makes one fine pillow."[2]

Lord, why should I do tonight what I can put off until tomorrow? Help me relinquish my worries, trusting that you will enable me to face them with faith and grace in the morning light.

FAULTY ALARMS

I am not afraid of ten thousand enemies who surround me on every side.

PSALM 3:6

Here's a list of the things my children have already survived: automobile accidents, bird flu, cancer, and kidnapping. If you think that's impressive, listen to what I've managed to live through: bankruptcy, an airline crash, a stroke, robbery, and attempted murder—yes, murder! Okay, well, maybe not. It's just that all these are things I've worried about at times, my anxious mind propelling us into disasters that never happened. Can you relate?

Most of us waste precious time and energy dealing with threats that never materialize. Still, worry can be useful if it wakes us up to impending problems, motivating us to seek solutions in response. Worry is a good thing when it serves as a helpful alert. The problem comes when worry morphs into a faulty alarm that won't stop ringing.

Here are a few practical tips for turning off your worry alarm.

1. Since worry is often powered by thoughts that develop below the surface, slow down and think about what you are thinking. Write down whatever undercurrents are powering your anxiety.
2. Once you have these thoughts on paper, examine them rationally. Pretend you are a trial lawyer, looking for holes, distortions, and inaccuracies in your thinking. Are you taking the whole picture into account or only emphasizing the most negative dimensions? What evidence refutes or supports your thoughts?
3. Based on your rational examination, formulate a response that is more realistic than your original thoughts. For example, you might conclude, "Just because my son received an F on his last algebra test doesn't mean he's going to flunk out of school."

Perhaps the most effective way to deal with worry is to "de-catastrophize" it. We do this by facing it squarely, asking ourselves what's the worst that could happen. Then we think about what we would do to cope with the situation. Doing so may help diminish our anxiety and give us a sense of healthy control.[3] As you take these steps, be sure to ask God to guide your thinking through the power of his Spirit.

Lord, remind me today that you are stronger than any enemy I will face—real or imagined.

FIXATED

> *Seek the Kingdom of God above all else, and live righteously,*
> *and he will give you everything you need.*
>
> MATTHEW 6:33

Have you ever tried shining a small laser beam to see if your dog will play with it as it bounces across the floor? This little prank inspires gales of laughter from my oldest daughter, who delights in finding dogs that are compulsive enough to take the bait. It is amusing to watch them pounce—first this way, then that—in their quest to capture the elusive red light. The only problem is that playing with dogs in this way seems to increase their compulsiveness.

Human beings can act as compulsively as puppies at times, becoming fixated on things we think will make us happy. You see it in the lives of celebrities who wreck their lives and relationships in pursuit of success. Or business executives who, despite their wealth, are consumed with greed. And what about ordinary people like us? Some of us suffer from small compulsions—feeding an addiction to shopping, for instance—because it yields a burst of positive feelings. Others among us may fixate on finding the right man, bouncing from relationship to relationship or refusing happiness as a result of this obsession.

Fixations are like targets attached to a brick wall. No matter how many times we aim at the bull's-eye, even the sharpest arrows fall to the ground.

I must confess that I have my own fixations. Their names are Katie and Luci. I want my daughters to be happy, good, successful, prosperous. The trouble is, no matter how hard I try, I can't make their lives conform to my ideal, regardless of how much I pray for them, plead with them, or try to help them. Perhaps it's time to take the target off the wall, lay down my bow, and ask God to dismantle the brick wall. Doing so doesn't mean I stop working and praying on behalf of my children; it simply means I am choosing not to fixate on a goal I'm not capable of achieving.

What about you? What targets are you aiming for? Have they kept you from knowing more of God's peace? If so, tell God you want him to tear down those targets so you can instead take aim at things like seeking first his Kingdom and doing his will.

> *Father, help me to give up lesser fixations for the one fixation*
> *that will bring me peace—loving and living for you.*

October 6

OUR DAILY BREAD?

Give us today the food we need.
MATTHEW 6:11

My friend Christine was surprised by her daughter's tears. "Emma, what's wrong?" she asked.

"I'm afraid I won't be able to go to college," she sobbed.

"But, honey, your grades are great. What are you worried about?"

"You and Dad say college is getting so expensive and the economy is terrible," Emma said. "I'm afraid there won't be enough money."

It took time, but Christine was able to address her daughter's fears, assuring her that they had been saving for her education and that there would likely be financial aid as well.

This incident reminds me of something in the Lord's Prayer. Jesus urges his disciples to ask for many lofty things. He begins by teaching them to address God as their Father in heaven and urges them to make his name holy, or hallowed. He teaches them to pray for God's Kingdom to come and his will to be done. Then, in the middle of the prayer, he veers in a far more practical direction, teaching them to pray for daily bread. By using the term *bread*, he is referring to food in general.

New Testament scholar Kenneth Bailey points out the uncertainty about the translation "daily" because it is based on the Greek word *epiousios*, a word that appears nowhere else in recorded Greek writings. Basing his interpretation on a very early translation of Scripture, he makes a persuasive case that this phrase is best translated not as "Give us this day our daily bread" but as "Give us today the bread that does not run out." While the first form of prayer asks for enough for today, the second asks God to relieve us of the ongoing anxiety that we will not have what we need. Yes, we may get bread today, but what about tomorrow and the day after that?

The next time you pray the Lord's Prayer, remember that you are asking your heavenly Father to deliver you from the fear of not having what you need. By alleviating that fear, God helps us enjoy a sense of peace and well-being, not only about today, but also about tomorrow and the day after that.

Our Father, who art in heaven, hallowed be thy name. Thy Kingdom come, thy will be done on earth as it is in heaven. Give us today "the bread that does not run out," and forgive us our trespasses, as we forgive those who trespass against us. And lead us not into temptation, but deliver us from evil.

CUSTODY OF THE EYES—AND EARS

Turn my eyes from worthless things, and give me life through your word.

PSALM 119:37

A friend of mine was assailed by sexual temptation whenever he walked across the University of Michigan Diag, a large open space in the center of campus. Why? Because in warm weather, hoards of scantily clad coeds would pass through on their way to class. His solution? He simply took off his glasses, which transformed his Diag experience into a complete blur. Though he didn't know it, he was practicing what classic spiritual writers have called "custody of the eyes."

This discipline of monitoring what we allow ourselves to focus on can be useful for dealing with a variety of situations—at the beach, for instance, or when reading or watching television or movies. Though it may sound quaint in our sex-saturated society, it's a discipline based on the practical recognition that visual cues can introduce powerful temptations. The same is true of listening to gossip or certain kinds of music. Instead of maintaining complete openness to every kind of stimuli, we guard ourselves against whatever might negatively impact our spiritual health.

That means we also need to guard against extreme violence or obscene materialism. The former can lead to heightened anxiety or tolerance of violence, while the latter can lead to a lust for more. That's why I refuse to watch horror movies and why I canceled my subscription to *Architectural Digest*. The triggers may be different for you than they are for me, but the point is we need to identify them and limit our exposure. Contrary to what we might think, visual and auditory stimuli are not necessarily neutral. They can shape our thoughts and actions in surprisingly powerful ways.

Lord, thank you for the gifts of seeing and hearing, and the richness they bring to life. Help me use my senses in ways that are redemptive, that will lead me toward peace rather than away from it. Give me the strength to deal decisively with things that tempt my eyes and ears.

People with understanding control their anger; a hot temper shows great foolishness.

PROVERBS 14:29

I remember having a power struggle with one of my children that centered on whether or not she was going to make her bed. I won't go into the details, but I assure you it wasn't pretty. I can't remember whether I won. The only thing I remember is how awful I felt afterward. I didn't want to give in because I thought more than a neat bedroom was at stake. It seemed to me that if my daughter failed to obey me in this one instance, she would find it easy to do so in others. While that may have been true, I think I could have used other techniques that would have done less damage to our relationship and that wouldn't have ended in the dreaded power struggle.

It takes wisdom to know where to invest our emotional resources. My guess is that most of us err on the wrong side of the equation, becoming emotional about things we should either ignore or learn to handle more calmly.

Robert Sapolsky, a professor of biology and neurology, reminds us of the physiological toll that chronic stress takes, promising that "if you experience every day as an emergency, you will pay the price."

Sapolsky goes on to explain, "If you constantly mobilize energy at the cost of energy storage, you will never store any surplus energy. You will fatigue more rapidly, and your risk of developing a form of diabetes will even increase. The consequences of chronically activating your cardiovascular system are similarly damaging: if your blood pressure rises to 180/100 every time you see the mess in your teenager's bedroom, you could be heading for a cardiovascular disaster. . . . If you are constantly under stress, a variety of reproductive disorders may ensue. In females, menstrual cycles can become irregular or cease entirely.[4]

Body and soul, mind and emotions—we are complex interweavings, fearfully and wonderfully made but sometimes all-too-easily broken. Today, let us ask God for wisdom in preserving the health he has given us.

Lord, it's easy to blame my stress on others. Help me to see that I do have choices. Give me the wisdom and self-discipline to make the right ones.

October 9
ROUGH EDGES

*I will brighten the darkness before them and smooth out the road ahead
of them. Yes, I will indeed do these things; I will not forsake them.*

ISAIAH 42:16

All of us have rough edges, places in our lives that need smoothing out.
Let me offer a superficial example. Most women I know have little difficulty finding something negative to say about their hair. I have more excuse
than most because I have what some people kindly call naturally curly hair.
If left to go its own way, particularly in high humidity, my kind of hair is
capable of inflicting psychic damage on small children. I know this because
I once unwisely opened the door to neighborhood children who, seeing my
untended hair, promptly exclaimed, "Wow, it's the Bride of Frankenstein!"

Last week I tried an expensive shampoo, touted to calm frizzy hair.
What I didn't know was that instead of smoothing out my hair, it acted as a
volumizer. Imagine someone seriously overweight donning a fat suit, and you
will get an idea of how this product affected my hair. It brought back the earlier conviction that my curly-haired parents should never have been permit-
ted to marry. Allowing two such people to mate, I am convinced, constitutes
a form of child abuse.

Over the years I've found that using a flatiron helps the most.
Sometimes I have trouble getting all the kinks out in back, so I simply do a
few quick swipes on the surface and let it go at that. The problem with such
a strategy is that the kinks beneath the surface insist on asserting themselves,
exposing the pretense that I have soft, manageable hair.

What's the point of my bad hair complaints? Simply that each of us
has our own set of rough edges to work out. True, we can make some surface changes. But these don't really deal with underlying character flaws that
keep asserting themselves despite our most determined efforts to hide them.
Willpower by itself cannot contend with problems like low self-esteem, a
quick temper, stinginess, stubbornness, laziness, judgmentalism, and negativity. The only power strong enough to straighten out the twisted elements in
our lives comes from God. Today let's ditch strategies that depend only on us,
so we can follow God's strategies for growing in his peace and grace.

*Holy Spirit, kindle in me the fire of your love. Change, renew,
and transform me from the inside out, I pray.*

Don't you realize that your body is the temple of the Holy Spirit, who lives in you and was given to you by God? You do not belong to yourself, for God bought you with a high price. So you must honor God with your body.

1 CORINTHIANS 6:19-20

Who are you, really? Wife? Mother? Student? Housewife? Doctor? Lawyer?

Without realizing it, many of us define ourselves solely in terms of external influences. If we have struggled with chronic illness, we may think of ourselves as sickly. If we have enjoyed great success, we may think of ourselves as winners. If we have failed, we may think of ourselves as losers. If we have suffered abuse at the hands of others, we may think of ourselves as victims. Often we slip into these and other roles without really being aware of them. But by defining ourselves merely in relation to others, we have adopted stories that may contradict the one story that should define us. That is the gospel story—the one that tells us we are sinners loved by God and saved by grace for a gracious purpose.

I like the way Miroslav Volf puts it. He says that "by opening ourselves to God's love through faith, our bodies and souls become sanctified spaces, God's 'temples,' as the apostle Paul puts it (1 Corinthians 6:19). The flame of God's presence, which gives us new identity, then burns in us inextinguishably . . . at times a temple in ruins, but sacred space nonetheless. Absolutely nothing defines a Christian more than the abiding flame of God's presence, and that flame bathes in a warm glow everything we do or suffer."[5]

As you go about your day-to-day routine, try visualizing the truth of who you are—a temple. A temple in ruins, perhaps, but still a place of great sacredness where God is pleased to dwell.

Father, how can I thank you for making me a holy place where you can dwell? Please touch others through your presence in my life.

FORGIVING THOSE CLOSEST TO YOU

If [Onesimus] has wronged you in any way or owes you anything, charge it to me. I,
PAUL, WRITE THIS WITH MY OWN HAND: I WILL REPAY IT. AND I WON'T
MENTION THAT YOU OWE ME YOUR VERY SOUL! *Yes, my brother, please do*
me this favor for the Lord's sake. Give me this encouragement in Christ.

PHILEMON 1:18-20

Isn't it interesting how those we love the most have the power to hurt us
the most? For those of us with children, we may find they know exactly
how to push our buttons. That was the case for Marcy, a mother whose
adopted son had hurt her deeply by his defiant, disrespectful behavior. One
day, after he had thrown yet another tantrum, Marcy asked God to help her
let go of the unforgiveness she felt.

She began reading Paul's letter to a slave owner by the name of
Philemon. Paul was begging Philemon to welcome back a runaway slave
named Onesimus, who had stolen from his master. While he was with Paul,
Onesimus had become a believer.

Words Paul spoke to Philemon jumped out at her: "If he has wronged
you in any way or owes you anything, charge it to me. . . . I will repay it. And
I won't mention that you owe me your very soul!" Marcy felt as though Jesus
was using the lips of Paul to speak directly to her. With tears running down
her cheeks, she forgave her son on the spot, deciding that forgiveness would
characterize her dealings with him from now on. Each time he offended,
she would forgive again, silently praying, *Jesus, I charge it to you.* Because she
was able to forgive her son, he didn't suffer from her judgments anymore.
Eventually he gave his life to Christ.[6]

If you have been hurt by your children or someone close to you, take a
moment now to take your disappointment to God, asking him for the grace
to forgive. Then ask for the strength to keep on forgiving.

Lord I forgive _____. *Help*
me to keep forgiving, trusting the results to you.

October 12

A FUTURE AND A HOPE

"I know the plans I have for you," declares the LORD, "plans to prosper you and not to harm you, plans to give you hope and a future."

JEREMIAH 29:11, NIV

The book *When Moms Pray Together* tells the story of a mother whose daughter suffered from bulimia. Thinking herself fat and ugly, Becky would binge and purge. She began cutting herself in high school, once so deeply that she had to be hospitalized. After months of intensive therapy, her emotional pain started to ease. Finally, after attending a retreat, she experienced the reality of God's love for her. After that she was able to share her story publicly in the hope of keeping others from heading down the same dark path.

Here's what her mother had to say about what it was like to deal with Becky's struggles: "Although I can rejoice now," she says, "I didn't know how this story would turn out. . . . At times in my frustration and impatience with her slow progress, I tried to take charge of her spiritual life. It was then that Becky clearly told me that this was her spiritual life and that I couldn't live it for her. . . .

"One of the verses that I clung to during this painful period was Jeremiah 29:11. . . . I clung to the words *hope* and *future*. And when fear and worry began to cloud my mind, I remembered what God had done for us in the past. . . . I took my focus off my circumstances and redirected it to Him who is my hope and future. Then I would pray the same verse for Becky, asking that she would believe that God had plans for her—good plans, not necessarily easy ones, but plans to give her a bright future and hope."[7]

What fears do you have for your loved ones and your children? Ask God to redirect your eyes to him rather than to their circumstances. Remember what he has already done for you. Then pray with renewed hope and confidence that God will be at work, making his plans for them come true.

Lord, I need to know I am not alone as I try to help my children and loved ones. Please come with your light and your power to push away the darkness and enfold them in your love. Let them see the light of your face, I pray.

STOP FRETTING ABOUT GOD'S WILL

Now I am bound by the Spirit to go to Jerusalem. I don't know what awaits me.

ACTS 20:22

S top asking God to show you his will for your life." That's Francis Chan's unorthodox challenge to earnest Christians seeking to know God's plan. As Chan points out, all that seeking, praying, talking, and fretting about God's will may be signs that you are not looking for ways to glorify God but for ways to stay safe and avoid making mistakes. You want the security of knowing you are on the "right path" of following God's perfect will for your life.

Here's how Chan puts it: "I think a lot of us need to forget about *God's will for my life*. God cares more about our response to His Spirit's leading today, in this moment, than about what we intend to do next year. In fact, the decisions we make next year will be profoundly affected by the degree to which we submit to the Spirit right now, in today's decisions."

Chan goes on to say, "It's much less demanding to think about God's will for your future than it is to ask Him what He wants you to do in the next ten minutes. It's safer to commit to following Him *someday* instead of *this day*."[8]

Of course, Chan is not counseling us to go our own way or to discard the notion that God has a plan for our lives. He's just pointing out the obvious—that God doesn't disclose all that much about the future. Even someone like Joseph, who had fabulous dreams about his future, had no idea how the details would unfold. He didn't realize that he would be falsely accused, thrown into an Egyptian jail, and exiled from home and family, and that every twist and turn would lead to the fulfillment of God's plan.

Peace comes not from being given a divine blueprint for our lives but from saying yes to God in this very moment.

Father, forgive me for seeking security in knowledge. Help me to simply say yes to what you are asking of me right now. I know you have a good plan for my life, and I entrust the details to you.

October 14

FEELING EDGY?

Be thankful in all circumstances, for this is God's will for you who belong to Christ Jesus.
1 THESSALONIANS 5:18

Have you ever noticed how easy it is to distract a toddler by handing him a toy in exchange for the dog bone he just picked up? Distraction is a time-honored parenting technique—one that works so well we really ought to try it on ourselves, especially when we start becoming frustrated and irritable.

Say, for instance, that you are feeling energetic enough to tackle your monthly bill-paying responsibilities. (That would be me last night.) But before you begin, you remember the TV is on the blink. You fiddle with it for five minutes, concluding that you need to call your service provider. You hold the phone for five more minutes until a lovely, lilting voice comes on the line with the promise of help.

Over the next forty-five minutes, you do everything she tells you to, answering questions, pushing buttons, checking connections, and observing blinking lights on modems while she tries to find a fix from eight thousand miles away. Then you're put on hold. You glance at your watch to discover that fifteen more minutes have elapsed. Then the woman comes on the line again, telling you she may need to schedule a technician. She asks if it would be okay if she sent you a new receiver. You say yes, and it takes a mere ten minutes to arrange. By now you know that with everything else you still have to do, there is no way you are going to get those bills paid tonight.

Normally I find situations like this frustrating. But last night I was able to distract myself by asking the woman where she was located. Her answer: the Philippines. I expressed concern about recent flooding there. She told me it was still raining hard and a few of her coworkers hadn't been able to get to work. Then it occurred to me that I am fortunate to have a phone, a TV, and a dry roof over my head. When we finally hung up, I felt at peace, though the bills hadn't been paid and the TV hadn't been fixed.

We all face unexpected problems that eat away at our precious time and energy. If we want to remain peaceful at such times, we can do so by distracting ourselves with gratitude. Positive distractions can prevent negative thoughts from growing and festering. Feeling edgy? Go ahead, distract yourself!

Lord, help me find practical ways to reshape my thoughts in a more positive direction.

TAKE THE PLUNGE!

When you fast, comb your hair and wash your face. Then no one will notice that you are fasting, except your Father, who knows what you do in private. And your Father, who sees everything, will reward you.

MATTHEW 6:17-18

Most of us find it relaxing to spend a few minutes soaking in a bath or a hot tub. But have you ever tried submersing your body in fifty-degree water for any length of time? It feels like being encased in a giant ice pack. Though this kind of therapy is popular in Europe and goes back to ancient Roman times, Americans have been slow to catch on. But the pleasure of soaking in a cold plunge doesn't just come from the relief you feel once you're out of it. Patients who use this therapy report decreased pain, even several hours later.

A recent convert to cold plunge therapy, I have learned about some of its touted benefits, which include improved circulation, less inflammation, a strengthened immune system, and a better mood. Though not recommended for pregnant women or people with heart conditions, cold plunge therapy is a natural way to get healthy and stay healthy. But if you're anything like me, you have to try it before you believe it.

Something similar happens when it comes to spiritual disciplines like fasting. Abstaining from food for any length of time can seem like torture, especially if you are just beginning. But if you make fasting a regular part of your life, you will find that it can increase your spiritual awareness, underlining the seriousness of your prayers and helping you develop more self-control. But don't do it to impress God or others. That's a downward path. Do it because you love the Lord and because you want him to know how hungry you are for the peace he promises.

Father, you haven't called me to a comfortable life. Help me to develop the courage to be uncomfortable if doing so will advance your Kingdom and increase your peace in my life.

October 16
WHEN BAD THINGS HAPPEN

The LORD is my strength and shield. I trust him with all my heart.
PSALM 28:7

I magine that you are a five-year-old girl. In the course of a week, six things happen that affect your perception of who your father is: (1) he surprises you with a shiny bike on your birthday, (2) he takes you to breakfast on his day off, (3) he says you are beautiful and he loves you, (4) he refuses to get you a dog, (5) he tells you that your mother has left and she may not be coming back, and (6) he says he has to leave you in the care of relatives for a while so he can take care of important business.

How would you deal with receiving three good things from your father's hand and three bad things? Would you accept both the positive and the negative as coming from a father who can always be trusted, or would you let the bad things overshadow the good, making you feel abandoned and unprotected?

Now think about how you might feel if you were fifteen and the same things happened. By now you realize that your mother cares for no one but herself, and despite your father's pleading, she has run off with another man. You also know your dad is going away for a few days so he can make a last-ditch effort to get your mother back. You realize, too, that he is right about the dog. Even being near a dog tends to throw you into an asthma attack.

At fifteen you understand circumstances that would have baffled your five-year-old brain.

What's the point of this little exercise? Merely to get you to think about how easy it is for us to misjudge God simply because we are human beings who are unable to comprehend all God's motives. As his daughters, we are called to grow in trust and confidence, knowing that whether life pays us back in positives or negatives, we can be confident we are being cared for by a Father who is always worthy of our trust.

Father, you haven't once let me down, though I may have thought so at times. Even now you hold me in your loving arms. Help me to trust you, I pray.

October 17

HAPPY ENDINGS

Hope in the LORD; for with the LORD there is unfailing love. His redemption overflows.
PSALM 130:7

I am a sucker for happy endings. A few years ago I read an early twentieth-century classic in which the main character suffers a fall from the moneyed class into social degradation and a tragic, untimely death. Though I loved elements of the story and the writing, I closed the book in a huff, feeling I had been cheated. After investing precious time and emotional energy into a story about a character I cared about, I discovered there was nothing redemptive about her story. She was doomed from the start.

Though I was surprised by how affronted I felt, I realized where my sense of indignation was coming from: I do not believe in bleak endings.

This world does not always produce happy endings. But as a believer in Christ, I cannot embrace a story that does not allow for the possibility of hope. Hence my addiction to stories with happy endings, like the movie *Dolphin Tale*. At the lowest point of the narrative, when all the other characters have fallen into despair about the possibility of saving the life of a dolphin called Winter, a father reminds his son of a poem they used to recite together:

> *I must down to the seas again,*
> *to the lonely sea and the sky,*
> *And all I ask is a tall ship*
> *and a star to steer her by.*[9]

As the two reminisce, the father says to his son, "Just 'cause we haven't got to where the star is taking us doesn't mean it's the wrong star." This line is the turning point of the movie. It injects hope and galvanizes the characters to achieve what had seemed impossible only moments earlier.

No matter how bleak things may look, our story is going to end well as long as we trust Christ. The excruciating details of the life we now live are not building toward a tragic ending but toward a redemptive finale in which every one of God's promises will be fulfilled.

No wonder we're wired for happy endings. God has stitched hope into our souls, giving us the strength to go on.

Father, thank you for the hope you've given me. Please renew it
when circumstances in my life conspire to crush me.

DON'T IGNORE THE SIGNS

Have compassion on me, LORD, for I am weak.
Heal me, LORD, for my bones are in agony.

PSALM 6:2

Have you ever noticed an area of dead or browning vegetation where the surrounding area is green? Or a rotten egg smell in the yard? Or hissing or blowing sounds coming from beneath the earth? Or dirt blowing into the air? Or bubbling in a flooded area? Or fire coming out of the ground? If so, don't ignore these signs. If you do, *boom!* Everything in your world might suddenly explode, simply because you didn't pay attention to the signs of a natural gas leak.

Similarly, a pattern of ignoring signs that something is not right in our own lives can create enormous destruction, hurting ourselves and others. Here are a few signs, for instance, that married couples should never ignore:

- yelling and name calling
- violent disagreements
- feeling misunderstood most of the time
- rarely or never having sex
- constant television or computer use
- repetitive conflicts with no resolution
- rarely engaging in meaningful conversation
- desire to escape

Ignoring these and other symptoms of marital discord can create bigger problems that may eventually destroy the marriage.

Similarly, whether you are single or married, you can't afford to ignore emotions and behaviors that are often symptoms of deeper problems, things like frequent crying spells, overeating, undereating, irritability, indecisiveness, drug or alcohol abuse, isolation, anxiety, forgetfulness, or fatigue.

It can be hard to face up to the tension and stress that's building inside us. We'd rather ignore it. But doing so makes it impossible to get the help we need—and there is help. Today, if you sense something is not right, ask God for the courage to face it and the wisdom to know where to get help.

Lord, thank you for knowing me better than I know myself. Help me recognize problems that are boiling beneath the surface of my life so that I can, by your grace, do something about them.

ONE DROP OF PEACE AT A TIME

The word of God is alive and powerful. It is sharper than the sharpest two-edged sword, cutting between soul and spirit, between joint and marrow. It exposes our innermost thoughts and desires.

HEBREWS 4:12

Akiva was an illiterate second-century shepherd. Though he hadn't sprouted from a long line of Jewish scholars, he became one of the most famous rabbis in history. According to a rabbinic tale, this is how his story began:

"He was forty years old and had not yet learned a thing. Once, he stood at the mouth of a well and asked, 'Who hollowed this stone?' He was told, 'Is it not the water which constantly falls on it day after day?'"[10] Akiva realized that if water could carve away stone, then the Scripture could carve a way into his heart, transforming him from an ignorant man into a sage.

Many centuries later, another rabbi pointed out that the stone could only have been hollowed out by water falling drop by drop. Had the water poured out all at once in a torrent, it would have run quickly over the rock, leaving no trace behind.[11]

The metaphor of water and rock is a good one for us to apply to our own journey toward peace. Biblical peace, as we have established, is far more than simply a feeling of calm or a cessation of conflict. *Shalom* involves those things and more, including healing, wholeness, well-being, completeness, soundness, safety, success, perfection, and good relationships between people and nations. Peace in our world is a goal we lean toward, like plants toward sunshine. As we steep ourselves in Scripture and yield ourselves to God, we experience shalom in ever-deepening measures.

Try opening the Bible today and imagining yourself as that rock. Ask God to pour out his life-giving water as you read his words and apply them to your life.

Father, may your Word be to me like water on a rock, a steady stream of wisdom and grace to shape my heart toward the peace you promise.

October 20

CHASING FEATHERS

*The heart of the godly thinks carefully before speaking; the
mouth of the wicked overflows with evil words.*

PROVERBS 15:28

Author Lois Tverberg recounts an entertaining story of an inveterate
gossip who had decided to mend his ways. Regretting the damage he'd
done, the man approached the village rabbi, asking what he should do to
make things right.

As the story goes, the rabbi simply told him to go home and fetch a
pillow. When the man returned, the rabbi commanded him to slit the pillow
open and then scatter its feathers to the wind.

As the feathers blew every which way, over housetops and through
fields, the rabbi turned to the man and said, "Now, go gather all the feathers
again and put them back in the pillow."

"But that's impossible," the man objected.

"In the same way," the rabbi said, "it's impossible to repair all the damage that your words have done."[12]

The problem with words is that they tumble out of our mouths so
effortlessly, often before we've had a chance to consider them. But reckless
words can wreck the peace, spreading like a contagion from person to person.
If you have been guilty of passing on a juicy bit of gossip, don't despair. There
is still time to change. True, you can't pick up all the "feathers" you've already
scattered, but you can keep the rest of them right where they belong—inside
the pillow.

Today, ask God to change your heart so you are no longer eager to listen to or spread gossip. Then show your resolve by saying something positive about people you've criticized in the past. Then ask God to keep your
lips pure in the future by helping you cultivate the habit of thinking before
you speak.

*Father, forgive me for passing on gossip or speaking in ways that hurt the reputations
of others. Give me the wisdom to know when to speak and when to keep quiet.*

EXTENDING THE PEACE

God blesses those who work for peace, for they will be called the children of God.
MATTHEW 5:9

Hailing from a town called Freedom, Pennsylvania, it's perhaps no coincidence that Linda Banks is concerned about a lack of freedom elsewhere in the world. On a visit to Pune, India, where her daughter and son-in-law are serving as missionaries, she met sixteen young girls who had been rescued from local brothels. As a result of her encounter with the Home of Hope, where the girls are living, Linda began praying and educating herself about human trafficking, asking God what she could do to help. The answer came in the form of an organization she founded, called the Praying Aunties Network.

The idea behind Praying Aunties is to connect one "auntie" with one girl. The auntie receives updates on the girl in order to know how to pray for her. She also meets monthly with other praying aunties in her area.

Linda's group of sixteen women prays for the sixteen girls and the staff members of the Home of Hope in Pune. Because of the problems associated with prostitution, it is not uncommon for rescued girls to return to their former lives. But this has not been the case in Pune, where all sixteen girls have accepted Christ and none have returned to their old way of life.

If you are serious about becoming a woman at peace, remember that God gives peace for a purpose. It's tempting to think that one person can't make much difference in a world that is filled with conflict. But Linda Banks and her praying friends have already made a world of difference to the young women they're praying for.

Why not ask God today whether you should join Linda's network (prayingauntiesnetwork.blogspot.com) or another similar organization, making an impact one life at a time? Don't let the sun go down on this day without sincerely asking God to show you how you can spread his peace in the world around you.

Jesus, I want others to know your peace. Lead me by your Spirit so I will know how and when to share the peace you've given me.

WHAT MIGHT HAPPEN?

Give all your worries and cares to God, for he cares about you.
1 PETER 5:7

Have you ever watched a boxer dancing around the ring, throwing punches at no one in particular? He's using a training technique called shadowboxing—sparring with an imaginary opponent. Now imagine that same boxer, but with a bizarre twist. While he's in the ring alone, his head thrusts backward again and again, as though someone were punching him in the face. But there's no one else around. Sounds crazy, doesn't it?

As strange as that scenario seems, it's an image of what can happen to us when we start sparring with imaginary ills. Our anxiety turns us into human punching bags, battered by thoughts not about what is, but about what might be. I might never get married. I might lose my job. My husband might leave me. My child might not graduate. My plane might crash. The economy might collapse. My mother might die. I might not have enough money to retire.

There are plenty of places in Scripture that tell us not to be anxious but to place our trust in God, who alone is our peace. One example is 1 Peter 5:7, which gives us a clear directive: "Give all your worries and cares to God, for he cares about you."

The next time you feel anxiety rising inside you like mercury in a thermometer, let it be the signal that you need to spend some time with God. Have a conversation with him. Tell him you want to focus on him rather than on all the what-ifs that assail you. Begin by praising and thanking him. Then lift up the people and situations that are troubling you. As you pray, imagine that God is in the room, which, of course, he is. Rest in his presence. If you make a habit of spending time with God daily, you will find that your anxiety will gradually be displaced by God's peace.

Lord, you are my Rock, the one who steadies me. Thank you for your great faithfulness. I remember the things you have already done for me—forgiving, loving, and protecting me. Because you care about what happens to me, I can entrust the future to you.

October 23

OVERWHELMING VICTORY

Despite all these things, overwhelming victory is ours through Christ, who loved us. And I am convinced that nothing can ever separate us from God's love. Neither death nor life, neither angels nor demons, neither our fears for today nor our worries about tomorrow—not even the powers of hell can separate us from God's love. No power in the sky above or in the earth below—indeed, nothing in all creation will ever be able to separate us from the love of God that is revealed in Christ Jesus our Lord.

ROMANS 8:37-39

If you were going to climb Mount Everest, would you pick a guide who had already completed the climb or someone who had read a lot of books about it? If it were my life on the line, I'd go for the guy who had actually succeeded in making the climb. That's why I place great stock in the words of the apostle Paul. If anyone had credentials to speak about peace, it was Paul. Why? Because by his own account he experienced imprisonment, whipping, beating, stoning, shipwreck, hunger, nakedness, and persecution in his commitment to live for Christ.

Despite these hardships and more to come, Paul's writings are bursting with optimism about the future. He proclaims that anyone who belongs to Christ can look forward not simply to winning a few battles but to experiencing "overwhelming victory." The odds, as Paul sees it, are completely in his favor—and ours.

Note that Paul prefaces this promise with the phrase "despite all these things." Just prior to the passage above, he speaks of the long list of troubles and calamities he faced. But Christ had already been so faithful to Paul in the midst of these challenges that he had no doubt about the future.

Why not join me today in taking Paul as your guide, memorizing this passage from the book of Romans? Hide it in your heart and let it strengthen you so that when calamity threatens, you will remember that nothing in heaven or on earth can ever separate you from God's love.

Lord, I know that neither angels nor demons, not my fears for today or my worries about tomorrow can separate me from your love. Hide that truth in my heart so I can stand in your peace when trouble comes.

*Don't copy the behavior and customs of this world, but let God transform
you into a new person by changing the way you think. Then you will learn
to know God's will for you, which is good and pleasing and perfect.*

ROMANS 12:2

Ever try *not* thinking a particular thought? The harder you try, the likelier you are to think it. I appreciate the way one woman deals with her propensity to think in negative ways. "My negative thoughts," she says, "are like impatient toddlers jumping up and down and screaming, 'Look at me, look at me.' Jesus and I take the negative 'toddler thoughts' and send them to time-out so we can focus on the good thoughts. Sometimes they don't obey. They get up out of the chair and once again scream for attention. Then Jesus and I take those thoughts back to the time-out chair, but this time we tie them up!"[13]

Though no analogy is perfect (I am sure, for instance, that she isn't advocating tying children to time-out chairs), we can extend the comparison in helpful ways. For instance, whenever our "toddler thoughts" scream for attention, we can simply distract them or redirect them, calling to mind specific instances of God's faithfulness and his promises, and thanking him for gifts we have already received. Distraction works because if we fill our minds with positive thoughts, there is no room for negative ones.

Of course, I am not advocating that we ignore every negative thought. Sometimes we need to pay attention to them so we can solve problems. But most of us know the difference between problem solving and merely rehearsing doubts, complaints, and negativity, which only corrode our faith and rob us of the peace God promises.

*Lord, the next time I am thinking in ways that make it hard for me to
serve you, put a check in my spirit. Help me to refocus my thoughts
in ways that will reshape my soul and renew my mind.*

October 25

STAY IN THE GAME

Endurance develops strength of character, and character strengthens our
confident hope of salvation. And this hope will not lead to disappointment.

ROMANS 5:4-5

Last year my daughter played on a basketball team for the first time. I loved going to her games, though I had to tread carefully whenever I did. Not wanting to be embarrassed by an overly enthusiastic mother, Luci thought it would be best if I just sat quietly while watching the game. I did my best to behave, though every so often I couldn't keep myself from poking one of the mothers sitting beside me, asking her to cheer Luci on since I wasn't allowed to.

Over the course of the season, a couple of the girls struggled with their shooting. In the last couple of games, the coach did everything he could to make sure they had a chance to get the ball. During the final minute of the last game, something magical happened. That's when one of the girls experienced her Rocky Balboa moment. She was surrounded by a swarm of defenders, when suddenly, above the crowd of gangly girls, the ball arced up, rising high and then swishing straight into the hoop. That shot, her first successful one of the year, clinched the game! If she hadn't kept playing, hadn't kept trying, she never would have experienced the thrill of achieving that unforgettable shot.

It's the same with us. We may not think of ourselves as giants of the faith, as people who can stand strong in difficult times. Perhaps we have already given in to doubt on more than one occasion. But God says don't give up. Stay in the game. Keep believing, keep hoping, keep trying. Persevere and watch what God will do with your life.

Lord, help me today to persevere—to cling to you, draw strength from you,
and trust that even in my suffering you are doing something good with
my life, making me a woman who is growing into your shalom.

WHAT THE STRUGGLE LOOKS LIKE

Don't worry about anything; instead, pray about everything. Tell God what you need, and thank him for all he has done. Then you will experience God's peace, which exceeds anything we can understand. His peace will guard your hearts and minds as you live in Christ Jesus.

PHILIPPIANS 4:6-7

It's fine, you might say, to tell me not to worry, but how exactly do I do that? Here's how one woman handled the struggle when her teenager was going through a tumultuous time. "I remember lying in bed many nights," Linda Dillow says, "thinking, *Did I make the right decision? How do I stop this child from heading down the path of foolishness?* I would pray through Philippians 4:6-9 but find my mind worrying again. It was as if my mind was stuck in worry mode.

"I would pray, 'Lord, here I am again. I was just here ten minutes ago but it didn't take: I'm still worrying instead of possessing Your peace.' Again I would pray through my part and God's part in Philippians 4. Then I would start worrying again. At that point I would sit up, force my body out from under the warm covers, and go to my desk. With pen and paper in hand, I would list all the positive things the Lord had accomplished in my teenager's life in the past year. Then I'd pray over the list and thank Him that He had been at work and was still at work in her life. I'd shut off the light and go back to my cozy comforter, this time to a peaceful sleep."[14]

If you want God's peace to characterize your life, remember that peace is organic—it's a fruit of the Spirit. Like all living things, it grows—not according to your timetable, but according to God's. Jesus isn't discouraged by the fact that you have to keep coming back to him every ten minutes for the peace you seek. Doing so will simply keep you connected, allowing the Holy Spirit to accomplish his will in your life.

Lord, you are the vine and I am one of your branches. Help me to learn to abide in you.

PERSISTING

*Your heavenly Father already knows all your needs. Seek the Kingdom of God
above all else, and live righteously, and he will give you everything you need.*

MATTHEW 6:32-33

My thirteen-year-old daughter happily eats a variety of foods. Cheese,
bologna, tortillas, stir-fry, broccoli, chicken, rice, salami, shrimp,
pickles, peppers—you name it, and she will eat it. But she draws the line
when it comes to spinach, scrunching up her face and looking for an opportunity to dump it into the disposal when she thinks her mother isn't looking.
Last night Luci decided to spice up this odious vegetable with a little hot
sauce. The combination was so successful that she surprised me by asking for
seconds!

Why am I telling you about my daughter's conversion to spinach? Only
because it illustrates the power of persistence. It took repeated tries for Luci
to discover the breakthrough that would make eating spinach delightful. It
can be like that in our search for peace. We have to keep persevering, especially when it comes to turning away from our natural desires and staying
faithful to the teachings of Christ. Jesus says:

> "If someone slaps you on one cheek, offer the other cheek also. If some-
> one demands your coat, offer your shirt also." (Luke 6:29)
> "Love your enemies! Pray for those who persecute you!" (Matthew 5:44)
> "Do not judge others, and you will not be judged." (Matthew 7:1)
> "Don't worry about these things, saying, 'What will we eat? What will
> we drink? What will we wear?'" (Matthew 6:31)
> "I tell you the truth, if you have faith and don't doubt, you can do
> things like this and much more. You can even say to this moun-
> tain, 'May you be lifted up and thrown into the sea,' and it will
> happen." (Matthew 21:21)

When it comes to God's peace, Jesus asks so much, but he also delivers
so much. Let's continue to follow him, trusting that as we do, he will work
even deeper levels of *shalom* into our lives.

*Lord, thank you for not only telling me the way to live but
for showing me how. Make me like you, I pray.*

October 28

I DOUBT IT

Some time later, God tested Abraham's faith. "Abraham!"
God called. "Yes," he replied. "Here I am."

GENESIS 22:1

With characteristic humor, John Ortberg says that he is "skeptical of reports that Elvis is alive and well and working as a short-order cook at Taco Bell. I don't believe," he says, "that aliens periodically land on earth and give rides to humans—how come they never seem to land at MIT to give a ride to a physics professor?"[15]

Similarly, it can be a good idea to doubt when unscrupulous or ignorant preachers make claims that contradict biblical faith: "Send a donation to my ministry and you will be healed." "God wants you to be rich." "The world is going to end next month." With regard to these and other claims, it is not only a good idea to doubt but our duty to do so.

But there is a kind of doubt that is never advisable—doubting God and his clear promises. Entertaining such doubts can wreak havoc in our lives, sapping the energy and confidence God wants to give us. Still, most of us go through times when we find it hard to believe. Even Abraham, the father of our faith, had seasons of doubt. As Ortberg points out, "This great paragon of faith in the Old Testament is not doubt-free. Abraham laughs in disbelief. He lies about his wife, placing her in jeopardy to save his skin. He sleeps with his wife's servant because he wants to father a child at any cost. He gets a lot wrong. But he gets one thing right: He just keeps going. . . . Even when he doesn't fully understand, Abraham obeys God."[16] And that's the key. Even when we doubt, we need to obey God. That's the only way to become the women God calls us to be.

Having courage doesn't mean we have no fear. It just means we move beyond it. Similarly, having faith doesn't mean we are free from doubt; it just means we do what God wants us to do in the face of those doubts. We may get a lot wrong. But let's get this one thing right, realizing that obedience is not only the path to faith but also the path to peace.

Lord, when doubts assail me, remind me of your faithfulness. Help me to cling to your Word and do what you want me to do. Give me the grace to grow in certainty as I grow in obedience.

IS THERE AN AFTERLIFE?

*Don't let your hearts be troubled. Trust in God, and trust also in me. There is
more than enough room in my Father's home. If this were not so, would I have
told you that I am going to prepare a place for you? When everything is ready,
I will come and get you, so that you will always be with me where I am.*

JOHN 14:1-3

Since his death, Steve Jobs, cofounder of Apple, has been hailed as a pioneer, a visionary, a creative genius, an American business magnate, and
an amazing human being. He was all of those. Diagnosed with a rare form
of pancreatic cancer in 2003, Jobs decided to forgo conventional treatment
in favor of a course of alternative medicine, a decision he later regretted and
which doctors say led to his early death at the age of fifty-six.[17]

Walter Isaacson, Jobs's official biographer, tells of a fascinating conversation he had with Jobs toward the end of his life. "I remember," Isaacson
says, "sitting in his backyard in his garden one day and he started talking
about God. He said, 'Sometimes I believe in God, sometimes I don't. I think
it's 50-50 maybe. But ever since I've had cancer, I've been thinking about it
more. And I find myself believing a bit more. I kind of—maybe it's 'cause I
want to believe in an afterlife. That when you die, it doesn't just all disappear.
The wisdom you've accumulated. Somehow it lives on, but sometimes I
think it's just like an on-off switch. Click and you're gone. . . . And that's why
I don't like putting on-off switches on Apple devices.'"[18]

Now we know why it can be so hard to find that on-off switch on
certain Apple devices! And we know something else as well. As terrible as
a terminal diagnosis can be, it affords a person time to reflect on ultimate
questions—like whether there is life after death. As Christians, we believe
in the existence of an afterlife. Why? Because Christ, our brother, assures us
there is one. Furthermore, he has already done the hardest thing possible—
dying for us and then being raised from the dead. Because of him, we can
face our own death with hope, believing God will restore us to life.

*Lord, help me to trust you so that when I face death, I will not
be afraid but will be surrounded by your peace.*

"UNWANTED"

God created human beings in his own image. In the image of God
he created them; male and female he created them.

GENESIS 1:27

Once upon a time, there was a little girl named Nakusha. She was beautiful and bright, healthy and full of life. But though she looked fine on the outside, she was sad—very sad—on the inside. Nakusha tried everything she could think of to make herself feel better—dancing, joking, smiling, working hard, being helpful, looking beautiful. But nothing helped. She still felt depressed and worthless. And no wonder, because in Hindi, *nakusha* means "unwanted."

Incredibly this is a common name for girls all across India. These girls' families bestow the name, it would seem, in order to express their regret at ever having daughters. A few days ago, 285 girls—all named Nakusha— gathered in central India for a renaming ceremony. Each girl chose a new name. Some picked Vaishalie, which means "prosperous, beautiful, and good." Others adopted the name of a Bollywood star. One girl called herself Ashmita, which means "rock hard" or "very tough," perhaps a reflection of what she needed to be in order to survive in a society that devalues women and girls.[19]

I remember an experience I had in China when I was adopting one of my daughters. An attractive, well-dressed Chinese woman came up to me and asked me point-blank, with a look of complete puzzlement, "You mean you want to adopt a girl?" She couldn't believe that, given the choice, anyone would prefer a girl to a boy.

How can the world ever be at peace when attitudes like these prevail? As Christian women, we know we are cherished by the Father who loves us. Realizing who we are, let's stand up for others, linking arms with those who are doing something to elevate the status of women and children throughout the world. Commit today to volunteering your time and money to an organization that is spreading the Good News and improving the lives of the most vulnerable people on earth.

Father, I pray for women and children who are in poverty in my city, my country, and
throughout the world. Please break the chains of ignorance, poverty, and violence. Open
their hearts to the Good News, and bring them by the millions into your Kingdom, I pray.

SCARY PLACES

Jesus spoke to the people once more and said, "I am the light of the world. If you follow me, you won't have to walk in darkness, because you will have the light that leads to life."

JOHN 8:12

Have you ever walked through a haunted house? I'm thinking of the kind that pop up in the month of October, close to Halloween. The kind with creaky floorboards crammed full of creepy monsters waiting for the chance to make you scream.

Donald Miller uses the analogy of walking through a haunted house to talk about what it takes to lead people through fear. "For whatever reason," he says, "I sometimes feel like I need to be the guy out front. You know, the guy turning the corners first, feeling the walls, trying to find my way through the maze in the dark. But I assure you, I'm not feeling all that brave up there. I'm feeling terrified, to tell you the truth. . . .

"Leading is like that sometimes. You've got a gaggle of screaming, giggling friends behind you. . . . The trick," he says, "to leading a group through a haunted house is knowing the scary stuff can't actually kill you. The management won't let them.

"It's the same with all the scary stuff we have to deal with, all the fear of abandonment and loneliness and wounds we have to address. They aren't allowed to kill us. Sure we might feel some fear, and a lot of it. But in the end (even if it kills our earthly bodies), we don't die. We just come through the other side with a knowledge we faced our fears, and we got out of that haunted house alive, our screaming and giggling friends in tow."[20]

I think Donald Miller is right. The only method for dealing with fear is to walk through it, not on our own, but with Christ leading the way. The next time you're afraid, remember that Jesus is the safest way through the dark.

Lord, thank you for going first. Because of your courage and faithfulness, I am not afraid to follow you.

FLYING SNAKES

*I was hungry, and you fed me. I was thirsty, and you gave me a drink.
I was a stranger, and you invited me into your home.*

MATTHEW 25:35

My oldest daughter, a lover of reptiles, has yet to meet a snake she dislikes. She finds them fascinating, perhaps because they are so different from human beings. But it's that very difference that makes many of us afraid of them. By contrast, my youngest wants nothing to do with any kind of reptile, especially snakes. That's why I was surprised to see her handling Katie's pet snake the other night. For a few minutes, Luci managed to master her fear, tentatively holding the snake in her hands and then letting it crawl up and down her arms.

I was glad to see her feeling more comfortable around the snake. But my pleasant thoughts were soon interrupted by a little yelp. As I turned my head to see what was going on, I saw the snake flying through the air. It seems Luci had gotten so comfortable with her new friend that she made the mistake of squeezing him inside the crook of her arm. In a panic, the snake, who had never bitten anyone before, must have given her a little nip. Terrified, Luci gave out a yell and sent him flying. Fortunately, the snake survived his short flight, and I was able to retrieve him before he had a chance to slither away in a panic, never to be seen again.

That little interchange between two innocent but fearful creatures made me think about the damage fear can do in our relationships with others, distorting our perceptions and putting us on the defensive simply because people are different from us. Such fears keep us constantly on guard, making it difficult to establish relationships with those who are not like us. Instead of reaching across fences to bring more peace to the world, we shrink back, preferring to confine our relationships to those who look and act like we do.

If we want more peace in our world, we will have to start taking a few risks. Even if we do get "bitten" from time to time, chances are we won't suffer too much.

Why not decide today to look for ways to forge relationships with people who aren't just like you? Ask God to show you who to reach out to and how, and then pray that your efforts will produce a little more peace.

*Father, instead of withdrawing or misjudging others, help me to be open
to forging relationships with people who are different from me.*

CREATION AT PEACE

The wolf and the lamb will feed together. The lion will eat hay like a cow. But the snakes will eat dust. In those days no one will be hurt or destroyed on my holy mountain. I, the LORD, have spoken!

ISAIAH 65:25

I come from a dog-loving, cat-loving, snake-loving, monkey-loving, fish-loving, lizard-loving, turtle-loving, bird-loving family. At one time or another during my childhood, we had at least one such pet in our home. Whenever we felt the need for a new one, my siblings and I had only to find a way of luring my mother into a pet store and then showing her the latest fascinating animal. Once she even let us have a South American tortoise that dined on bananas.

I've since come to regret keeping some of those animals in captivity. But my experience with so many different animals convinces me of at least one thing: most animals have more feelings and intelligence than we think. Why do we miss this? I fear that for some among us, it's because admitting their capabilities would make it harder to exploit them.

But God calls us to be stewards of his creation. We are to take care of, not take advantage of, the creatures he has made. I'm not arguing that we should all become vegetarians, but I am saying that we have to treat other creatures with respect, sparing them unnecessary suffering whenever possible.

I love the story about Francis of Assisi and his encounter with a ravenous wolf that had been terrorizing a city in Italy. According to the story, Francis ordered the wolf to stop eating people and promised that, in return, the people of the town would feed him. According to the legend, the wolf complied, as did the people of the city, and there was never another incident. Sound preposterous? What if God had enabled Francis to perform such a miracle in order to offer us a glimpse of his original intention for how human beings should interact with other animals?

After all, Isaiah prophesied that wolves, lambs, lions, and venomous snakes would one day live together peaceably, without harm. As stewards of creation, let's ask God to show us how to take proper responsibility for the beautiful world he has made.

Lord, creation itself has been subjected to sin's destructive power. Help us as your redeemed people to care for nature as stewards that you have appointed. Awaken our understanding and our consciences that we may care for the earth in a way that reflects your glory.

DEVELOPING A SLOW MOUTH

The mouths of fools are their ruin; they trap themselves with their lips. . . .
Spouting off before listening to the facts is both shameful and foolish.

PROVERBS 18:7, 13

In the course of their quest to live peaceably and simply, the Amish have developed many wise proverbs. This is one of my favorites: "Swallowing words before you say them is so much better than having to eat them afterward."

Were I to attempt writing a proverb of my own, it would go like this: "If you desire more peace, let your ears be quick and your mouth be slow." Though I haven't always lived by that bit of practical wisdom, I have learned to be careful about spouting off on political or religious topics, because doing so often subtracts from the peace rather than adding to it. Responding too quickly often means speaking carelessly, without giving enough thought to what others are saying or to how they might respond to your words.

The familiar phrase "hold your peace" provides a useful visual. When we "hold our peace," we are maintaining our silence. Our decision to keep quiet unless and until it's time to speak gives us the ability to stay peaceful, helping to maintain the peace around us. Exercising this kind of self-control can also increase our influence, because people tend to listen to calm voices rather than anxious or angry ones.

Peace is something precious, something to be guarded and protected. The next time you find yourself in a situation in which you are tempted to respond with rapid-fire words, try imagining yourself "holding your peace." Do your best to think calmly, asking God for his wisdom to shape your response.

Lord, thank you for the peace you give. Help me to cherish and hold on
to it. Make me quick to listen so that I can know how and when to speak
in a way that will add to the peace rather than subtract from it.

November 4

REGRETS

*Jesus explained: "My nourishment comes from doing the will of
God, who sent me, and from finishing his work."*

JOHN 4:34

I have sometimes heard people say that they have no regrets. But I don't
believe them. Every life has its share of regrets arising from bad decisions,
lost opportunities, mistakes, and sins. There are some things we should
regret. In fact, regret can serve as a wise instructor, preventing us from making the same mistakes over and over.

But sometimes we get stuck in our regrets, unable to experience God's
peace because we cannot get free of them. What then? Charles Stanley
tells the story of a young woman who felt called to become a missionary in
Southeast Asia. Instead of pursuing her calling, she married a man who felt
no such call. For the next twenty-five years, the woman was mired in her
regrets. When she was forty-eight, she told her husband how she felt. A generous man, he encouraged her to undertake a short-term mission, promising
to support her in it for up to twelve months.

But all of the woman's efforts to forge an alliance with a missionary
organization failed. Finally she decided to fly to Southeast Asia and look for
a missionary who might welcome her help. After four months, she returned
home, dejected and in ill health. A wise pastor told her the truth: "That
boat sailed. God may have called you nearly thirty years ago to serve Him in
Southeast Asia. What you need to ask yourself is this: 'What is God calling
me to do right now?'"[1]

If you have made decisions or done things that you regret, don't let
your regrets continue to block God's peace. Instead, take each one to the
Lord, asking for forgiveness. Then ask God what he wants you to do right
now. Remember that he is both powerful and creative, still able to bring your
life—even after many failings—into perfect alignment with his purposes.

*Lord, forgive me for not doing what you wanted me to. I repent for going my own way.
Help me now to know your will and to do it, trusting in your mercy and forgiveness.*

JOY AHEAD

There is wonderful joy ahead, even though you have to endure many trials for a little while. These trials will show that your faith is genuine. It is being tested as fire tests and purifies gold—though your faith is far more precious than mere gold. So when your faith remains strong through many trials, it will bring you much praise and glory and honor on the day when Jesus Christ is revealed to the whole world.

1 PETER 1:6-7

We have already seen that God's peace has many facets to it. To grow in that peace is to grow into the likeness of the one we call the Prince of Peace. Since *shalom* contains the ideas of wholeness, well-being, serenity, healing, safety, satisfaction, and even prosperity, God's peace is something rich and deep that he works into our lives as we grow in greater maturity.

Like joy, peace is not something we merely feel but something that comes to characterize our lives regardless of circumstances. There will be times when we feel our lack of it acutely even though we are attempting to follow God faithfully. Seasons of difficulty will arise. Trials and tragedies will assail us. Such times may temporarily rob us of the sense that God is with us, making us vulnerable to fear. At these times, it may help to remember the things that lead to peace. I'm referring to things like

confessing our sin	resting
forgiving others	exercising
obeying God	praying daily
expressing gratitude	reading and studying
finding fellowship	Scripture
praising God	

Think of these as pearls on a string that together will make a beautiful necklace. While we wait for God's peace to adorn our lives, we can actively address any areas that may need shoring up, trusting that as we do, God will help us to grow in faith and trust.

Father, let me not ask why but how. How should I respond to what is happening right now? As I ask that question, give me confidence that you will provide the answer.

Be still, and know that I am God!

PSALM 46:10

How would you like it if someone called you a *motzi shem ra*? Huh? You might wonder if you had just been complimented or insulted. In fact, the phrase identifies you as the lowest of the low—someone who lies in order to give others a bad name. Jesus likely used this phrase when he said, "Blessed are you when people hate you, when they exclude you and insult you and *reject your name as evil*" (Luke 6:22, NIV, emphasis added).

Over the centuries, the Jewish people learned through painful experience how dangerous the tongue can be. Think of the pogroms that have been carried out against the Jews, often fueled by outrageous lies. So dangerous is the tongue, the rabbis say, that God designed it to be kept behind two protective walls—the lips and the teeth. Here are a few commonly cited examples of speech that may seem normal to us but that are forbidden to observant Jews:

> Don't call a person by a derogatory nickname, or by any other embarrassing name, even if the person is used to it.
>
> Don't ask an uneducated person for an opinion on a scholarly matter (because it would draw attention to the person's lack of knowledge or education).
>
> Don't refer someone to another person for assistance when you know the other person can't help (in other words, don't give someone the runaround).
>
> Don't deceive anyone, even if doing so does no harm.
>
> Don't compliment people if you don't mean it.[2]

Clearly, the rabbis have thought a lot about this issue. One way to combat the negative power of our tongues is to cultivate the discipline of silence. Dietrich Bonhoeffer recommended silence at the beginning and end of each day. Conscious and prayerful silence can open a space into which God may speak, giving him the first and the last word. Silence can also be a powerful tool against temptation. As Bonhoeffer pointed out, "Often we combat our evil thoughts most effectively if we absolutely refuse to allow them to be expressed in words."[3]

Father, help me to learn to be silent when silence is the best way to reflect your love.

November 7

SAD

God said, "Let there be light," and there was light.
And God saw that the light was good.

GENESIS 1:3-4

I can think of three reasons why summer is my favorite season. Reason number one: there is more light in a day. Reason number two: the sun rises earlier. Reason number three: the sun goes down later. But, you might object, that's only one reason, stated three different ways. Well, of course. Summer is all about light, isn't it? Given my enthusiasm for summer, it's no wonder that I approach fall and winter with a tiny bit of dread. Though I don't suffer from full-blown seasonal affective disorder, otherwise known as SAD, I do know that getting more light on those gloomy days can greatly improve my mood.

If you feel light-deprived, as I sometimes do, there are practical things you can do to stay cheerful even when the days are short. Researchers point out that melatonin supplements can improve sleep and relieve symptoms of depression in certain people. Just check with your doctor before taking it. Fish oil supplements, rich in omega-3 fatty acids, can also be a boon for your system. Here's another idea. Trimming overgrown bushes and tree branches around your house that block the sunlight will bring in more light, in addition to depriving would-be burglars of cover. Another way to add more light to your day is to make a habit of basking in the light of a lamp that simulates sunshine.

Finally, though you may not like strolling around in a snowstorm, you can make an effort to spend time outdoors most days. As one researcher explains, "The light we get from being outside on a summer day can be a thousand times brighter than we're ever likely to experience indoors. For this reason, it's important that people who work indoors get outside periodically." Even in winter, combining time outdoors with sleeping in total darkness at night "can have a major impact on melatonin rhythms and can result in improvements in mood, energy, and sleep quality."[4]

Uneasy about the onset of winter? Why not adopt a different approach this winter to see whether it improves your sense of well-being?

Lord, thank you for scientific advances that improve the quality of our lives. Help me to stay healthy through all the seasons, I pray.

THE PEACE OF KNOWING GOD'S WILL

Trust in the LORD *and do good. . . . Take delight in the* LORD, *and he will give you your heart's desires. Commit everything you do to the* LORD. *Trust him, and he will help you.*

PSALM 37:3-5

Sometimes I think we've tried to forge a Christian version of a crystal ball. It's called "knowing God's will." Afraid we might forfeit God's blessings if we miss his will, we avidly pursue it, agonizing over decisions like what school to attend, whom to marry, what job to accept. Though these decisions are important, and though it is always good to seek God's will, some of us are motivated more by fear than by a desire to glorify God. We want to be in control of the uncontrollable future, thinking perhaps we can assure a life of satisfaction and success.

But what if there is more than one way to do God's perfect will? What if he is not always as concerned about specific decisions as we are, knowing as he does that he can achieve his purpose in a variety of ways? Furthermore, why do we sometimes feel so anxious about finding his will, as though God has decided to make it impossible to discover?

Jerry Sittser, the author of *The Will of God as a Way of Life*, points out that the conventional approach to finding God's will, in which we think there is always only one perfect choice to make, betrays a faulty notion of God, implying that he is playing a celestial game of hide-and-seek. "Raising my own children," he says, "has changed my understanding of both God and the game of hide-and-seek. . . . I was better at hiding than my kids were. But I always gave them hints, like little squeaks or hoots, to help them find me. When they discovered my whereabouts, they would squeal with delight because they loved to find me. I never once wanted to hide so well that they would never find me, because the joy of the game came in being found, not in hiding."[5] Similarly, we can assume that God delights in revealing his will to us as we seek him.

The next time you are faced with a major decision, ask God to reveal his will. But don't get tied up in knots over it. Just point your heart toward his purposes and rest in the assurance that he will provide the guidance you need.

Father, I trust you to lead me, not into a future that I can control, but into one that will glorify you. I want to do your will, Lord. Guide me as I seek your face.

MORE ON GOD'S WILL

Seek the Kingdom of God above all else, and live righteously, and he will give you everything you need. So don't worry about tomorrow, for tomorrow will bring its own worries. Today's trouble is enough for today.

MATTHEW 6:33-34

Nowhere in the Bible does God lay down a complete blueprint for anyone's life. He didn't take Abraham aside, for instance, and tell him, "I want you to marry your half-sister Sarah, and then the two of you will move to a land that will someday be called Israel, but a famine will cause you to move to Egypt, and then you will bring back a slave girl by the name of Hagar who will bear you a son and there will be great strife in your household because of arguments between Sarah and Hagar and their children, and then I will ask you to sacrifice Isaac and to turn Ishmael out into the wilderness, and then you will acquire great riches, and then Sarah will die and you will remarry, and finally you will live to a ripe old age and three great religions will trace their beliefs to you." True, God did disclose some things to Abraham over a period of time, but there was much that Abraham simply didn't know about how life would unfold.

Surprisingly, the Bible doesn't offer a lot of guidance about our future, though it does offer considerable guidance about how we should conduct ourselves in the present. One thing Abraham did know was what God wanted him to do in the present, and, to his credit, he did it. To seek to know the future in detail would be like a first-year algebra student demanding to move straight from solving two-step equations to partial-fraction decomposition. It just won't work.

As Jerry Sittser points out, God has a plan for our lives. But he doesn't disclose it to us too far in advance. "We will discover that plan, however," Sittser tells us, "by simply doing the will of God we already know in the present moment. Life will then gradually unfold for us. We will discover at just the right time what we need to know and do. . . . We will discern God's will as naturally as we learned how to walk—one step at a time."[6]

Father, help me not to press against the limits you have placed in my life, seeking knowledge that you do not want to give. Help me to be content with what you have already revealed so I can do your will today.

YOUM AASL, YOUM BASL

I have learned how to be content with whatever I have. I know how to live on almost nothing or with everything. I have learned the secret of living in every situation, whether it is with a full stomach or empty, with plenty or little. For I can do everything through Christ, who gives me strength.

PHILIPPIANS 4:11-13

Journalist Annia Ciezadlo has covered wars in Lebanon and Iraq. Her memoir, *Day of Honey*, offers an unusual take on what it's like to live in the midst of a Middle Eastern war zone. Annia explains that whenever she travels, she also cooks "because eating has always been my most reliable way of understanding the world."[7]

"We all," she says, "carry maps of the world in our heads. Mine, if you could see it, would resemble a gigantic dinner table, full of dishes from every place I've been."[8] The title of her fascinating book is drawn from an Arabic phrase, *youm aasl, youm basl*, meaning "day of onion, day of honey." The point of this rhyming Arabic phrase is that some days will be bad and others will be good. People use it to comfort each other, as though to say that a better day will come.

Our lives are also filled with days of honey and days of onion, times when life is sweet and when it's anything but. Can we enjoy God's peace in both good days and bad? Paul seems to say that the answer is yes. One translation of his words to the Philippians says, "I have learned the secret of being content" (NIV).

I confess that I have yet to learn the unshakable contentment Paul speaks of. A day of onion can still transform my peace into discord. If you're more like me than the great apostle Paul, join me today in praying for the grace to become content in any and all circumstances.

Lord, I want to have the kind of unshakable faith Paul had. Please teach me how to trust you so that whether my circumstances are good or bad, I can rest in your faithfulness.

November 11

GENTLE

Don't be concerned about the outward beauty of fancy hairstyles, expensive jewelry, or beautiful clothes. You should clothe yourselves instead with the beauty that comes from within, the unfading beauty of a gentle and quiet spirit, which is so precious to God. This is how the holy women of old made themselves beautiful.

1 PETER 3:3-5

I confess that this has never been my favorite Bible passage. But I have come to realize there is something appealing about people, male or female, who are gentle and quiet at the core of their being. Such people have the ability to spread a sense of calm wherever they go.

The Amish have a reputation for being a peaceable people. Have you ever wondered what their secret is? One of their secrets to peace concerns a foundational value they call *gelassenheit*. Though it has no direct English equivalent, *gelassenheit* can best be understood, explains an Anabaptist minister by the name of Durand Overholtzer, through synonyms like "yieldedness, humility, calmness, composure, meekness, aplomb, tranquility, imperturbability, serenity, poise, sedateness, letting go, the opposite of self-assertion, a gentle spirit, submitting to God's will." *Gelassenheit*, he says, "is the union and agreement of the inner spirit with the outward response."[9]

While many of us are attracted to ideals of calmness, composure, poise, and tranquility, we are not so eager to embrace ideals like yieldedness, humility, meekness, and gentleness. But what if the second set is vital to developing the first, much like physical training is vital to becoming a successful athlete? Or what if the second set is like the thread that forms the pattern on a quilt, making it uniquely beautiful? Join me today in praying that God will thread his character onto the quilt that is your life, making you a woman of greater peace and deeper calm.

Father, help me to become a woman who is at the very core of her being gentle and quiet. Help me to remember that yieldedness, humility, and meekness bring peace. Through those qualities let me spread your peace.

November 12

CONFESSION

Confess your sins to each other and pray for each other so that you may be healed.

JAMES 5:16

If you want to experience more of God's peace, try doing exactly what James tells you. Make it a practice to confess your sins not only to God but to a mature sister in Christ. Confessing our sins to "someone with skin on" sounds like a recipe for creating more anxiety rather than more peace. You may wonder, *What will people think of me? Won't it make me feel worse about myself?* Contrary to what you may think, such a practice can be a tremendous step toward healing and a real stress reliever. Let me illustrate.

In his book *Rumors of Another World*, Philip Yancey tells the story of hearing author Keith Miller talk about his struggle to face the weakness and sin in his life. Determined to do so, he hit upon a plan, deciding to contact a Catholic priest who lived five hundred miles away in order to ask if he would hear his confession. It must have sounded like an odd request, coming as it did from a Protestant, but the priest agreed. As Miller prepared to meet with the priest, he made a list of everyone he had wronged and every character flaw and defect he could think of. When it came time to confess, he looked down at his list and read them to the priest out loud. Fearing to look up, he then held his head in his hands, awaiting a response. But as Yancey recounts, there was only silence. "Miller," he says, "kept expecting the blow to fall. Nothing. When he forced himself to raise his head, he saw that the priest was crying. 'My God, Keith,' he said, 'that's my list too.' A path opened toward healing."[10]

Perhaps in that moment, both men received healing, experiencing God's gracious presence as they spoke together honestly, openly, and with faith. Ask God today to show you whom you can confide in, and then make the request. Examine your conscience with the help of God's Spirit, and then do what James instructs: confess your sins and pray so that you may be healed.

Father, thank you for the mercy I have already experienced from brothers and sisters in Christ. Give me the courage and the wisdom to confess my sins and failings so that I may receive your peace.

November 13

MORE PEACE, LESS STUFF

Look at the lilies and how they grow. They don't work or make their clothing,
yet Solomon in all his glory was not dressed as beautifully as they are.

LUKE 12:27

Ever heard of the terms "hedonic adaptation" or "hedonic treadmill"? Both of these refer to the fact that in order to maintain the surge of pleasure that comes with every new gadget and thingamajig we purchase, we have to keep buying new things. Of the two phrases, I prefer the latter because it vividly captures the idea that we have to keep running farther and faster in order to achieve the same amount of happiness.

But what would happen if we were to step off the treadmill? That's what several people in the small house movement have done, building tiny homes so they can live more simply and cheaply. Such homes cost less to heat, cool, and repair and are much quicker to clean. One woman who lives in the tiniest of houses heats her home with solar panels and a propane tank, the kind the rest of us use to power our gas grills, making her heating bills about $5 per month. Her "refrigerator" is a small cooler. By having a small carbon footprint, small-house folks hope to have a big impact on the world around them, spending their time and money on causes, people, and experiences they care about. What a terrific counterpoise to the bloated houses many people have been building in suburbs across the country.

Though I have no desire to call a closet home, the idea of downsizing appeals to me because I've learned the hard way that owning lots of stuff usually works against my sense of peace and happiness.

You needn't move into a tiny house to achieve the goal of living simply. Just decide that you want the benefits simplicity can bring and start making decisions with your goal in mind.

Lord, help me to major on the majors and minor on the minors. Having lots
of stuff is minor. Dedicating my time and money to you is major.

November 14

THE FEAR MAGNET

Fear of the LORD is a life-giving fountain; it offers escape from the snares of death.
PROVERBS 14:27

Have you noticed how easy it is for all kinds of fear to coexist in your heart? You may, for instance, feel fearful for your children, your spouse, your friends, your finances, your future, and your health. You may be afraid of public speaking and taking tests and flying in planes and crossing bridges. When left unchallenged, fear can spread like a contagion inside us. Or maybe fear is something like a great big magnet, attracting more and more fear to our lives. If this is so, how can we neutralize its power?

Perhaps the only way to do this is to replace our fears with what I call a capital F kind of fear. I am thinking, of course, about what Scripture calls the "Fear of the Lord." But doesn't associating the word *fear* with the word *Lord* end up ramping up our fears, reviving all the old stereotypes about a wrathful God who is always angry? Not if we understand the term rightly. Scripture links fear of the Lord to many good things: wisdom, safety, long life, prosperity, and a sure foundation. Fear of the Lord can protect you from evil, death, bitterness, and ruin.

To fear the Lord is to revere him, to stand in awe of him, so much so that your primary aim is to please him above pleasing yourself or others. Like a young girl who feels secure while walking alongside her father, you heed his voice because you know that doing so will keep you from straying too close to the edge of a cliff or wandering off in the company of a stranger. You know that your heavenly Father has your best interests at heart. Fearing God produces a kind of foundational security, reducing and reordering the lesser fears that threaten you.

Scripture tells us that the fear of the Lord is a "life-giving fountain," the beginning of wisdom, and the door to friendship with God. By fearing God, we reduce the other fears that plague us, avoiding evil and courting blessing.

Lord, I want to fear you more than I fear anything in this world—financial loss, illness, sorrow, tragedy, even death. Help me to fear you in the right way that I might grow in the knowledge of your peace.

TOO MUCH EMPATHY?

*Our earthly fathers disciplined us for a few years, doing the best they knew how.
But God's discipline is always good for us, so that we might share in his holiness. No
discipline is enjoyable while it is happening—it's painful! But afterward there will be
a peaceful harvest of right living for those who are trained in this way. So take a new
grip with your tired hands and strengthen your weak knees. Mark out a straight path
for your feet so that those who are weak and lame will not fall but become strong.*

HEBREWS 12:10-13

I have a friend whose mother suffers from chronic anxiety. Always a worrier, her mom has grown more and more anxious with the years. Her mother's doctor recently prescribed an anti-anxiety drug, which she adamantly refuses to take. Because her mother's anxiety has provoked so many problems within the family, my friend recently quipped that if her mother won't take the pills then the rest of the family will have to—so they can stay calm enough to deal with her anxiety. My friend's tongue-in-cheek comment reveals something important about human dynamics. Many of us are easily infected by each other's emotional weaknesses. Sometimes the weakest member of a family is the one who exerts the strongest influence.

Take, for example, the child who easily whines and cries. Of course there's nothing wrong with crying, unless it becomes habitual or a method for children to get their way. As mothers, many of us are good at empathy. We understand and sympathize with our children's weaknesses. But sometimes our empathy can be an obstacle that makes it harder for them to grow up.

Edwin Friedman, a family therapist and leadership consultant, pointed out that people tend to mature more when the leader of an organization adapts toward strength rather than weakness. In that context, Friedman considered empathy an adaptation toward weakness. He counseled leaders to challenge those they lead as a way to help them grow and mature. As Friedman pointed out, there are some people whose real need is to *not* have their need fulfilled.

Perhaps that's why we don't always experience God being as empathetic as we might like. He knows exactly how we need to be challenged in order to become the kind of women who can lead others toward peace.

*Lord, help me to stop absorbing the emotions that are swirling around me.
Strengthen me so I can respond in a way that strengthens others.*

INTIMACY WITH GOD

Go and make disciples of all the nations, baptizing them in the name of the Father and the Son and the Holy Spirit. Teach these new disciples to obey all the commands I have given you. And be sure of this: I am with you always, even to the end of the age.

MATTHEW 28:19-20

In July 2007, twenty-three South Korean missionaries, sixteen men and seven women, were on a bus traveling from Kandahar to Kabul, when the driver allowed two armed men to board the bus. For the next month and a half, members of the Taliban held them hostage, moving them to a series of cellars and farmhouses in order to conceal them. Before they were split into small groups, all twenty-three rededicated their lives to Christ, pledging their willingness to die for his glory. There was even an argument about who might be given the privilege of dying first.

One of the missionaries had a small Bible, which was split into twenty-three sections so each person could have a portion of God's Word to strengthen and comfort them during the difficult days ahead. Two of the men were executed before a deal was reached to release the hostages.

Oddly enough, when the remaining hostages were safely back on South Korean soil, more than one of them would later comment, "Don't you wish we were still there?" Several spoke of experiencing a deep intimacy with God in the midst of their terrible ordeal—an experience they hadn't been able to recapture since their return to the safety and comfort of their own land.[11]

Why this dynamic? Perhaps because in the midst of their difficulties, God was fulfilling his promise that the Holy Spirit would be with those who would be brought to trial for the sake of the gospel. Perhaps also because desperation can excavate more space in our hearts for God. Instead of feeling full and satisfied, we recognize a need only Christ can fill. Very few of us will ever face the threat these men and women did. But we can take heart from their story, believing that God can give us courage for whatever we may face.

Lord, I have already experienced your closeness during times of great need. Thank you. Help me not to get so comfortable and so full that I forget I need you still.

November 17

EVEN BROKEN CAN BE BEAUTIFUL

Even a tree has more hope! If it is cut down, it will sprout again and grow new branches. Though its roots have grown old in the earth and its stump decays, at the scent of water it will bud and sprout again like a new seedling.

JOB 14:7-9

Today is my parents' anniversary. I can't remember the last time they celebrated, not just because my father passed away a few years ago, but because they were divorced many years before that. There were too many problems. Neither one of them knew how to conduct a "good" argument, for one thing. And both were strong willed. Pronouncing those two husband and wife was like putting Joe Frazier and Muhammad Ali in the ring and expecting a love fest. There was also the matter of my father's alcoholism. There was just too much brokenness and hurt for one marriage to survive.

And yet I feel like celebrating. Because of the great things God did—not to put the marriage back together, but to help two old people love each other to the end. Because that's how it was. My father finally reaching bottom and realizing he wasn't alone. God was there. The family gathering once again on holidays, my parents at both ends of the table. My brothers joking and laughing, embracing a father they had shunned for a time. And I losing all fear of him and feeling only affection. And then there was my mother, sitting every day at my father's bedside, fiercely protective as he struggled to pass from this life to the next.

My family was as fractured as many, but I give thanks for the way God pieced it back together, making it beautiful in its brokenness. It's a picture that will stay with me always, not just because it captures how God dealt with us, but because in a way, it's a picture of every life that belongs to God this side of heaven—beautiful in its brokenness because of the way his glory shines through.

Lord, thank you that nothing and no one is so broken that you can't come and make your home with them, rebuilding their hope, renewing their love, and pouring out your grace to let your glory shine through.

KNOWING GOD BY NAME

Then the Levite leaders called out to the people, "Stand up and praise the Lord your God, for he lives from everlasting to everlasting. Praise his glorious name! It is far greater than we can think or say."

NEHEMIAH 9:5, TLB

Did you know that the word *God* is a relatively recent invention? In fact, it is not used in any of the original versions of Scripture written in Hebrew, Greek, or Aramaic. Instead, the Jewish people used various names and titles to refer to God, names like *Yahweh, Elohim, El Shaddai, Adonai*, and many others. But why mention this in a book about knowing God's peace? Simply because our struggle to experience more peace is really a struggle to know God more intimately. One way to know God more is to ask him to reveal more of himself through his names and titles as they are revealed in the Bible. By learning just a little bit about each of his names and then meditating on various passages containing them, we may find our sense of peace growing.

Here are a few to get you started.[12]

- *El* [God, Mighty Creator] is not like people. He tells no lies. He is not like humans. He doesn't change his mind. When he says something, he does it. When he makes a promise, he keeps it. (See Numbers 23:19.)
- *Yahweh* [God's covenant name, the LORD] is merciful, compassionate, patient, and always ready to forgive. *Yahweh* is good to everyone and has compassion for everything that he has made. (See Psalm 145:8-9.)
- *Elohim* [God, Mighty Creator] is our *Machseh* [refuge] and strength, an ever-present help in times of trouble. That is why we are not afraid even when the earth quakes or the mountains topple into the depths of the sea. Water roars and foams, and mountains shake at the surging waves. (See Psalm 46:1-3.)

Yahweh, my God, thank you for revealing yourself to your people throughout the ages. Help me to grow strong in your peace by growing in my knowledge of you, I pray.

PEACE AMONG BELIEVERS

I pray that they will all be one, just as you and I are one—as you are in me, Father, and I am in you. And may they be in us so that the world will believe you sent me.

JOHN 17:21

Over the years I have had the privilege of knowing Christians from a wide variety of denominational and nondenominational backgrounds: evangelical, mainline, charismatic, Catholic, and Orthodox. I have sung the ancient hymns and joined in contemporary choruses. I have meditated in silence and prayed out loud. I have held hands, kept silence, and listened with wonder to sermons that touched my soul. I have prayed and been prayed over. I have worked alongside brothers and sisters from various churches to promote God's truth and love. Rubbing shoulders with Christians from different traditions has been for me an immeasurably enriching experience. It has encouraged, challenged, and taught me important things I might not otherwise have learned. Though I realize that the body of Christ is divided, I also know that Christ is with all of his people, whether or not we approve of them.

That's why I find it so painful to be around those who draw the tiniest of circles around their church or their version of Christianity, characterizing those who disagree with them, even on small points, as faithless. Yes, there are times when we have to contend for the faith, but we cannot make the mistake of acting as though disagreements regarding minor matters, like which translation of the Bible we read, are as serious as disagreements regarding core elements of our faith like the Incarnation and the Resurrection. Let's agree to disagree on the minors while we stand together on the majors. And while we are doing that, let's pray for each other and learn from each other and treat each other with respect, remaining together so Christ can be glorified and the gospel can be preached throughout the world.

Father, forgive me for ways I have been overly critical of other Christians. Help me to love and respect my brothers and sisters in Christ without feeling as though I have to agree with them on everything. Teach me to distinguish the difference between major and minor issues so I can be at peace with all who are faithful to you.

WHY DO THE WICKED PROSPER?

LORD, you always give me justice when I bring a case before you. So let
me bring you this complaint: Why are the wicked so prosperous?

JEREMIAH 12:1

Author Charlie Shedd once received a letter from a high school student in Nebraska, asking a difficult question. "We are having a hard time on the farm this year," she explained, "because of no rain. My father is worried about paying the bills and the bank. All the farmers are worried.

"My folks are good people," she went on to say. "We go to church, my mom and I sing in the choir, and my father is a deacon. My parents do so many good things. They grow more food than we need and give to poor people.

"I guess what bothers me most is *why does it rain on my uncle's farm?* He lives seventy miles away, and his crops are looking good. I probably shouldn't say this, but my uncle is mean. I don't see how my aunt stands him; he is so awful to her. He is awful to my cousins too, and nobody likes him. He swears a lot, and he doesn't go to church. I am not sure he even believes in God. So why does he get rain and we don't? Do you know what I'm asking? Do you think it's fair?"[13]

In his response, Charlie didn't lecture this earnest young girl about the fact that good behavior doesn't ensure an easy life or that geographical factors may have been affecting weather patterns, but he did remind her of the story of a man called Job, the poor guy who lost his children, his servants, and his wealth in just a few hours. Then Job's body broke out in horrible sores. In the end, after enduring days of bad advice from three so-called friends, Job received something better than a buttoned-up answer to his sufferings—a visitation from a God so magnificent that his questions no longer mattered. He also received twice as many blessings as he had before.

"Why do the wicked prosper?"—it's a question that will always be asked. Our task is not to keep searching for easy answers but to keep believing that God is good no matter what. As Charlie Shedd pointed out, the story of Job ends on a positive note: "The LORD blessed the latter part of Job's life more than the former part" (42:12, NIV). Each of us can expect the same, even if the "latter part" doesn't begin to unfold in this life.

Lord, hear my cry to you. Help me to be faithful, remembering
your goodness in the midst of many trials.

HEAL ME!

Inside the city, near the Sheep Gate, was the pool of Bethesda, with five covered porches. Crowds of sick people—blind, lame, or paralyzed—lay on the porches. One of the men lying there had been sick for thirty-eight years. . . . Jesus told him, "Stand up, pick up your mat, and walk!" Instantly, the man was healed!

JOHN 5:2-5, 8-9

As the result of a diving accident, Joni Eareckson Tada was paralyzed at the age of seventeen. Shortly after that, a friend sat by her bed and read the passage about the man Jesus healed at the pool of Bethesda.

"It was the part about being an invalid for thirty-eight years that got me," Joni remembers. "Please Lord, I can't live without use of my hands or legs for three days, let alone thirty years. I'm not like that man by the pool at Bethesda. Be compassionate to me, like you were to him. Heal me!"

But Joni's prayer for a miracle seemed to go unanswered. Thirty years later as she rounded a corner while touring Jerusalem with her husband, Ken, she came face-to-face with the ruins of that pool. Looking at her husband, the tears welling up, she said, "Jesus didn't pass me by. He didn't overlook me. He answered my prayer: He said, 'No.'"

And then came the astonishing confession. "And I'm glad," she said. "A 'no' answer has purged sin from my life, strengthened my commitment to him, forced me to depend on grace, bound me with other believers, produced discernment, fostered sensitivity, disciplined my mind, taught me to spend my time wisely, stretched my hope, made me know Christ better, helped me long for truth, led me to repentance of sin, goaded me to give thanks in times of sorrow, increased my faith, and strengthened my character. Being in this wheelchair has meant knowing him better, feeling his strength every day."

"Are you ok?" her husband asked.

"Yes," she sniffed and laughed. "I can't believe that I'm crying and laughing at the same time. There are more important things in life than walking."[14]

Thank you, Joni, not only for telling us what peace is, but also for showing us what it looks like. Let's take heart from the example of this remarkable woman, so that whether the answer is yes or no, we can experience the deep peace that comes from knowing God is faithful.

Lord, I lift up my prayers to you, confident that you will answer them in the best way possible.

LET'S STOP PRETENDING

Because of Christ and our faith in him, we can now come
boldly and confidently into God's presence.

EPHESIANS 3:12

Last night the power went out at our house. It seems that a squirrel had suffered an unfortunate collision with a transformer, leaving a swath of the city without power. Fortunately our emergency generator kicked in and we feasted on light and power while our neighbors' houses were shrouded in darkness. Then my cell phone rang. It was a friend who lives a few blocks away.

"Do you have any power?" she asked.

"Yes, the generator is on," I said. Since it was dinnertime, I asked if she would like to come over.

"No, thanks. I think I'll just stay home and make a salad. I really don't want to go out because I worked at home all day and haven't put on any makeup."

Now, I respect the need for makeup as much as the next woman. When my children ask me why I bother wearing it, I tell them it's because I don't like scaring people. But, seriously, wouldn't it be great to venture out into the world without the need for pretense? I like what Brennan Manning has to say about the fact that none of us need to pretend when we come into the presence of the Lord.

"Whatever our failings may be," he says, "we need not lower our eyes in the presence of Jesus. . . . Jesus comes not for the super-spiritual but for the wobbly and the weak-kneed who know they don't have it all together, and who are not too proud to accept the handout of amazing grace. As we glance up, we are astonished to find the eyes of Jesus open with wonder, deep with understanding, and gentle with compassion."[15]

Let's stop thinking we can't come into God's presence because we aren't spiritual enough or good enough or holy enough or passionate enough. Instead, let's trust him, believing that he welcomes us—the wobbly and the weak-kneed—receiving us with compassion and understanding.

Lord, like the old song "Just As I Am," I sing: Just as I am, though tossed about with many a conflict, many a doubt. Fightings and fears within, without, O Lamb of God, I come, I come.

November 23

A SINGLE SPARK

Those who control their tongue will have a long life.

PROVERBS 13:3

Last year, a serial arsonist was on the loose in a neighborhood near my house. His specialty was setting fire to garages in the middle of the night. One evening the flames in an attached garage quickly spread to the house where several people were sleeping inside. Fortunately no one was injured. This troubled man terrorized the neighborhood for several months before he was finally caught and charged with as many as ten fires. At one point, investigators even brought in an accelerant-sniffing dog to help with the case.

When it comes to accelerants, the Bible doesn't have anything to say about the common ones: acetone, kerosene, gasoline, lacquer, or lacquer thinner. Instead, it talks about an item that is small but ubiquitous. Every household has at least one and sometimes several. Though it may seem innocent enough, this accelerant can do tremendous damage when activated. What am I talking about? The human tongue, of course. Listen to how the book of James characterizes it: "The tongue is a small thing that makes grand speeches. But a tiny spark can set a great forest on fire" (3:5). One ill-considered word can quickly shatter the peace. The Bible compares the tongue to a sharp razor, and it uses adjectives like "twisted," "lying," "gossiping," and "deceitful" to describe it. The tongue is such an expert deceiver that it can even fool the person who wields it. It's so easy to rationalize our words, creating a thousand reasons to justify our unkindness. Like the serial arsonist, some of us are guilty of causing great harm because of our habit of letting our tongues control us.

Peace comes, at least in part, from learning how to control the incendiary power of the tongue. Today, take a step in that direction by reviewing the conversations you've had over the past week. Did your words promote healing and peace or strife and difficulty? If you discover traces of gossip, rage, slander, deceit, or unkindness, go to the person or the people who heard them and apologize. Then ask God to help you develop greater sensitivity to how your words affect others.

Father, thank you for the gift of speech, a gift I have not always used well.
Please forgive me for speaking in ways that have harmed others and give me
the power to recognize and break any unhealthy patterns of speech.

WHY PEOPLE CAN'T FLY

Wise words satisfy like a good meal; the right words bring satisfaction. The tongue can bring death or life; those who love to talk will reap the consequences.

PROVERBS 18:20-21

M om, why can't people fly?" my daughter asked me one day.
Never one to shy away from attempting to answer the unanswerable, I ventured a guess, pointing out that God had already granted human beings incredible powers. Flying, I explained, would give us an enormous, unfair advantage. It wouldn't be fair, for instance, if hunters were able to pull alongside a flock of ducks and then pick them off one by one. And who would want to live in a world where burglars or Peeping Toms could fly, to say nothing of kids intent on toilet papering your house? The truth is, we have enough trouble managing the powers we do have.

Take the power of our tongues. Scripture tells us that our words have incredible power. It goes so far as to say that the power of life and death is in our tongues. We can use them to bless or to curse, to encourage or to demoralize. Who hasn't regretted spitting out angry words that are impossible to retract? How can we bring our tongues under greater control so they will add to the peace of our world rather than detract from it?

The key to controlling our mouths, of course, lies in the way we control our minds. Remember how Paul advised the believers in Rome, saying, "Letting your sinful nature control your mind leads to death. But letting the Spirit control your mind leads to life and peace" (Romans 8:6)? Paul is saying that controlling our minds is not primarily a matter of willpower but of Spirit power. Today, as you seek to control the power of your tongue, ask God to inhabit your thought life through the transformative power of his Spirit.

Father, I want my words to bless and build up rather than to hurt and tear down. Please help me welcome your Spirit today, surrendering my thoughts and judgments to you.

November 25

MY NUMBER ONE WORRY

Four men arrived carrying a paralyzed man on a mat. They couldn't bring him
to Jesus because of the crowd, so they dug a hole through the roof above his head.
Then they lowered the man on his mat, right down in front of Jesus.

MARK 2:3-4

If someone asked you to name your number one worry, what would you say? Like many mothers, I would have to confess that my top worry and the target of many of my prayers is my children. I realize that my aspirations for them far outpace my ability to help them. There are some things a mother just can't do, no matter how well-intentioned she may be.

A story in the Gospels is instructive, pointing out a way to deal with worry, whether it's worry about our children or about others we care for. You probably remember the four men who lowered a paralyzed man into Jesus' presence so the man could be healed. Fern Nichols, founder and president of Moms in Prayer International, points out that intercessors are a lot like those four men who were bold enough to climb onto another man's roof, dig a hole through it, and then lower the paralyzed man into Christ's presence.

"Many of our children," she says, "are paralyzed by sin, and the weight of that reality is too much for a parent to bear by herself. We become weary when we don't see any change, when we don't spy even a glimpse of an answer to prayer.

"Imagine a mom pulling one corner of a mat, as she slowly drags her two-hundred-pound football player of a son to Jesus. But then another mom comes alongside and picks up a corner. The prayers of the second mom spark faith. Then another mom and another come alongside, each gathering up a corner. Hope returns, as she hears the believing prayers of the other moms."

Fern knows just how effective a group of praying women can be. We may not be able to save a single soul or perform a miracle in answer to our worries about loved ones. But we can do something vital, linking arms in prayer as we bring those we love into the presence of the only one capable of keeping them safe and giving them peace.

Lord, help me to find other women to pray with so I can become "a mat carrier,"
not taking on the whole burden but sharing it with others who love you.

Too much talk leads to sin. Be sensible and keep your mouth shut.

PROVERBS 10:19

I've never been a whiz at making small talk. Give me something meaty to talk about like the elusiveness of peace in the Middle East or the prospect of an economic turnaround in the next year, and I usually have something to say. My fallback for making small talk is to ask people obvious questions like, "How's work been going?" That's the question I recently pitched to an acquaintance, who stammered out the answer that she had just quit her job. Not wanting to probe, I said something stupid like, "Well, I'm sure something better will come along soon." (Keep in mind that I made this remark despite knowing that the unemployment rate in my state was at 13 percent.) My awkward comment was followed by an even more awkward silence.

A few days later I mentioned this woman's situation to a mutual friend. The friend replied that she knew exactly what had happened . . . but she wasn't at liberty to tell me. From the tone of her voice, I knew there were juicy details. Remember those old cartoons depicting a devil squatting on one shoulder while an angel is sitting on the other? For a split second the little devil on my shoulder whispered in my ear: "If you knew more about what was going on, I'm sure you could pray for her better." But then the angel on my other shoulder replied, "Oh, sure. That's the only reason you want all the gory details, so you can pray better! Now I've heard everything."

Fortunately my "skeptical angel" prevailed and I kept quiet, resisting the temptation to probe. I already knew everything I needed to know in order to pray for the woman who had left or lost her job. I could leave the gory details where they belonged, between her and the Lord.

Sometimes peace comes from knowing less than you would like to. Knowing less about office politics can help you stay focused on your job. Knowing less about the failings of others can keep you from judging them. Listening to gossip may offer its share of momentary pleasures, but it will not bring you peace, nor will it help you become a peacemaker.

Father, give me the grace to be content with knowing only what I need to know, especially when it comes to the failures of others. Help me to protect their peace by minding my own business.

DON'T BE ASHAMED
OF YOUR WEAKNESS

To keep me from becoming proud, I was given a thorn in my flesh, a messenger from Satan to torment me and keep me from becoming proud. Three different times I begged the Lord to take it away. Each time he said, "My grace is all you need. My power works best in weakness." So now I am glad to boast about my weaknesses, so that the power of Christ can work through me.

2 CORINTHIANS 12:7-9

Have you ever wondered about the Bible's reliability? How true are the stories it tells? One thing that makes the Bible so believable is the way it portrays its major characters. Very rarely do you run across anyone in the pages of Scripture who has it all together. Sarah was consumed with jealousy, Rachel and Leah couldn't get along, Miriam chafed under Moses' leadership, Abraham lied because he was afraid, David committed adultery and then murder, and Solomon had an insatiable appetite for women. If the Bible were a puff piece, its characters would be far more heroic. Instead, it displays their weaknesses honestly, revealing the kind of raw material God had to work with.

And work with it he did. As Rick Warren points out, "The great missionary Hudson Taylor said, 'All God's giants were weak people.' Moses' weakness was his temper. It caused him to murder an Egyptian, strike the rock he was supposed to speak to, and break the tablets of the Ten Commandments. Yet God transformed Moses into *the humblest man on earth.*'

"Gideon's weakness was low self-esteem and deep insecurities, but God transformed him into a *'mighty man of valor.'* Abraham's weakness was fear. Not once, but twice, he claimed his wife was his sister to protect himself. But God transformed Abraham into *'the father of those who have faith.'* Impulsive, weak-willed Peter became *'a rock,'* the adulterer David became *'a man after my own heart,'* and John, one of the arrogant 'Sons of Thunder,' became the 'Apostle of Love.'"[16]

What about you? What are your greatest weaknesses? Ask God for the grace to face them honestly. But don't let them weigh you down. No amount of weakness can keep you from becoming the woman God wants you to be if you will keep following him, trusting him to transform you as you do.

*Lord, let my weakness become your opportunity. Transform
me into a living example of what you can do.*

DON'T FORGET

*Can a mother forget her nursing child? Can she feel no love for the child she
has borne? But even if that were possible, I would not forget you!*

ISAIAH 49:15

My daughter had just returned from school. After a few minutes, I heard
her voice calling plaintively up the stairs: "Where's the dog? I looked
everywhere, but I can't find Kallie. She's not in the house."

My first thought was that I had forgotten to let the dog in from the
backyard. How long had she been out there? I really couldn't remember. But
now our beloved dog had gone missing, and I was to blame!

I raced out to the backyard. Just as I feared, there was no sign of Kallie.
No Kallie in the front yard, either, and no Kallie racing happily toward me
as I desperately shouted her name. I ran back inside and grabbed my coat,
intending to drive around the neighborhood, shouting her name. I didn't
care what the neighbors thought. I knew the girls would never forgive me
if anything happened to their dog. "Please, God, help me get Kallie back,"
I prayed.

Wait a minute, I thought. *Shouldn't I look for tracks in the snow to tell me which way
she had headed when she exited the backyard?* I looked on either side of the car and up
and down the driveway but found nothing, not a single paw print. That was
strange. If Kallie wasn't in the backyard and if she hadn't been through the
front yard, where was she? Then it hit me! She was exactly where I had left
her after making a quick trip to the bank.

In the car!

While I had been desperately calling her name, scanning the driveway
for paw prints, Kallie had been staring out at me from the backseat of the car,
no doubt wondering what all the fuss was about.

Ah, forgetfulness. It should be my middle name. And speaking of forgetfulness, how much more peaceful would our lives be if we could remember that no matter where we are or what we are going through, God will
never forget us?

*Father, sometimes I lose my peace because I think you've forgotten all about
me. Help me to realize that when you say something, you mean it. May
I learn to rest in the truth that you will never fail or forget me.*

November 29

BREAKING THE CHAINS

God has not given us a spirit of fear and timidity, but of power, love, and self-discipline.

2 TIMOTHY 1:7

Remember those paper chains you used to put together as a child? All you had to do was insert a strip of paper into the last link and stick the ends together. Then it was time for the next link. Before you knew it, you had a nice, long chain. According to one source, people have been making paper chains since at least 225 BC. But we've been making emotional and spiritual chains far longer than that. Unfortunately, these chains can create enormous impediments to God's peace.

Many of us, for instance, are overweight. We say yes to one little brownie after another, and then we wonder why we can't seem to lose weight. We know we lack self-control, but we've given up doing anything about it.

Author Joanna Weaver admits to a lifelong struggle with weight. Last time I saw her, however, she looked lovely—tall and svelte. Let's listen in on how she learned to let God lead her in the fight to break the chains that held her. "Instead of helping me handle my weight issue," she says, "the Lord began to convict me of my choice of reading material.

"You see, at the time I was basically addicted to Christian fiction.

"Now, there is nothing wrong with a wholesome story. The problem lay in the fact I couldn't read just one novel at a time—much less a few pages before bed. No, I was a binge reader. Which meant one book right after another. Forget housework, forget cooking, and 'Don't bother me! I'm reading.'"

So Joanna stopped reading fiction for a year. And guess what, the discipline she gained from fasting from fiction spread into other areas of her life, particularly her eating. "When I obeyed God in the specific area He pointed out," she says, "it was as though a single link in the chain that bound me snapped. But soon other links lost their power as well, and I began walking in a freedom I'd never experienced before."[17]

As Joanna points out, the secret to living in greater freedom involves letting God choose our battles and then playing the role he assigns us. That's the way to both break the chains and to experience the peace we desire.

Father, don't let me ignore the voice of your Spirit speaking through my conscience. Help me to pay attention and to do what you are asking.

SPIN

When [the devil] lies, it is consistent with his character; for he is a liar and the father of lies.

JOHN 8:44

You may think that "spin" is something that was invented by modern media. But a closer look reveals that the practice dates back to the Garden of Eden. God said to Adam in Genesis 2, "You may freely eat the fruit of every tree in the garden—except the tree of the knowledge of good and evil" (verses 16-17). But by Genesis 3, the message had already become distorted. Here's what the serpent said to Eve: "Did God really say you must not eat the fruit from any of the trees in the garden?" (verse 1). See how it works? Satan takes a bit of the truth, adds a falsehood to it, and then produces a plausible lie that will insinuate itself into your heart as a question, causing you to distrust God.

Here's how spin might work on you today. God says he has forgiven you because you belong to Christ. But you know you are far from perfect. You told a lie, you yelled at your children, you gossiped. Even worse, you've done these things repeatedly. Instead of repenting and receiving God's forgiveness, you listen to the voice that tells you sin is despicable. True enough—sin is despicable. But then the voice takes it a step further, implying that *you* are despicable and that God can't possibly forgive you. Listening to Satan's spin on your sins will separate you from God's mercy.

Or how about this? God says he hears your prayers and will help you. He tells you he will bring good out of even the worst circumstances because he loves you and you love him. Yet your husband lost his job last year and can't find another or your child is ill and not getting any better. After a while, you stop listening to God's promises and start tuning in to the voice that says, "God doesn't care. Give it up. You're on your own." Listening to this voice rather than to the voice of the Spirit will spin you into a spiritual depression that separates you from God's love and peace.

The way to resist the spin Satan wants to put on your life is to lean into the promises God has made—promises to give you a future full of hope. Ask God today to help you listen to the message of his truth so you can faithfully cling to his promises.

Father, Satan wants to manipulate me with lies in order to destroy my faith. But your only objective is to love and save me. Help me to trust your words, not his.

December 1

GOD SEES YOU

Philip went to look for Nathanael and told him, "We have found the very person Moses and the prophets wrote about! His name is Jesus, the son of Joseph from Nazareth." . . . As they approached, Jesus said, "Now here is a genuine son of Israel—a man of complete integrity." "How do you know about me?" Nathanael asked. Jesus replied, "I could see you under the fig tree before Philip found you."

JOHN 1:45, 47-48

What is so remarkable about seeing someone sitting under a tree? When I was in Nazareth a few years ago, I saw a fig tree that made this story from John's Gospel come to life. The tree was covered with enormous leaves attached to branches that extended low to the ground. To snatch a few moments of peace and quiet, all you had to do was sit quietly beneath the tree. Even people passing within inches of the tree would not know you were there. That's what Nathanael must have been doing.

Notice that Jesus saw Nathanael sitting beneath the tree, but he also saw further than that—into the secret places of his heart, pronouncing him an honest man. Nathanael's encounter with Jesus reminds me of a story in the Hebrew Scriptures in which a homeless woman encounters God and names him "the God who sees me." It's a wonderful story of how the Lord cared for Hagar and her child in the midst of a brutal wilderness. To find out more about this story, take a look at Genesis 16 and Genesis 21:8-21.

Jesus' encounter with Nathanael assures us that nothing is hidden from the Lord's penetrating gaze. Not our struggles or our joys, not our fears or our dreams. He knows us as no one else does. Take time today to worship Christ and decide, as Nathanael did, to follow where he leads.

Jesus, you know me and you love me. Help me today to hear your voice, to trust it, and to follow you.

FINDING THE RIGHT TEACHER

You have been taught the holy Scriptures from childhood, and they have given you the
wisdom to receive the salvation that comes by trusting in Christ Jesus. All Scripture
is inspired by God and is useful to teach us what is true and to make us realize what
is wrong in our lives. It corrects us when we are wrong and teaches us to do what
is right. God uses it to prepare and equip his people to do every good work.

2 TIMOTHY 3:15-17

I love history. My favorite trips have been to places where there is a pro-found connection to ancient history, like Israel or Greece. Similarly, I love to read biographies of people like Teddy Roosevelt or Winston Churchill because of what their stories reveal about the past.

But don't count on me when it comes to solving math problems. That's just not my thing, which is why I can relate to Pastor Jim Cymbala's self-described struggles. "I took geometry," he says, "during my sophomore year in high school, and for the life of me, no matter what that teacher said, I couldn't figure it out. I didn't know an isosceles triangle from a bagel with cream cheese. None of it made sense. Then about two months into the semester, the teacher got sick and a new teacher replaced him. Under her tutelage, suddenly, the light went on for me. For the first time, I understood triangles, angles, and parabolas. (Well, maybe not the parabolas.) I had to give credit for my newfound understanding to the new teacher. It was the way she explained things that helped me understand geometry."

Cymbala goes on to say we need the best possible Teacher when it comes to reading Scripture and applying it to our lives. This means that whatever our bent, whether we love reading this ancient book or not, we all need the guidance of the Holy Spirit. He is the one who makes Scripture come to life so we can understand and apply it.

As Paul says, Scripture "corrects us when we are wrong," which is another way of saying it brings us to a place where we can experience more of God's peace.

Lord, I want to read your Word with understanding, applying it to my life
in the ways you want me to. Help me to make space in my life to read the
Bible daily. As I do, send me your Spirit to guide me into the truth.

December 3

ANXIETY WRAP

The LORD is my light and my salvation—so why should I be afraid? The LORD is my fortress, protecting me from danger, so why should I tremble?

PSALM 27:1

My family used to have a wire fox terrier that was terrorized by thunderstorms. Sweet Pea (yes, that really was her name) was trained to stay in the kitchen unless someone invited her into other rooms in the house. But with the first clap of thunder, her training would fly out the window. Racing through the house, she would look for the closest lap to shelter in. On more than one occasion, a storm sent our poor dog into a seizure. We might have helped Sweet Pea by fitting her with a Thundershirt, had it been available back then. This is a garment that wraps around dogs like a coat, applying gentle, constant pressure, which works to calm them down. It is also called an Anxiety Wrap.

Strange as it may sound, this technique also works for some children with autism who wear weighted vests for a few minutes each day to calm their overstimulated nervous systems. No doubt the same principle is at work with infants who are swaddled. The pressure makes them feel more secure.

While most of us don't need weighted vests, we could all do with our own version of an Anxiety Wrap. Here is the one I've developed: whenever I become anxious or fearful, I talk about my concerns with close friends, enlist their prayers, pray, and read Scripture. I also consciously remember how God has helped me in the past, and I thank him for his faithfulness. The more I focus on God and on doing his will, the more peaceful I become. As God wraps me in his grace, I am able to calm down in his presence.

Lord, I want my life to be characterized not by fear but by faith. Wrap me in your love and faithfulness today, changing my anxiety into confidence so I can do your will.

EDITING

*The Lord—who is the Spirit—makes us more and more like
him as we are changed into his glorious image.*

2 CORINTHIANS 3:18

A few months ago I finished a book I'd been working on for over a year.
When I handed it in to my editor, I thought it was in pretty good shape.
Good thing, because I needed to take a break from writing so I could get to
the thousand and one things I'd put aside while completing the book.

Weeks passed before the next step in the publishing project, when an
editor delivers her critique of the manuscript. Though most writers will tell
you they welcome constructive criticism, what they don't tell you is that in
the heart of every writer (especially tired ones), there is the secret dream
that the editor will read the manuscript and respond that it can't possibly be
improved.

Since my editor didn't make my dream come true, I had to roll up my
sleeves and dig back into the writing, spending much more time on revisions
than I had planned. But the final manuscript was so much better than the
one I had initially turned in that I later thanked her for not living up (or
down) to my secret dream.

A good editor, of course, performs a difficult balancing act between
encouragement and critique. Err on one side or the other, and a writer may
become either complacent or frustrated. The editor's role is to help the
writer produce the best work possible. In this regard, editors are a little like
therapists or, better yet, like the Holy Spirit. Why? Because the Holy Spirit
both encourages and stretches us, giving us hope and convicting us of wrongdoing in order to produce the best life possible.

If the Spirit is uncovering an area of weakness in your life right now,
don't give in to discouragement. If change is called for, then believe change is
possible. Embrace it with all the energy and faith you can muster, confident
that God will help you to do whatever he is asking you to do.

*Lord, help me to be sensitive to your Spirit. I want to be open to how you want to
correct and encourage me. Whatever your guidance, help me to trust you.*

STANDING OVATION

There is more than enough room in my Father's home. If this were not so,
would I have told you that I am going to prepare a place for you?

JOHN 14:2

How many funerals have you been to that ended with a standing ovation? I just returned from one. It was for my neighbor Dale. He had fought and eventually lost a long battle with cancer. But his life had borne great fruit, touching many people. Dale was a man who loved God and served him humbly as a deacon in his church. I was struck by how everyone who spoke at his funeral talked about Dale in the present tense, as though he hadn't passed away.

It wasn't just a case of feeling his lingering influence; rather, most of those gathered believed Dale was still alive. In fact, the pastor who preached the sermon remarked how much he disliked hearing anyone described as "dead." People die, of course, but the pastor reminded us that death is an event, not a destination. It's the point at which we make the transition into another life—one that will last forever. The applause at the end of the funeral for this former college football player, father, grandfather, great-grandfather, and deacon was given in honor of a life well lived and as a celebration of the life Dale is enjoying right now, face-to-face with the God he loves.

One of my neighbors had the privilege of witnessing the moment of Dale's passing. His large extended family had gathered in his living room. She watched as they all were drawn to the bed the moment Dale died. Then they knelt down and began to sing. She told me it was the most beautiful thing she had ever witnessed—to see this family's reaction as their father and grandfather passed into heaven.

I won't see Dale for a while, unless, of course, my time on earth is shorter than I imagine. But when I do see him, I hope God will welcome me into his peace with the same words I believe he has spoken to Dale: "Well done, my good and faithful servant" (Matthew 25:21).

Lord, the peace we enjoy now is just a foretaste of the peace we will enjoy
forever. Help me to remember that as I seek your peace for this day.

December 6

SPIRITUALLY AMBIDEXTROUS

I have learned the secret of living in every situation, whether it is with a full stomach or empty, with plenty or little. For I can do everything through Christ, who gives me strength.

PHILIPPIANS 4:12-13

What do Roberto Alomar, Mickey Mantle, Pete Rose, and Eddie Murray all have in common? If you're a fan of Major League Baseball, you may know that each was a talented switch-hitter, able to slug a baseball either right-handed or left-handed, depending on which would prove most advantageous against a particular pitcher. While many switch-hitters have to train themselves to use their nondominant hand, some have an inborn talent for it. These players are, of course, ambidextrous.

In his book *A Grace Revealed*, Jerry Sittser mentions a desert father by the name of Abba Theodore, who used the word *ambidextrous* to apply to believers who had learned to take both prosperity and adversity in stride. Given the choice, I'm pretty sure I would always choose prosperity over hardship. As Sittser puts it, prosperity "makes God seem good, the world seem right, and faith seem natural, as natural as writing with the dominant hand. Obviously," he says, "adversity does the opposite, making life hard for us. Temptation overruns us, doubt plagues us, routine bores us."[1]

Even if we could chart a course toward perpetual prosperity, it is doubtful such a course would produce the peace we long for. Why? Because prosperity has its pitfalls. It can make us fat and dull, turning us into people of mediocre faith.

To the early Christians, Abba Theodore offered this wise counsel: "We shall then be ambidextrous, when neither abundance nor want affects us, and when the former does not entice us to the luxury of a dangerous carelessness, while the latter does not draw us to despair, and complaining; but when, giving thanks to God in either case alike, we gain one and the same advantage out of good and bad fortune."[2]

In the end, becoming spiritually ambidextrous is primarily an exercise in trust. We trust not in our circumstances but in the goodness of a God who loves us even more than we love ourselves.

Father, I am not yet at a point in my life when I can take both prosperity and adversity in stride. Help me learn not to seek one or the other but to seek your Kingdom and your glory, come what may.

FUTURE-THINK

Sell your possessions and give to those in need. This will store up treasure for you in heaven! And the purses of heaven never get old or develop holes. Your treasure will be safe; no thief can steal it and no moth can destroy it.

LUKE 12:33

The next time you meet with an investment counselor, don't be surprised if you are handed a photo of how you will look twenty or thirty years hence. In the category of "What will they think of next?" Hal Ersner-Hershfield and a team of researchers at Northwestern University conducted a study to see whether people would save more money if they could imagine how they would look in the future. They hypothesized that most of us don't save enough for retirement because we don't empathize strongly enough with our future selves. We know we are going to get old, but we can't seem to make an emotional connection with our future selves.

To remedy that, they utilized off-the-shelf software aimed at video game developers and employed an age-progression algorithm to alter photos of people participating in the study. The result? According to the study, participants who came face-to-face with their future selves were willing to set aside more than twice as much money for retirement as those who only saw their current selves.[3]

Of course, Jesus was no stranger to the idea of investing in the future. At one point he even offered his listeners a fail-safe investment plan—one that is neither vulnerable to scamming nor subject to market turmoil. According to him, when we share our resources with the needy, we will have treasure in heaven—riches that can never be stolen or destroyed. Faith, not the latest software, is what will help us envision our future lives. As you ask God for greater faith, act on the faith you do have by giving generously to the poor.

Father, help me to live with an open hand rather than a closed heart. When it comes to the way you want to use me now, help me to be an optimist, not a pessimist. Let me entrust my future to you.

REDEFINING YOUR EXPERIENCE

Moses protested to God, "Who am I to appear before Pharaoh? Who am I to lead the people of Israel out of Egypt?" God answered, "I will be with you."

EXODUS 3:11-12

A friend of mine is a physical therapist. With her no-nonsense personality, she never hesitates to challenge her patients to go beyond what they think they can do in order to achieve greater strength and healing. Whenever her clients object to a particular exercise, she encourages them by saying, "That's not pain, it's stretch!" This simple phrase enables her patients to reframe their experience, helping them realize that what they thought would hurt them will instead benefit them.

It's the same in our relationship with the Lord. Sometimes he allows us to experience difficult circumstances because he knows it's the only way for us to achieve the purpose for which he made us. But often our first instinct is to protect ourselves. If we can begin to realize that many of our challenges will stretch us but not harm us, we will be able to face them with greater trust and confidence.

Let me offer an example from the life of an Old Testament hero. Moses has just spotted a bush engulfed in flames. Then he hears a voice calling, "Moses! Moses!"

God's voice speaks to him out of the bush, telling him he has been chosen to lead his people out of slavery in Egypt.

Shaking with fear, Moses wails, "Who am I, that I should go to Pharaoh and bring the Israelites out of Egypt? And why should the elders listen to me? Besides, I have never been good at speaking. O LORD, please send someone else to do it."

But God doesn't allow Moses' fear to disrupt his plan. And in the end Moses allows himself to be stretched, doing exactly what God asks. Because of that, he is able to stand at the edge of the Red Sea after watching the waves crash over his enemies and raise this victory shout: "The LORD is my strength and my song; he has given me victory. This is my God, and I will praise him—my father's God, and I will exalt him!" (Exodus 15:2).

Lord, I don't want to shrink back from the challenges you place in my path. Give me the courage to move forward, experiencing peace as I trust you to use every difficulty to achieve your purpose for my life.

December 9

PLUNGING INTO THE DARKNESS

Both day and night belong to you.

PSALM 74:16

Jerry Sittser tells of an experience shortly after he lost his wife, his mother, and his four-year-old daughter in a tragic accident. As he stood in the funeral home looking at three open coffins, he felt himself slipping into dread and oblivion even as people tried to comfort him.

Days later, he says, "I dreamed of a setting sun. I was frantically running west, trying desperately to catch it and remain in its fiery warmth and light. But I was losing the race. The sun was beating me to the horizon and was soon gone. I suddenly found myself in the twilight. Exhausted, I stopped running and glanced with foreboding over my shoulder to the east. I saw a vast darkness closing in on me. I was terrified by that darkness. I wanted to keep running after the sun."

Though Jerry found the dream unsettling, his sister later pointed out that "the quickest way for anyone to reach the sun and the light of day is not to run west, chasing after the setting sun, but to head east, plunging into the darkness until one comes to the sunrise."[4]

That was a turning point—the moment Jerry realized he could not run from his sorrow; he had to face the darkness of his grief. Three years later he wrote a book that has become a classic on the topic: *A Grace Disguised: How the Soul Grows through Loss.*

As I write this, it is early December. The days grow shorter. The light wanes. Try as I might, I cannot run back to summer, reliving its warmth. The only way forward is to head into deepest winter. In a few days' time, those of us in the Northern Hemisphere will reach the winter solstice, the point in the year with the least amount of daylight. Each day after that will bring more light until we are once again basking, enjoying the brightness.

As in Jerry's dream, as with the rhythm of the year, sometimes the only way into the light we long for is straight through the darkness. We go there, not alone, but in the keeping of the God the psalmist acclaims: "To you the night shines as bright as day. Darkness and light are the same to you" (Psalm 139:12).

Faithful God, lead me where you choose, and make me who you want me to be, even if it means I need to go through times of darkness to get there.

*The people who sat in darkness have seen a great light. And for those who
lived in the land where death casts its shadow, a light has shined.*

MATTHEW 4:16

The tears were welling in my eyes, my heart a mixture of wonder and sadness. Wonder that so many had gathered to pay tribute to my neighbor Dale, a man whose life had touched many. Sadness that he was gone, taken down by cancer. When my daughter asked about my tears, I had to explain that they weren't coming from a heart completely filled with sorrow. The tears were also expressing a deep joy that came from watching people love each other and remind each other of the truth.

The funny thing about our hearts is that they are capable of holding more than one emotion at a time, even when those emotions are polar opposites. The darkness is like that, too, often yielding treasures that will produce more light. As Jerry Sittser observed when he faced the terrible grief of losing three of the people he loved most, darkness invaded his soul. "But then again, so did light," he says. Both contributed to his transformation.

He goes on: "In other words, though I experienced death, I also experienced life in ways that I never thought possible before—not after the darkness, as we might suppose, but *in* the darkness. I did not go through pain and come out the other side; instead, I lived in it and found within that pain the grace to survive and eventually grow. I did not get over the loss of my loved ones; rather, I absorbed the loss into my life, like soil receives decaying matter, until it became a part of who I am. Sorrow took up permanent residence in my soul and enlarged it."

The key for Jerry—and for all of us—is not whether there will be times of darkness but how we will respond to the darkness when it comes. As he says, "We do not always have the freedom to choose the roles we must play in life, but we can choose how we are going to play the roles we have been given."[5]

*Lord Jesus, you are the Light of the World. And yet you faced into the darkness
of death and crucifixion, trusting the Father to deliver you. Shine your
light into my darkness, and help me to find peace in the midst of it.*

December 11

GO, GRANDPA!

He will shelter you with his wings. His faithful promises are your armor and protection.
PSALM 91:4

Peter Secchia is a successful businessman and former U.S. ambassador to Italy. A few years ago, when he was sixty-seven, he and his three-year-old granddaughter, Thea, were walking down a Seattle street. As they headed toward a shop selling cinnamon buns, Thea was startled when a thirty-eight-year-old man tried to grab hold of her hand, identifying himself as a policeman and saying she had to come with him.

Secchia, a former Marine, wasted no time. He punched the man as hard as he could. Then he held him down between two parked cars until police arrived. Afterward a detective from the Seattle police force remarked, "Anybody who's read the [police] report is going, 'Yeah! Go, grandpa!' That's the kind of grandpa I want my granddaughter to have."[6]

Jim Cymbala tells a similar, though less dramatic, story. "Some years ago," he says, "I was taking my granddaughter Susie on a walk when a couple of homeless men came walking toward us. Their scruffy appearance made her afraid. In her little mind, she thought she was about to be harmed. She was already holding my hand, but instantly I felt her push her body into mine as she grabbed onto my pant leg. 'Papa!' she whispered. Of course, I put my arm around her and said that everything was going to be all right. The men passed us on the sidewalk without incident.

"Inside, my heart was brimming. That instantaneous reflex of reaching out for my aid meant that she thought I could handle anything and everything. . . . She showed that she had a deep faith in me. I would come to her rescue. I would meet her urgent need. I would take care of her."[7]

Jim Cymbala and Peter Secchia—two grandfathers whose love provides a glimpse of the Father's love for us. Let's make God glad by pressing into him whenever we feel anxious or afraid, trusting he will meet our urgent need.

Father Almighty, I trust you to care for me. Help me to be
quick to turn to you whenever I am afraid.

BRAIN TILT

Always judge people fairly.
LEVITICUS 19:15

Anyone who has ever been misjudged—and who hasn't?—will appreciate this instruction from the book of Leviticus about the importance of judging fairly. Jewish tradition takes this ideal a step further by speaking of the obligation to "judge others favorably." Perhaps it is no surprise that Jewish rabbis developed this teaching, given the long history of persecution and discrimination their people have suffered.

Most of the judgments we make against others happen in fairly mundane circumstances. Imagine, for instance, that you're at a middle-school event and your son is talking to a friend. You've noticed that the friend's shoelaces are untied, so you mention it, expecting the boy to bend down and tie them. But he just smiles and keeps on talking. Even though his mother is standing nearby, she says nothing. *What's wrong with her?* you wonder. *Doesn't she care if he trips and falls?*

If you had been a Jewish woman, steeped in that ethical tradition, you might have stopped yourself from making the negative judgment. Instead, you would have reminded yourself that this boy is a good kid from a good home. Though you can't fathom why his mother doesn't act as you would expect her to, you acknowledge that she may have a good reason for her silence.

Now consider the mother of the boy who won't tie his shoes. Having heard the woman's suggestion, she senses her son's embarrassment. She knows he won't bend down to tie his shoes because he can't. Her son suffers from cerebral palsy, which makes tying his own shoes a challenging task to master. But his condition is so mild that most people don't even realize he has a problem. Of course his mother cares whether he trips over his shoelaces, but she keeps quiet so as not to embarrass her son further.

Sound far-fetched? This is what happened to a friend of mine. How much more peaceful would our lives become if we could make a habit of tilting our brains in a positive direction, judging others favorably until there is definite evidence that we should not?

Father, you are the only one who knows everything about the people who populate my world. Keep me from judging them unfavorably. Help me instead to be generous in my judgments, willing to extend the benefit of the doubt whenever possible.

December 13

CELEBRATE YOUR FREEDOM!

You have six days each week for your ordinary work, but the seventh day is a
Sabbath day of rest dedicated to the LORD your God. On that day no one in your
household may do any work. This includes you, your sons and daughters, your male
and female servants, your livestock, and any foreigners living among you.

EXODUS 20:9-10

I magine that you live in a country without any kind of labor laws. You and
your family are dirt poor, forced to work for someone who doesn't know
the meaning of a day off. Day after weary day you perform heavy labor for
long hours and little pay, with no hope of a better future. Then something
extraordinary happens. A rich man comes along and takes pity on you. He
tells you he has an incredibly fertile piece of property that he intends to give
you, lifting you out of your poverty. As a landowner, you will be able, for the
first time in your life, to hold your head high. You will be able to support
yourself.

But then the man makes a curious request—a demand, really. He
tells you that he doesn't want you, your spouse, your children, your future
employees, or even your animals to do a lick of work one day a week. What
do you do? Having been treated as a slave for most of your life, do you still
retain the mentality of a slave, convinced that if you take a day off you will
not be able to pay the bills?

This, of course, was the challenge facing the Israelites when God led
them out of Egypt and promised them a land of milk and honey. Would they
emulate their Egyptian oppressors by making work their first priority, or
would they trust the God who freed them to provide for their needs as they
observed the Sabbath rest?

Even though we are no longer bound to keep the strict Sabbath rules
outlined in the Hebrew Scriptures, we can benefit from observing a Sabbath
rest, putting God first and trusting him to provide what we need. Why not
celebrate your freedom and your dignity as a daughter of God by giving yourself a day of rest this week?

Father, I'm not used to thinking of "sacred days." Help me to taste the goodness
of a day spent resting in your presence and celebrating your generosity.

THE PEACE OF FORGIVENESS

Peter came to him and asked, "Lord, how often should I forgive someone who sins against me? Seven times?" "No, not seven times," Jesus replied, "but seventy times seven!"

MATTHEW 18:21-22

I t's an early morning in October, and a mother is busy preparing for the day ahead—making breakfast and getting her children ready for school. As she kisses each child good-bye, she has no idea of the tragedy that looms. Later that day a man will break into her daughter's school just after morning recess. This man will leave behind a suicide note explaining his anger at God at the death of his infant daughter, perhaps as a twisted explanation for the crimes he is about to commit.

Dismissing the boys, along with some others who are visiting the school, he orders the remaining children—ten girls between the ages of six and thirteen—to lie facedown on the floor of the schoolroom. Then he binds their ankles with wire and plastic ties. According to a surviving younger sister, the oldest girl asks the gunman to shoot her first, hoping he will spare the others. At 11:07 a.m. he begins shooting. When it is all over, Charles Carl Roberts IV has killed himself and five young girls.

Here's how the deputy coroner of Lancaster County, Pennsylvania, described the mayhem inside that school: "There was not one desk, not one chair, in the whole schoolroom that was not splattered with either blood or glass. There were bullet holes everywhere, everywhere."

What would you or I do if we had been the mother of a child who had been murdered at the Old Order Amish West Nickel Mines School? I might have responded with bitterness or a desire for vengeance. But one mother shocked the world by joining others in her community in forgiving the murderer and extending grace to his family. To make it real, she attended his funeral and sent meals and flowers to his widow.

Where does a mother get the grace and courage to do something like that? At the foot of the cross of the extraordinary man who said, "Father, forgive them, for they don't know what they are doing" (Luke 23:34).

Father, please give me grace to forgive even as I have been forgiven. As I do, grant me your peace.

December 15

DOMINOS

[Jesus] called his twelve disciples together and began sending them out two by two.

MARK 6:7

Stack a bunch of dominos close together and then flick the first in line, and the entire line will quickly collapse. That's the image behind a political idea called the domino theory. Popularized in the latter half of the twentieth century, the theory is based on the idea that if one nation were to fall under the spell of Communism, surrounding nations were likely to topple and become Communist as well.

Though the theory has its critics, there is no doubt the principle can be applied to other areas of life. Richard Stearns, president of World Vision, invokes this idea in a positive way when he says, "I believe that this is how God works in history. Two thousand years ago, Jesus Christ set up just 12 dominos, mentored them, and led them in his way. He empowered them with the Holy Spirit and then sent them off to go and do likewise. Two thousand years later there are more than two billion followers of Christ in the world. That's a lot of dominos!

"As Christians, we are all dominos in the chain reaction set off by Jesus. The amazing thing about dominos falling is that the chain reaction always starts small—with just one seemingly insignificant domino."[8]

You and I have spent nearly a year together reading about, praying about, and seeking to follow God as he leads us toward greater peace. As in all good things that come from God's hand, the peace he gives is meant not to be hoarded but to be shared. Today let's thank him for ways that he has worked in our lives and ask him to make us that first domino, willing and able to spread his peace to others. What will that mean? It might involve giving a gift to an organization like World Vision or praying for someone in turmoil or starting a ministry or loving your family in practical ways. It could mean a thousand different things, depending on how the God of peace is leading you. Ask him and you will find out.

Father, thank you for the peace you have given me. I praise you for reordering my heart and sharing your peace. Now use me, Lord—one small domino to spread your peace to others.

December 16

IS GOSSIP GOOD FOR YOU?

*Does anyone want to live a life that is long and prosperous? Then keep
your tongue from speaking evil and your lips from telling lies! Turn away
from evil and do good. Search for peace, and work to maintain it.*

PSALM 34:12-14

"If you can't say something good about someone, sit right here by me," Alice
Roosevelt Longworth used to quip.[9] And plenty of people did.

Recently the media headlined a study indicating that gossip might actually be good for you. But a closer look at the data reveals that only so-called positive gossip or chitchat is good for you, as in when you say something nice about someone else. Those who were critical of others experienced a 16 percent drop in positive emotions and a whopping 34 percent increase in negative emotions. So what's the "good for you" part of gossip? In the short term it may result in a certain amount of social bonding. You're part of an in-group that knows something others don't. But this effect produces a rather shallow set of social connections. Additional studies indicate that most people dislike and distrust gossips and wouldn't want to be considered one.[10]

So if gossip is bad for you and if no one wants to be called a gossip, why do so many of us keep flapping our tongues? Joseph Telushkin points out that gossip is primarily a game of social status. Ask yourself, he says, if you've ever heard people whispering the intimate details of their cleaning lady's life.[11] Most of us haven't. We gossip, he says, not about our social inferiors but about those of similar or higher social status in an attempt to elevate our own status. Gossip can be a way of being "in the know" or of delighting in the fact that other people have problems too.

When you look at it like this, gossip is a game for the weak, not the strong. It's the underdog trying to get the upper hand by passing on some juicy tidbit. The next time you're tempted to watch a celebrity gossip show on TV or engage in gossip with friends, remind yourself that negative speech hurts at least three people: the person who spreads it, the person who listens to it, and the person who is the brunt of it.

*Father, I confess that I like to be "in the know." Help me to redirect my curiosity
to matters I need to know about rather than ones I want to know about.*

SPIRITUAL FORMATION

*I will give you a new heart, and I will put a new spirit in you. I will take out
your stony, stubborn heart and give you a tender, responsive heart.*

EZEKIEL 36:26

In his wonderful book *Renovation of the Heart*, Dallas Willard points out
that spiritual formation happens to everyone, whether or not they know
it. Even atheists undergo a process of formation whereby their spirits are
formed in a particular direction, making them who they are. He also points
out two important truths: first, that all of us are more ruined than we think,
and second, that all of us have more potential for goodness and glory than
we think.

"Sin," he explains, "does not make [the soul] worthless, but only lost.
And in its lostness it is still capable of great strength, dignity, and heartbreaking beauty and goodness—enough so to hide from the unenlightened,
or those who do not wish to understand, the horror it has become and is
becoming."[12]

The trajectory of ruin is this: "In the ruined soul, the mind becomes a
fearful wilderness and a wild intermixture of thought and feeling, manifested
in willful stupidities, blatant inconsistencies, and confusions, often to the
point of obsession, madness, or possession."[13]

But the trajectory of redemption is transformation into Christ's image.
This way leads, as Willard points out, to "a fuller and ever fuller restoration
of radical goodness to the soul. It accesses incredible, supernatural strength
for life."[14] The well-ordered soul, he says, is capable of responding to life in
ways that are right and good. No more lashing out in anger, no more saying
one thing and doing another because everything within us will be wholly
directed toward God. This describes the soul that is filled with *shalom*.

Is such a life possible? Yes, if we can learn to prefer God's will to ours—
not just sometimes, but always. As God's Spirit fills and guides us, each day
will take us closer to this goal, healing the divide inside so we can become the
women God created us to be.

*Father, I want to be like your Son in every way. I pray you will so fill me with your
Spirit that I will be able to lay down my life and take on yours. Make me, Lord, a woman
with a well-ordered soul, able to respond in ways that are always good and right.*

RUN YOUR OWN RACE

I have fought the good fight, I have finished the race, and I have remained faithful.
2 TIMOTHY 4:7

I've been using the treadmill a lot lately—usually walking at a brisk pace but occasionally breaking into a full-scale run. This morning I managed to run for four minutes! I know that sounds pathetic, but as someone who hates to perspire, even a few minutes full speed ahead is an accomplishment.

Now consider three world-class female runners. Lolo Jones holds two World Indoor titles in the one-hundred-meter hurdles. Paula Radcliffe set the world record in the London Marathon in 2003. Gladys Burrill is the oldest woman ever to complete a marathon. She was ninety-two at the time.

Three women—each unique and each famous for her achievements. Now imagine what would happen if the three were to compete with each other. Lolo Jones wouldn't come close to Paula Radcliffe's record-setting performance in the marathon, and Paula would be left in the dust as she ran behind Lolo in the one-hundred-meter hurdles. Each woman has to run the race for which she is suited and trained.

I emphasize the obvious because many times we make the mistake of trying to run someone else's race—comparing our lives to others' and feeling as though we come up short. Perhaps we have children who struggle with special needs and we compare ourselves to a woman who has well-behaved, perfectly successful children. Why can't our children be as happy or thriving as hers? Or we know someone who is constantly offered leadership positions at church or at work, and we wonder why we are not.

But God is calling us to run our own race. He knows the gifts he has given us, the circumstances we live in, the personalities we have, the unique opportunities and challenges we face. We are the only ones who can run the race he has set before us.

I like what Gladys Burrill said when asked for her advice: "Just get out there and walk or run. I like walking because you can stop and smell the roses," she said, "but it's a rarity that I stop."[15] With an attitude like that, it's no wonder they call her the "Gladyator."

Lord, help me to focus on the race you've set before me. Give me the peace that comes from not comparing myself to others and from being faithful to the tasks you've given me.

December 19

FACES

*[Moses] would give the people whatever instructions the LORD had given him,
and the people of Israel would see the radiant glow of his face. So he would
put the veil over his face until he returned to speak with the LORD.*

EXODUS 34:34-35

O scar Wilde once said that by the time people are forty, they have the face they deserve.[16] I suspect he meant that a lifetime of choices will shape our souls in a particular direction, which will be tellingly reflected in our faces.

Perhaps you've heard of a nineteenth-century Christian by the name of George Müller. A remarkable man who cared for more than 10,000 orphans and established 117 schools, educating more than 120,000 children, Müller apparently did his job so well that some people faulted him for educating the poor beyond their station in life. With that kind of heart for the underprivileged, it's no wonder someone once remarked that Müller "had the twenty-third psalm written in his face."[17]

But as a youth, Müller made choices that were shaping him not toward grace but toward ruin. While his mother lay dying, fourteen-year-old Müller was roving around half-drunk with friends. A liar and a thief, he was imprisoned for stealing when he was only sixteen. But as a college student, he gave his life to Christ as the result of being influenced by Christian friends.

Though Müller published the answers to his many prayers for God's provision, thereby influencing people to give, he never directly asked anyone for money to support his orphanage. The donations came pouring in unsolicited, often just in the nick of time. On one occasion, when there was no food, Müller gathered the children around the table to say grace. As they finished praying, a baker knocked on the door with more than enough bread to feed everyone.

Müller's primary purpose in establishing an orphanage was to encourage Christians to believe that God could supply their needs. He wanted to make a public display of God's faithfulness by showing how the Lord would provide for the children in his care.

Today let us thank God for revealing his faithfulness through the life of this good man. And let us ask God to shape our souls into the likeness of his Son so we can reflect his peace to others as well.

*Father, give me the grace to desire one thing—to do your will. In the process,
let me reflect the face of Christ to others so they may know you.*

I CAN'T DO THIS!

I can do everything through Christ, who gives me strength.
PHILIPPIANS 4:13

Author and pastor John Van Sloten remembers his response to the news that his infant son Edward had Down syndrome. Driving home from the hospital after visiting his wife, he could no longer keep it together. "I couldn't stop crying. . . . When I got home I ran down the hallway, fell face-first onto my bed, and screamed out to God, 'I can't do this . . . there is no way in the world I can handle this. . . . I cannot do it!'

"'You're right. You can't, John,' was the response. 'But I can.'"[18]

It wasn't until three months later, during a weeklong trip to Rochester, New York, that Van Sloten began listening to what God was trying to tell him. During that trip he had three surprise encounters with young men diagnosed with Down syndrome, each of whom seemed to be a living contradiction of the fears he had for his young son.

"The night after arriving home," he says, "I sat down to journal about my amazing Rochester adventure. Then it hit me. That night, three months ago, while I was lying in bed running all those awful scenarios of how terrible being Edward's dad was going to be, God already had the events I'd just experienced in mind. God knew. Right down to the last detail, each of my anxious imaginary scenes was recast, retold, and redeemed."[19]

Not long afterward Van Sloten felt the call of God on his life and began the transition from land developer to church pastor. Years later he reflected on how God had transformed his worst day into his best. "Many times over the course of my life," he says, "I've experienced this retrospective recalibration of painful events. Time would bring a perspective that sometimes brought about a dramatic redemption of the situation. I wonder if, in the end, we will all experience one big retrospective moment before the very face of God."

What is it you are having a hard time accepting right now? Ask God to help you listen to what he is saying. Trust him to "recalibrate" even your worst day—to recast, retell, and redeem it in a way that brings him glory.

Father, you know where I struggle most. Help me to listen for your voice, to trust you, and to rest in the peace you give.

MEMORY LOSS

I recall all you have done, O LORD; I remember your wonderful deeds of long ago. They are constantly in my thoughts. I cannot stop thinking about your mighty works.

PSALM 77:11-12

Memory loss is something many people fear, not just because it's inconvenient to forget everything but because forgetfulness can be a sign of encroaching decrepitude. Increasing forgetfulness can signal that a mind once agile and quick is now on the decline, encased in a body that has also seen better days. Anyone who has dipped a toe into old age, or knows someone who has, realizes that whoever invented the phrase "the golden years" deserves the Pulitzer Prize for fiction. There's nothing golden about the loss of so many of our basic faculties.

Scripture repeatedly speaks of the importance of remembering, no matter how young or old you are. Remember, God says, that I rescued you from Egypt. Remember that I led you through the desert. Remember to follow my commandments. Remember to be kind to strangers because you were once strangers. Remember my promises. I will always remember you. With God and in God and through God we remember the love story of salvation—a story that is both ours and his to commemorate and to live.

Mark Buchanan points out that faith without memory will quickly morph into something less than faith. "Our faith," he says, "is rooted in memory, so much so that one of the key works of the Holy Spirit is the ministry of reminding (see John 14:26). The day we forget the works of God, from ages past until this very morning, is the day our faith starts to deform into something else—mythology, ideology, superstition, dogmatism, agnosticism, fanaticism. Remembering well is essential to an authentic, living faith."[20]

Today let us ask the Spirit to stir up the memory of all God has done for us from ages past until this very morning. And let us enjoy the peace that comes from knowing that God still remembers us.

Father, never let me forget what you have done for me. Help me begin each day by thanking you for at least one great thing you have done.

You must love the LORD your God with all your heart, all your soul, and all your mind.

MATTHEW 22:37

Children are good at exploring. But sometimes their curiosity leads to painful lessons. Take the toddler who sticks out his tongue to "taste" a frozen lamp post. Ouch! It's not fun to peel your tongue away from a subzero piece of steel.

Spiritual writers sometimes use the word *attachment* to describe what happens when we become so stuck to things or to people that these connections separate us from God. Because we've given our hearts to them, we are not free to give our hearts to God.

Chuck De Groat points out that *attachment* describes "a heart 'nailed' to something or someone, bound to it, enslaved to it."[21] I think that's a pretty good picture of what can happen when we commit our affections to things that lead us away from Christ. It could be anything—pleasures, relationships, expectations, beautiful objects, money, success, food. We humans are good at stuffing ourselves to the brim with all kinds of substitutes. The trouble is, they never satisfy our longings.

The bad thing about getting stuck to anything except God is that we lose our freedom. If you feel dissatisfied, ask yourself whether you might be attached to something—or someone—that is interfering with your relationship with God. If the answer is yes, turn to God, asking him to free you. It may be that some difficulty or challenge will form the environment for God to free you. Whatever the circumstances, be willing to do what it takes to regain your freedom in Christ.

> *Lord, I know you are not willing to share my heart with anything or anyone else. Show me if I have any unhealthy attachments, and help me to get free from these so I can be fully attached to you.*

THE PLACE OF DESIRE

Blessed are the pure in heart, for they will see God.
MATTHEW 5:8, NIV

Mother Teresa and Janis Joplin: two women whose names rarely end up in the same sentence. In fact, the two might seem a universe apart. But author Ronald Rolheiser manages to pull them together, observing that the lives of both were powered by great energy directed toward great desire. Mother Teresa's all-consuming desire was to love God by serving the poor. It was a singular, passionate longing that shaped the course of her life.

Janis Joplin was a woman whose passionate desires also shaped the course of her life. But as Rolheiser points out, "Joplin could not will the one thing. She willed many things. Her great energy went out in all directions and eventually created an excess and a tiredness that led to an early death. But those activities—a total giving over to creativity, performance, drugs, booze, sex, coupled with the neglect of normal rest—were her spirituality. . . . In her case, as is tragically often the case in gifted artists, the end result, at least in this life, was not a healthy integration but a dissipation. She, at a point, simply lost the things that normally glue a human person together and broke apart under too much pressure."[22]

In truth, most of us fall somewhere between Mother Teresa and Janis Joplin. Though we hope we are closer to the former, we sometimes act in ways that betray our divided hearts, causing further disintegration in our personalities and in our relationship with God and others.

The more we are transformed by the Holy Spirit, the more our many desires will be reordered into the one great desire to know God, loving him as we are loved. As Søren Kierkegaard has famously said, "Purity of heart is to will one thing." And as Jesus has said, "Blessed are the pure in heart, for they will see God" (Matthew 5:8, NIV).

Lord, this peace you promise is the peace that comes from ordering all my desires into one great desire so my energy will be spent on loving you—body, mind, and spirit. Do this in me, I pray.

December 24

CHRISTMAS EVE PRAISE

Look! The virgin will conceive a child! She will give birth to a son, and they will call him Immanuel, which means "God is with us."

MATTHEW 1:23

What hymn has been performed by more than three hundred artists, including Enya, Boys II Men, Linda Ronstadt, Elvis Presley, Bing Crosby, Mariah Carey, Mahalia Jackson, and Mannheim Steamroller? I'll give you a hint: the Bing Crosby single sold more than ten million copies. Another clue—the music was composed and sung on Christmas Eve nearly two centuries ago in a small town in Austria. And another—the lyrics were written by a priest who was the illegitimate son of a poor woman and a mercenary who had deserted both the army and his family. And one more—the melody was written by an obscure composer who studied music secretly because of his father's opposition. If you guessed the hymn "Silent Night," you're right.

The lyrics were penned by Joseph Mohr in 1816. Two years later, on Christmas Eve, he asked his friend, a teacher and church organist by the name of Franz Xaver Gruber, to set his poem to music. Gruber produced a melody and a guitar arrangement for the song, which the two men sang on that night in 1818, backed by a choir in front of the main altar at St. Nicholas Church in Oberndorf. By the time the hymn became famous, the melody was variously attributed to Mozart, Haydn, or Beethoven. It wasn't until 1994 that Gruber was authenticated as the composer.

Why not spend this Christmas Eve meditating on the lyrics of the most popular Christmas carol ever written?

Silent night, holy night,
All is calm, all is bright.
Round yon virgin mother and Child.
Holy Infant so tender and mild,
Sleep in heavenly peace,
Sleep in heavenly peace.

Silent night, holy night,
Son of God, love's pure light.
Radiant beams from Thy holy face,
With the dawn of redeeming grace,
Jesus, Lord, at Thy birth,
Jesus, Lord, at Thy birth.

Lord, quiet my heart this night, that I might ponder the mystery of your coming—to a poor couple in Bethlehem, to shepherds in a field, and to me, here in this place.

December 25
THE GREATEST SURPRISE

Suddenly, an angel of the Lord appeared among them, and the radiance of the Lord's glory surrounded them. They were terrified, but the angel reassured them. "Don't be afraid!" he said. "I bring you good news that will bring great joy to all people."

LUKE 2:9-10

If someone were to ask me what the greatest surprise of my lifetime has thus far been, I would have to say that it was the shock (and that is not too strong a word) I felt when I encountered God's love for the first time. I was in my twenties, recently graduated from college and struggling with any number of confusions. Into this mess, God made himself known in a way beyond my imagining or hope. Before that, I had thought of God—if I thought of him at all—as a distant figure. I wasn't too sure he existed. If he did, I was pretty certain he would not want anything to do with me. That the opposite was true took me off balance and disarmed me. That he would reveal a deep tenderness toward me was even more shocking.

It is now Christmas Day, many years after that initial discovery.

We are familiar with the glitter of the season, but we often miss its glory. That God would decide on a solution to the sin problem that involved becoming one of us should continue to surprise and shock us. It should challenge the things we think we know about God, especially any designation of God as unloving, distant, or uncaring. And it should rattle our assumptions that we or anyone else is unlovable or beyond his help. To harbor such thoughts is to disregard the evidence. It is to be disloyal to the one who made us and disloyal to ourselves as women who are loved and cherished by the most important person in the universe.

This year, as you ponder the meaning of Christmas, ask God to help you penetrate the mystery of the Incarnation more deeply. Tell him you want to celebrate all he has done. Then ask him for the grace to be ready—for he is coming again!

Lord, your ways are far beyond anything I can imagine. Just as the heavens are higher than the earth, so your ways are higher than my ways and your thoughts higher than my thoughts. No wonder I am always surprised by you.

A child is born to us, a son is given to us. The government will rest on his shoulders. And he will be called: Wonderful Counselor, Mighty God, Everlasting Father, Prince of Peace.

ISAIAH 9:6

One of my favorite Christmas songs is one I hadn't even heard of until a few years ago when I listened to James Taylor singing it on his Christmas album. About this time of year, I find myself humming it wherever I go, perhaps because it's such a perfect fit for our Michigan winters with their landscape of hard, white earth set beneath a lid of thick, gray skies. And yet so much wonder and worship attend the song that it cheers my spirits. The song is called "In the Bleak Midwinter," and its lyrics were written by Christina Rossetti, a famous English poet. The poem wasn't set to music until twelve years after she died.

With or without music, it makes a beautiful prayer:

In the bleak midwinter, frosty wind made moan,
Earth stood hard as iron, water like a stone;
Snow had fallen, snow on snow, snow on snow,
In the bleak midwinter, long ago.

What can I give Him, poor as I am?
If I were a shepherd, I would bring a lamb;
If I were a Wise Man, I would do my part;
Yet what I can I give Him: give my heart.

Yes, Lord, I give you my heart.

December 27

FUTURE PEACE

I heard a loud shout from the throne, saying, "Look, God's home is now among his people! He will live with them, and they will be his people. God himself will be with them. He will wipe every tear from their eyes, and there will be no more death or sorrow or crying or pain."

REVELATION 21:3-4

No matter how much peace you and I taste in this world, it will not be enough, not nearly enough. The shortfall comes from the fact that we are still living in a broken, disordered world—a place in which children are trafficked for sex and where greed causes financial meltdowns and where politicians grub for power and where we are not all we should be. For perfect peace, we need a reckoning—a true and perfect judgment that will only come, Scripture says, when Christ returns.

The final judgment is that moment when God will say, "Enough!" Enough chances, enough choices, enough time to turn and do the right thing. What have we done? How have we lived? His judgment will be both a seal and a sentence—a period at the end of our story and a verdict on how well we have lived it.

The last judgment is not something Christians should anticipate with terror. Instead, we should welcome it. As N. T. Wright observes, "In a world of systematic injustice, bullying, violence, arrogance, and oppression, the thought that there might come a day when the wicked are firmly put in their place and the poor and weak are given their due is the best news there can be."[23]

But knowing our own sins and failings, how can we look forward to judgment? Wright points out that future judgment is "good news, first, because the one through whom God's justice will finally sweep the world is not a hard-hearted, arrogant, or vengeful tyrant but rather the Man of Sorrows, who was acquainted with grief; the Jesus who loved sinners and died for them; the Messiah who took the world's judgment upon himself on the cross."[24]

Meanwhile, as women who have tasted God's mercy, we are called to spread the Good News while there is time for people to respond. Then, when judgment comes, they will, instead, find mercy.

Lord, thank you for your promise to make the world a place in which justice will one day flourish. Give me wisdom and courage to do what is just so others can know your peace.

December 28

A FINANCIAL FAST

Honor the LORD with your wealth and with the best part of everything you produce.
Then he will fill your barns with grain, and your vats will overflow with good wine.

PROVERBS 3:9-10

If I were to draw a pie chart labeled "My Worries" in order to track the source of my anxieties, 50 percent would probably be allotted to my children, 30 percent to family and friends, and 20 percent to financial worries. What about you? What would your chart look like?

Michelle Singletary is a columnist and the author of a book entitled *The Power to Prosper: 21 Days to Financial Freedom*.[25] Her answer to financial stress is to hit it head-on by undertaking a twenty-one-day financial fast. The basic idea, field-tested by members of her church, is to put yourself on a spending diet for three weeks, during which time you promise not to use any credit or debit cards; to buy only what you absolutely need (like food and medicine); to use only cash; to forgo looking at retail catalogs, visiting malls or stores, or shopping online; and to refrain from eating out. The idea is to evaluate where you are spending your money so you can use your resources in a way that glorifies God and brings greater freedom to your life.

The world promises that purchasing new things will make us happy or hoarding resources will make us feel secure. But God's Word is counter-cultural—it's only when we give what we have back to God that we can have true peace of mind.

If financial worries comprise 10 percent or more of your "worry pie chart," why not consider reading Michelle's book and starting the new year by undertaking a financial fast? Doing so will likely present its share of challenges, but it may be just what you and I need in order to experience more of God's peace in the future.

Lord, help me to become more intentional about my finances. I want to stop being anxious about money so I can become more generous and peaceful.

December 29

GENTLE AT ALL TIMES

The wisdom from above is first of all pure. It is also peace loving,
gentle at all times, and willing to yield to others.

JAMES 3:17

How many people can stand on a blue whale's tongue?" My daughter loves stumping people with bizarre questions about animal facts, and this is one of her favorites. You can't dodge the question by pointing out that no one can stand on the tongue of the largest animal in the world and live to tell the story. Unless you answer fifty, you will flunk her quiz.

But here's another question: who has a tongue that's even more powerful than that of a mega-ton whale? The answer, of course, is that we do. Good old *Homo sapiens*—the species with the most powerful tongue in the world. James observes with frustration, "People can tame all kinds of animals, birds, reptiles, and fish, but no one can tame the tongue. . . . Sometimes it praises our Lord and Father, and sometimes it curses those who have been made in the image of God. And so blessing and cursing come pouring out of the same mouth. Surely, my brothers and sisters, this is not right!" (James 3:7-10).

Yesterday I was reading a book about all kinds of high-minded ideals, like loving others even when they don't deserve it. The book made me feel good, as though I had become more virtuous simply by reading about virtue. But then a quarrel broke out in the kitchen. Irritated that my peaceful Sunday was being disrupted by two children who couldn't stop arguing, I yelled at them, telling them in no uncertain terms that I had had enough! As my words trailed off, it occurred to me that the virtuous feelings that had filled me just a few seconds earlier had been replaced by a whole lot of anger. My daughters weren't the only ones in the house guilty of breaking the peace.

Like James, I am frustrated, aware that I can praise God one minute and then speak harshly the next. But James also says that the wisdom of heaven is "peace loving" and "gentle at all times." Today I pray that God's wisdom will do in me what I cannot possibly do in myself—make me gentle at all times.

Father, I know gentleness is a strength, not a weakness. I pray that a
deeper wisdom will pervade my life and transform it, enabling me to
be peace loving and gentle, rather than harsh and impatient.

December 30
TWO OLD WOMEN
SITTING ON A BENCH

Even in old age they will still produce fruit; they will remain vital and green.

PSALM 92:14

My mother has lived to a ripe old age, but not, of course, without suffering her share of losses. One of these concerns her growing confusion and forgetfulness. But despite her decline, she has not lost her instinct to care about others.

Not long ago, one of the residents in her retirement community got lost, despite the fact that they live in a very small apartment complex with only two floors. Suffering from advanced dementia, this woman made her way to the office and announced that she had locked herself out of her apartment. Would someone let her back in? The woman behind the desk told her she had a key and would be happy to help. But no amount of persuasion would convince the elderly woman to step onto the elevator that would carry them both to her second-floor apartment. "No," she insisted, "my apartment is on the first floor. I've never lived on the second floor!"

After repeated attempts to convince her otherwise, the woman in the office finally gave up and called a family member to come and help. But the relative she called could not come for at least another hour. Noting the situation and her elderly friend's agitation, my mother assured the staff member that everything was going to be all right. Because she knew it was futile to try to convince her friend she had always lived on the second floor, she didn't even try. Instead she simply settled her arthritic back onto a bench outside the office, sitting beside her friend until help arrived.

I like that story because it says something important about the comfort we derive from each other. Often we don't want people to solve our problems as much as we want them to sit down beside us, comforting us with their presence. Two elderly women, both confused, sitting quietly on a bench together. That speaks to me of the gift we can be to each other, even in our weakest moments.

Father, help me to remain open to ways I can be a gift to others, even when I'm busy or burdened. Don't let me underestimate the comfort I can bring since your Spirit is alive within me.

December 31

UNDAUNTED

The LORD passed in front of Moses, calling out, "Yahweh! The LORD! The God of compassion and mercy! I am slow to anger and filled with unfailing love and faithfulness."

EXODUS 34:6

Three months after France and Great Britain declared war on Germany, on Christmas Day 1939, King George VI broadcast an address to the nation. By this time, Austria, Czechoslovakia, and Poland had already fallen to the overwhelming power of the Nazis.

Rallying people amid the gathering darkness, the king concluded his speech with these words:

A new year is at hand. We cannot tell what it will bring. If it brings peace, how thankful we shall all be. If it brings us continued struggle, we shall remain undaunted. In the meantime I feel that we may all find a message of encouragement in the lines which, in my closing words, I would like to say to you:

I said to the man who stood at the Gate of the Year: "Give me a light that I may tread safely into the unknown."
And he replied: "Go out into the darkness, and put your hand into the Hand of God. That shall be to you better than light, and safer than a known way."

Then the king said, "May the Almighty Hand guide and uphold us all." It would be another six years of war before peace was finally restored.

As George VI told his people, none of us know what the new year will bring. If it brings safety, healing, prosperity, wholeness, and joy, we will praise and thank the Lord. But if it brings continued struggles, we will remain undaunted, not because we are strong or have it in our own power to remain faithful, but because our God is strong and more than able to keep us in his peace.

Lord, help me to take hold of your hand today, staying close to you in the coming year. No matter what happens, may the peace you promise come to characterize my life in a way that will bring you glory. Amen.

Notes

JANUARY

1. Stephen R. Covey, *The 7 Habits of Highly Effective People* (New York: Free Press, 2004), 99.
2. Jim Cymbala, *Spirit Rising* (Grand Rapids, MI: Zondervan, 2012), 43.
3. Etty Hillesum, *The Letters and Diaries of Etty Hillesum, 1941-1943* (Grand Rapids, MI: Wm. B. Eerdmans, 2002), 535–36.
4. For a more complete discussion consult Lois Tverberg, *Listening to the Language of the Bible* (Holland, MI: En-Gedi Resource Center, 2006), 3–4.
5. I first encountered this insight in a reflection by Carol Knapp in *Daily Guideposts 2011* (New York: Guideposts, 2011), 14.
6. Carol Kuykendall in *Daily Guideposts 2011* (New York: Guideposts, 2011), 26.
7. Martin Luther King Jr., "Where Do We Go from Here" (address to the Southern Christian Leadership Conference, August 16, 1967).
8. The story is told in Fern Nichols, *Every Child Needs a Praying Mom* (Grand Rapids, MI: Zondervan, 2003), 21–24.
9. The story is told in Charles Stanley, *Finding Peace: God's Promise of a Life Free from Regret, Anxiety, and Fear* (Nashville: Thomas Nelson, 2003), 72–73.
10. Jim Cymbala, *Fresh Faith* (Grand Rapids, MI: Zondervan, 1999), 93.
11. "Largest Game of Chinese Whispers," *Guinness World Records* (blog), July 14, 2008, accessed February 7, 2011, http://community.guinnessworldrecords.com/_Largest-game -of-Chinese-whispers/BLOG/493418/7691.html.

FEBRUARY

1. Rick Warren, *The Purpose Driven Life* (Grand Rapids, MI: Zondervan, 2002), 201–2.
2. Judith Viorst, *Alexander and the Terrible, Horrible, No Good, Very Bad Day* (New York: Simon and Schuster, 1972).
3. Jim Cymbala, *Spirit Rising* (Grand Rapids, MI: Zondervan, 2012), 106–7.
4. John Van Sloten, *The Day Metallica Came to Church: Searching for the Everywhere God in Everything* (Grand Rapids, MI: Faith Alive, 2010), 33–35.
5. Francis Chan, *Forgotten God: Reversing Our Tragic Neglect of the Holy Spirit* (Colorado Springs: David C. Cook, 2009), 123–24.
6. Catherine Whitmire, *Practicing Peace* (Notre Dame, IN: Sorin Books, 2007), 28–29.

7. Mark Regnerus, "Sex Economics," *Christianity Today*, February 2011, 26–28.

8. David Germain, "'King's Speech' Writer Has His Own Stutter Story," Associated Press, February 16, 2011, accessed February 24, 2011, http://today.msnbc.msn.com/id/41619818/ns/today-entertainment.

9. Ibid.

10. Paul Tripp, *What Did You Expect? Redeeming the Realities of Marriage* (Wheaton, IL: Crossway, 2010), 35.

11. Philip Yancey, *Rumors of Another World: What on Earth Are We Missing?* (Grand Rapids, MI: Zondervan, 2003), 239.

12. Hannah Whitall Smith, *Daily Secrets of the Christian Life* (Ann Arbor, MI: Vine Books, 1985), 3.

13. Hannah Whitall Smith, *Daily Secrets of the Christian Life,* ed. Ann Spangler (Grand Rapids, MI: Zondervan, 1985), 25.

14. Joanna Weaver, *Having a Mary Spirit* (Colorado Springs: Waterbrook, 2006), 153, 155.

15. Paul Tripp, *What Did You Expect? Redeeming the Realities of Marriage* (Wheaton, IL: Crossway, 2010), 25.

16. Ibid., 24.

17. Marie Carlson, "God's 'A' Plan," in *Stories of Comfort for a Healthy Soul*, compiled by Christine M. Anderson (Grand Rapids, MI: Zondervan, 2001), 38–40.

18. Wayne Muller, *Sabbath: Restoring the Sacred Rhythm of Rest* (New York: Bantam Books, 1999), 82–83.

19. Oswald Chambers, *My Utmost for His Highest*, ed. James Reimann, updated edition (Grand Rapids, MI: RBC Ministries, 1935, 1992), July 29 devotional.

MARCH

1. John Ortberg, *The Life You've Always Wanted* (Grand Rapids, MI: Zondervan, 2002), 11–12.

2. Philip Yancey, *Rumors of Another World: What on Earth Are We Missing?* (Grand Rapids, MI: Zondervan, 2003), 146.

3. Joanna Weaver, *Lazarus Awakening* (Colorado Springs: Waterbrook, 2011), 14.

4. Eugene Peterson, *A Long Obedience in the Same Direction* (Downers Grove, IL: InterVarsity, 2000), 42.

5. Ibid., 87.

6. Chuck DeGroat, "On John Piper and Tornadoes Sent by God . . . ," *The New Exodus* (blog), August 12, 2009, http://www.drchuckdegroat.com/2009/08/on-john-piper-and-tornadoes-sent-by-god.

7. Jay Alabaster, "Tsunami Hit Towns Forgot Warnings from Ancestors," Associated Press, April 6, 2011, http://news.yahoo.com/s/ap/20110406/ap_on_re_as/as_japan_earthquake_warnings_in_stone.

8. Ibid.

9. Ibid.

10. Charles Stanley, *Finding Peace: God's Promise of a Life Free from Regret, Anxiety, and Fear* (Nashville: Thomas Nelson, 2003), 221–22.

11. If you want help with the spiritual disciplines, read Richard Foster, *Celebration of Discipline* (San Francisco: HarperSanFrancisco, 1988) or Dallas Willard, *The Spirit of the Disciplines* (San Francisco: HarperOne, 1998).

12. Suzanne Woods Fisher, *Amish Peace* (Grand Rapids, MI: Revell, 2009), 111.

13. Robert M. Sapolsky, *Why Zebras Don't Get Ulcers* (New York: Henry Holt, 2004), 5.

14. Ibid., 144.

15. "Musical Order," *I Am Neurotic* (blog), June 6, 2008, http://iamneurotic.com/2008/06/06/musical-order.

16. "Clean Chalkboard = Sane Students," *I Am Neurotic* (blog), April 19, 2011, http://iamneurotic.com/2008/06/18/clean-chalk-board-sane-students.

APRIL

1. Genelle's remarkable story is told in Jim Cymbala, *Breakthrough Prayer* (Grand Rapids, MI: Zondervan, 2003), 69.
2. Larry Crabb, *Connecting* (Nashville: Thomas Nelson, 1997), 179.
3. Pema Chodron, *The Places That Scare You* (Boston: Shambala Publications, 2002), 18.
4. Ibid., 19.
5. L. B. Cowman, *Streams in the Desert* (Grand Rapids, MI: Zondervan, 1999), 192.
6. Philip Yancey, *Rumors of Another World: What on Earth Are We Missing?* (Grand Rapids, MI: Zondervan, 2003), 147.
7. Dallas Willard, *Renovation of the Heart: Putting on the Character of Christ* (Colorado Springs: NavPress, 2002), 65.
8. Ibid., 65.
9. Miroslav Volf, *The End of Memory: Remembering Rightly in a Violent World* (Grand Rapids, MI: Wm. B. Eerdmans, 2006), 27.
10. Quin Sherrer, *A Mother's Guide to Praying for Your Children* (Ventura, CA: Regal, 2011), 97.
11. Søren Kierkegaard, *Eighteen Upbuilding Discourses*, ed. and trans. Howard V. Hong and Edna H. Hong (Princeton: Princeton University Press, 1990), quoted in Miroslav Volf, *The End of Memory: Remembering Rightly in a Violent World* (Grand Rapids, MI: Wm. B. Eerdmans, 2006), 169.
12. Jim Cymbala, *Fresh Faith* (Grand Rapids, MI: Zondervan, 1999), 91.
13. Joseph Telushkin, *Words That Hurt, Words That Heal* (New York: William Morrow, 1996), 23.
14. Though this explanation may at first seem improbable, read Kenneth Bailey's convincing exegesis in *Jesus through Middle Eastern Eyes: Cultural Studies in the Gospels* (Downers Grove, IL: InterVarsity, 2008), 217–26.
15. Ibid., 224.
16. Michael Hyatt, "Where to Find Peace in Turbulent Times," *Michael Hyatt Intentional Leadership* (blog), February 28, 2011, http://us2.campaign-archive1.com/?u=52d5c7778a3ad fda535c3b349&id=c17029a0c2&e=53afb51cde.
17. Abraham Joshua Heschel, *The Sabbath* (New York: Farrar, Straus and Giroux, 1979), 90.
18. Wayne Muller, *Sabbath: Finding Rest, Renewal, and Delight in Our Busy Lives* (New York: Bantam, 1999), 98.
19. Dietrich Bonhoeffer, *Life Together: The Classic Exploration of Faith in Community* (New York: Harper & Row, 1954), 112.
20. Ibid., 113.
21. Robert M. Sapolsky, *Why Zebras Don't Get Ulcers* (New York: Henry Holt, 2004), 376–77.

MAY

1. Tom Rademacher, "Students Share All on 'Speak Wall,'" *Grand Rapids Press,* May 6, 2011.
2. John Piper, "How Do You Remain Humble?," *The Christian Post,* May 6, 2011, accessed May 13, 2011, http://www.christianpost.com/news/how-do-you-remain-humble-50129.
3. John Piper, quoted in Josh Etter, "Learn the Secret of Gutsy Guilt," *Desiring God* (blog), accessed May 13, 2011, http://www.desiringgod.org/blog/posts/learn-the-secret -of-gutsy-guilt.
4. Timothy Keller, *The Reason for God* (New York: Dutton, 2008), xvi.
5. Wendy Beckett, *Sister Wendy on Prayer* (New York: Harmony Books, 2006), 83.
6. Wayne Muller, *Sabbath: Finding Rest, Renewal, and Delight in Our Busy Lives* (New York: Bantam, 1999), 69.
7. Abraham Joshua Heschel, *The Sabbath* (New York: Farrar, Straus and Giroux, 1979), vii.

8. Ibid., viii.

9. Ibid., xiv.

10. For more information on the Sabbath and ideas for celebrating it, read chapter 7 of my book *The Peace God Promises* (Grand Rapids, MI: Zondervan, 2011).

11. Joseph Telushkin, *The Book of Jewish Values: A Day-By-Day Guide to Ethical Living* (New York: Bell Tower, 2000), 441.

12. Dietrich Bonhoeffer, *Life Together*, trans. John W. Doberstein (New York: Harper and Row, 1954), 86.

13. Wayne Muller, *Sabbath: Finding Rest, Renewal, and Delight in Our Busy Lives* (New York: Bantam, 1999), 127.

14. Suzanne Woods Fisher, *Amish Peace* (Grand Rapids, MI: Revell, 2009), 42.

15. Parker Palmer, quoted in Catherine Whitmire, *Plain Living: A Quaker Path to Simplicity* (Notre Dame, IN: Sorin Books, 2001), 143.

16. An excellent discussion of the meaning and significance of *shema* can be found in Lois Tverberg, *Walking in the Dust of Rabbi Jesus* (Grand Rapids, MI: Zondervan, 2012), 31–41.

17. Wayne Muller, *Sabbath: Finding Rest, Renewal, and Delight in Our Busy Lives* (New York: Bantam, 1999), 84.

18. John Ortberg, Laurie Pederson, and Judson Poling, *Groups: The Life-Giving Power of Community* (Grand Rapids, MI: Zondervan, 2000), 50.

19. Ibid., 52–53.

20. Jo Farrow, quoted in Christine Whitmire, *Practicing Peace* (Notre Dame, IN: Sorin Books, 2007), 110.

JUNE

1. Stormie Omartian, *The Power of a Praying Parent* (Eugene, OR: Harvest House, 1995), 16.

2. Ibid., vii.

3. Paul Tripp, *War of Words* (Phillipsburg, NJ: P&R Publishing, 2000), 230.

4. Ibid., 71.

5. Mark Buchanan, *The Rest of God* (Nashville: Thomas Nelson, 2006), 190.

6. Charles Stanley, *Finding Peace: God's Promise of a Life Free from Regret, Anxiety, and Fear* (Nashville: Thomas Nelson, 2003), 193–94.

7. Joseph Telushkin, *The Book of Jewish Values: A Day-By-Day Guide to Ethical Living* (New York: Bell Tower, 2000), 29.

8. Larry Crabb, *Connecting* (Nashville: Thomas Nelson, 1997), 175.

9. Miroslav Volf, *The End of Memory: Remembering Rightly in a Violent World* (Grand Rapids, MI: Wm. B. Eerdmans, 2006), 76.

10. Based on an unpublished sermon by Mart De Haan (Maranatha Bible and Missionary Conference, Muskegon, MI, July 17, 2011).

11. *Genesis Rabbah* 1:10, quoted in Lois Tverberg, *Walking in the Dust of Rabbi Jesus* (Grand Rapids, MI: Zondervan, 2012), 156.

12. Winston Churchill, (speech, given at Harrow School, Harrow, England, October 29, 1941), quoted in *Churchill by Himself* (New York: Public Affairs, 2008), 23.

13. Quoted in the July 29, 2011, readings, taken from *The Liturgy of the Hours*, 4 vols (New York: Catholic Book Publishing, 1974), divineoffice.org.

14. *Young Frankenstein*, screenplay by Gene Wilder and Mel Brooks (20th Century Fox, 1974).

JULY

1. Augustine, *The Confessions of Saint Augustine*, trans. Edward B. Pusey (New York: P. F. Collier, 1909), 135.

2. Ronald Rolheiser, *The Holy Longing: The Search for a Christian Spirituality* (New York: Doubleday, 1999), 202.

3. Keven McQueen, "Carrie Nation: Militant Prohibitionist" in *Offbeat Kentuckians: Legends to Lunatics* (Kuttawa, KY: McClanahan Publishing House, 2001).

4. Amanda Way's story is told in Catherine Whitmire, *Practicing Peace* (Notre Dame, IN: Sorin Books, 2007), 212–13.

5. Nancy Guthrie, "Healing My Heart," Beliefnet, http://www.beliefnet.com/Love-Family /Holidays/Mothers-Day/Healing-My-Heart.aspx.

6. Jonathan Sacks, "Tikkun Olam: Orthodoxy's Responsibility to Perfect G-d's World" (address to the Orthodox Union West Coast Convention, December 1997).

7. Ibid.

8. Ken Sande, *The Peacemaker: A Biblical Guide to Resolving Personal Conflicts* (Grand Rapids, MI: Baker Books, 2004), 37.

9. whizzer75, August 10, 2006 (8:34 p.m.), comment on aldaric, "Squirrels eat tomato's? [*sic*]," posted on "Tomato Pests and Diseases," iVillage Garden Web, accessed August 16, 2011, http://forums.gardenweb.com/forums/load/tompests/msg0819534428839.html.

10. Laura Hibbard, "Humpbacked Whale Puts on a Show for the Men Who Saved Her," *Huffington Post*, July 13, 2011, accessed August 17, 2011, http://www.huffingtonpost.com /2011/07/14/humpback-whale-video_n_898859.html.

11. Ibid.

12. AFP, "Sinkhole Forms under Guatemalan Woman's Bed," Google News, July 19, 2011, http://www.google.com/hostednews/afp/article/ALeqM5hEAjEe8vStGMO iswAxDcxXi_d_DQ?docId=CNG.832a4bd5d343e4861527751b5e0d9c50.ad1.

13. Adapted from Ken Annan, *Following Jesus through the Eye of the Needle: Living Fully, Loving Dangerously* (Downers Grove, IL: InterVarsity, 2009), 174.

14. Ibid., 175.

15. Miroslav Volf, *The End of Memory: Remembering Rightly in a Violent World* (Grand Rapids, MI: Wm. B. Eerdmans, 2006), 9.

AUGUST

1. Katherine Welch, "The Work of the Week," *A Just Walk (Run, Hike, Etc . . .)* (blog), August 19, 2011, accessed August 30, 2011, http://justawalk.wordpress.com/2011/08/19 /the-work-of-the-week/.

2. Leslie C. Allen, *A Liturgy of Grief: A Pastoral Commentary on Lamentations* (Grand Rapids, MI: Baker Academic, 2011), 5.

3. Ibid., 6.

4. Augustine, *Confessions*, 9.10.26.

5. Ibid., 9.12.29.

6. Ibid., 9.12.33.

7. Nicholas Wolterstorff, *Lament for a Son* (Grand Rapids, MI: Wm. B. Eerdmans, 1987), 56.

8. Ibid., 26.

9. The experiments are described in Robert M. Sapolsky, *Why Zebras Don't Get Ulcers* (New York: Henry Holt, 2004), 255–56.

10. Rick Warren, "A Time for Reconciliation," session 3 of *The Purpose of Christmas: A Three-Session, Video-Based Study for Groups and Families* (Grand Rapids, MI: Zondervan, 2008), DVD.

11. Brett McKay and Kate McKay, "Bookend Your Day: The Power of Morning and Evening Routines," *The Art of Manliness* (blog), September 5, 2011, accessed September 6, 2011, http://artofmanliness.com/2011/09/05/bookend-your-day-the-power-of-morning-and -evening-routines/.

12. Abraham Joshua Heschel, *The Sabbath* (New York: Farrar, Straus and Giroux, 1979), 13.

13. Lois Tverberg, *Walking in the Dust of Rabbi Jesus* (Grand Rapids, MI: Zondervan, 2012), 113–14.

14. Rosamund Lupter, *Sister: A Novel* (New York: Broadway Books, 2010), 117.

15. Charles H. Spurgeon, "A Mystery! Saints Sorrowing and Jesus Glad!" (sermon, Metropolitan Tabernacle, London, August 7, 1874), transcript, Spurgeon Gems, accessed November 18, 2011, http://www.spurgeongems.org/vols10-12/chs585.pdf.

16. Walter Mosley, "Mosley's 'Last Days' Restores Memory, but at a Cost," interview by Terry Gross, *Fresh Air*, December 6, 2010, transcript and audio, 18:43, NPR, http://www.npr.org/2010/12/06/131848211/mosley-s-last-days-restores-memory-but-at-a-cost.

17. Diane Bartholomew, "Snapshots of My Early Life," in Wally Lamb, *Couldn't Keep It to Myself* (New York: Harper Perennial, 2003), 332.

18. See Peace Pilgrim, "Steps toward Inner Peace," Wikisource, last modified July 26, 2008, accessed September 14, 2011, http://en.wikisource.org/wiki/Steps_Toward_Inner_Peace.

19. Peace Pilgrim, "My Spiritual Growing Up: My Steps toward Inner Peace," chap. 2 in *Peace Pilgrim: Her Life and Work in Her Own Words*, Peace Pilgrim website, accessed September 14, 2011, http://www.peacepilgrim.com/book/chapt2.htm.

20. For more on this strange plot, read Ben Macintyre, *Operation Mincemeat: How a Dead Man and a Bizarre Plan Fooled the Nazis and Assured an Allied Victory* (New York: Harmony Books, 2010).

21. Donald Miller, "Want to Be Happy? Forgive Your Enemies," Donald Miller's blog, May 26, 2011, accessed September 29, 2011, http://donmilleris.com/2011/05/26/want-to-be-happy-forgive-your-enemies.

SEPTEMBER

1. Sally Lloyd Jones, *The Jesus Storybook Bible* (Grand Rapids, MI: Zondervan, 2007), 347.

2. Ken Sande, *The Peacemaker: A Biblical Guide to Resolving Personal Conflicts* (Grand Rapids, MI: Baker Books, 2004), 34.

3. Kenneth E. Bailey, *Jesus through Middle Eastern Eyes: Cultural Studies in the Gospels* (Downers Grove, IL: InterVarsity, 2008), 91.

4. George Guitton, *Perfect Friend: The Life of Blessed Claude la Colombière*, trans. William J. Young (St. Louis: B. Herder Book Company, 1956), 326, quoted and paraphrased in Bert Ghezzi, *Adventures in Daily Prayer* (Grand Rapids: Brazos Press, 2010), 59.

5. Thabiti Anyabwile, "Anxiety-Free Christianity," Christianity.com, accessed September 20, 2011, http://www.christianity.com/Home/Christian%20Living%20Features/11651516.

6. Philip Yancey, *Reaching for the Invisible God* (Grand Rapids, MI: Zondervan, 2000), 56.

7. Ibid.

8. Drawn from David W. Cox, "The Edwin Friedman Model of Family Systems Thinking: Lessons for Organizational Leaders" (essay, 2006), accessed September 22, 2011, http://www.vredestichters.nl/page6/files/artikel%20Edwin%20Friedman.pdf.

9. Paul Tripp, *Forever: Why You Can't Live without It* (Grand Rapids, MI: Zondervan, 2011), 203.

10. Ibid., 37.

11. Ibid, 34.

12. Heather Rowe, "My Husband Has Asperger Syndrome," *Women Alive*, accessed September 26, 2011, http://www.womanalive.co.uk/articles?articleaction=view&articleid=546.

13. N. T. Wright, *Surprised by Hope* (San Francisco: HarperOne, 2008), 208.

14. Gail Sheehy, "Girlfriends Are Key to Women's Optimism," *USA Today*, October 4, 2011.

15. Joseph Telushkin, *The Book of Jewish Values: A Day-By-Day Guide to Ethical Living* (New York: Bell Tower, 2000), 34.

16. Steve Jobs (commencement address, Stanford University, Stanford, CA, June 12, 2005), "'You've Got to Find What You Love,' Jobs Says," prepared transcript, Stanford University News, accessed January 15, 2009, http://news-service.stanford.edu/news/2005/june15/jobs-061505.html.

17. Kathy Cronkite, *On the Edge of Darkness* (New York: Delta Trade Paperbacks, 1994), 2–3.

18. Temple Grandin, *Thinking in Pictures: And Other Reports from My Life with Autism* (New York: Vintage Books, 2006), 122.

19. Temple Grandin, "Temple Grandin Talks about Her Upcoming HBO Biopic," *Beef*, October 31, 2008, accessed October 6, 2011, http://beefmagazine.com/cowcalfweekly /1031-temple-grandin-hbo-biopic/.

20. Quoted in Elizabeth Scott, "Funny Stress Quotes to Brighten Your Day," About.com, last modified September 26, 2011, accessed September 27, 2011, http://stress.about.com/od /humorandstressrelief/a/Funny-Stress-Quotes-To-Brighten-Your-Day.htm.

21. Norman Cousins, *Anatomy of an Illness as Perceived by the Patient* (New York: W. W. Norton, 1979), 43.

OCTOBER

1. Mark Buchanan, *The Rest of God* (Nashville: Thomas Nelson, 2006), 150–51.

2. Philip Gulley, *Hometown Tales: Recollections of Kindness, Peace, and Joy* (San Francisco: HarperSanFrancisco, 2001), 161.

3. These practical suggestions are drawn from William Sanderson, "Why Do People Worry and How One Can Overcome It?," interview by Cheryl Washington, *Good Day New York*, Fox Network, July 14, 1992, transcript, accessed October 10, 2011, http://www.ctcli.com /worry.html.

4. Robert M. Sapolsky, *Why Zebras Don't Get Ulcers* (New York: Henry Holt, 2004), 13.

5. Miroslav Volf, *The End of Memory: Remembering Rightly in a Violent World* (Grand Rapids, MI: Wm. B. Eerdmans, 2006), 79.

6. Quin Sherrer, *A Mother's Guide to Praying for Your Children* (Ventura, CA: Regal, 2011), 109.

7. Fern Nichols, *When Moms Pray Together* (Carol Stream, IL: Tyndale House Publishers, 2009), 40–41.

8. Francis Chan, *Forgotten God: Reversing Our Tragic Neglect of the Holy Spirit* (Colorado Springs: David C. Cook, 2009), 120.

9. John Masefield, "Sea Fever," in *Salt-Water Ballads* (New York: Macmillan, 1913), 59.

10. *The Fathers According to Rabbi Nathan* 6:2, quoted in Joseph Telushkin, *The Book of Jewish Values: A Day-By-Day Guide to Ethical Living* (New York: Bell Tower, 2000), 1.

11. This analogy was made in the nineteenth century by Rabbi Israel Salanter, as pointed out in Telushkin, *The Book of Jewish Values*, 1.

12. Lois Tverberg, *Walking in the Dust of Rabbi Jesus* (Grand Rapids, MI: Zondervan, 2012), xx.

13. Linda Dillow, *Calm My Anxious Heart* (Colorado Springs: NavPress, 2007), 32–33.

14. Ibid., 31–32.

15. John Ortberg, *The Life You've Always Wanted* (Grand Rapids, MI: Zondervan, 2002), 215.

16. Ibid., 215–16.

17. Jon Swaine, "Steve Jobs 'Regretted Trying to Beat Cancer with Alternative Medicine for So Long,'" *The Telegraph*, October 21, 2011, accessed February 2, 2012, http://www.telegraph .co.uk/technology/apple/8841347/Steve-Jobs-regretted-trying-to-beat-cancer-with -alternative-medicine-for-so-long.html.

18. Walter Isaacson, "Steve Jobs: Revelations from a Tech Giant," interview, *60 Minutes*, CBS News, October 23, 2011.

19. Associated Press, "285 Indian Girls Shed 'Unwanted' Names," *USA Today*, last modified October 23, 2011, accessed October 24, 2011, http://www.usatoday.com/news/world /story/2011-10-22/India-women-names/50869628/1.

20. Donald Miller, "Leaders Lead People through the Fear," Donald Miller's blog, September 23, 2011, accessed September 28, 2011, http://donmilleris.com/2011/09/23/leaders-lead -people-through-the-fear/.

NOVEMBER

1. Charles Stanley, *Finding Peace: God's Promise of a Life Free from Regret, Anxiety, and Fear* (Nashville: Thomas Nelson, 2003), 109.

2. Adapted from Tracey R. Rich, "Speech and Lashon Ha-Ra," Judaism 101, accessed June 15, 2011, http://www.jewfaq.org/speech.htm.

3. Dietrich Bonhoeffer, *Life Together*, trans. John W. Doberstein (New York: Harper and Row, 1954), 91.

4. Russel J. Reiter, quoted in Meredith Melnick, "5 Ways to Beat the Winter Doldrums," *Time*, November 5, 2010, accessed October 5, 2011, http://healthland.time.com/2010/11/05/5-ways-to-beat-the-winter-doldrums/#sadcropped.

5. Jerry Sittser, *The Will of God as a Way of Life* (Grand Rapids, MI: Zondervan, 2004), 25–26.

6. Ibid., 39–40.

7. Annia Ciezadlo, *Day of Honey* (New York: Free Press, 2011), 8.

8. Ibid., 7.

9. Quoted in Suzanne Woods Fisher, *Amish Peace* (Grand Rapids, MI: Revell, 2009), 108.

10. Philip Yancey, *Rumors of Another World: What on Earth Are We Missing?* (Grand Rapids, MI: Zondervan, 2003), 150.

11. Francis Chan tells the story of meeting one of the missionaries on a trip to South Korea in *Forgotten God: Reversing Our Tragic Neglect of the Holy Spirit* (Colorado Springs: David C. Cook, 2009), 107–8.

12. If you want to locate more, you can find them in my books *Praying the Names of God* (Grand Rapids, MI: Zondervan, 2004) or *Praying the Names of Jesus* (Grand Rapids, MI: Zondervan, 2006) or listed in *The Names of God Bible*, a version of God's Word Translation (Grand Rapids, MI: Revell, 2011).

13. Charlie W. Shedd, *Brush of an Angel's Wing* (Ann Arbor, MI: Servant Publications, 1994), 151–52.

14. Joni Eareckson Tada, "Please Heal Me!" in *Stories of Comfort for a Healthy Soul*, compiled by Christine M. Anderson (Grand Rapids, MI: Zondervan, 2001), 38–40.

15. Brennan Manning, *The Ragamuffin Gospel: Good News for the Bedraggled, Beat Up, and Burnt Out* (Sisters, OR: Multnomah, 2000), 28.

16. Rick Warren, *The Purpose Driven Life* (Grand Rapids, MI: Zondervan, 2002), 275–76.

17. Joanna Weaver, *Having a Mary Spirit* (Colorado Springs: Waterbrook, 2006), 190–91.

DECEMBER

1. Jerry Sittser, *A Grace Revealed* (Grand Rapids, MI: Zondervan, 2012).

2. Ibid.

3. Benjamin Carlson, "Facing the Future," *The Daily*, March 14, 2011.

4. Jerry Sittser, *A Grace Disguised* (Grand Rapids, MI: Zondervan, 1995), 33.

5. Ibid., 36–37.

6. Kyla King, "Secchia Wallops Man Who Menaced Grandchild," *Grand Rapids Press*, February 21, 2004.

7. Jim Cymbala, *Fresh Faith* (Grand Rapids, MI: Zondervan, 1999), 48.

8. Richard Stearns, "Spiritual Dominos," *World Vision News*, Winter 2011, 3.

9. Pamela Paul, "Is Gossip Good for You?" *New York Times*, October 8, 2010, accessed February 15, 2011, http://www.nytimes.com/2010/10/10/fashion/10Studied.html.

10. Ibid.

11. Joseph Telushkin, *Words That Hurt, Words That Heal* (New York: William Morrow, 1996), 36.

12. Dallas Willard, *Renovation of the Heart: Putting on the Character of Christ* (Colorado Springs: NavPress, 2002), 46.

13. Ibid., 33.

14. Ibid., 75.

15. Mark Niesse, "Gladys Burrill, 92-Year-Old Woman, Oldest Ever to Finish a Marathon," *Huffington Post*, April 4, 2011, accessed November 14, 2011, http://www.huffingtonpost.com/2011/04/05/oldest-woman-to-finish-a-_n_844972.html.

16. Dallas Willard, *Renovation of the Heart: Putting on the Character of Christ* (Colorado Springs: NavPress, 2002), 16.
17. Ibid., 71.
18. John Van Sloten, *The Day Metallica Came to Church: Searching for the Everywhere God in Everything* (Grand Rapids, MI: Faith Alive, 2010), 40.
19. Ibid., 45, 47–48.
20. Mark Buchanan, *The Rest of God* (Nashville: Thomas Nelson, 2006), 197–98.
21. Chuck DeGroat, "Risk Much. Fail Often. The Wisdom of the Desert," *The New Exodus* (blog), August 26, 2009, accessed April 21, 2011, http://www.drchuckdegroat.com /2009/08/risk-much-fail-often-the-wisdom-of-the-desert/.
22. Ronald Rollheiser, *The Holy Longing: The Search for a Christian Spirituality* (New York: Doubleday, 1999), 8.
23. N. T. Wright, *Surprised by Hope* (San Francisco: HarperOne, 2008), 137.
24. Ibid., 141.
25. Michelle Singletary, *The Power to Prosper: 21 Days to Financial Freedom* (Grand Rapids, MI: Zondervan, 2009).

The One Year®
Devo Reader App

FREE App Includes Thirty Days of One Year Devotions

Start any day The One Year way! This 365-day iPhone/iPad devotional-reader app will help you stay on track as you explore the inspiring and life-changing devotionals that will help make Bible reading a priority.

You will also be able to

- write and organize notes for each devotional;
- tap referenced Scriptures to read them in the app;
- share inspiring quotes via text message, e-mail, and Facebook; and
- access devotionals through relevant topics and Scripture passages.

The One Year Devo Reader comes with five-day samples from all available iPhone/iPad One Year devotionals. Get this free app, decide on a devotional you want, and purchase it effortlessly using in-app purchase!

Now available from iTunes—just open the iTunes store and type in "one year devo" in the search field.

THE ONE YEAR® WAY

Do-able. Daily. Devotions.

START ANY DAY THE ONE YEAR WAY.

Do-able.
Every One Year book is designed for people who live busy, active lives. Just pick one up and start on today's date.

Daily.
Daily routine doesn't have to be drudgery. One Year devotionals help you form positive habits that connect you to what's most important.

Devotions.
Discover a natural rhythm for drawing near to God in an extremely personal way. One Year devotionals provide daily focus essential to your spiritual growth.

For Women

*The One Year®
Devotions for
Women on
the Go*

*The One Year®
Love Language
Minute Devotional*

*The One Year®
Devotions for
Moms*

*The One Year®
Women of the
Bible*

*The One Year®
Coffee with God*

OTHER BOOKS BY ANN SPANGLER

Men of the Bible (coauthored with Robert Wolgemuth)
The Names of God Bible (Ann Spangler, general editor)
Praying the Names of God
Praying the Names of Jesus
Sitting at the Feet of Rabbi Jesus (coauthored with Lois Tverberg)
The Tender Words of God
When You Need a Miracle
Women of the Bible (coauthored with Jean Syswerda)

You can reach Ann at http://annspangler.com.